ROUTLEDGE LIBRARY EDITIONS: COLONIALISM AND IMPERIALISM

Volume 42

RACE, POWER AND SOCIAL SEGMENTATION IN COLONIAL SOCIETY

RACE, POWER AND SOCIAL SEGMENTATION IN COLONIAL SOCIETY

Guyana After Slavery, 1838–1891

BRIAN L. MOORE

LONDON AND NEW YORK

First published in 1987 by Gordon and Breach Science Publishers

This edition first published in 2023
by Routledge
4 Park Square, Milton Park, Abingdon, Oxon OX14 4RN

and by Routledge
605 Third Avenue, New York, NY 10158

Routledge is an imprint of the Taylor & Francis Group, an informa business

© 1987 Gordon and Breach Science Publishers Inc.

All rights reserved. No part of this book may be reprinted or reproduced or utilised in any form or by any electronic, mechanical, or other means, now known or hereafter invented, including photocopying and recording, or in any information storage or retrieval system, without permission in writing from the publishers.

Trademark notice: Product or corporate names may be trademarks or registered trademarks, and are used only for identification and explanation without intent to infringe.

British Library Cataloguing in Publication Data
A catalogue record for this book is available from the British Library

ISBN: 978-1-032-41054-8 (Set)
ISBN: 978-1-032-45618-8 (Volume 42) (hbk)
ISBN: 978-1-032-45620-1 (Volume 42) (pbk)
ISBN: 978-1-003-37788-7 (Volume 42) (ebk)

DOI: 10.4324/9781003377887

Publisher's Note
The publisher has gone to great lengths to ensure the quality of this reprint but points out that some imperfections in the original copies may be apparent.

Disclaimer
The publisher has made every effort to trace copyright holders and would welcome correspondence from those they have been unable to trace.

RACE, POWER AND SOCIAL SEGMENTATION IN COLONIAL SOCIETY

Guyana After Slavery, 1838–1891

by

Brian L. Moore

Department of History
University of the West Indies
Mona Campus, Jamaica

GORDON AND BREACH SCIENCE PUBLISHERS
New York London Paris Montreux Tokyo Melbourne

© 1987 by Gordon and Breach Science Publishers Inc. Post Office Box 161, 1820 Montreux 2, Switzerland. All rights reserved.

Gordon and Breach Science Publishers

Post Office Box 786
Cooper Station
New York, New York 10276
United States of America

Post Office Box 197
London WC2E 9PX
England

58, rue Lhomond
75005 Paris
France

14-9 Okubo 3-chome
Shinjuku-ku, Tokyo 160
Japan

Private Bag 8
Camberwell, Victoria 3124
Australia

Library of Congress Cataloging-in-Publication Data

Moore, Brian L., 1948-
    Race, power, and social segmentation in colonial society.

    (Caribbean studies, ISSN 0275-5793; v. 4)
    Bibliography: p.
    Includes index.
    1. Social classes — Guyana — History — 19th century.
2. Guyana — Race relations — History — 19th century.
3. Guyana — Social conditions. 4. Power (Social sciences)
I. Title. II. Series.
HN330.3.Z9S665   1987   305.5'0988'1   87-17694
ISBN 0-677-21980-6

No part of this book may be reproduced or utilized in any form or by any means, electronic or mechanical, including photocopying and recording, or by any information storage or retrieval system, without permission in writing from the publishers. Printed in Great Britain by Bell and Bain Ltd., Glasgow.

*For Farah Monique
and all the other children
of Guyana*

TABLE OF CONTENTS

List of Illustrations		ix
Introduction to the Series		xi
Acknowledgements		xiii
	Introduction	1

HISTORICAL AND THEORETICAL BACKGROUND

Chapter 1	Plantation Societies, Pluralism and Social Stratification	9
Chapter 2	The Plantation System and the Challenge of Emancipation	31

WHITE MINORITY DOMINANCE

Chapter 3	Colonial Politics and the Institutionalization of Planter Hegemony	51
Chapter 4	Race and Imperialism in the Colonial Polity	77

THE BLACKS AND COLOUREDS IN SOCIETY

Chapter 5	The Political Subordination of the Black Villages	93
Chapter 6	Second Class Subjects: The Socio-Economic Status of the Blacks and Coloureds	109

TABLE OF CONTENTS

THE INCORPORATION OF IMMIGRANTS

Chapter 7   Secondary Colonists: The Rise of the Portuguese Immigrants   139

Chapter 8   The Subjugation of the Indian and Chinese Immigrants   161

THE ORGANIZATION AND STRUCTURE OF THE TOTAL SOCIETY

Chapter 9   The Stability and Unity of the Society: Consensus or Coercion   191

Chapter 10   Conclusion: Race, Power and Social Segmentation   213

Notes and References   225
Appendices   273
Bibliography   277
Index   301

LIST OF ILLUSTRATIONS

I. A multiracial scene. Taken from Charles W. Eves' *The West Indies* (London, Sampson Low, Marston, Searle & Rivington, 1889)

II. Map of the coast of Guyana showing Plantation Belt

INTRODUCTION TO THE SERIES

The purpose of this series is to provide a forum in which the major themes and trends affecting the entire region will be explored in depth. Thus, while the island-specific approach is not eschewed, the aim is to develop perspectives on problem-solving in the area as an entirety, both on the local level and in the international context. Hence the emphasis is on the qualitative and quantitative interpretation of the economic and political culture in which the modern Caribbean operates. Historical, demographical and sociological issues, when relevant to the central focus of the series, will also be examined.

Caribbean Studies publishes the research of academic scholars working within the region, as well as Caribbeanists working internationally. Simultaneously, it is hoped that the monographs function as a reference data source for libraries, foundations and government agencies with an interest in the Caribbean either exclusively or peripherally.

It is the coeditors' hope that the series will increase comprehensive Caribbean studies internationally, and will similarly stimulate innovative research and development of methodology suitable to comparative perspectives. Only when the Caribbean is evaluated in its broadest panorama can the true global importance of the region be appreciated.

Manuscripts may be sent to either of the two coeditors, who are assisted by an advisory board of internationally recognized scholars.

ACKNOWLEDGEMENTS

Over the years an enormous debt has been accumulated in the preparation of this study. Both institutions and individuals have played very important roles in facilitating my research and writing. Firstly, I would like to express my sincere appreciation to the staffs of the following research institutions and libraries where I conducted my work: the University of the West Indies library (Mona); the Institute of Social and Economic Research library (U.W.I., Mona); the Institute of Jamaica; the Guyana National Archives; the University of Guyana library; the Georgetown Public Library; the Public Record Office, London; the British Library; the University of London library; the libraries of the Institute of Historical Research, and of Commonwealth Studies, London; the Royal Commonwealth Society library; the library of the West India Committee; and the New York Public Library. In addition, several missionary organisations in London made their valuable records available to me viz., the Society for Promoting Christian Knowledge, the Congregational Council for World Mission, the Society of Jesus (English Province), the Methodist Missionary Society, and the United Society for the Propagation of the Gospel.

Since most of the material for the book formed part of my doctoral thesis of 1973 (U.W.I.), my indebtedness extends a long way back. In particular, I cannot fully express the tremendous sense of gratitude that I feel in respect of the late Professor Elsa Goveia who was the principal supervisor of my thesis, and who thereafter encouraged me to do further research with a view to publishing this work. That, however, was postponed by a six-year absence from academic life. I also owe a great deal to Professor Edward Brathwaite who, as cosupervisor of the original thesis, has been associated with this project for as long as it has been in existence.

A very special word of thanks must be reserved for Professor Barry Higman, without whose material assistance this study may never have seen the light of day, and who, moreover, very generously read and offered constructive criticism of two drafts. I cannot be too profuse in my expression of gratitude to Dr. Bridget Brereton who, at very short notice, so willingly and thoroughly read and provided me with a very detailed critique of the manuscript, causing me to rethink a number of issues and conclusions. In addition, the work would not be nearly as complete as I hope it has become without the valuable comments and advice of Dr. Roberta Delson, the editor of this series of Caribbean Studies.

I wish also to thank Mr. James Rose of the University of Guyana who kindly furnished me with very useful data to fill some gaps in my historical material; and especially Miss Marjorie Dinnall who cheerfully, willingly and efficiently typed two drafts of this book. Finally, a very special debt is owed to my wife, Pamela, who not only actively encouraged and supported my efforts throughout, but also assisted tangibly by meticulously proofreading each draft. To all those other persons, too numerous to mention individually, who contributed in various ways, thanks very much.

Brian L. Moore

INTRODUCTION

The writing of Caribbean social history is coming under fresh review by professional historians. Barry Higman's recent paper on "Theory, Method and Technique in Caribbean Social History"[1] is an excellent beginning that will undoubtedly inspire future analyses. Such reassessments are critical for identifying problems and deficiencies in Caribbean historiography, and for encouraging the development of new methods to solve them.

This study of Guyanese society after slavery aims to focus on one problem area of Caribbean historiography that deals with social classes and ethnic groups. While in part seeking to do for Guyana what works such as Wood and Brereton have done for Trinidad,[2] van Lier for Surinam,[3] and Curtin for Jamaica to a lesser extent,[4] it also focusses on the theoretical issues in the debate on pluralism versus stratification and provides a detailed interdisciplinary analysis of the process of structural change in a composite colonial society over a significantly long historical period — over half a century. It is this focus that partially differentiates it from two of the more outstanding monographs on 19th Century Guyana, i.e., Alan H. Adamson's *Sugar Without Slaves*[5] and Walter Rodney's *History of the Guyanese Working People*.[6] While these studies are also concerned with classes and social groups, that interest stems largely from primary economic and political considerations arising from the emphasis on the plantation as the dominant economic institution in Adamson's analysis, and on capital as the pivotal element in the formation of social classes in the case of Rodney. The study of social groups has just received a fresh input by Mary Noel Menezes' new documentary book on the Portuguese in Guyana.[7] But in its primary concern with just one ethnic group, its scope is somewhat restrictive.

The works of Adamson and Rodney are easily the most professional and scholarly that have been written on post-emancipation Guyana, but there are other modern publications of some importance to the social history of that period. Jay Mandle's *The Plantation Economy*[8] is essentially an economic history that covers the period from 1838 to 1960, though its coverage of the post-emancipation 19th Century is rudimentary and relies to some extent on secondary sources for its statistics. Mohammed Shahabuddeen's *Constitutional Development of Guyana since 1621*[9] is a very meticulous compilation of historical data on the political system. While essentially descriptive rather than analytical, it loses its objectivity by its attempt to justify the recent constitutional changes in Guyana and to legitimize the present regime. Finally, an earlier work by Alan Young (1958) treated the politico-legal developments in local government from 1838 to the 1950s[10] but, like Shahabuddeen, Young was not a professional historian, and his work lacks analytical depth. Moreover, his bias toward British colonialism is clearly reflected in his views.

Most of the recent professional social histories of 19th Century Guyana are in the form of unpublished Ph.D. dissertations and theses. The works of Ramnarine,[11] Bisnauth,[12] and Potter[13] on the Indian immigrants; of Wagner on the Portuguese;[14] of R.J. Moore on race relations between blacks and Indians;[15] and of Fraser on education,[16] are excellent examples. In addition, a number of useful M.A. theses have come out of the University of Guyana graduate programme.

The issues raised by Barry Higman[17] on the general state and direction of Caribbean social history seem to me to be pertinent to this work. As regards method, he notes that a general reluctance exists among historians of the English-speaking Caribbean to employ the methods of what he calls "social science" or the "new" social history. This entails the application of sociological and anthropological theory and analytical methods to social history. In identifying the reasons for this reluctance, Higman points to the claim by some historians that the historical data is not sufficiently precise to lend itself to such rigorous theoretical analysis as used in the modern social sciences. This is true in some instances, but ought not to serve as a deterrent because the application of such methods can and does raise many new questions which, even if the historical evidence cannot supply conclusive answers, can serve as a guide to the direction of future research.

There is also the fact that many historians find the terminology and theories of the social sciences highly "specialized" and not easily grasped by the "outsider". This becomes increasingly so as new theories are built on old ones which means that unless one has some grounding in the discipline or is prepared to acquire it (almost like learning a new language) then one is perpetually at sea. Many social science theories that ought to be applied to social history are thus studiously eschewed by some historians. That might also be in part conditioned by the apprehension of opening oneself to the criticism of writing neither good social history, sociology nor anthropology.

This study, however, attempts to overcome some of these conservative attitudes to the writing of Caribbean social history. It explicitly employs social science theory and method as analytical tools and applies them to the Guyanese case. This does not necessarily mean that all the questions raised by such methodology are fully or even partially answered; for where the data is unavoidably sparse, one is left with impressionistic rather than rigorous scientific conclusions. But the use of social science method has provided a more systematic framework within which the historical analysis could be undertaken. Whether this extends our understanding of the form and structure of post-emancipation Guyanese society beyond the strict limits of the historical evidence is a matter for independent assessment.

Higman observes that historians have generally been borrowers of theory.[18] This is true for this study as well, which in fact seeks not only to apply social science theories, but also to test their validity in relation to one Caribbean society over a critical period of its historical development. But the study goes further to try to draw certain general theoretical conclusions and to posit new ways for applying those theories to similarly structured societies.

Of course, there is a risk of possibly adopting outdated theoretical disputes and controversies in applying social science theory to social history.[19] In the context of this study, the debate over the structure of Caribbean societies, whether stratified or plural, apparently lost its edge during the 1970s, since none of the new writings seems to have significantly advanced the frontier of theory. Yet no one can pretend that the debate is moribund. Any perusal of the recent contributions of Stuart Hall,[20] Raymond Smith,[21] Harmannus Hoetink,[22] Leo Despres,[23] Carl Stone,[24] Malcolm Cross,[25] Adam Kuper,[26] Percy Hintzen,[27] *et al.* clearly demonstrates the contrary; the recent *Culture, Race and Class in the Commonwealth Caribbean* of M.G. Smith[28] (one of the most articulate proponents of the pluralist argument) has been so provocative in its rebuttal of his critics, both old and new, that it has stoked the flames of the controversy anew.

The theoretical debate thus lives on, and is as vibrant as ever. While this work is not sufficiently ambitious to pretend to resolve the differences, it does hope to make an important contribution to that debate. But at its base, it is a work of history, and as such I hope not only to add to the theory and method of Caribbean social history, but also to the growing body of historical knowledge about Guyanese and Caribbean society.

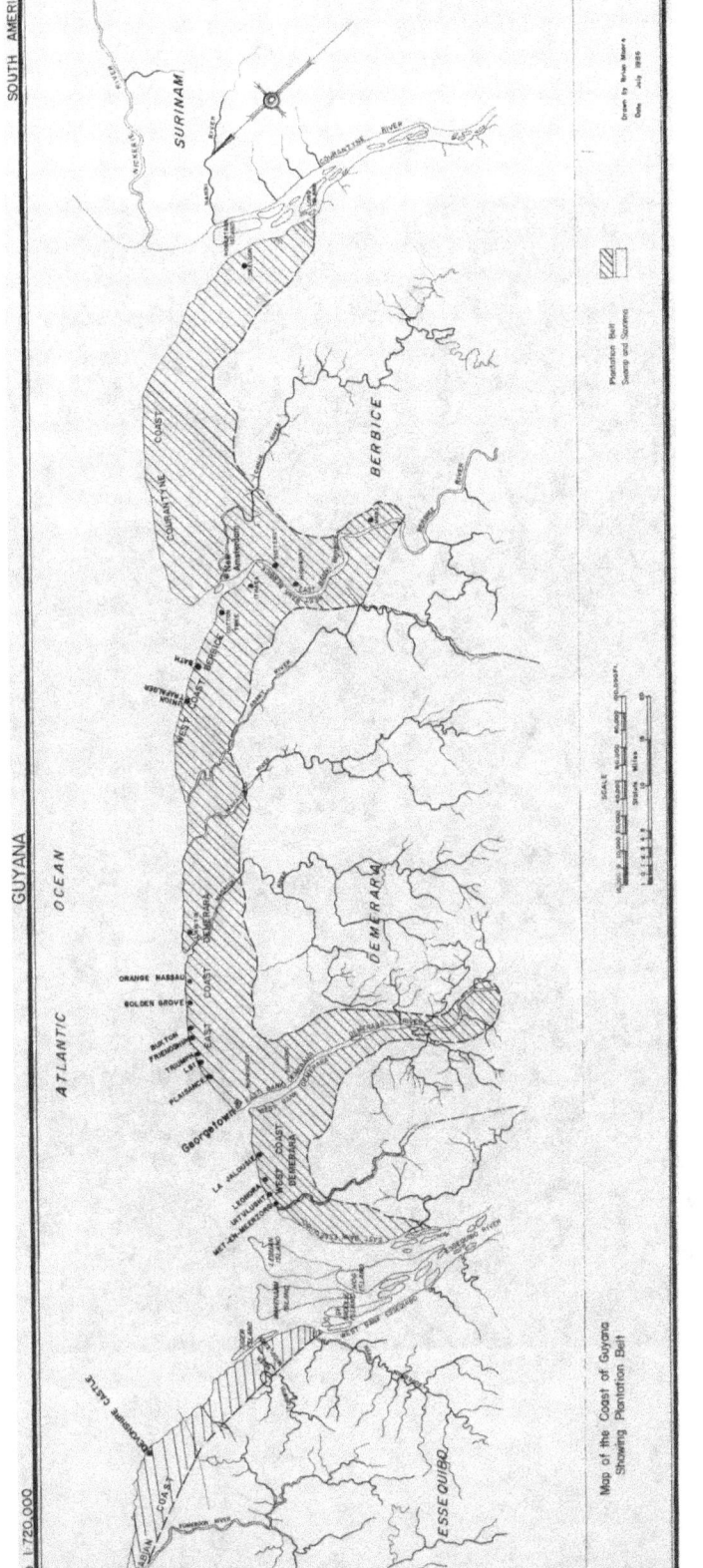

"They mix but do not combine." — Furnivall. Street Scene in Georgetown, Demerara. Reproduced (by kind courtesy of the Royal Commonwealth Society) from Charles W. Eves, The West Indies (London, 1889) housed in the *West Indies Collection*. Main Library, University of the West Indies, Mona, Jamaica.

HISTORICAL AND THEORETICAL BACKGROUND

CHAPTER 1

PLANTATION SOCIETIES, PLURALISM AND SOCIAL STRATIFICATION

Although plantation systems have been found in parts of Asia, Africa, the Mediterranean and the Pacific, they had their earliest and most pervasive development in tropical America, particularly in the Caribbean. The label "Plantation America" has been given by Charles Wagley to this so-called culture sphere which, though stretching from northeastern Brazil and the Guianas, through the Caribbean, to the southern United States, exhibits basically similar features consequent on the socio-economic primacy of the plantation and the system of slavery upon which it was built. According to Wagley, this culture sphere is characteristically coastal, tropical and, at least in its formative period, economically monocultural.[1]

It is the absolute dominance of the plantation which allows analysts to consider such societies as a special type. Elena Padilla claims that a plantation society can be heuristically defined as a 'kind of class-structured society whose major economic institutions are geared to large-scale production and marketing of an export crop or crops for profit, and whose population depends directly or indirectly on the plantation for its livelihood and the realization of its economic wants'.[2] Edgar Thompson further observes that wherever the plantation attained socio-economic dominance, it established its own regimen designed to perpetuate its supremacy and either obliterated the indigenous social and economic forms while subjecting the native peoples to its regime, or imported vast numbers of unfree labourers to fulfil its labour requirements. Thus he asserts that 'it is actually the introduction of such an industrial army of occupation that gives the plantation its character'.[3]

Wolf and Mintz have classified certain general, historically-derived characteristics of the establishment and continued operation of the plantation system. Among the "initiating conditions" are the availability of sufficient capital to secure the necessary factors of production; land in sufficient quantity and of satisfactory quality to facilitate adequate production and probable expansion; a large supply of cheap labour for profit maximization; sufficiently high technology to permit large-scale production and improved transportation; and sanctions of a politico-legal sort to regulate the distribution of surpluses, and to maintain a disciplined work force. The "continued operation" of the plantation system depends on a continuous supply of capital which the plantation must be capable of absorbing; an assured large-scale industrial market; the scope for physical expansion through further land acquisitions; a regular or seasonal oversupply of labour; the utilization of improved technology for greater profit; and an impersonal, standardized, commercial control over the labour force reinforced by sanctions of state power, including military force.[4]

It is this exercise of state power which Thompson sees as the crucial element in ensuring the continued domination of the society by the plantation; and he notes that ultimately every institution in the society becomes involved in the support of the plantation system.[5] This idea of a society dominated by a single institution, the plantation, which in turn leads to the development of a special type of social structure and political organization, has more recently been pursued by George Beckford. He sees the plantation system as a total system which controls the economic resources and relegates all other enterprise into a subsectoral position in relation to the dominant system. This economic dominance of the plantation system is paralleled by the socio-political hegemony of the planter class which owns and controls it. This hegemony is not confined to the authority structure on individual plantations, but extends to the political institutions of the state. Hence 'the supreme authority of the planter on his estate is paralleled by the concentration of state power in his class, and by a highly centralized form of government'.[6]

Denis Benn, however, has queried the theoretical validity of the idea of "plantation society". In particular, he attacks the notion of "totality" which underscores Beckford's conceptualization, arguing that even if the plantation system could be perceived as a totality during slavery, this condition was not true after emancipation.[7] That, however, only pertains to some Caribbean territories. In places such as Barbados and the Leewards, for instance, the plantation system still retained a "closed-resources" situation (in the Nieboerian sense) which perpetuated as near a "total system" of control as was possible in a theoretically "free" society. Even in the much larger Guyana as will be seen later, the planters and their imperial overlords were able to reimpose a similar situation after the mid-century.

What is evident, however, is that the exceptions to the "rule" are sufficient to devalue the usefulness of the "plantation society" as espoused by Beckford as a general theory. But that does not invalidate its value as a descriptive term in reference to societies dominated by the plantation system and exhibiting those general features and characteristics outlined by the writers cited above (including Beckford but, of course, without the condition of totality which he imposes on it). This study, therefore, employs the term in such a general and descriptive manner.

Both Wagley and Beckford have stressed the multiracial character of plantation societies. Referring specifically to "Plantation America", Wagley observed that 'everywhere there are a multitude of "social race" categories — categories based not upon scientific fact but upon social values for given characteristics". He furthermore pointed out that in these societies, race relations is an important focus of interest to all people.[8] Beckford indicates that wherever located, whether in Africa, Asia, or the Pacific, plantation systems are associated with multiracialism. Hence, he asserts that 'the dominance of plantations in any particular situation is alone (sic) a necessary and sufficient condition for the existence of a mixed population base', though multi-racial societies do exist where plantations are not dominant.[9]

Beckford, however, goes further to establish a direct link between multi-racialism and pluralism in plantation societies. Hence, for him, 'Cultural pluralism is a characteristic feature of all plantation societies because the plantation brought together people of different races and cultural backgrounds to carry out the task of production'.[10] Not surprisingly, therefore, he concludes that plantation society is a plural society since 'it consists of different racial and cultural groups which are brought together in the realm of economic activity'.[11]

This assertion of a necessary relationship between multi-racialism and pluralism in plantation-dominated societies is, however, open to critical examination, and forms an important aspect of this study. The concept of pluralism and its applicability to certain types of composite societies have aroused considerable debate among sociologists and social anthropologists without any sign of an emerging consensus. In fact, Leo Kuper notes that the term "pluralism" is actually used to classify two radically different socio-political traditions. One relates to certain types of society founded in imperialistic conquest or economic expansion, and is characterized by ethnic diversity, rigid segmentation into racially and culturally exclusive sections, political domination by one section (often a minority), lack of consensus, instability and conflict, and held together mainly by coercion and possibly by asymmetrical interdependence within a common economic system. The other is identified with democracy, and is characterized by a plurality of organizations and interest groups with overlapping membership, which are bound together by a competitive balance of cross-cutting loyalties, an adherence to common values, and a respect for the rules which govern the conduct and limits of such competition. Kuper thus labels the first the "conflict model" of pluralism, and the second the "equilibrium model".[12]

Without necessarily accepting Kuper's labels, it is the first model with which this study is concerned. This conceptualization of pluralism was first formulated by J.S. Furnivall in his studies of the colonial economies of Southeast Asia. Furnivall was fascinated by the ethnic diversity of these societies. According to him:

> the first thing that strikes the visitor is the medley of peoples — European, Chinese, Indian and native. It is in the strictest sense a medley, for they mix but do not combine. Each group holds by its own religion, its own culture and language, its own ideas and ways. As individuals they meet, but only in the market-place, in buying and selling. There is a plural society, with different sections of the community living side by side, but separately, within the same political unit. Even in the economic sphere there is division of labour along racial lines.[13]

According to Furnivall, the plural society is further characterized by the absence of any common social will or demand. The highest common factor is the economic factor, and the only test that applies in common is the test of cheapness. Outside the economic sphere, each racial group lives apart and continually tends to fall apart unless held together by the colonial regime. The sections, however, are not segregated: 'the members of the several units are intermingled and meet as individuals; the union is not voluntary but is imposed by the colonial power and by force of economic circumstances, and the unit cannot be dissolved without the whole society relapsing into anarchy'. Furnivall was at pains to point out that not only is the society divided, but the ethnic sections are themselves fragmented. 'Each section ... is a crowd and not a community, ... an aggregate of individuals rather than a corporate or organic whole; and as individuals their social life is incomplete'. 'In each section, the sectional common social will is feeble ...'[14]

Julius Boeke's subsequent work on Southeast Asia also dealt with aspects of pluralism, or "dualism" as he termed it, which he perceived as the clashing of an imported social system with an indigenous social system of another style. The term "dual society" he reserved 'for societies showing a distinct cleavage of two synchronic and full grown social styles which in the normal, historical evolution of homogenous societies are separated from each other by transitional forms, as for instance, pre-capitalism and high capitalism by early capitalism, and which do not coincide as contemporary dominating features'.[15]

It was another Dutchman, R.A.J. van Lier, who first applied the concept of pluralism to Caribbean plantation society. He spoke of "segmentarianism", and considered Caribbean societies to be the oldest colonial segmentary societies. But he did not significantly develop the concept beyond Furnivall's formulation. He held that:

> If there is little solidarity in a society composed of segments, we speak of a segmentary society or segmentarism. Its individual members are thus lightly held together by very few bonds. Collective ideas and values which lend unity to a group are almost completely absent. The individuals are influenced by notions which they possess as members of their particular segment. Cooperation occurs chiefly in the political

and economic spheres. Yet even there they remain separate groups, either lined up next to one another or in opposition. Social processes are controlled by the economic motive. Social values originate, but only in so far as these may be economically advantageous ... Such societies possess a minimum of expansive force. Aside from that which is performed by the authorities very little is accomplished. They are held together by state power, which is usually monopolized by members of one of these segments.[16]

It was not until the late fifties and early sixties that attempts were made to reconstitute the concept of pluralism into a systematic theory. The leading figure in this development, M.G. Smith, considers only territorially distinct units having their own governmental institutions as societies. Hence he equates society with the political state. Following Malinowski, Nadel and Linton, he sees the core of a culture as its institutional system:

> Each institution involves set forms of activity, grouping, rules, ideas and values. The total system of institutions thus embraces three interdependent systems of action, of idea and value, and of social relations ... The institutions of a people's culture form the matrix of their social structure.

Smith groups those institutions which deal with the same phases of life (e.g. marriage, family, extended kinship forms, etc.) into systemic clusters or subsystems. Together, these subsystems form the total institutional system. Hence for him, it is institutional differences that distinguish cultures and social units.[17]

Smith asserts that all institutions have two analytically distinct, but intimately connected aspects, i.e., the cultural and the social. 'Culture and society are equally rooted in the institutional system on which each human aggregate depends for its inner cohesion, distinctive identity, membership and boundaries'. Hence, institutional homogeneity, heterogeneity, and pluralism respectively involve corresponding social and cultural homogeneity, heterogeneity, and pluralism. But this does not mean that culture and society are at all times coterminous or interdependent since certain aspects of culture, e.g., ideas, language, aesthetic styles, etc., can be transferred across social boundaries with little social effect. Thus systems of social relations can persist despite substantial shifts in their cultural content or explicit orientations.[18]

Smith further distinguishes basic or compulsory, alternative, and exclusive institutions. The basic or compulsory institutions are those common to all members of a social unit and embrace kinship, education, religion, property and economy, recreation, and certain sodalities. Alternative institutions are optionally participated in by people of certain categories such as social classes; while exclusive institutions are shared by members of specialized social categories e.g., occupational groups. The role which these institutional variations play in the social system determines the type of the society. In his view, a homogeneous society is one in which all members share a common institutional system. In a heterogeneous society, the members share the same basic institutions, but practise differing alternative or exclusive institutions. The plural society is distinguished by the absence of shared basic institutions.[19]

In order to differentiate more clearly between heterogeneous and plural societies, Smith also employs Meyer Fortes' distinction between the kinship or private and the politico-jural or public domains. Although recognizing that most basic institutional systems are represented unequally and variably in either domain according to the society, he places great emphasis on the institutional structure of the public domain to differentiate between the two types of society. In his view, all societies depend for their boundaries, organization, and internal order on the scope and character of their corporate structure which is explicitly centred in the public domain. Since institutional differentiation among cultural sections in a society signifies pluralism, then if such differences are confined solely to the private domain, a condition of cultural pluralism is operative i.e., the society is heterogeneous. If, however, those differences occur in the public domain, then there is social pluralism.[20]

The forms of pluralism may be further indicated by the societal modes of incorporating the culturally differentiated sections. If the society is dominated politically by one cultural section, then the subordinate sections are differentially incorporated within that 'common political society' with unequal rights and status. In such a case, a condition of structural or hierarchical pluralism exists. If, however, the differentiated cultural sections coexist alongside one another with equal political rights, privileges and status then, although clearly segmented socially and institutionally, there are no fundamental structural inequalities. Hence the sections are incorporated to form a "consociation" in which citizenship is determined by membership of one of the constituent sections. In this instance, a condition of social or segmental pluralism is said to exist.[21]

Alternatively, where social and political rights, privileges and status are accorded to individuals without reference or primary identification with any cultural section, there is universalistic societal incorporation. In this case, whatever institutional divergences there may be are confined to the private domain without corresponding corporate social differences. Thus there is a condition of cultural pluralism or societal heterogeneity. Smith notes that

> though cultural pluralism may prevail without social or structural pluralism, these latter forms of pluralism cannot obtain without commensurate degrees of cultural pluralism. Moreover, while structural pluralism entails social and cultural pluralism, the converse is not necessary.

He further asserts that in some cases, the conditions of structural and segmental pluralism can exist simultaneously. But there is no fixed relationship between any of the levels of pluralism and any mode of societal incorporation. Instead they can be combined in various ways to form differing types of complex regime.[22]

Smith's differentiation between culture and society is not sufficiently distinct for Leo Despres, who also challenges the former's definition of society as a political unit rather than as a socio-cultural system. Despres, however, concurs with Smith on the central role of institutional differences in distinguishing differing cultures and social units, though he fundamentally disagrees with the classification of compulsory, alternative, and exclusive institutions. In his view, if a culture is an integrated pattern of social usages, then Smith's distinction is spurious. He does acknowledge, however, that society and culture are not coterminous, though not entirely independent of each other.[23]

In order to overcome Smith's difficulty in differentiating clearly the plural from the heterogeneous society, Despres has employed functional analysis. Thus when institutional activities maintain cultural differentiation between groups at the local level, such groups are *minimal* cultural sections. When such differentiation occurs at the national level, the groups form *maximal* cultural sections. A society with minimal cultural sections is socially and culturally heterogeneous; one with maximal cultural sections is a plural society. In this context, he considers both the heterogeneous and the plural society to be ideal types on a continuum of socio-cultural integration.[24]

Similarly, Despres distinguishes between two types of institutions by their functions. Local institutions integrate separately differentiated cultural groups at community level, whereas broker institutions perform a similar function for the minimal cultural sections at the societal level. The first type includes language (dialects), family and kinship, work, religion, socialization, recreation, associational and communal activities. The second type includes markets (labour and consumption), corporations, labour unions, government agencies, political parties, school, religious, social and civic, and ethnic associations.[25]

One major problem of the pluralist thesis as adumbrated by both Smith and Despres has been their conceptualization of society essentially in terms of the form or function of its institutional system without focussing on social action either between or within cultural sections. Morever, as Malcolm Cross has observed, the thesis does not treat the process of institutionalization by which some patterns of behaviour perdure to become accepted institutional practices while others do not. Similarly, the thesis is restricted to the identification of institutional differences in a society which marks it as plural at a given time without explaining the process of acculturation by which such differences might be reduced.[26]

This, as Lloyd Braithwaite has noted, tends to encourage a merely quantitative estimate of what are "similar" and "different" in institutional practices and beliefs and to ignore the main point, which is that certain of these values are central and others peripheral to the social system.[27] Stuart Hall also criticized the pluralist thesis for subordinating factors such as race/colour, class, etc. to culture in determining the social structure. Since, he argues, these factors all coincide with one another to a high degree, it is not analytically sound to ascribe priority to any one. Rather 'it is [the] over-determined complexity which constitutes the specificity of the problem requiring analysis'.[28] This criticism strikes at the root of the pluralist theory as conceived by Smith and Despres.

As a further objection, Hall also claims that the plural model 'blurs the distinction between parallel or horizontal, and vertical or hierarchical segmentation'. This criticism, however, was evidently made without reference to Smith's differentiation between structural/hierarchical and social/segmental pluralism. In any event, to assert (as Hall does) that hierarchical segmentation does not signify true pluralism[29] is to prejudge the issue without proper examination. While this might well be true of some societies, it certainly does not apply to all composite or Caribbean societies at all stages of their historical development (e.g. Guyana and Trinidad in the 19th century).

Representing a synthesis of sorts, the approach of van den Berghe, in my opinion, appears to go a long way towards neutralizing these criticisms of the general theory of pluralism, though it does make the term "plural" somewhat nebulous. Rejecting the idea of institutional diversity as an essential condition for pluralism, he treats it as a variable and includes cases of stratification based on race, caste, estate or class as instances of pluralism, even though the constituent sections share the same general culture. Thus, two basic features signify a greater or lesser degree of pluralism:

1. segmentation into corporate groups that frequently, though not necessarily, have different cultures or subcultures;
2. a social structure compartmentalized into analagous, parallel, non-complementary but distinguishable sets of institutions.

Other characteristics of pluralism include a relative absence of consensus, a relative presence of cultural heterogeneity, a relative degree of inter-group conflict, relative sectional autonomy, the relative importance of coercion and economic interdependence as integrative elements, the political dominance of one corporate group, and the primacy of segmental, utilitarian, non-affective, and functionally specific relationships *between* corporate groups, and of total, non-utilitarian, affective, diffuseties *within* such groups.[30] This approach renders the concept of pluralism less restrictive and at the same time highlights the interaction of social roles without losing sight of the importance of cultural institutions.

The segmentation which is said to characterize the structurally plural society raises a number of questions regarding the maintenance of its form and stability. Central to the pluralist theory is the view that in the absence of a collective social will or consensus, the political domination of one corporate section is necessary to preserve the total social order. According to Smith, 'Given the fundamental differences of belief, value, and organization that connote pluralism, the monopoly of power by one cultural section is the essential precondition for the maintenance of the total society in its current form'. This dominant power is held by a distinct numerical minority organized as a corporate group. The entire state apparatus is thus under the exclusive control of this cultural minority and is employed in a systematic way to subjugate the other cultural sections by denying them political rights, citizenship, and opportunities for their own organization as corporate groups. Though forming a majority of the population, these subordinated people are not citizens but subjects, and the state becomes the representative political organ of the dominant ruling minority. 'The result is a characteristically oligarchic regime based on systematic political and social inequality designed to preserve and perpetuate the institutional conditions for the sectional dominance with which it is identified.'[31]

While recognizing the central importance of such political domination by one corporate section and its employment of coercion to maintain the structural inequalities among the constituent sections, some writers have been critical of Smith's concentration on this domination in the political institutional system,[32] and his consequent classification of "property and economy" as institutions which might differ among the cultural sections.[33] Using the Gramscian concept of hegemony, Hall asserts that 'imperative coordination [in composite societies] ... is achieved via the hegemonic domination of one sector over all the others in every feature of organised life'. However, he argues that the plural model falls short of this by concentrating 'on plural cultural values, but not on the structure of legitimation',[34] which presumably would include, *inter alia*, (in Marxist terms) control of the means of production i.e., of the dominant economic institutions.

In a similar manner, van den Berghe also considers control of the political institutions to be insufficient to ensure compliance among the subordinated sections (and thus social stability), and instead regards economic interdependence within a common economy as one of the few integrative elements in a plural society. Since this interdependence is asymmetrical,[35] however, it endorses Hall's notion of an all-embracing sectional hegemonic domination extending beyond the political institutions. Yet it is evident that by distinguishing between collective domination which is effected through the political institutions, and individual domination which occurs when segments of the subordinate population are placed under the direct control of individuals of the dominant group (e.g., serfdom, slavery, peonage or indenture),[36] Smith also implicitly recognizes the pervasiveness of minority dominance in the plural society.

The issue of race is a thorny problem in the theoretical formulations of the plural model. Though acknowledging that most plural societies, especially those characterised by differential incorporation, are multiracial and that the racial sections tend to be culturally distinct, Smith does not consider race to be a condition of pluralism. 'To do so is to mistake the social myth for reality, and thus to miss the structure that underlies it and gives it both force and form'.[37] On the contrary, however, both John Rex and Harmannus Hoetink regard race as an integral part of the social reality of a segmented society since it reinforces cultural differences and perpetuates social segmentation.[38]

Rex in fact adds a further historical dimension by pointing out that with the abandonment of legal inequality in colonial societies, racism assumes even more salience as the ideological basis for maintaining the structural inequalities which differentiate the constituent social groups.[39] In his rethinking of pluralism, Smith has recently appeared to accord greater importance to race in determining sectional differentiation and status, though he still continues to subordinate it to culture.[40]

It is van den Berghe, however, who has attempted to develop a firm theoretical relationship between race and pluralism. He treats race as an independent criterion in determining social segmentation. 'Since race is a more rigid basis of cleavage than ethnicity, social pluralism can subsist longer and, indeed even in the nearly total absence of cultural pluralism, whereas the converse is not true.'[41] Accordingly, he formulated an elaborate framework which relates the form of pluralism with the type of race and power relations in the segmented society.

Within this framework, paternalistic systems of race relations are dominated by a racial minority, and are further characterized by sharp role and status differentiation along racial lines, great social distance between racial categories, and a lack of social mobility. Here the underlying bases of social pluralism are the wide differences in status, power and wealth. Such a system is partially maintained by force and economic interdependence. But despite the great social distance, there is close symbiosis and even intimacy without any diminution of status inequalities. Physical segregation is, therefore, not a major element of social control, and consequently there is much scope for the development of value consensus around an acceptance of the superiority of the dominant section, and through acculturation. Hence, social pluralism is preserved while there is a gradual reduction of cultural pluralism.[42]

On the other hand, competitive systems of race relations are dominated by a majority or a large minority of over 20 percent. A colour bar still persists and racial membership remains ascribed, but there is a wide range of class differentiation within the racial sections and less status differential between them. Hence, although particularistic-ascriptive values persist, greater social and occupational mobility is fostered by a shift towards universalistic-achievement values as required in certain economic sectors. This, however, causes a decrease in social distance and an erosion of the value consensus around the acceptance of the superiority of the dominant section. Consequently social pluralism is perpetuated and consciously reinforced by segregation and discrimination in order to counterbalance integrative tendencies at the economic and cultural levels.[43]

Social segmentation, lack of consensus, political domination by one section, coercion — all these characteristics point to a climate of inherent instability in the structurally plural society, and most proponents of the theory seem to admit that intersectional conflict is probable. M.G. Smith argues that 'since the plural society depends for its structural form and continuity on the regulation of intersectional relations by government, changes in the social structure presuppose political changes, and these usually have a violent form'. In fact, the very structure of the plural society, whether it assumes the form of differential incorporation under the political dominance of a cultural minority or of a consociation uniting equally autonomous segments of different structure, size, ethnic and institutional background, interest, need and power, is conducive to instability and conflict.[44] Van den Berghe concurs with the view that conflict is inherent in plural societies.[45] But while admitting the presence of conflict, Despres does not see it as a product of pluralism. Instead, he argues that the patterns of plural integration can be manipulated to form different types of social alignment between the sections which might be conflict-producing.[46]

The issue of conflict in the plural society lies at the heart of the debate between the advocates and critics of the theory. Central to this issue is the absence of common social values. Lloyd Braithwaite argues, however, that every society must have a certain amount of common or shared values in order to preserve its unity. Thus he claims that the pluralists' tendency to ignore the ties of common sentiment leads to an over-emphasis of sectional cultural differences, and of the essentiality of economic and coercive elements to hold the society together.[47] Another critic, H.I. McKenzie, has suggested that conflict might be produced by the very creation of a common value system consequent on the breakdown of the plural order.[48]

Using Caribbean plantation society as their point of reference, Braithwaite, Raymond T. Smith and others have articulated their own theories of class stratification in contraposition to the pluralist theory. They argue that the common value system around which the society is integrated is the general acceptance of the superiority of the scale of values and culture of the superordinate social system. R.T. Smith points out, however, that the sharing of this common value system does not imply the absence of social and cultural differentiation or the lack of opposition to the dominance of one social grouping. Rather it simply means that everything in the society is judged by comparison with the values of the dominant European social system, so that the whole structure of society, including the ranking system, acquires "legitimacy" in terms of those values. Accordingly, the "subcultures" of the subordinate groups are correspondingly devalued.[49]

R.T. Smith and Hall call this process of integration "creolization". It is not a simple process of acculturation to the dominant culture, but involves two major processes: firstly, the creation of some area of common culture corresponding to the social relations in which people of varying ethnic groups are involved; secondly, the stressing of differences between the groups identified as "racial" groups. 'Thus creole culture, while encouraging some level of common cultural participation, also emphasized cultural differences and resulted in the participation of socially exclusive groups at every level of society.'[50] This has caused Braithwaite to point to the continued importance of differences of racial identity within the context of societal integration.[51]

This in large measure accords with the concept of creolization espoused by historian Edward Brathwaite, which is based on the 'notion of an historically affected socio-cultural continuum, within which ... there are four inter-related and sometimes overlapping orientations' viz., European, Euro-creole, Afro-creole (or folk), and creo-creole (or West Indian). 'A common colonial and creole experience is shared among the various divisions, even if that experience is variously interpreted.'[52] Into this "traditional" creole matrix were integrated after emancipation the Asian and other immigrant groups who, though with very different "great traditions", were likewise creolized.[53]

What is interesting about Brathwaite's variant of the creole model, however, is the notion of "incomplete creolization" among all the socio-cultural groups in the society,[54] both old and new immigrants. This has meant that each group expresses its own variant of the common creole culture which unites them as a total society. Like R.T. Smith and Hall, therefore, Brathwaite recognizes differences within the Creole whole whose unity he poetically describes as "submarine".[55]

According to the consensus thesis, such social and cultural differences as exist within the society do not constitute pluralism in the Furnivallian sense. On the contrary, it is held that during slavery Caribbean plantation society was characterized by a graduated hierarchy of social stratification based on particularistic-ascriptive values of race and colour by which whiteness was ascribed a superior status and placed the individual at the top of the social pyramid, while blackness was equated with inferiority and relegation to the bottom of the social structure. In Vera Rubin's words, 'given the system of social stratification, race and ethnicity were associated with social class and the cultural correlates of class. Stated inversely, socio-cultural correlates of colour have been significant status variables in the West Indies'.[56] Hall refers to this social structure as a "caste-status" system based on race and colour in which the cultures and institutions of master and slave are 'rigidly differentiated' but adapted to the slave society context. Hence, 'the "world" of the slave house and the village and the "world" of the plantation great house are two socio-cultural "worlds" which form differentiated parts of a single socio-economic system: they are not plural segments of parallel but distinct cultures'.[57]

After slavery, however, it is argued that universalistic-achievement values such as education and occupation increased in importance as determinants of social status and mobility, though not to the exclusion of ascriptive criteria.[58] For this reason, Hall sees the emancipation 'as the transition point between caste and class society in the Caribbean', with indenture serving as "a water-shed" between the two social sturctures. Following Braithwaite, he sees 'a tilting of the ethnic composition of class and status groups ... [signifying] a degree of social mobility across race-colour frontiers'. Thus a system of stratification emerges in which 'race, colour, status, occupation, power and wealth overlap and are ideologically mutually reinforcing'. But although it is the first three criteria which form the basic stratification matrix, the society cannot be classified as an 'ethnic or race-based or even race-colour based social system, but a social class stratification system in which the race-colour elements in the stratification matrix constitute the visible index of a more complex structure'.[59]

This class stratification thesis thus treats differences of culture among the ethnic sections as "subcultures" coexisting within a society integrated around a common system of shared values. This does not deny the importance or validity of racial or cultural differences in determining the social structure. In fact, it recognizes ethnic cleavages while focussing on the forms of social interaction which promote social and cultural integration. Nor does it assume complete social consensus. R.T. Smith even admits that coercion is a very important element in the stabilization of this society.[60] Likewise, it does not postulate the absence of conflict; for Braithwaite asserts that the common value of ethnic superiority/inferiority is inherently productive of tensions, and creates a tendency to disintegration within the social system particularly when this value is challenged.[61]

Although this approach is radically different from the pluralist theory outlined by M.G. Smith and Despres, it is by no means incompatible with van den Berghe's conceptualization of pluralism. In fact, as articulated by R.T. Smith, it bears the hallmarks of what van den Berghe identifies as minimal cultural pluralism with accompanying social or racial pluralism. Braithwaite himself makes the observation that in a general sense every society has pluralistic aspects.[62] In fact, he has gone even further to express some doubt about the applicability of consensus theory to Guyana and Trinidad:

> The question really arises as to how far these countries have developed a sufficient common culture, ... understanding, ... tolerance, a sufficient body of institutions in which everybody has confidence so that a political system can endure. To some extent, of course, this has been achieved, but ... the issue is still in doubt.[63]

These apparent theoretical convergences, however, merely obscure the fundamental differences between the two basic approaches.

The class stratification thesis is, of course, premised on the Weberian concept of class which embodies three analytically distinct criteria, viz., wealth, status and power.[64] But there is another theoretical persuasion which has influenced the work of some Caribbeanists, i.e., Marxism. Marx posited a far more economic determinist approach to society, and identified classes by their relations to the means of production. His conceptualization of the transformation over time of "classes *in* themselves" into "classes *for* themselves" as they develop a consciousness of distinctly common interests and act together to promote and defend them, is the crux of his theory. For Marx, it is this identification and pursuit of divergent material interests stemming from the differentiated relations to the means of production which generates "class conflict".[65]

This theoretical, methodological and analytical approach has influenced several Caribbeanists, most recently Post and Beckford & Witter on Jamaica, and Rodney on Guyana. The latter, for instance, saw the fundamental class conflict in 19th century Guyana as being one between capital (identified mainly with the planter class) and labour (both full- and part-time workers). At the same time, however, he could not be too zealous in his application of Marxist theory to 19th century Guyana because he recognized that the plantation colony was still in certain respects pre-capitalistic. This meant that the conditions did not exist for the formation of clear-cut and well-defined economic classes except perhaps for the planter class as the owners of the dominant means of production. The biracial middle strata were seen to vacillate between the two primary and mutually antagonistic "classes". Because of this economic class deterministic approach, all of these writers regard(ed) racial conflict as a contradiction, historical residue, aberration, etc.[66]

John Rex sees value in both the class stratification and pluralist theses for the development of sociological theory. But he does not think that all composite colonial societies could realistically be grouped together and classified as either plural or stratified. Rather he distinguishes three types of such societies. The first is characterized by the existence of a large settler population including farmers and employed workers. The farmers form an economic class in the Marxist or Weberian sense and defends its interests both in the market place and in the political sphere. Native labour forms a separate class without control over the means of production, and without the capacity to defend its interests because of restrictions imposed by the political regime which represents the dominant, politically organized class. Such a situation exists in South Africa.[67]

Rex, however, notes that 'while relation to the basic means of production is an important source of differentiation and class position ... there are also other aspects of the total economic, political and legal systems which differentiate men from one another and produce roles which are often performed by culturally or racially distinct groups, each of which has its own distinct system of legal rights'.[68] In fact, he argues that there is no reason why economic class cannot also function as estates and status groups.[69] These considerations have led him to his second type of colonial society composed of groups of different national or ethnic origin which are to some degree occupationally specialized in a caste-like or estate system, though the groups are bound together by the same economic system. These distinct ethno-occupational groups are separately composed of peasants, slaves, serfs, and indentured workers; secondary traders; settler capitalists, workers and farmers; freed slaves, coloureds, and poor whites; colonial administrators; and missionary and clergy. Each group represents a distinct legal and political entity.[70]

This social system appears to approximate the plural model, and indeed M.G. Smith has been quick to observe that it 'leads us back to the politically grounded racial orders on which all plantation societies are based, and so to their prerequisite and historic pluralism, their major sections being institutionally differentiated as regards family and kinship, socialization, education, religion, political institutions, technology, ecology and economy, recreation, and language'.[71]

Far more cautiously, however, Rex deliberately designates it a "colonial estate system" or "ethnically plural estate system" because that nomenclature suggests that more is at stake than mere cultural and institutional differences among the constituent social sections. He does, however, agree with the pluralists that the stability of such societies depends on a monopoly of the means of legitimate power and violence in the hands of one corporate section, in this case the colonizing power, upon the withdrawal of whom conflict is likely unless there is some agreement over the division of political and economic power.[72]

The third type of composite society is the product of a biological-cum-cultural integration. Rex notes that in all composite societies, there is the emergence of a biologically mixed group which speaks the language and practises with variations the culture of the dominant section. This merger of physical types and cultures results in a stratified system integrated by a shared culture which incorporates two completely distinct groups at its extremes, and which allows for an infinite number of intermediate gradations.[73] This approximates the type of stratified society conceptualized by Braithwaite, Raymond Smith, Brathwaite, Hall, *et al.*

This biological-cum-cultural concept has been taken to its

logical conclusion by Hoetink. He argues that the plural society idea is in reality approximated only at the moment of origin of the society. Immediately thereafter, the process of dissolution of pure social and cultural pluralism begins, and progresses gradually towards ultimate racial and cultural homogenization, unless a commonly accepted ideology supportive of the perpetuation of the existing social segmentation is developed e.g., the ideology of caste in India.[74]

Thus, short of the elimination of one (or more) segment(s) by another, homogenization would be effected by ultimate racial and cultural fusion. But this depends on whether the different sections consider it a desirable ideal for the total society. The process is conditioned by "the somatic norm image" which is 'the complex of physical (somatic) characteristics which are accepted by a group as its norm and ideal'. In other words, it is the yardstick of aesthetic evaluation and ideal of the somatic characteristics of members of the group.[75]

Hoetink argues that the somatic norm image forms an independent factor in moulding attitudes towards race distinct from normal social milieu factors. The pace at which racial homogenization will occur thus depends to a large degree on the somatic norm images of the respective groups concerned, though that of the dominant group is crucial to the process. Since it is inevitable that inter-sectional acculturation or cultural homogenization will centre around the practices and values of the dominant group, their adherence to a cultural ideology which stimulates (or rejects) biological-cum-social mingling will ultimately lead to its incorporation as an ideal in the cultural fabric of the subordinate groups, and will promote (or retard) the process of biological or racial homogenization.[76]

Hoetink's idea of racial and cultural homogenization constitutes an ideal social situation. But his conceptualization of this process is useful for its insight that social integration in a composite society requires a shared value system which is not merely socio-cultural in nature, but which has psychological and racial dimensions as well. This is not to deny the perpetuation of social segmentation in some instances based on an accepted ideology; but this differs from pluralism which for him exists only at the hypothetical "first moment" of a society.

It is evident from the foregoing that there is no integral

relationship between multiracialism and pluralism as suggested by Beckford. Multiracial societies are not necessarily plural, nor are plural societies necessarily multiracial. But, the fact remains, as M.G. Smith has claimed, that most differentially incorporated plural societies *are* multiracial. At the same time, we can concur with Rex in the view that composite colonial societies cannot realistically be grouped together as either plural or class stratified. For it is evident that these societies may exhibit features characteristic of both types in varying combinations. Hence there is considerable value in treating them as variables along a continuum in which both plural and class stratified societies are ideal types, with M.G. Smith's structurally plural society at one pole and Hoetink's racially and culturally homogenized society at the other. In fact, Hoetink himself seems to have arrived at a similar conclusion when he notes that the two theoretical persuasions 'are not mutually exclusive, but rather they have to be viewed as poles of a continuum'.[77] This is not the same as treating them all as variably plural as does van den Berghe,[78] because that renders the term "plural" somewhat imprecise.

Before any classification can be made of composite societies, therefore, they should be analysed separately with a view to establishing whether their structural features are characteristic of either plural or class stratified societies, and also to determining at which point along the societal continuum they might fall. Such systematic analysis is important in order to provide more empirical data for the further development of social theory in this field, as well as for the comparative study of these societies. The present study of post-slavery plantation-dominated Guyana is precisely such an analysis of a composite colonial society during a critical period of its historical development.

In the following chapters, therefore, those aspects and features of composite societies which emerged from the preceding theoretical discussion as central to their form and structure are subjected to detailed examination and analysis. In particular, attention will be focussed on the distribution and use of power in the political system, intra-sectional and inter-sectional activities and relations, and their effect on the degree of social segmentation and/or integration; the extent to which the stability and unity of the total society is maintained by consensus and/or coercion; and, the degree and nature of change which the society undergoes in the period under consideration. What is critical is the fact that no study of a multiracial society can be complete without an assessment of the importance and role of race as an independent determinant of the socio-political structure.

CHAPTER 2

THE PLANTATION SYSTEM AND THE CHALLENGE OF EMANCIPATION

The fundamental conditions and criteria for the development and continued operation of the plantation system outlined by Wolf and Mintz (see chapter 1) achieved their maximum fulfilment in the Caribbean by the mid-eighteenth century. The system was fully established particularly in the old British and French colonies of Barbados, Antigua, St. Kitts, Jamaica, Martinique, Guadeloupe and St. Domingue, and was rapidly developing in other territories. Everywhere the plantation system utilized most of the arable land suitable for the large-scale production of staples, accounted for most of the capital invested and technology imported into the territories, and was virtually solely responsible for the introduction of a vast amount of unfree labour from West Africa. Furthermore, in each island society, the planting interest assumed political and social hegemony by the concentration of state power in their hands, which was used to perpetuate the dominance of the plantation system. Although in the French colonies power was concentrated in the crown, it was used to the same end.

By the early 19th century, however, the British Caribbean plantation system was showing signs of incipient decline. After the abolition of the British slave trade in 1807, the supply of labour became increasingly problematic, and was further exacerbated by the manumission policy during the 1820s. Furthermore, with the end of the Napoleonic Wars, the British West Indian planters encountered stiff competition in Europe from Brazilian and Cuban sugar producers, and even found their monopoly in the British market gradually eroded by their East Indian counterparts. This contraction of both the labour supply and markets curtailed further expansion, except in the newly acquired territories where fertile land was more readily available and costs of production lower. Thus the profitability of the British Caribbean plantation system, especially in the older colonies, was under severe threat; and this naturally affected the flow of investment capital and the acquisition of new technology. This meant that the basic operating conditions of the plantation system became increasingly difficult to fulfil as slavery drew to a close in the British West Indies.

The final emancipation in 1838 thus merely served as the catalyst for the long impending socio-economic crisis which the plantation system encountered. The system of unfree labour upon which the plantations had depended for two centuries no longer existed. In addition, much of the politico-legal sanctions and regulations which had been employed to suppress and control the slaves were no longer appropriate in post-emancipation society. Consequently, the spectre of widespread chaos and destruction in a blind quest for revenge by the ex-slaves loomed large in the minds of the plantocracy.[1] Then, as if to seal the ruin of the plantation system, the British government, in pursuit of its free trade policies, permitted foreign free-labour sugar to enter the British market in 1844; and two years later passed legislation designed to equalize the duties on all sugar imported into Britain. For the embittered plantocracy, not even the handsome slave compensation award of £20 million made by the British government could offset the damage inflicted by such "disastrous" policies.

The effects of emancipation and of the British free trade policies were not, however, uniform throughout the Caribbean. Local conditions, geographical and demographic, political and economic, played a vital part in determining in what form and to what extent the plantation system would survive. Green shows that where land was scarce in relation to labour, the planters found that the plantation system could be maintained with minimum adjustment, aided by the compensation award. Thus in the older settled, smaller and most densely populated islands such as Barbados, Antigua and St. Kitts (with over 300 persons per square mile), the effective utilization of most of the arable land by the plantations prevented any significant withdrawal of the ex-slaves from plantation labour, and consequently, sugar production was actually increased after emancipation: from about 19,000 tons in 1834 to 41,000 tons in 1865 in Barbados, from 8,000 to about 10,000 tons in Antigua, and from 4,000 to about 8,000 tons in St. Kitts in the same period.[2] Not surprisingly, therefore, the dominance of the plantation was preserved and the planters remained virtually unchallenged in their social and political supremacy in these islands.

Circumstances were somewhat different, however, in the middle and low density territories comprising Jamaica, the Windward Islands, Trinidad and Guyana. With population densities varying from as high as between 150 and 180 persons per square mile in Grenada and St. Vincent, between 50 and 75 in St. Lucia and Jamaica, just 12 in Trinidad,[3] to as low as about one per square mile in Guyana,[4] the plantation system in these territories encountered enormous difficulties in its quest to adjust to the new economic and social environment created by emancipation. These difficulties centred around two main factors: firstly, the scarcity of finance capital, particularly in the first decade of freedom, which affected the entire British Caribbean economy; and, secondly, a shortage in the supply of regular, cheap labour which affected essentially the middle and low density territories.

The situation in Guyana was typical of the crisis which the relatively less densely populated territories experienced. Between 1838 and 1844, plantation production fell dramatically: coffee production was down 64.4 percent, sugar by 29.5 percent, rum by 36.5 percent, and molasses by 25 percent; while cotton had virtually gone out of production altogether.[5]

The real crisis came after the passage of the sugar duties act in 1846, coupled with a severe economic recession in Europe in 1847-48. The bottom literally fell out of the market as prices slumped drastically from 34s.5d. per cwt. in 1846 to 28s.3d. in 1847, and still further to 23s.8d. in 1848.[6] This occasioned enormous losses to the West Indian planters who found their bills of exchange for produce already shipped to metropolitan merchants worthless since many West India houses had crashed. What was worse was the fact that credit which had even before the recession been scarce,[7] practically dried up in the crisis. Many plantations, already heavily encumbered with debt, were thus forced to be mortgaged to metropolitan principals or were abandoned and sold at execution sales.[8]

In these circumstances, property values depreciated greatly, changing hands in many cases fully 50 percent below 1840 prices.[9] By 1846, not one-third of the Guyanese plantations was free from mortgage debts,[10] and between 1847 and 1850 at least one-quarter was sold at execution sales at prices which brought land to an average of 40 shillings ($9.60) per acre, inclusive of buildings, machinery and all invested capital.[11] This situation was also reflected in Jamaica and to a lesser extent in Trinidad.[12]

The plantation system in the British Caribbean found itself in a process of contraction during the first decade after emancipation, being unable to attract sufficient finance capital, or to introduce improved technology, or to expand production and maximize profits, or even to procure an adequate and regular supply of labour. Hence, in Jamaica, the number of estates declined from 646 in 1834 to 330 by 1854.[13] In Guyana, the figure dropped from 308 in 1838 to 196 by 1849.[14]

It was in fact the labour supply which, as far as the West Indian planters were concerned, presented the greatest problem. Particularly in the middle and low density territories, the availability of land for settlement by the ex-slaves seemed to offer them an opportunity to establish a way of life independent of the plantations. Thus wherever there was unused land which could provide basic subsistence, the ex-slaves sought to purchase and/or occupy it. Rawle Farley attributed this craving for land to slavery itself. He noted that the same desire for personal liberty which had been the root cause of slave revolts and the establishment of maroon settlements was responsible for the land purchases after emancipation and the formation of peasant villages. 'The rise of the village settlements was symbolic of the continuation of the revolt against the plantation system by free labour, reinforced after 1838 by the advantages denied them under slavery.'[15]

This land hunger was visible particularly in the Windward Islands, Jamaica, Trinidad and Guyana. Despite attempts to hinder this process in most of these territories either through restrictive Crown lands legislation or outright reluctance of the planters to sell unused private lands to the exslaves, the latter were able to acquire land either through direct purchase or indirectly with the intervention of sympathetic missionaries. Riviere notes that in Trinidad, the emancipated people owned 53,000 acres by 1854; in Jamaica, the number of freeholds increased from 2,000 in 1838 to 27,379 in 1845, and still further to about 50,000 in 1861. A similar, though less spectacular development occurred among the ex-slaves in the Windward Islands. In St. Lucia, freeholds increased from 100 in 1841 to 2,343 in 1853; in Tobago, from 658 in 1845 to 2,367 in 1853; and, in Grenada, from 1,947 to 3,571 between 1845 and 1853[16].

Guyana witnessed one of the greatest expressions of land hunger among the ex-slaves of the region. Settlements sprang up along the entire sea coast from the Corentyne river in Berbice, through Demerara, to the Arabian coast in Essequibo. Not only were there purchases of small plots of land, but more remarkably, whole plantations were bought by large groups of ex-slaves who became joint-stock holders of the purchased estate. By the end of 1840, the ex-slaves had nominally acquired 121 land titles in Berbice,[17] and 475 in Demerara and Essequibo.[18] So great was their demand for land that by 1842, the lowest price paid was $240 (£50) per acre, and in many areas $480 (£100) per acre was not unusual.[19]

By 1848, there were already 32,717 people resident on freehold lands in Guyana.[20] In 1850, there were 7,329 plots, varying between one-quarter and five acres, and amounting to 6,413 acres, for which the 7,023 proprietors had paid an estimated $631,701. In addition, there were 25 plantations with a total acreage of 9,049.5 acres under collective ownership, which cost $373,835. Thirteen tracts of Crown land comprising 1,387 acres had been bought for $6,658. Hence between 1838 and 1850, the ex-slaves of Guyana had spent about $1,012,194 on land alone; and it was estimated that a further $1.5 million were spent on the building of 10,544 houses and on agricultural and other improvements. Thus the total value of property in the hands of the ex-slaves after just one decade of freedom amounted to almost $2.5 millions.[21]

What was very striking about these land purchases in Guyana was that in spite of the availability of vast amounts of Crown lands in the hinterland beyond the plantation belt at a price (£1 or $4.80 per acre) far lower than those paid for private lands, the ex-slaves generally declined to buy them, preferring instead to remain within the cleared, settled, better drained, cultivated parts of the country, where they could also benefit from proximity to markets, churches, schools, and of course the plantations in order to supplement their incomes by wage labour.[22] The ex-slaves in Guyana, therefore, enjoyed greater flexibility and scope in the process of land acquisition than their counterparts in the smaller, more densely populated islands.

But did population density determine the availability of land to the ex-slaves in the Caribbean? Pointing to Belize where there was a low population density, but where the ex-slaves were still not able to acquire substantial amounts of land, Bolland argues that it is necessary to go beyond the pure demographic factors and examine the total system of white domination, especially their control of the land, to determine the access of the ex-slaves to land resources. Thus the availability of land is primarily determined by the power structure.[23] Green, however, counters this by claiming that the Belize case is too greatly different from the sugar colonies to make a meaningful comparison.[24]

The Guyana case throws some light on this little debate. It demonstrates that while the system of white domination apparently remained intact after emancipation, the ex-slaves were nevertheless able to acquire very substantial amounts of land; and this was in spite of the new crown lands regulations which were intended to inhibit this process. The question, therefore, is whether this land was (made) available simply on account of the fact of low density of population or something more fundamental.

The evidence suggests that it was largely economic factors which determined the availability of land to the ex-slaves. The lands which the ex-slaves purchased were not the lower priced, and more remote crown lands; but rather the far more highly priced private lands. These became available because of acute economic distress encountered by the planters during the 1840s which forced many of them reluctantly to cut their losses and exploit the land hunger of the ex-slaves. One might thus argue that economic conditions weakened the control of the planters over land (and labour) and thereby made private land available to the ex-slaves. In that sense one important area of the white power structure was breached.

As will be seen later on, however, during and after the 1850s when conomic conditions improved, white control over land (both private and state-owned) was firmly reasserted by leagal restrictions on group purchases, an increase in the price of crown lands, and the appointment of superintendents of rivers and creeks to root out squatters from Crown lands. Thus although village lands became relatively worthless due to poor drainage, the white power structure was able by legislative, pricing and policing mechanisms to effectively prevent the ex-slaves and their descendants from acquiring more land. This was true in spite of the fact that Guyana has always remained a low density country (see chapters 5 & 6).

The availability of land in Guyana did not lead, however, to a wholesale withdrawal from plantation work as the planters feared though, as in the other middle and low density territories, it did affect the quantity and regularity of labour supply. By the mid-1840s there were about 38,000 ex-slaves still at work on the plantations, [25] about 43 percent of the work force at emancipation. The fact was that new opportunities for alternative employment arose; there was a new freedom to determine how best to dispose of one's time and labour; and new interests and responsibilities diverted the ex-slave's attention from the sole preoccupation with plantation labour. Men who bought land had to devote some time to its cultivation and to the erection of houses. In addition, women performed household duties and took care of their children, and there was a tendency to withdraw children from plantation work and send them to school instead.[26] The result was not a definitive stoppage in the supply of labour to the plantations, but no less problematical, a considerable irregularity in that supply. This was the case as well in Trinidad and Jamaica.[27] The planter, therefore, could not be certain of the same number of workers in the field from day to day; and even when in the field, many workers left to attend to their own business interests after a short time at work.[28]

The supply of labour was also influenced by the attitude and solvency of the planters. Where tact and moderation were exhibited, where planters were prepared to pay their workers fairly and punctually, and perhaps to provide a few judicious indulgencies, there was generally no shortfall in the supply or performance of labour.[29] In Guyana, some planters prudently built schools and chapels, and paid missionaries to remain on the spot in the hope of enticing their workers to settle near or on the plantations.[30] The ex-slaves themselves were not slow to devise tactics to augment their earning. In Guyana, itinerant task-gangs became popular, moving under a headman to plantations in different parts of the countryside to perform highly paid, strenuous tasks where labour was scarce.[31]

In Nevis and the Windward Islands, particularly St. Lucia, Tobago and Grenada, several planters sought to overcome their labour problem by adopting the share-cropping or *métairie* system. By this system, the planter supplied the plants, transportation and machinery, while the *métayer* provided the labour. At the end of the crop season, the sugar produced was shared between the parties according to contract. Marshall observes that this system was considered by the Windward planters as a 'desperate expedient', and that they never perceived it as 'a system of land tenure or a permanent feature of industrial activity'.[32] So although it remained the principal means of production in those islands until the end of the century, it was not very successful in practice.[33]

When tried in Jamaica and Guyana, the system was even more shortlived as the planters were much less enthusiastic than their Windward counterparts.[34] In Guyana, those who had capital to pay for labour were loathe to share their profits with *métayers*. Although the system did save some plantations from total abandonment during the worst phase of the economic recession, most planters who adopted it repudiated it when circumstances improved. Besides, many disputes arose between the planters and *métayers*. Shares were arbitrarily fixed by planters varying from a half for each party to as low as one-third for the *métayers*; and coupled with accounting irregularities arising over advances of money made to the latter during the cultivation period, and fluctuating market prices, it proved extremely difficult to inspire the mutual trust and confidence so very necessary to the success of the experiment.[35]

The general failure of the *métairie* system reflected the inability of the post-emancipation Caribbean to determine how to operate a free-labour economy. Accustomed to exercising absolute control over bonded labour, many planters were at a total loss without the use of artificial means of compulsion;

while, for their part, many ex-slaves attempted to maximise their newly gained bargaining power to extract concessions of one sort or another from the planters. Planters bemoaned the loss of contrl over their labour force, and apportioned all blame for the economic decline squarely on the shoulders of the ex-slaves on account of their irregular labour.[36]

Not surprisingly, therefore, some planters attempted to turn the clock backwards by resorting to their "time-honoured" methods of coercion in order to compel the freed workers to remain in plantation employment. In Guyana, for instance, just after emancipation, the Essequibo planters tried to increase the working day from seven to nine hours, but retreated in the face of resolute resistance from the ex-slaves. In fact, on one estate where the plan was actually implemented, practically all the workers left *en masse*.[37] The following year, the Guyanese planters attempted to pass a trespass bill to curtail the freedom of movement of the ex-slaves by empowering local justices of the peacs or any person in authority on a plantation to apprehend and imprison any stranger on the sole grounds that he did not being to a given estate, and had refused to leave when ordered to do so. The bill, however, was annulled by an order-in-council (6 October 1838) prohibiting such restrictions.[38]

Throughout the Caribbean, however, the most commonly employed method of coercion was the iniquitous tenancy-at-will system. It was common practice to combine rents and wages, and to charge exorbitant rents with a view to forcing the worker to labour long hours on the plantation in order to earn enough to pay the rents. If workers sought to escape such quasi-peonage by working elsewhere, they were subject to summary eviction.[39]

Riviere notes that this system was employed with considerable effectiveness in Dominica, Nevis, Montserrat, St. Lucia, Tobago, St. Vincent, and Antigua; but although operated with great severity in Jamaica, the ex-slaves were so successful in resisting it there that by 1842 the planters were obliged to change their approach and to separate rents from wages.[40] The Guyanese planters were no less vicious in their practice of the system. In 1840, for instance, some workers at Plantation Tuschen de Vrienden in Demerara, even after having vacated their cottages, were physically attacked by their former manager, overseer, and some Indian labourers while they awaited transportation to the capital.[41] In another instance, the manager of Plantation Henry was actually convicted in January 1842 of "ill-usage, harsh and improper conduct" towards some of his workers after ejecting them from their cottages without reasonable notice.[42]

In Trinidad and more so in Guyana, the planters felt the need to resort to more drastic collective action in order to cut labour costs and regularize the supply. In 1841, the Guyanese argued that their costs of production exceeded the market price by 14.36 percent, which they attributed mainly to excessively high wages, irregular labour, poor work, and allowances such as gratuities, housing, and medical care. Thus both they and their Trinidad counterparts decided to impose certain rules and regulations from the beginning of 1842 to govern the conduct and remuneration of labour.[43]

In Guyana, these included wage deductions for lateness; a rent penalty for absence from work; dismissal for engaging in occupations not connected with the plantation; prohibition from rearing livestock or hunting, fishing, picking fruit and cutting grass on the plantation; and confiscation of provisions cultivated on the estate on removal or eviction therefrom. Most importantly, wages were fixed at 32 cents a day in the field, and 40 cents in the factory.[44]

Such rules and regulations, however, were not enforceable by law unless voluntarily agreed to by the workers, who displayed no such inclination. In Guyana, they remonstrated to the governor, struck work wherever the rules were imposed, and general civil unrest ensued throughout Demerara and Essequibo, even resulting in a riot at Plantation Blankenburg.[45] Since the planters in Berbice did not follow suit, they were spared similar unrest and strikes. The result was that by the end of January 1842, the Demerara and Essequibo planters were forced to concede defeat and to abandon the scheme.[46] Their Trinidad counterparts did not seem to have achieved any greater success, and it was not until 1844 that they were able to enforce a general wage reduction even in the face of labour strikes.[47] The Guyanese planters had to wait a few more years before experiencing similar success.

The West Indian planters also made full use of the machinery of state to compel the freed workers to labour on the plantations. In Jamaica, Trinidad, and Guyana, masters and servants acts were passed for precisely this purpose. Such an ordinance, passed in 1846 in Guyana, presumed a worker to be contracted for one month in the absence of a long term contract. If he wished to stop working before, he was required to provide fourteen days' written notice. He could also be fined $24 for "wilful misconduct" or "ill-behaviour" while at work; and the magistrate was empowered to stop all or a part of the wages of a convicted person and hand it to the employer for his own use. Finally, the iniquitous system of tying wages to rents was practically legalized by empowering an employer to forfeit a day's rent from the wages of a worker for each day absent from work.[48] Except, therefore, for instituting a wage reduction, this law to all intents and purposes embodied the basic elements which the planters had unsuccessfully tried in 1842 to impose by extra-legal means.

It was not until 1848, however, that the Guyanese planters were able to achieve a direct wage reduction similar to what was successfully imposed in Trinidad four years earlier. The pretext was the acute economic recession of 1847; and they were able to persuade the governor to use the stipendiary magistrates as agents to convince the workers of the necessity for such austerity measures, or risk the alternative of large-scale closure of plantations, widespread unemployment, and lapsing into barbarism. This threat of doomsday was clearly rejected by the workers who promptly struck work again.[49]

Unlike 1842, this strike enveloped the whole colony, including Berbice, and endured for three months from January to March 1848. But as in Trinidad, the whole white section was united on this occasion — planters, merchants, colonial officials, and even the non-conformist missionaries who had previously supported the emancipated people. Eventually the latter were forced into submission, and had to accept wage reductions varying from ten to thirty-three percent.[50] But it was a bitter defeat, marked by violence — acts of incendiarism, and even the murder of plantation watchmen — which persisted well into the following year (1849).[51] No less important was the fact that race relations between white and black deteriorated to their worst state since the emancipation,[52] and placed the issue of race into a new position of prominence, which allowed it to dominate social and political relations for the rest of the century.

This heightening of racial tension achieved even greater

significance since it coincided with the introduction of large-scale immigration to satisfy the labour demands of the plantations. From the outset of this immigration scheme, the ex-slaves were resentful of being taxed to finance in part a scheme which would introduce a mass of alien workers to undermine and weaken their bargaining power in the labour market and to lower wages. The fact that many of these aliens were of different racial stock did not help matters; and the problem was further exacerbated during the 1848 strike when Portuguese and Indian immigrant workers contributed to the defeat of the ex-slaves by keeping several plantations in operation. This consequently generated the animosity of the strikers who intimidated and attacked the immigrant strike-breakers.[53] This early souring of race relations between the Creoles and immigrants set a pattern which persisted for the rest of the century and beyond.

Attempts to introduce immigrants into the British Caribbean began even before the final emancipation in 1838. Interest appeared to be greatest in the three largest territories of Jamaica, Guyana, and Trinidad, although many Windward Island planters were no less keen. The West Indian planters appeared eager to encourage white immigration, although they did not (especially those in Guyana and Trinidad) close their eyes to other sources. White immigration was desirable mainly for two reasons: (1) to create a middle class both economically and socially, and thus force the freed blacks to continue working on the plantations for wages; (2) to augment the white population in the interest of racial security.

Between 1834–38, Jamaica received some 2,371 European immigrants, Trinidad a few Portuguese, and Guyana over 1,000, mainly from the British Isles (including Ireland), Madeira, Malta, France, and Germany. Yet despite their general unwillingness to remain on the estates and excessively high mortality due to disease, poor medical facilities, bad accommodation, and poor diet, only Jamaica was prepared to concede that European immigration was a failure.[54] In 1841 Guyana, and later on Trinidad, St. Vincent, and Grenada began to offer a bounty equivalent to the cost of the passage to promote immigration from Madeira. Some 6,967 Madeirans emigrated to Guyana in 1841–42 before excessive mortality forced a stoppage to this immigration in May 1842.[55] However, after some evidence of successful acclimatization by the survivors, Madeiran immigration into Guyana under the bounty system was resumed in September 1846, resulting in a great influx of 9,730 Madeirans by the end of 1847.[56] Again, however, excessively high mortality attended this immigration; and in 1850 a propaganda campaign in Madeira against emigration to Guyana tended to discourage prospective migrants especially after the famine which had stimulated the initial exodus thence began to subside.[57]

Notwithstanding difficulties between 1835–50, a total of 17,098 Madeirans went to Guyana, while from 1851 to 1882 when Guyana stopped paying the bounty, a further 13,535, emigrated. In addition, 164 Azoreans also migrated to Guyana.[58] The smaller Caribbean territories, however, were far less successful in attracting Portuguese immigrants. According to Laurence, Antigua received just 2,500, St. Vincent and St. Kitts-Nevis each got 2,100, and Jamaica, Grenada, and Dominica a few hundred each.[59]

European immigration was thus hardly adequate to satisfy the labour requirements of the Caribbean plantation system after emancipation. Consequently, the planters particularly in Guyana and Trinidad stopped at nothing to procure labour from any part of the world. They again sought to look to Africa to solve their problem. Despite its sensitivity to any charge of reopening the slave trade under a new guise, the British government allowed itself to be persuaded by the West Indian planters in December 1840 to permit a scheme of bounty-paid immigration from Sierra Leone. But not many Africans who had been liberated from slave ships and sent to Sierra Leone were inclined to risk voluntary migration across the Atlantic, and in fact a number of ships returned empty to the Caribbean in 1841. Even after the British government undertook in 1843 to assume full responsibility for West African emigration, the response among the people was lukewarm. Approximately 500 Africans went to the British Caribbean in 1841–42, the vast majority (475) going to Guyana; and between 1843–45, only 3,448 people went from Sierra Leone to the region, of whom 2,128 went to Guyana.[60]

In 1846, the West Indian planters pressed the British government to approve a scheme to recruit immigrants from the Kroo coast of Liberia. In addition, liberated Africans were imported from the island of St. Helena, as well as from the slave centres at Rio and Havana. Yet the number of these

African immigrants was not very substantial so that between 1841–67, only 36,120 liberated Africans went to the British Caribbean. Of these 12,810 went to Guyana, about 8,000 to Trinidad, 11,000 to Jamaica, and 5,000 to Grenada, St. Vincent, St. Lucia, and Dominica.[61] Guyana also received 819 Africans from Portuguese Cape de Verde,[62] but these should not be confused with the liberated Africans. As Laurence notes, however, even though their number was not very large, the Africans made an important contribution to the continued operation of the plantations in the early post-emancipation years before large-scale Asian immigration became a reality.[63]

The low density territories of Guyana and Trinidad also benefitted from immigration from the smaller, more densely populated West Indian islands, and to a far lesser extent from the United States. A privately funded Voluntary Subscription Immigration Society (VSIS) established in Guyana in 1839 only managed to attract thirty black Americans to that colony;[64] but between 1839–47, Trinidad secured over 1,300 black Americans.[65]

Immigration from the smaller Caribbean islands, particularly Barbados and the Leeward Islands, was more substantial. Recruiting agents were sent by Guyana and Trinidad to these islands offering high wages and generous allowances to prospective emigrants, despite the efforts of the irate island governments to restrict the practice. The VSIS in Guyana managed to attract 2,900 Barbadians in 1840.[66] Between 1835–63, 7,707 West Indians went to Guyana, mainly from Barbados; and this excludes a considerable number of individuals and family groups of between ten and twenty persons who paid their own passages, but of whom no accurate record was kept.[67] Trinidad, between 1839–49 alone, received some 10,278 West Indians.[68] Immigration from the West Indian islands into Guyana received a further stimulus when in 1864 a bounty system was started which accounted for the arrival of 27,223 West Indians until 1885 when it was stopped;[69] but another 853 West Indians migrated to Guyana under renewed bounty in 1890–91.[70]

The revival and expansion of the plantation system, particularly in Guyana and Trinidad, is generally attributed largely to the influx of Indian immigrants. The first group of 396 was introduced into Guyana by the planter John Gladstone in 1838 under five-year contracts and with the promise of a return passage at the end of that period. However, on account of the high mortality and reports of ill-treatment which were publicised by the Anti-Slavery Society, the Council of India suspended any further emigration pending investigation.[71] In 1844, the West Indian planters persuaded the Secretary of State, Lord Stanley, to reopen this source of immigrants with the promise of return passages after five years. The following year, large-scale Indian immigration commenced to Guyana, Trinidad, and Jamaica, only to be discontinued when these colonies cancelled their orders for Indian immigrants — Jamaica in 1846, Trinidad and Guyana in 1848 — on the heels of the credit squeeze and the economic recession.[72]

It was not until 1851 that Indian immigration was resumed to the Caribbean and then only after the British government provided a loan of £500,000 to help finance immigration. [Even so, Jamaica could not make use of this facility immediately, and it was not until 1860 that Indian immigration was resumed into that island but only for a few years. In fact, for most of the century Jamaica imported Indian immigrants in spurts, and consequently not nearly as many went there as to Guyana and Trinidad.]

Indian immigration into the Caribbean lasted until 1917, with Guyana receiving the largest number, some 238,909 between 1838–1917, while Trinidad received 143,939, Jamaica 36,412, Grenada 3,200, St. Vincent 2,472, and St. Lucia 4,354.[73]

The final category of immigrant workers brought into the region was the Chinese. Their introduction had been discussed since 1843, yet an ordinance passed by the Guyana legislature (the Court of Policy) to make provision to receive them came to nothing.[74] In 1851, the Guyanese immigration agent, James White, visited China to promote emigration to the British Caribbean; and this mission eventually yielded some fruit when 988 Chinese emigrated to Trinidad, 647 to Guyana, and 267 to Jamaica between 1852–54.[75] The scheme broke down from an administrative standpoint, and it was not until 1859 that Chinese immigration into the British Caribbean was resumed. Between 1859–66, 11,282 Chinese went to Guyana, and 1,557 to Trinidad.[76] Treaty disagreements between the British and Chinese governments, however, put a halt to this immigration in 1866, and further attempts to revive it were only partially successful. Hence, in 1873, only 388 Chinese went to Guyana;[77] and these were followed in 1879 by the final arrival of 515 Chinese immigrants.[78]

The effects of this programme of large-scale immigration were far-reaching both in economic and social terms. It provided the plantation system, particularly in Guyana and Trinidad, with an abundant and regular supply of dependent labour which ensured its revival, expansion and prosperity after the economic crisis of the 1840s. Immigration thus enabled the planters to recapture full control of the labour market and to reduce the price of labour. Together with the gradual improvement in the market price of sugar after the mid-fifties, it contributed significantly to the increased profitability of the sugar industry, thus enabling the planters to attract more capital for expansion and investment in new technology such as vacuum pans, pneumatic pans, steam clarifiers, and especially in Guyana (where there was a drainage problem), steam draining pumps.

The plantation system which emerged from the 1840s, therefore, was significantly transformed in production technique and better able to compete in the British commodity market with foreign sugar. Although the number of casualties was great, it had been mainly the smaller, inefficient, and least profitable plantations, encumbered with debt, which went out of existence. Many were in fact taken over by larger capitalist companies with headquarters in the metropolis, a process which continued for the remainder of the century. Hence, in Guyana the number of plantations declined still further from 173 in 1851 to 95 in 1890. This, however, was accompanied by an increase in the acreage under sugar cane cultivation from 48,087 in 1855 to 79,243 by 1890. Similarly, with the aid of immigrant labour, production increased from 29,584 tons in 1841 to 105,484 tons in 1890.[79] Trinidad, likewise, experienced a marked increase in production from 14,312 tons in 1838 to 55,327 tons in 1882.[80]

However, neither Jamaica nor the Windward Islands could apparently afford to finance the importation of immigrant workers in sufficiently large numbers to materially reverse the economic decline of their plantation systems. This is one of the reasons why sugar production in Jamaica fell so drastically from 52,659 tons in 1838 to 19,934 tons in 1894, Likewise, St. Vincent's production declined from 10,006 tons between 1834–38 to 2,727 tons in 1894; Tobago's from 4,363 to 599 tons in the same period; Grenada's from 8,408 to a mere three tons in 1894. Indeed, of the Windward Islands, only St. Lucia experienced an increase in production from 2,591 tons in 1834–38 to 7,506 tons in 1882, though this fell sharply to 4,485 tons by 1894.[81]

If the economic impact of large-scale immigration was differential within the British Caribbean, it nevertheless had a profound effect in social terms. Indeed, immigration may be said to have ushered in a new Caribbean society characterized essentially by wide ethnic diversification. To the traditional biracial composition which characterized the slave period and which indeed persisted in several islands after slavery (e.g. Barbados and the Leewards) were added the entirely new racially and culturally differentiated categories of Indians and Chinese particularly in Guyana, Trinidad and Surinam.[82] Caribbean plantation society as a whole was thus characterized by a widely diversified multiracialism after emancipation, a condition which was very strikingly manifested in Guyana. It is in this context that the ensuing analysis of post-slavery Guyanese society is undertaken, since Guyana provides one of the best examples of the new societal composition emerging in the British Caribbean during the half-century after emancipation.

WHITE MINORITY DOMINANCE

CHAPTER 3

COLONIAL POLITICS AND THE INSTITUTIONALIZATION OF PLANTER HEGEMONY

The distinction has been made between two basic types of colonies established by the European imperial powers in different parts of the world. According to Leonard Thompson, the exploitation colony is typically tropical, and is dominated by a minority of transient white administrators, soldiers, managers of plantations and commercial houses, and missionaries. These are all members of institutions with headquarters in the metropolis which they regard as "home", and return thence on retirement. The settler colony on the other hand is typically temperate, and is dominated by a substantial, though not necessarily a majority, white settler community which considers itself as belonging to the colony. Thompson further notes that it is not just a difference of numbers, but 'a question of permanence, self-perpetuation, identification, commitment, and purpose' which differentiates the settler colony from the colony of exploitation. This does not, however, render the two types mutually exclusive; for as Knight observes, to a certain extent each embodies an element of the other.[1]

Plantation colonies were manifestly exploitation colonies *par excellence*, established for the sole purpose of producing one or a few staple commodities, mainly sugar, cotton, coffee and tobacco, for export to the metropolitan markets. The white colonists naturally dominated the society by virtue of their absolute control and management of the principal economic, political, and social institutions, viz., plantations, commercial houses, government and church. Thus in Guyana, they consisted mainly of planters and estate personnel, colonial officials, professionals, merchants, priests and missionaries, soldiers and sailors. "Home" was Britain, in particular England and Scotland, as well as Ireland. There was also a small, steadily declining number of Dutch and North American residents.[2] Finally, there was a body of local-born whites, many of whom were psychologically transients since they too regarded their presence in the colony to be accidental and impermanent, and considered the metropolis as home.

This dominant group of white transient colonists formed a very small minority in the colonial society, never exceeding three percent of the total population. Their numbers increased from 2,776 (2.8 percent) in 1841 to 4,551 (1.6 percent) in 1891.[3] Yet, despite its relatively small numerical composition, the white section did not constitute an organic whole. Differences of origin, wealth, and occupation determined one's class and status. Broadly speaking, British-born whites enjoyed greater prestige than local whites, for the colonial officialdom and most of the other influential whites were British-born. But more specifically, it was the wealthy resident planters and attorneys representing metropolitan principals who dominated the colonial society and formed a kind of aristocracy with a quasi-monopoly of political and social power. They were the main employers of labour and the main patrons of the professions.[4] The colony was practically their fiefdom, and everyone paid them homage and obeissance. They personified the immense dominance which the plantation system held over the entire society.

Only slightly less influential than the planters and attorneys were the plantation managers, whose day to day control of the practical operations of the plantations not only gave them direct power over hundreds of workers of different races and cultures on individual plantations, but also gave them considerable influence for miles around. Indeed, many justices of the peace were resident managers, and in several parts of the country the functions of that office were performed exclusively by them. Overseers stood cap in hand in their presence, while neighbouring gentry, doctors, parsons, and even some government officials were deferent to them. As one contemporary writer put it:

The word manager means a whole pageful of such words as favours, conveniences, power and autocracy. All kinds of privileges and things desirable are in his gift.... At his word hundreds laugh or cry, from his dictum there is no appeal. A benevolent providence has placed labour, homes, surroundings, and life moral, social and otherwise of hundreds in his hands.[5]

Thus the supreme authority of the planters, attorneys and managers on the plantations was reflected in their social pre-eminence. Ranking below them were the merchants, professionals, clergy, junior government officials, and the subaltern officers of estate management. Both Edgar Thompson and George Beckford have pointed out that this social pre-eminence of the plantocracy is parallelled by the concentration of state power in them as a class. This is a necessary condition for preserving the dominance of the plantation system over the society.[6] In Guyana, it assumed the appearance of a despotism of a highly organized oligarchy of sugar barons[7] whose political dominance was institutionalized in the colonial constitution and underwritten by the imperial government.

The constitutional framework thus became a critical component of this planter hegemony. Its origins dated back to 1795 when the Dutch colonists drafted their *Plan of Redress*, and it was preserved by the British after they took possession of Demerara and Essequibo in 1803, under the terms of the "Articles of Capitulation".[8] By this *Plan*, three distinct political authorities were established apart from the judicial bodies. These were the Governor, the Court of Policy, and the College of Kiezers, to which was later added the College of Financial Representatives.[9]

The governor was appointed by the imperial government, and was the chief executive officer, in charge of the overall civil and military administration of the colony. He was automatically president of the legislature, the Court of Policy, and no meeting of that body could be convened in his absence, nor could any bill be introduced or any measure discussed therein, except at his suggestion or with his consent. Moreover, he had the power of suspending any proceeding or discussion, and of voting on any question. In event of a tie, he was empowered to vote again to create a majority.[10] This "casting vote" of the governor was an important element of the

Crown's legislative power in the colonial polity (see chapter 4).

The Court of Policy was originally composed of four ex-officio members including the governor, and four colonial members, two each from Demerara and Essequibo. After Berbice was joined to form the united colony of British Guiana in 1831, an additional member was added to each section of the legislature. One colonial member from each province alternately was required to retire annually according to seniority.[11] Whenever such a vacancy arose in the colonial section, two candidates were nominated by the electoral college, the College of Kiezers, from whom the legislature itself selected one to fill the vacant seat. The electoral college was thus interposed between the colonial legislators and the electorate. Its membership, fixed at seven in 1831, was elected for life by the eligible voters of the colony as one constituency.[12]

The College of Financial Representatives had a membership of six who were to be adjoined to the governor and Court of Policy in Combined Court for the specific and sole purpose of voting on all matters concerning the raising of taxes and the examination of accounts. These financial representatives were elected biennially by the same constituency as the kiezers.[13]

The constitutional provisions which created the political dominance of the plantocracy were the qualifications for the franchise and for membership of the political institutions. After 1831, the franchise had been limited to the holders of 25 slaves.[14] After the abolition of slavery, however, a monetary value was established, viz., the payment of taxes on an annual income of 2,001 guilders (approx. £143), or the payment of 70 guilders (£5) in direct taxes.[15] But since taxation in the colony was chiefly indirect, these qualifications effectively restricted the franchise to a comparatively very small class,[16] and precluded the extension of the vote to the ex-slaves.

Although the idea of extending the franchise to include some of the emancipated people was from time to time aired both by the governor and the Colonial Office,[17] nothing concrete materialized until 1849 when by Ordinance No.15, the franchise was extended:

(a) to freeholders with three acres of cultivated property

valued at $96 (£20) per annum in the country, or with property valued at $500 (£104) in the towns;
(b) to rural leaseholders of six acres of cultivated land valued at $192 (£40) per annum, or to urban leaseholders paying an annual rent of $120 (£25); and
(c) to persons paying taxes on an income of $600 (£125) per annum, or $20 (£4) a year in direct taxes.[18]

The issue of race had figured prominently in the planters' opposition to the proposed extension of the franchise for fear that it would enfranchise the black and coloured majority and result in a "reversion to barbarism".[19] In effect, however, the 1849 franchise proved harmless to the political dominance of the white plantocracy. In each county, the new voters with an income exceeding $600 (essentially whites) far exceeded those who possessed a freehold valued at $96 per annum, even if one presumed that all of the latter were Creole villagers. The governor, Henry Barkly, noted that since no less than 11,000 out of a total population of about 110,000 were proprietors of small lots with houses, representing with their families probably half the total number of inhabitants, the new qualifications could not be considered beyond what was calculated to *prevent* an undue preponderance of the democratic element. The electoral statistics for 1849 demonstrated this vividly: out of 544 votes in the rural districts, only 167 were held by virtue of the dreaded freehold qualifications.[20] And although the number of voters nearly doubled from 561 in 1847 to 962 in 1851, they still constituted a small privileged category, less than one percent of the total population.[21]

The political dominance of the plantocracy was further engineered by election rigging, which became a "time-honoured tradition" in Guyana. The leading sugar firms virtually controlled the election to the political institutions. A few clerks in these firms wrote up voting forms equal to the number of voters in the firms' employ to whom they were dispatched in the country for signature. Governor Light claimed to have seen about 300 to 400 votes in the same handwriting in one election.[22] Thus one or two firms which controlled the purse-strings of two-thirds of the voters could practically determine the outcome of an election.[23]

Such abuses were made more feasible by the system of proxy voting which further bolstered the control of the planters. This system was littered with corruption; votes were cast by attorneys, sequestrators, executors, trustees and guardians for minors, lunatics, husbands on behalf of their wives,[24] aliens, foreigners, etc. They were allegedly manufactured by the dozen in the name of absentee proprietors and thrust into the ballot boxes by attorneys or agents who, not wishing their principals to know the use made of their names, never bothered to register them publicly. It was not uncommon, therefore, for one attorney to submit 50 or 60 proxy votes under different denominations or categories.[25]

Despite the overwhelming evidence of the corruption and abuses under the proxy system, it was nonetheless retained by the 1849 franchise law, provided the absentee proprietors were properly qualified as if resident in the colony. The Colonial Office had resisted its abolition on the grounds that to do so would impair the security and hazard the interests of absentee property, and thus militate against further investment of British capital in the colony.[26] But once again it was the factor of race which seemed to be the final determinant in retaining the proxy system. Governor Barkly admitted that the proxy vote was designed to lessen the possibility of a preponderance of Creole freeholders in the electoral system. Particularly since there had been little educational progress among them, Barkly thought that to abolish the proxy system because it had given rise to abuses would have been suicidal policy.[27]

As a further safeguard against black majority power and to preserve planter dominance, the 1849 law retained the electoral college. This institution had long been recognized to be one of the main pillars supporting the planter oligarchy since its life membership created an irresponsible exercise of power in support of narrow planter interests.[28] However, it was recognised that so long as the franchise remained limited, the abolition of the Kiezers and direct election of the colonial legislators was unlikely to break that oligarchy. On the contrary, it might conceivably even strengthen it by giving it the appearance of a popular mandate. Yet, rather than simply lower the franchise substantially, the Colonial Office favoured the retention of the electoral college with high property qualifications for its life members, while reducing the franchise qualifications minimally. This was calculated to give a few black and coloured property-holders ("the lower orders") the right to choose representatives essentially from among the white section ("the higher orders") without threatening the dominance of the plantocracy.[29] Race was thus an important element in preserving planter hegemony, although in the absence of overt racial disqualifications of the black and coloured majority high property qualifications and the literacy test were designed to be an effective debarment of the non-white population.

Thus, the 1849 franchise ordinance, without extending the franchise to create a significant black constituency, nonetheless preserved the electoral college as an extra safeguard interposed between the electorate and the legislators, while establishing a high property qualification for membership of the college to ensure the continued monopoly of power by the white minority. These qualifications were fixed at the possession of 80 acres of land, half of which were to be cultivated; or the leasehold of property valued at $1,440 (£300) per annum; or the possession of a clear annual income of $1,440. These applied as well to membership of the Financial College.[30]

Since overt racial criteria would not have been permitted by the imperial authorities explicitly to bar the non-white population, high income and property qualifications and the literacy test were the next best options available to the ruling white minority to preserve their political dominance. The preservation of the electoral college was intended to complete the screening process by exercising greater selectivity on those who entered the legislature.

The problem, however, was that the manipulation of such electoral mechanisms was not a foolproof method of keeping out non-whites if only because, short of imposing wider discriminatory restrictions on the non-white population, wealth and education were colour blind. In fact, the exclusion of women, despite the fact that some were substantial property holders in their own right, was more explicit and effective than the provisions to keep out non-whites.[31] In this way, the acquisition of an apparently abandoned estate, Broomhall[32] on the Mahaica-Mahaicony coast, enabled the wealthy coloured merchant, politician, and ex-mayor of Georgetown, Richard Haynes to qualify for membership of the Court of Policy; and with the support of such powerful white "liberals" as Peter Rose, manager of the Colonial Bank, he was able to enter that body in January 1850.[33]

It is worthy of note, however, that when he was renominated for a seat in 1855, he was by-passed in favour of a white landowner, John Gordon who, despite his disinclination to accept the seat, was required to do so by the legislature which stated that his non-acceptance 'would inevitably lead to great public inconvenience',[34] i.e., Haynes' re-entry. No non-white subsequently gained entry into the legislature until after the 1891 constitutional reforms.

What is evident, therefore, is that by the mid-1850s, the doors were being closed on non-white political participation at the state level, particularly as the economic base of white power and dominance was strengthened with the return of prosperity for the plantations. As we shall see later, an amendment of the landed qualifications for membership of the legislature in 1864 effectively put paid to the issue of any future non-white representation by sealing the one loophole through which Haynes had temporarily breached the dam of exclusive white planter power.

In a plantation-dominated society, the distinction has to be made between white supremacy and planter dominance. Though the qualifications for membership of the elective institutions ensured the former, that was not synonymous with planter domination. The extension of the franchise to certain categories of taxpayers favoured the wealthier urban interests (predominantly white but also including a few coloureds), since there was no direct taxation or any other fiscal system in the rural districts which could serve as a basis for qualification. The planters thus feared that this would exclude a large portion of potential voters dependent upon them in the rural districts, and tilt the balance of power into the hands of the urban voters.[35] This apprehension was not unfounded since under the 1849 law, Georgetown alone had over 40 percent of the total registered voters in the colony, while New Amsterdam had over two-thirds of the voters in Berbice.[36]

To counteract this development, the planters advocated the creation of local constituencies to give the rural districts a majority of seats and so retain their political dominance. Hence by the 1849 law, two Kiezers and one Financial Representative were allotted to Georgetown, and one of each to New Amsterdam; whereas rural Demerara and Berbice each secured one representative to each elective college, and Essequibo was allocated two to each.[37] Thus the planting interest was theoretically assured a majority of four to three in the College of Kiezers, and four to two in the College of Financial Representatives through the rural representation.

Once again, however, the issue of race served to justify the further entrenchment of the planter hegemony by means of the local constituencies. Fearful of a possible enfranchisement of a considerable number of black and coloured householders, most whites were further alarmed at the prospect of arousing them throughout the colony every time a vacancy arose in either elective college, as would be the case if the whole colony remained as one single constituency. Rather than risk the spectre of widespread political excitement and agitation among the emancipated people, the white section acquiesced in the introduction of local constituencies which thereby permitted the further entrenchment of planter domination.[38]

Planter apprehension over the rising challenge to their dominance from the wealthy urban interests was not without foundation. Although in the first election of financial representatives under the new franchise law, 'gentlemen of as high standing and of as extensive property were chosen members by the newly formed constituencies' as before,[39] within a decade the planter hegemony was under serious threat. By 1863, five of the six financial representatives were white merchants, one of whom was replaced by a city lawyer; while the members of the electoral college were by then chiefly white merchants as well. Moreover, as the rural planters could rarely attend meetings of the electoral college, the influence of the white urban interests increased proportionately.[40] The growing confrontation between these two white groups, came to a head in 1863 when the urban party in the electoral college pushed the nomination of a city lawyer (who did not have the requisite landed property) for a vacancy in the Court of Policy, which was for all practical purposes the exclusive preserve of the plantocracy.[41]

No qualification for membership of the Court of Policy had ever been fixed. It had always been assumed that since the old Dutch constitution, the *Plan of Redress*, had vested the franchise in the planters alone (i.e., persons with 25 or more slaves), it was intended that membership of the legislature should likewise be restricted to the planters only. The *Plan* had used the word *Colonisten* to describe those who were eligible for membership of the Court. Though translated as "colonists", it was argued that it was meant in the sense of "planters" or "cultivators" of the soil, and that that was the interpretation of the term by established precedent and usage.[42] Previous attempts by the Kiezers to nominate landless candidates had failed. But they had effectively circumvented the legal obstacle by nominating men who had bought abandoned plantations specifically for the purpose of getting seats in the legislature.[43] It was by this means that the coloured merchant, Richard Haynes, had managed to gain entry into that body in 1850.

The planters had made two abortive attempts to close this loop-hole by fixing high qualifications for membership of the legislature. During the passage of a disallowed reform bill in 1852 (no.8), they had rejected a mere income qualification because it would have permitted the urban interests too great a political influence, and insisted on the possession of eighty acres of land for membership.[44] But because this was unduly favourable to the planters and injurious to other interests, it was disapproved by Secretary of State Pakington.[45] To overcome his objection, the planters opted during the passage of a subsequent reform bill in 1855 (no.19) to accept the same income qualification as for membership of the financial college as a compromise alternative to the possession of 40 acres of cultivated land.[46] This would most certainly have been approved by the imperial government had the other provisions of the bill proven acceptable.[47]

Thus there was still no clearly stipulated qualification for membership of the Court of Policy in 1863 when the political crisis arose. The imperial government actually found itself in a serious dilemma. For whereas official policy frowned on any fresh attempt to restrict representation in the legislature to a single class, the Colonial Office were nonetheless legally bound to uphold a constitutional convention. Hence after considerable deliberation, they felt obliged to approve a measure (Ord. No.1/1864) which set the qualification for membership at the high level of ownership of 80 acres of land with half under cultivation.[48] This practically guaranteed a planter monopoly of the colonial seats in the legislature and, in particular, closed the door on non-white entry into that body.

It is evident, therefore, that the political structure of post-slavery Guyana exhibited the classic characteristics of a typical plantation system — white minority dominance with state power being vested in an even smaller planter oligarchy whose political ascendancy was institutionalized. Moreover, race played a vital role in preserving this planter hegemony, for the alternative to a prosperous dominant planting interest was seen to be black majority rule, barbarism, and the creation of a totally outcast state like Haiti.[49] This view was shared by the plantocracy and the colonial/imperial authorities and obscured whatever differences they might have had as to how political power should be divided between them.

In treating the issue of planter hegemony, one needs to make the point very clearly that its influence was far more pervasive than mere dominance in the elective institutions of the colonial state. As Rodney correctly pointed out, it extended to all the statutory boards e.g., sea defence, drainage, the vestries, village administration, health, and so on.[50] It also extended to the local armed forces (police, militia and volunteer forces), and also to the judiciary. Former chief justice Joseph Beaumont asserted that 'when the acts of the Executive Government or the interests or privileges of the planters come into question, no judge or magistrate can decide adversely to them, without being exposed to the risk of punishment'.[51] And apart from their ownership of the dominant socio-economic institution, the plantation, which controlled most of the arable coastal land, the planters also exerted tremendous influence on Crown lands policy. Finally, although they did not monopolize the press, the two oldest and longest surviving newspapers, the *Royal Gazette* and the *Berbice Gazette*, forcefully articulated their views and prejudices and considerably influenced colonial opinion.

This means that any analysis of political activities instigated against this planter hegemony ought not to be confined solely to the constitutional sphere. All acts of civil and industrial disobedience against planter oppression or exploitation should be interpreted as political acts, whether they occurred on the plantations, the villages or the towns; whether they took the form of formal petitions or of acts of violence such as riots and incendiarism. The following chapters treat the behaviour of the subordinate ethnic groups in this context, but here, however, we will confine ourselves to politics in the constitutional sphere and the efforts of the middle-class to weaken the political dominance of the planters.

Ironically it was the pursuit of greater political power by

some of the leading planters which ushered in a period of public campaigning for political reform during the 1840s aimed at breaking the dominance of the planters themselves. A series of public meetings was organized in August 1842 by a number of planters and wealthy merchants including Peter Rose, manager of the Colonial Bank. These meetings were also attended by radical "small whites" such as John Taggart (town councillor), and John Emery (journalist); wealthy coloureds such as Richard Haynes (merchant and town councillor); and independent missionaries such as E.A. Wallbridge of the London Missionary Society (L.M.S.).[52]

The meeting of August 12th was adjourned after the passage of resolutions by the planters and their cohorts calling for a "free democratic constitution", but with high qualifications for membership of the legislature in order to preserve their political dominance. The "small white" and coloured minority, however, mobilized the support of the new village freeholders on the east coast of Demerara for the next meeting of the 19th, when they used their majority turn-out to cancel the previous week's resolutions and to call, albeit lamely, on the imperial government to amend the constitution as it thought fit.[53]

This fundamental divergence of position between the planters and major import-export merchants on one hand and the less wealthy middle-class white and coloured merchants/ store-keepers, professionals and property holders on the other nullified the efforts to achieve political reform. It was not until 1845 that fresh efforts were made to form an organization aimed at bringing about political change. This took the form of a Reform Association whose directorate was drawn mainly from the white and coloured middle-classes under the chairmanship of Richard Haynes who became mayor of Georgetown in 1846.[54]

This organization campaigned for representative government with a legislative assembly and executive council similar to those of the older British Caribbean colonies. It campaigned vigorously among the new village smallholders much to the consternation of both the colonial authorities and the conservative planters,[55] who were firmly opposed to representative government. These planters argued that the emancipated people were not ready for such privileges and that the growing multiracial diversity of colonial society would pose special problems to its functioning[56] — in short, they feared being subordinated as a racial minority in a representative system.

Whether the Association solicited the support of the wealthy members of the banking and mercantile sector is not clear; but it certainly did attract a few "liberal" elements from that sector, the most notable of whom was the influential Peter Rose who was also a member of the Court of Policy. Rose's affiliation with the Reform Association certainly enhanced its prestige and influence as a political party. But it also caused divisions within the movement. Rose did not believe that representative institutions necessarily entailed such an extension of the franchise and membership of the political institutions as would undermine planter hegemony (and white minority rule). So in 1849 he proposed a scheme for a two-tier representative system which attempted to put his ideas into law.

His proposed 39-member assembly was to consist of five seats for the villages where the franchise requirements would be met by ownership of a house valued at $500 (£104) plus literacy; five seats for Georgetown and New Amsterdam with the same franchise as for the municipal elections (property valued at $1,200 or £250); and 29 seats for the rural counties where the franchise was to be based on the tax on an income of $667 (£139). It was further proposed that qualification for membership would be the possession of land whose produce was valued at $1,440 (£300) or an income of $2,400 (£500) per annum.[57]

These proposals, however, brought the divisions within the movement into the open; for under the guise of liberal representative institutions they were evidently calculated to concentrate power in the hands of the planting interest and the wealthy merchants. The planters would have continued to be dominant through the vast preponderance of rural county seats, while the lower qualifications for membership of the assembly would have extended representation to the wealthy merchants and some professionals in the urban and village seats. Nor would there have been much change in the electorate. Since the proposed franchise was the same as that for elections to the electoral and financial colleges, only a few leading attorneys of absentee owners would have continued to elect 75 percent of the assembly. The rural electorate would have been limited to about 600 voters, while in the towns it would have been restricted to about 1,500, mainly merchants and professionals on account of the exclusion of leaseholders. As the franchise for the villages was the same as for the towns, in addition to the literacy requirement, there might have been about two or three voters in each village, the doctor and perhaps one or two storekeepers.[58] For all practical purposes, this scheme would have continued to exclude the black and coloured smallholders from the political process, while admitting the wealthy merchants and professionals to a small share of power; but political dominance would have been retained by the plantocracy. In short, it was designed to extend the political rights of the white minority section as a whole, and grant *minority* political participation to the coloured elite, while continuing to deny same to the majority of blacks and coloureds.

Through his management of the Colonial Bank, Rose acquired enormous political clout among the planters and merchants who depended on bank credit. This enabled him to win some support among the elected members of the legislature for his scheme, even though most of the plantocracy still remained sceptical and apprehensive about the growth of mass politics encouraged by the Reform Association.[59] But his proposals caused serious divisions within the party which became quite open after he proposed that the council should be elected, like that of the Cape Colony, by a constituency possessing an even higher pecuniary qualification than for the assembly.[60] This would have placed the planters in unchallengeable control of the legislative process.

The result was that the more radical wing of the Association, composed mainly of the black and coloured smallholders, "small" whites like Taggart, and the independent missionaries most notably E.A. Wallbridge and Joseph Ketley (both L.M.S.) took to the streets and the rural villages to whip up public support for more radical reform than embodied in either the Rose scheme or the 1849 franchise ordinance. In the Court of Policy, Richard Haynes openly warned of a possible recurrence of the 1823 uprising if radical reform was not implemented.[61]

The campaign resulted in a petition to the Court of Policy in October 1850 with 2,500 names,[62] and culminated in the first ever mass open-air meeting in Georgetown in November

1850 which was attended by an estimated 2,000–2,500 people including women. Out of this meeting emerged yet another petition calling for representative institutions and an extension of the franchise with 2,482 names which were collected in less than a week — 'a demonstration of public feeling altogether unprecedented in the political history of this colony'.[63]

This show of popular support for the radicals did nothing to heal the divisions in the party. In fact from 1850 onwards it appeared that the two wings of the Association were on collision course. When, for instance, at a public meeting in April 1850, a resolution calling for the enfranchisement of the smallholders was proposed, it was rejected by the wealthy members present whose spokesman, J.T. Gilbert (a lawyer), argued that it was going rather too far.[64] The breach, however, became irreparable by June 1851 when Rose openly declared in the legislature that neither he nor a large majority of his colleagues in the Association had ever wished the elective franchise to be lower than it was under the 1849 ordinance.[65]

Similarly the pro-reform *Colonist* newspaper argued that to think that "full, free and popular representation" meant universal adult suffrage was an utterly absurd and monstrous proposition. On the contrary, it saw the franchise as a boon and a benefit to be conferred only on those who had by 'honest industry and labour' raised themselves one or more degrees above the level of the lower class of labouring population. "Full, free and popular representation" meant:

> a representation founded on a franchise which shall embrace all classes of the community, whenever the members composing those classes shall have acquired a certain amount of property either in land or money, or by their course of industry and manner of life, shall be found to contribute to the general taxation for the efficient maintenance of the local Government.[66]

This was perhaps the clearest statement yet on the political position of the reform leaders. They stood for the political participation of the propertied and salaried middle-class ostensibly without regard to race. In this context they clearly sought to distance themselves from those, particularly within the plantocracy and also among the colonial officialdom, who wished to preserve the racial principle as a reason for denying political rights to the non-white majority. But in practical terms, because of the close correlation in early post-emancipation society between race/colour and class, the effect of the reform programme would have been similar in so far as it would have excluded the vast majority of Creole smallholders and workers from the political process. Not surprisingly, therefore, although the wealthy coloureds remained committed to the reform programme, the black smallholders dismissed it as "buckra story".[67]

Therefore, while considerations of race, disguised by "open" property and income qualification prerequisites continued to bolster the political hegemony of the plantocracy, the organized opposition was divided along colour-class lines. With the withdrawal of black smallholder support, the Reform Association slumped into rapid decline,[68] and by 1852 its public meetings failed to attract large gatherings.[69] By 1863–64 when the disqualification of J.T. Gilbert for a seat in the legislature occasioned a political controversy, attempts to mobilize anew public support for a petition for political reform could muster only 400 signatures mainly from among the urban middle-class. The vast majority of smallholders remained aloof because they stood to gain nothing from the reformers who clearly stated that they had no wish to lower the franchise requirements.[70]

By 1870, those groups who saw themselves ill-served by the wealthy middle-class leadership began to organize their own political activities. The establishment of the *Liberator* newspaper was one such shortlived attempt intended to politicize the black and coloured masses to fight for equal civil and political rights.[71] In 1871 a group of east coast villagers submitted a petition with 1,013 names protesting against planter hegemony, discriminatory taxation, and calling for political reform. The leaders were a printer/typesetter named Dummett (formerly with the *Colonist*, and then foreman at the Portuguese newspaper, the *Watchman*); James Rodney, one of the leading opponents of government control of village administration (see chapter 5), and Stephen Richards.[72] These men represented precisely those smallholders whom the biracial middle-class leaders had perpetually overlooked.

It is quite probable that Dummett *et al*. might have been influenced by the Portuguese who, in 1870–71, separately mounted two petitions against the restrictions and abuses which affected two main areas of their economic enterprize viz., the woodcutting and retail spirit trades. They considered themselves to be discriminated against as a socio-economic group by the planter dominated Combined Court, and also demanded political rights to look after their interests.[73] They also established Portuguese language newspapers to politicize their group.[74]

That the Portuguese should in 1870–71 have opted to petition the government as an ethnic group is revealing since, during the political agitation of the late forties, some of them were signatories to the petitions in support of the Reform Association,[75] and they were also among the few retailers who signed the 1864 petition.[76] However, their economic prosperity after 1850 marked them as targets of government taxation on one hand, and as economic collaborators of the dominant whites in the exploitation of the non-white population on the other; and although some were very wealthy indeed, they were nonetheless excluded from the political process by their foreign nationality (see chapter 7). By 1870, the Portuguese felt the need to organize themselves politically as a separate interest group although they clearly shared similar class interests with the biracial middle-class. For these settlers, therefore, race and ethnicity had, by that date, superceded class in determining their political behaviour and action.

As regards the Indian and Chinese immigrants, their essentially transient outlook rendered them marginal to the formal political process. In any event, their effective subjugation by means of the indenture system which placed them under the direct domination of individual planters, led to their being denied any political rights. But their continuous struggle against planter oppression and exploitation on the plantations did play its part in the gradual weakening of planter hegemony. The intensification of their resistance, work stoppages/strikes, acts of incendiarism and violent disturbances during the 1870s and 1880s (see chapter 8) must be interpreted as political acts aimed at bringing about change in the overall structure of planter hegemony.

By the 1880s, Guyanese society had undergone significant change and the impact on politics was considerable. Perhaps the most profound structural change was the growth of the previously insignificant black and coloured middle-class. This was composed of individuals who had been able to achieve upward social mobility through education (despite the grave deficiencies of that system), technical training/apprenticeships, professional/occupational achievements, acquired wealth in the form of higher incomes and property, and by assimilating creolized white culture and values. In this way, they were gradually able to overcome various forms of racial discrimination to make significant inroads into spheres of activity that had previously been considered preserves of the whites (see chapter 6).

Though only a few could afford the expense of higher education in Britain to become lawyers and doctors, many entered the lower ranks of the civil service or became teachers, clerks and bookkeepers, parsons, journalists, mechanics and artisans. In addition, although still sharply differentiated ethnically, some of the leading members of the Portuguese business community had also by the 1880s begun to realize that their best chances of attaining political influence was in alliance with the white and Creole middle-classes.

It was this considerably broadened biracial middle-class which agitated for reform during the 1880s. In 1881, it was reported in the press that 'some of the most prominent citizens' had started a campaign for the abolition of the electoral college,[77] which was followed in 1883 by the formation of a Constitutional Reform Association (C.R.A.) seeking the abolition of the electoral college and a reduction of the franchise requirements.[78] This movement coincided with a similar one in Jamaica calling for a restoration of representative institutions.[79]

As in the 1840s, deteriorating economic conditions contributed largely to a growing demand for political change. The severe economic depression of the 1880s occasioned by the slump in the market price of sugar created high under- and unemployment particularly among Creole workers whose growing discontent could be channelled in support of the middle-class demands for political change. A public meeting of taxpayers at the Philharmonic Hall in Georgetown in April 1886 demonstrated the growing support for representative government,[80] and encouraged a group of middle-class coloureds and blacks to form the Political Reform Club (P.R.C.) in June 1887.[81] The brainchild of David Straughn (journalist), its leadership included D.M. Hutson (lawyer and later solicitor-general), J.A. Murdoch and J. van Ryck de Groot (lawyers), J.D. Fileen and S.E. Wills (schoolmasters), and W.H. Hinds (journalist).[82]

It was the growth of the black and coloured middle-class which encouraged these men to form the P.R.C. virtually as an ethnic party, a departure from the traditional biracial middle-class opposition to planter hegemony. They made vigorous efforts to promote political consciousness among the black and coloured population to urge those who possessed the required property and income qualifications for the franchise to register and thus participate in the political process.[83] In this drive they were very largely successful, and managed to increase the number of registered voters by 60% from 1,233 in 1886 to 1,973 by 1890,[84] which in turn even enabled a few non-whites to be elected to the political institutions.

Thus, before the 1892 general elections, which were based on the reformed constitution, there were two coloureds in the electoral college, and two coloureds and one black in the financial college. No non-white, however, was able to get into the Court of Policy.[85] At the same time, however, the black and coloured elites came to the realization that they could not effect political change on their own, and thus sought to close ranks with the wealthier (mainly white) reformers of the C.R.A. Finally in 1889 the two groups merged as the reconstituted C.R.A. under the chairmanship of Robert Drysdale, a white merchant (ex-planter).[86]

It is often said that history does not repeat itself; yet this merger is reminiscent of the situation in the 1840s when Peter Rose and his cohorts joined (and indeed captured the leadership of) the old Reform Association. But as in the 1840s, from the standpoint of practical politics, the forging of such a biracial middle-class alliance lent substance (wealth) and influence to the reform movement, as it incorporated some of the wealthier mercantile interests and even the odd planter.[87]

Very importantly, too, it incorporated the wealthy Portuguese business interest[88] who, also recognizing that they could not achieve political benefits on their own as an ethnic group, opted to cast their lot with people of similar socio-economic class in the C.R.A. This decision was taken in spite of the existence of strong racial animosity among the rank and file of both the Portuguese and Creole communities which had erupted in large-scale violence as late as 1889 in Georgetown (see chapter 7). What this demonstrates is that by 1890, at least at the elite or leadership levels of both socio-racial groups, common class affiliation (in the Marxist/Weberian sense) was allowed to take precedence over racial differences in pursuit of common political goals i.e., the quest for equal political rights and privileges.

Both the C.R.A. and the P.R.C. had used the press to good effect to push their campaign for political reform during the 1880s. Indeed that decade witnessed a proliferation of newspapers of various shades of political opinion. To the old newspapers (the *Royal Gazette*, the *Berbice Gazette*, the *Colonist* which ceased publication in 1884, and the *Creole* which ceased in 1882) were added the *Demerara Daily Chronicle* and the *Argosy* in 1881, *the Daily Chronicle* (1885), the *Echo* (1887), the *Nugget* (1888), and *the Reflector* (1889). In addition there were two Portuguese language newspapers, *O Portuguez* (1880) and *A União Portugueza* (1889). Of these only the two *Gazettes* and the *Argosy* stood against the reform movement. In short, therefore, the public was subjected to an intense level of politicization in the press.

It was therefore in a highly charged atmosphere of heightened political activity that a constitutional crisis broke in 1887. This was occasioned by the publication of a medical report by Dr. A.W. Williams critical of conditions in the hospitals and dwellings on the plantations.[89] The governor's decision to permit Williams to go abroad on leave, despite the planters' demand to delay his departure until they were satisfied with his explanations, so infuriated them that they refused to raise taxes for the 1888 Estimate or to conduct business in the legislature unless the governor publicly withdrew the report.[90] This effectively brought the government to a standstill, and Governor Irving determined to end the deadlock by seeking to force a reform of the constitution with a view to widening political representation and breaking the political hegemony of the planters.[91]

More than anything else perhaps, this narrow-minded action by the planters served to give the reform movement its momentum, and set in motion an irreversible process towards political change despite the reluctance of the Colonial Office.[92] The reformers pushed their public campaign in the "streets" as well as in the press.[93] The P.R.C. in particular was very active mobilizing mass support for political reform by organizing public meetings throughout the country. A petition sponsored by them calling for "freer, fuller, wider and more popular and direct representation" in government succeeded in procuring as many as 4,647 names[94] and thus forced the issue on a reluctant Colonial Office.[95] Even the planter representatives in the colonial legislature felt the wisdom of at least paying "lip-service" to the notion of political reform.[96]

This broad-based biracial reform movement called, *inter alia*, for the abolition of the existing political institutions and the substitution of an executive council consisting of the governor as president and six members nominated by the Crown of whom no more than three should be officials, as well as a legislative assembly consisting of five officials and sixteen members elected by secret ballot. An income qualification for membership of the legislature was proposed at $1,440 (£300) per annum, while it was suggested that for the franchise it should be $300 (£62.5) per annum. The C.R.A. also suggested that the colony should be divided into 16 electoral districts, five of which would be in the urban centres of Georgetown and New Amsterdam.[97]

This programme made no attempt to disguise the limited middle-class objectives of the reformers. The qualification for membership of the legislature would have excluded all but the planters, wealthy businessmen and well-to-do professionals. The requirements for the franchise would have admitted a small number of skilled artisans, clerks, schoolmasters, civil servants and professionals. Certainly the vast majority of Creole and immigrant workers would still have remained disfranchised.[98]

Despite the very modest nature of these reform proposals, however, they would have meant an end to planter hegemony. But the planters were not about to relinquish power without a fight. They utilised every political resource at their disposal to limit the proposed reforms and found an ally in the governor, Lord Gormanston, who was too timid to confront them,[99] and a Colonial Office which was still dependent on their goodwill to approve a civil list to pay the salaries of government officials and judges.[100] But most significant was the fact that despite the broad-based biracial character and numerical strength of the opposition groups, their demands and proposals on reforming the constitution[101] could be and were safely ignored in the drafting of the final document,[102] which in the final analysis was the product of compromise between the planters on one hand, and the colonial and imperial governments on the other. Nor should this surprise us since the middle-class leaders were far too narrow in their objectives and refused to make proposals that would incorporate the mass of the working people into the political process of the state institutions.

Thus, despite three years of negotiations, discussions and public agitation, when the 1891 law was finally promulgated its impact was anticlimactic. In its final form, ordinance No. 1 of 1891 reflected, to a considerable degree, the limited changes which the planters felt they could make without substantially undermining their political power. The abolition of the electoral college was certainly a blow to their authority, but this was more than compensated by the other provisions. An Executive Council was established to assume the executive functions of the Court of Policy and, as it was composed of the governor as president, with two official and two unofficial members,[103] the planters could be reasonably sanguine that their interests would receive sympathetic consideration in that body.

Retaining its ancient title, the legislature was expanded to consist of the governor, seven official and eight elected members in accordance with the planters wishes, with the governor retaining his casting vote. The increased membership was calculated to give the urban interests some representation through the three seats assigned to Georgetown and New Amsterdam; but the remaining five elective seats reserved for the rural districts was clearly designed to preserve a planter majority among the elected membership of the legislature. The Financial College with its membership of six was also retained to be joined in Combined Court with the legislative members on financial and fiscal matters.[104]

The qualifications for membership of the Court of Policy similarly reflected the opinions of the plantocracy. Although the proposal of the C.R.A. to equalize the qualification for membership of the Court of Policy with that of the Financial College (i.e. an income of £300 per annum) had actually been passed by the legislature in the disallowed ordinance of 1855 and was currently favoured by the Colonial Office, the strong objections of the planters effectively became a veto when they threatened to refuse to grant an extended civil list. Consequently, they were allowed their way in having the qualification for membership of the legislature made the ownership of immoveable property other than land valued at $7,500, or the rental of a house and land at $1,200 per annum as an alternative to the high existing land qualification of eighty acres with forty under cultivation.[105] This in effect succeeded in limiting membership only to the planters and the very wealthy non-planting interests. Moreover, since membership of either institution was restricted to natural born or naturalized British subjects, this effectively excluded a substantial number of Portuguese immigrants.[106]

Likewise, despite both the C.R.A's proposal that the franchise be halved,[107] and even the request of the Colonial Office that it be reduced below the £100 income qualification proposed by the planters,[108] it was the latter who triumphed by including their proposal as part of a deal with the government for approving an extended civil list. In fact, this political deal amounted to nothing short of an unprincipled sell-out by the Colonial Office, since they sacrificed precisely those elements which both they and the colonial reformers had considered essential to any meaningful package of political reforms, viz., a substantial reduction of the elective franchise requirements and the adoption of the secret ballot.[109] In effect there was only a token reduction of the franchise prerequisites to an income qualification of £100 per annum and notwithstanding its adoption in other British colonies, the ballot system was not introduced.[110]

Taken as a whole, the political reform of 1891 hardly altered the structure of colonial politics or significantly affected the political dominance of the plantocracy. The high property qualifications for membership of the legislature were calculated to maintain a planter majority in the elective section, even though the wealthy urban merchant and professional interests, which by 1890 included several of the black and coloured elite, achieved representation in that body for the first time. Similarly, the small reduction in the income qualification for the franchise hardly altered the composition of the electorate. The number of registered voters increased by only 3.7 percent from 1,973 in 1890 to 2,046 in 1891;[111]

and by 1896 they numbered just 2,479 (0.9 percent of the population) or 1 in 111, whereas the proportion in Jamaica, for instance was 1 in 14, and in Bermuda 1 in 13.[112] Moreover, in such a small electorate, the system of open voting enabled the powerful plantocracy to exercise unfair influence on voters in the interest of preserving their political power.[113] The effect was vividly demonstrated in the 1892 election which returned a majority of the planting interest to the legislature.[114] As in the Bahamas, where such a system of open voting existed well into this century, it facilitated the continuation of white minority dominance even after the franchise had been extended. It was not until 1896, after further vigorous and intensive campaigning and lobbying by its proponents, that the secret ballot was finally introduced.[115] This signalled a decisive break of the political hegemony which the planters had for so long enjoyed and of white minority dominance, and marked the rise of the black and coloured elite in the political spectrum.[116]

This break in white planter dominance towards the end of the century was endorsed by contemporary obsevers such as Henry Kirke who, writing in 1897, noted:

> Thirty years ago the planters were the great men in the colony; they were aristocrats on their own estates and for miles around; they were J.P.s, and sat on the bench with the judge at the Inferior Criminal Courts; ... they took precedence to stipendiary magistrates; storekeepers bowed before them; and bankers did them reverence. But all that was changed ... the old style manager had disappeared.[117]

The success of the biracial middle-class reform movement between 1880 and 1896 ultimately signified a triumph for the principle of political equality without regard to race. After 1896 white minority dominance could no longer be maintained by the manipulation of political mechanisms, but rather power was to be distributed by means of open and shared economic class criteria. The system of white planter hegemony was replaced by one in which access to power was open to individuals of all ethnic sections so long as they could meet certain class-based economic requirements, were British subjects, and were literate in English.

Yet although this symbolized a very significant sociopolitical change in which race receded in importance as a determinant of political status, in practice the change benefitted only a relatively small minority of subordinate elites, while the vast majority of the black and coloured population remained disfranchised and outside the formal constitutional process. Likewise, the great mass of Indian and Chinese immigrants and a substantial number of less well-to-do and/or non-naturalized Portuguese were denied political participation or representation. And, it was still obvious that the planters retained enormous political and social influence even though their legitimized domination was at an end.

This historical analysis is of great significance in the wider theoretical debate under consideration. On one hand, the incorporation of the black and coloured middle-class elites into the colonial political system as full and equal participants based on broad socio-economic class, rather than racial, affiliation can be interpreted as evidence of social integration around the development of a single set of interests and values — in short, the growth of a class stratified society in which racial and cultural differences were subordinated to common class interests.

On the other hand, it can be argued that the full incorporation of these subordinate elites into the public domain on the basis of shared political, economic, social and cultural interests represented an extension of the system of sociopolitical dominance by a *cultural* minority; that is, through a process of sociocultural assimilation and individuation by the subordinate elites, the latter came to share the same values and interests as the white minority which enabled them to participate in the colonial political institutions as an integral part of that dominant cultural minority. One might suggest that the subordinate elites extended the social boundaries of that cultural minority which could now no longer be defined exclusively by racial criteria.

Taking this analysis one step further, this educated elite would have become politically indistinguishable from the dominant white cultural section, and by the same token politically differentiated from the vast majority of blacks and coloureds who continued to use alternative methods to defend and promote their own sectional political interests, ideas and actions. In short, the incorporation of the Creole elites into the dominant cultural minority section would have alienated them from the vast majority of their socio-racial kith and kin, again resulting in a segmented society, albeit along cultural rather than racial lines.

Because the analysis of the colonial political system can be interpreted to suit either the theory of stratification or of pluralism, it is necessary to examine the broader socioeconomic roles and relationships of the constituent ethnic groups within the colonial society in order to determine the extent to which they reinforce the divergent theoretical interpretations outlined above. Critical to this assessment, however, is the role of the imperial power in the colonial polity which must be thoroughly analysed.

CHAPTER 4

RACE AND IMPERIALISM IN THE COLONIAL POLITY

M.G. Smith's definition of society as a territorially distinct unit with its own governmental institutions poses some analytical problems when one is dealing with a colonial society such as Guyana whose governmental institutions were not autonomous or independent, but in which the imperial government participated directly through their colonial officials, and exercised a superordinate power over the colonial government. It can thus be argued that the political state extended beyond the strict territorial boundaries of the colony, and so to equate the society with it, as Smith does, is to conceive some form of greater society which would include certain groups and institutions in the metropolis with direct interest in the colonial society,[1] e.g., the Colonial Office, the British parliament, absentee planters and mercantile firms involved in trade with and investment in the colony, churches and missionary societies, and so on. One has to be careful, however, not to treat the colonial society as a mere extension of the metropolitan society, but as a separate and distinct entity with its own character and identity.

In this study of 19th century Guyanese society, a clear distinction must be made between the internal socio-cultural dynamics of that society, and the external or imperial forces which exercised a superordinate influence in the shaping of power and status relationships within the colonial society. Thus while Guyanese society is generally treated in this book as a system of socio-cultural relationships among its constituent members, special attention will be paid in this chapter to the pivotal role of the imperial power as an agent of continuity and/or change in the colonial society.

The political constitution of Guyana was unique within the context of the British Caribbean. As noted earlier, the basic institutional framework was inherited from the Dutch in 1803 and preserved unchanged under the terms of the Articles of Capitulation until 1891. Although Guyana was technically a Crown colony like Trinidad, St. Lucia and, after 1865, most of the rest of the British Caribbean except Barbados and the Bahamas, there was a strong "representative" tradition which not only enabled the planters to have voice in the formulation of colonial legislation, but more importantly accorded them control over the colonial budget. This is what made the Guyanese polity unique. Throughout the 19th century, therefore, the relationship between the planters and the imperial government centered on questions relating to the control of colonial finances and, as seen in the preceeding chapter, to the political franchise.

All of this has very direct bearing on the theoretical debate. If the imperial government was prepared to use its legislative power to extend the franchise and thereby incorporate elements of the non-white majority into the public domain, it could play a very important role in promoting societal integration and the development of political alignments among socio-economic classes with shared interests and values. On the other hand, if the imperial government preferred simply to preserve the *status quo* and support the political hegemony of the planters, or, alternatively, if it sought to augment its own power through its officials in the colony — in short, to impose *full* Crown colony government akin to the other Caribbean colonies after 1865 — then white socio-political dominance would be perpetuated, and the non-white majority would continue to be excluded from political participation in the public domain. The latter options would thus have preserved institutional differences at the political level between the white minority and the non-white majority sections.

Two underlying factors determined the attitude and role of the imperial authorities in the colonial power structure — race and imperialism. The issue of race was used to deny the black and coloured majority the right of political participation, while their consequent non-representation was in turn used to justify the need to maintain the supremacy of the authority and power of the imperial Crown in the colonial polity. Thus race and imperialism went hand-in-hand with the preservation of white political domination in the colonial society.

The prime assumption which dictated Colonial Office thinking on the colonial power structure was that the black and coloured majority were not sufficiently intelligent to exercise political power. Consequently, no political rights could be extended to them until they firstly asked for them, and secondly, demonstrated beyond a doubt their readiness and ability to exercise them responsibly. Since they were considered unsteady, excitable and shallow, it was argued that they would require more education than other races of men before they could be assessed fit to exercise political power. Hence, there could be no question of granting them political rights and franchises before they had attained the required level of mental and political development.[2]

Limited experiments had been tried in other West Indian colonies by moderately reducing the franchise requirements to include mainly the coloured perople and very few blacks; but the results were considered very unpredictable. It was claimed that in Jamaica, for instance, when the coloureds were granted equal political rights they tended to align with the whites against the blacks. Recent research, however, has demonstrated how over-simplified this assessment of the actions of coloured politicians was.[3] On the other hand, in Dominica, the coloureds were equally simplistically seen as allies of the blacks against the whites which in the view of the Colonial Office was largely responsible for that island being in the worst social state in the British Caribbean.[4] Hence they were disinclined to repeat that experiment in Guyana. Until the blacks were deemed sufficiently advanced in "civilization" and capable of exercising power so as to render it safe to broaden the franchise enough to make the legislature a truly representative body, no change would be made in the existing constitution.[5]

Hence, despite its obvious defects and shortcomings, the Colonial Office maintained the colonial political system, even with its institutionalized planter oligarchy provided, of course, that the latter was not pitted against the government.[6] One senior official, Henry Taylor, even regarded the Court of Policy under normal circumstances to be the most efficient legislature in the West Indies.[7] But at the same time, it was recognised that this system could not endure permanently because the planter oligarchy had become increasingly incompatible with, and unrepresentative of, the idea of a "free" society after emancipation, and irreconcilable with the principles of government in the metropolis. Consequently, the Colonial Office, perceived as its main objective the preservation of a strong imperial power in the colonial political system ostensibly to facilitate the protection, instruction and guidance of the unrepresented classes who would ultimately rule.[8]

Imperial trusteeship was thus considered necessary to protect those who had been deliberately excluded from the political process on the basis of race. As it was assumed that it would require a protracted period of time and a system of public instruction long and sedulously administered before the black population could be granted political rights, it was considered essential that the power of the Crown should be supreme. For the Colonial Office, the choice was not between a popular government and one in which the power of the Crown would predominate;

> but between an independent irresponsible oligarchy on the one hand, and on the other an exercise of power by the Crown under the immediate observation of a body of colonists, and subject to control by Parliament, where those colonists would be certain to find a competent advocacy against abuse.[9]

In short, there had to be some form of white rule, either that of the planters or that of the Crown. Although there was a danger of concentrating all power in the hands of the governor and the colonial officialdom by upholding the supremacy of the Crown, the Colonial Office considered it the least evil which could be readily prevented or remedied by the planters' access to the imperial parliament. This would present an effective check to any arbitrary proceedings of the colonial government.[10]

That the blacks were not thought fit to govern is not surprising. Such views were very much in keeping with contemporary Victorian attitudes towards non-white colonial peoples, and in particular blacks. Whether in Africa or the Caribbean, blacks were regarded as being both racially and culturally inferior to whites. Not only were they physically and phenotypically different, but blacks were considered ignorant, savage, indolent, and liars.[11]

These overtly racist attitudes assumed a particularly virulent form in the West Indies by the late 18th century, reflected in the writings of Edward Long who "established" the link between the African and the orang-outang.[12] Although the humanitarian movement did a great deal to counteract such racist notions, most of its supporters still held the black man to be culturally inferior.[13] Besides, a strong residue of racist sentiment towards the African still persisted, as reflected in the writings of Thomas Carlyle,[14] Anthony Trollope[15] and Charles Kingsley,[16] and attained a new prominence after the Morant Bay riot in Jamaica in 1865.[17]

These racist views achieved more credibility by the development of a number of pseudo-scientific race theories during the 19th century propounded by Cuvier, Carus, de Gobineau, Hunt, and others. But undoubtedly the most influential race theory in the later 19th century was social Darwinism which sought to apply Charles Darwin's theory of evolution to the human species. This seemed to offer scientific proof that blacks had not evolved to the same level of human development as whites.[18]

The influence of such theories and racial attitudes were very much in evidence in the writing of English historian, James Froude on the Caribbean,[19] and in the works on Guyana by James Rodway (also English born and bred).[20] What is very striking about all of these writers on the Caribbean mentioned above (from Carlyle to Rodway) is their translation of the idea of black racial inferiority to mean black incapability to govern, and hence the need for strong centralized white rule. These ideas also permeated the Colonial Office. Taylor's reference to Dominica as the worst British Caribbean colony was intended as a warning against extending the franchise to permit black-coloured majorities in the West Indian legislatures on the ground that they were not fit for such political responsibility. Haiti with its frequent political upheavals was generally seen as tangible proof of this,[21] and the Jamaican "rebellion" of 1865 seemed to endorse that view.[22]

The Colonial Office, however, exhibited genuine interest in not abandoning the ex-slaves, to the mercy of the uncontrolled power of the planters. Thus they had to be "protected" because the planters could not be trusted with the exercise of exclusive political power in the altered state of West Indian society after emancipation. Roy Augier has argued that

> It is true to say of the black that he was then unfit, but in all the senses in which this judgement is true and relevant, it is also true of the white. In both cases their disabilities were due to their being creatures of a slave society. Therein lies whatever justification there was for allowing the British Government a role in the affairs of the society. An effective role would have, for a time, put both communities at an equal political disadvantage.[23]

That, however, did not happen in Guyana (or elsewhere in the Caribbean) because the imperial government's idea of its role as "trustee" was predicated upon a mixture of racism, paternalism and arrogance. Thus on one hand it disfranchised the blacks; on the other it simply tried to temper the excesses of the whites. There was no pretence of even-handedness in disadvantaging both communities. It was always claimed that no British parliament would have agreed to the Crown assuming full political control in Guyana: hence the imperial government had to continue to share power with the planters. But of course the 1928 imposition of full crown colony government when the coloureds and blacks were in political ascendancy in the legislature gives the lie to that claim. In any event even where, as in Trinidad or in Jamaica after 1865, the Crown did enjoy full political control, there was still not equal political disadvantages for black and white.[24]

Nevertheless even the mild objective of tempering the excesses of the vested white colonial interests threatened from time to time to lead to head-on collision since the colonial plantocracy was not about to relinquish power to any interest, colonial or imperial. Although the Colonial Office had decided to preserve the existing constitution, the delicate balance of power which it created between the imperial and colonial (planter) interests was always liable to break down in the face of either side continually seeking to gain ascendancy over the other, and thus to exercise total control over the colonial political system. For whereas in the Court of Policy there was an official majority by virtue of the governor's casting vote (see chapter 3), in the Combined Court there was a colonial majority through the addition of the six financial representatives.

Consequently, the imperial Crown enjoyed an affirmative power over legislation and, with the governor's veto and the royal prerogative of affirmation or disallowance of colonial acts, a negative power as well. On the other hand, the planters possessed control over the colonial finances (initially only taxation, but subsequently expenditure as well), and after slavery over the salaries of colonial officials on the civil list. Thus the key issues in the power struggle between the imperial power and the planter representatives were colonial taxation and expenditure, the civil list, and the power of legislation. Not surprisingly, the issue of race intruded to become a critical element in the power equation. In fact, it is important to note that in the struggle for supremacy between the planters and the Crown, that issue not only set the parameters of the dispute, but in the final analysis took precedence over all other issues in the political relations between the two interests.

Already by the time of emancipation in 1838, the planters had assumed effective control over taxation and expenditure as well as the civil list. When the constitution was formed in 1795, the financial representatives were to be adjoined to the legislative members in Combined Court for the sole purpose of voting on all matters concerning the raising of taxes and the examination of accounts 'without any other power whatever'.[25] But consequent on some unauthorized constitutional amendments implemented by the acting governor, Major-General Carmichael, in 1812,[26] the Combined Court were able to assume control over colonial expenditure surreptitiously.[27] They exercised that power until 1831 when the original constitutional regimen was restored.[28]

The planters were not, however, prepared to relinquish the power which they had exercised for so long without a fight, and consequently refused to raise taxes in 1832–33 unless it was restored to them.[29] In order to obtain revenue, Governor D'Urban was obliged to allow the Combined Court to discuss the items of expenditure provided it was not used as a precedent to prejudice the decision on the question of right. His successor, however, was unable to reach accord with the planters; and in 1835 the issue had to be arbitrated by the governor of Barbados, Sir Lionel Smith, who negotiated a deal[30] which permitted the Combined Court to discuss 'in detail, freely and without reserve' the items of expenditure in exchange for their granting a civil list in order to pay the salaries of senior colonial officials.[31] Thus, the colonial representatives legitimately acquired the power of control over colonial expenditure, at least for the duration of the civil list.[32]

This was the first of several occasions on which the imperial authorities were obliged to yield power or abandon principle in order to obtain a civil list, and it demonstrates the extent to which they considered it essential to the functioning of the colonial administration. The problem of the civil list first arose as a direct result of the abolition of slavery, when the revenues of the King's Chest, which had previously been raised by a capitation tax on slaves, dried up and the salaries of the colonial officials, including the governor, were placed in jeopardy. This circumstance automatically enhanced the power of the planter representatives in the Combined Court who had to be approached by the imperial authorities for a civil list. The new control which the planters acquired over the salaries of the heads of government departments not only subjected the latter to the temptation of shaping their conduct to suit the wishes and interests of the planters, and even of individual members of the Court, but was also liable to bring the conduct of government business to a complete standstill. Recognising the threat posed to the independence and supremacy of the Crown by this circumstance, it became a principal objective of the imperial authorities for the remainder of the century to extract a permanent civil list from the colonial representatives.[33]

Fully cognisant of the vital significance of this new source of power at their disposal, the planters were not prepared to grant a permanent civil list;[34] neither, on the other hand, were the imperial authorities prepared to grant them as a permanent right the power to determine colonial expenditure.[35] Thus these two matters, which formed the basis of the 1835 deal, became the main elements of subsequent political compromises between the government and the planters, which were renegotiated septennially. This, of course, did not prevent the planters from continuing to use their power over taxation to bring the conduct of government business to a halt by refusing to raise taxes whenever they were locked in dispute with the colonial and imperial authorities. This occurred between 1840–42 when the governor resisted a proposed reduction of official salaries and pensions, and the imposition of a tax on British goods, and refused to guarantee free immigration from any part of the world.[36] Again in 1848–49, another attempt by the planters to reduce official salaries by 25 percent, and to forestall the discussion of the annual Estimate led to confrontation with the governor and their refusal to raise taxes.[37] But nearly forty years elapsed before the planters once more felt the need to resort to this action in the political dispute of 1887 over the Williams report on estate hospitals.[38]

A number of factors accounted for this long hiatus. Firstly, the plantation system was free from the acute economic depressions after the 1840s until the 1880s. Secondly, the plantocracy enjoyed supreme political dominance between 1850 and 1880 unchallenged by the large-scale popular movements for political reform which marked both the forties and the eighties. But perhaps the most important factor was the opinion of the Parliamentary Select Committee to which the dispute of 1848–49 had been referred. It was argued that its recommendation that any changes in the constitution should be decided upon in friendly concert with the colonial authorities, and that such changes should concede to the legislature greater control over the conduct of public affairs, put an end to any notion which the Colonial Office might have harboured of imposing imperial supremacy in fiscal and financial matters. (Of course the 1928 "rape of the constitution" gave the lie to that notion.) At the same time, however, the Select Committee sounded a clear note of warning to the planter oligarchy that constitutional changes should proceed only on the basis of extending the elective franchise as far as practical.[39] The planters thus realised that to bring about a political crisis by refusing to raise taxes would signal a threat to their continued dominance by an extension of the franchise; and in fact this is precisely what happened in the late eighties and early nineties when they did precipitate a crisis.

Although the Select Committee's report did not augment imperial power in the colonial polity, it had the effect of strengthening the hand of the colonial and imperial authorities vis-a-vis the planters. Significantly, the factor which made the difference was the issue of race. Recognising that the planters were most decidedly opposed to enfranchising the blacks and coloureds (which ironically the Crown was not prepared to contemplate either), the Colonial office could always threaten in the event of a future crisis to go back to parliament and premise the question of supremacy on the distinct assertion that the black people were and had to be unrepresented, and so required and had to have the protection of the Crown. This would have presented the planters with the choice between a significant extension of the franchise and the maintenance of the imperial power: that is, between real representation of the people and an effective control of the imperial government. It was felt that in such a circumstance the planters would, as they did in Jamaica in 1865,

> prefer the control of the Crown to control by the Negroes, and they will not be disposed to force the intervention of Parliament, because in the House of Commons, a low franchise would probably meet with more favour than an oligarchy of planters.[40]

So by clever exploitation of the race factor, the Colonial Office was successfully able to use the black and coloured population as pawns to contain the plantocracy in the struggle for political supremacy.

The third major issue in this power struggle between the planters and the imperial authorities was the power of legislation. This consisted of two elements, namely, the official majority in the Court of Policy occasioned by the governor's casting vote, and the governor's power of veto. This issue attained great prominence after the 1849 Select Committee's recommendation that constitutional changes should concede greater control of public affairs to the legislature. Not surprisingly, this aspect was seized by the planters who, in 1850 eagerly supported a scheme proposed by Governor Barkly, himself a plantation proprietor, to increase the elective section of the legislature by one seat, thereby giving them a majority.[41] This proposal was endorsed by a meeting of absentee planters in London in 1851, who also called for the abrogation of the governor's veto to prohibit the introduction or stop the progress of any bill, and for all members to be given the right to introduce bills.[42] These proposals thus formed the basis of a political reform bill (no.8) of 1852.[43]

Similarly in 1855, another constitutional reform bill (no.19) was passed in the legislature which sought to abolish the governor's casting vote and his veto power.[44]

The effect of these proposed changes would have been to transfer the power of legislation from the Crown to the planter representatives who, with their control over colonial finances, would have assumed absolute political supremacy. Indeed, they almost succeeded in 1852, for the majority opinion in the Colonial Office, including Secretary of State Earl Grey, entertained no objection to an elective majority in the colonial legislature, though Grey decided to retain the governor's casting vote to block bills which the Crown disapproved of (such as those that might affect the well-being of the disfranchised masses).[45] A change of administration, however, resulted in Grey's replacement by Sir John Pakington who strongly objected to a planter majority in the legislature; and, urged by Henry Taylor, the archangel of imperialism, he disallowed the 1852 reform bill.[46]

It was in fact Taylor's cogent views which informed and ultimately shaped imperial policy on the colonial power structure in the post-emancipation period. Recognizing that an elective majority in the legislature was only a representative government in the narrowest sense (since the planters alone were represented), he considered it undesirable to place the government of about 120,000 people in the hands of seven planters representing less than 1,000 people. He further argued that with an elective majority of just one, the planters would feel that their power depended on unity, and would thus form a more effective opposition to the Crown than if there were a large and less cohesive elective majority. He considered these factors particularly vital in the probable eventuality of further reforms, whose outcome would depend entirely on whether the legislature was dominated by an official or planter majority.[47]

This touched on the essence of the Crown's power of legislation, its *affirmative* power of legislating for the colony in non-financial matters despite the combined opposition of all the elected members.[48] This was the power which the bills of 1852 and 1855 sought to abrogate. Taylor argued that although the governor could always withhold the Crown's assent from a measure passed by an elective majority, that was merely a negative power which, though important enough not to be surrendered,[49] should not be the sole element of imperial power in the colonial polity. Hence, while he could not anticipate what might occasion the exercise of the Crown's supremacy over legislation in the future, he was convinced of the necessity for positive powers of legislation remaining vested in the Crown. Though it wa only in some extreme situation that he could envisage the government attempting to pass legislation in the face of the unanimous opposition of the elected members, such a situation might arise in reference to the welfare of the unrepresented black and coloured majority or the immigrants.[50]

Taylor thus exploited the racial factor to buttress his argument in favour of retaining the existing political constitution and the supremacy of the Crown within the colonial power structure. According to him, to abrogate the legislative powers of the Crown was to deviate from the broad principle of imperial policy that either the power of the Crown should be maintained or a really popular constituency be created.[51] Like his colleagues in the Colonial Office,[52] he considered the black and coloured majority so ignorant and barbarous as to preclude popular representative government. For this reason he advocated the retention of the existing power structure in which the Crown purportedly acted as the representative of the disfranchised non-white majority and controlled the planter oligarchy, while the British people through their parliamentary representatives in turn controlled the Crown.[53] This vividly demonstrates the vital role which the imperial government and parliament were expected to play within the power structure of the colonial polity.

Thus, although the white section and, in particular, the plantocracy exercised a dominant political influence in Guyana, supreme political power remained vested in the imperial Crown. This imperial involvement in the colonial polity played a very decisive role in the socio-political development of the colonial state, and constituted a crucial element in the total political domination of the colonial society by the small white minority. At the same time, however, the maintenance of imperial supremacy in the colonial political system conflicted with the ever-increasing aspirations of the plantocracy for more political power in order to preserve the ascendancy of the plantation system in a "free" society: hence the inevitability of their confrontations and political dealings over expenditure and the civil list with the colonial and imperial authorities.

But this power struggle between the planters and the government masked a unanimity of opinion by both sides on the fundamental issue upon which the division of power between them was predicated. That was the unquestioned presumption of the unsuitability and undesirability of the black majority to exercise political power and responsibility. It was this racial factor which served to rationalize both the continued dominance of the plantocracy in colonial politics, as well as the necessity to maintain the political supremacy of the Crown ostensibly to protect the disfranchised majority. Thus, in the final analysis, race was the single most important element in preserving the colonial power structure characterized by white minority dominance subject only to the supreme authority and power of the imperial Crown.

In the context of the debate on pluralism versus stratification, what this chapter demonstrates is that in its unwavering opposition to enfranchising the non-white majority, the imperial power not only bolstered white minority rule in Guyana, but functioned as an obstacle to the political integration of the several socio-racial sections. This prolonged exclusion of the non-white majority from the political institutions at the colonial state level meant that with the exception of the biracial middle-class each section was forced not only to pursue its own political interests separately and independently, but also to employ alternative institutions and modes of political action to defend or promote those interests. Extra-parliamentary political action in post-emancipation Guyana was thus as important, if not more so, than intra-parliamentary activity. In this context, therefore, the struggle for village autonomy and self-government, petitions to the Crown, protest meetings and demonstrations, and ultimately riots and other forms of civil disobedience formed a critical aspect of that extra-parliamentary activity by the non-white majority.

THE BLACKS AND COLOUREDS IN SOCIETY

CHAPTER 5

THE POLITICAL SUBORDINATION OF THE BLACK VILLAGES

In plantation-dominated societies the concentration of state power in the hands of the planter class is accompanied by a highly centralized form of government.[1] This is also considered an integral feature of the plural society, and forms part of its institutionalized inequalities. A highly centralized system of administration is thus essential to the maintenance of the political domination of the cultural minority. At the same time, in order to minimize threats to its regime, the dominant section, through its political organization, actively discourages or suppresses extensive organizations by which the subject population can convert itself from an acephalous, institutionally disprivileged category into a coherent corporate group capable of effective political and social action.[2] This also results in the development of loosely organized local communities which exhibit a weak sense of social cohesion.[3]

In Guyana after 1838, it was the newly established village communities along the coast which provided the institutional framework for organizing the black and coloured section into a coherent corporate group. They were the vehicle by which the disfranchised majority could develop the organizational structure and leadership with which to challenge the political and social dominance of the white minority. The villages thus assumed enormous significance as "broker institutions"[4] for integrating the black and coloured section at the societal level. If the development of the villages as political institutions could facilitate the full participation of the blacks and coloureds in political affairs in the public domain, then they would have served an integrative function by promoting political participation without regard to race or culture. If, on the other hand, they remained separate and isolated, they could still perform an important though limited function of ethnic group organization. But as political institutions serving only sectional interests they would promote or perpetuate socio-political segmentation along racial and cultural lines. The final possibility is that the villages as political institutions might simply be emasculated and subordinated to the direct control of the central government, losing all semblance of self-rule. This would represent an extreme form of incorporation of their inhabitants into the colonial polity — what M.G. Smith terms "differential incorporation", one of the prime indicators of structural pluralism.[5]

In post-emancipation Guyana, the key factors which determined the viability of the villages as socio-political cum economic institutions were the system of land ownership and the problem of coastal drainage. Problems of allotment and titles for each plot arose almost from the inception of the communal villages, which had been bought as single units by a number of shareholders. Among other things, emancipation led to the full incorporation of the ex-slaves into the capitalist money economy, which in fact was expanded by their new buying power. Thus although the communal villages were established as cooperative ventures, this philosophy and spirit ran counter to the dominant capitalist ideology which emphasized individualism and materialism. This was reflected in the process of individualization of land ownership. Thus very soon after the purchase of the communal villages, the shareholders sought to acquire their own individual plots in accordance with their shares.

The problem, however, was that the divisions were not made by survey; rather a friendly arrangement seems to have sufficed in delineating the plots for each proprietor for which no title-deed was drawn up.[6] Moreover, instead of allotting one block of land to each proprietor, several small plots were allotted in different parts of the estate to ensure that no shareholder obtained better land than the others.[7] Thus individualization was accompanied by an even greater problem — the parcellization of land into small plots.[8]

Land parcellization coupled with subdivisions and alienations of land without proper legal titles resulted in chaotic land tenure. Questions of inheritance further complicated the matter especially if they involved illegitimacy and unregistered births,[9] and the existing system of Roman-Dutch law did not simplify the issue. By this system the widow and children, unless expressly barred by prematrimonial settlement, each inherited a specific but undivided share of the deceased's land. One can thus imagine the confusion which would have arisen in such cases and, not surprisingly, disputes over land were rife.[10]

As important as the problems caused by the chaotic land tenure was the question of drainage. The Guyana coastlands lie in part below sea level and require an elaborate system of dams, dykes, sluices and drainage canals to effect and maintain a proper system of drainage. This problem was made particularly acute in the mid–19th century by the formation of large mud banks along the east coast of Demerara which compelled most of the plantations in that locality to employ steam-draining engines to pump out the flood waters.[11] In addition, behind the coastland there lies a belt of savannah and swamp which is another source of floodwater to the coast unless protected by more dams and canals. Flooding might also result from the very heavy rainfall to which the country, bordering the equatorial belt, is periodically subjected. The elaborate network of drainage infrastructure was and is very expensive to erect and maintain, and was consequently beyond the meagre resources of the villagers. Thus for want of adequate drainage facilities, the villages literally sank beneath the floodwaters in the rainy seasons to become the breeding ground of diseases associated with tropical swamplands and a polluted water supply.[12]

These two factors — the chaotic land tenure system and bad drainage — provided the opening for the intervention of the central government in village affairs. The management committees which had been set up by the original proprietors to administer these villages lacked the legal authority to attempt a rationalization of the land tenure system, and were powerless and without the necessary financial resources to undertake the drainage works required to improve their communities.[13] Nor did the central government make any effort to grant them the legal powers and financial support to effect such public works. Instead, for the first decade after emancipation, the villages were simply left to flounder helplessly into an abject state of physical decay and stagnation because Governor Light did not think that the black inhabitants were sufficiently enlightened to exercise municipal functions, or that they possessed the requisite aptitude. Moreover, he feared that the granting of municipal powers to the villages would provide them with the sort of corporate organization and leadership which might pose problems for the government.[14] Hence, from the outset the race issue was employed to discourage the organization of the black villages as a corporate group and to keep them acephalous.

But by the time of Light's departure from the colony in 1848, it was patently evident that some form of local government was necessary,[15] and even the villagers themselves began to demand municipal powers. Hence, in 1850 a limited experiment in local government was started at Plaisance on the east coast of Demerara where six commissioners (four of whom were elected) were empowered to deal with the maintenance of drainage and public roads, and to assess and levy local rates to meet the costs.[16] Underlying this structure, however, was the basic principle upon which government policy towards the villages was based, that is, that the villages should from their own resources bear the full costs of local public works, particularly drainage, under the supervision of the central government.[17] It was the excessive financial burdens imposed in fulfilment of this principle which ultimately resulted in the political subordination of the black villages to the direct authority of the central government.

So far as the land tenure system was concerned, its need for rationalization had been evident since the mid-forties,[18] not least of all by the villagers themselves who demanded the establishment of a legal framework for partitioning an estate among the proprietors and bestowing proper titles to them.[19] Thus in 1851, the mechanism for effecting this process was implemented in Buxton,[20] and extended the following year to all communal villages. In 1856, the legislature was empowered to partition any estate which had been purchased by more than ten persons based on the application of a single co-proprietor. At the same time, however, a sinister move was made in 1852 to discourage further land acquisitions by groups of blacks and coloureds by prohibiting joint purchases by more than twenty persons; and it was made more stringent in 1856 by limiting such purchases to ten people.[21] This, as will be seen in the following chapter, appeared calculated less to prevent joint ownership than to hinder the blacks from acquiring more land.

Simultaneously, an attempt was made by the central government to assert indirect control over village administration. Ordinance No. 33 ruled that subdivided villages could opt for incorporation by law under the administration of two commissioners and a salaried overseer elected by the proprietors. The catch was that these village officials were subordinate to a district registrar appointed by the governor, and the registrar could appoint commissioners if the villagers refused to elect any. Moreover, the villagers were again burdened with the entire costs of local public works (drainage, roads, bridges, etc.), village partitioning, and the overseer's salary, through rates on assessed property.[22] Not surprisingly, very few villages availed themselves of the opportunity to become incorporated; in fact, by 1862, just 17 out of over 200 villages had been incorporated;[23] and in any event, these did not experience any improvement in their general condition. Drainage, health, and roads remained in a dreadful state,[24] and village lands depreciated so greatly for want of proper drainage that it was more profitable to rent drained estate land at £5 per acre than to cultivate the former.[25]

The problem of drainage intensified, eventually becoming the pretext for the assumption of direct control of village administration by the central government during the sixties; the race issue served as an important underlying factor. This is not to propose any crude hydraulic theories to explain the move towards centralization. Colonial authoritarianism was not born in bad drainage; rather the latter merely served as an excuse for resorting to the former. The reality is that the deplorable condition of the villages was attributed to the inherent incapability of the black inhabitants to govern themselves effectively, and it was argued that the elected village commissioners possessed neither the necessary qualifications nor the authority to enable them to exercise properly the administrative functions with which they were entrusted. It was even claimed that the black villagers themselves were quite conscious that without direct government interference and supervision, their affairs would remain hopelessly mismanaged. As a step toward countering this condition, it was decided that, under the control of the central government, steam-draining engines would be made available to the villages through government loans to cover their costs, and these would be repaid over a period of years by rates on the assessed value of village property.[26]

The brainchild of Governor Hincks, this scheme was first implemented on an experimental basis in the three east coast villages of Buxton, Friendship and Beterverwagting during the years 1862–63. A Special Improvement Board was established for each village, comprising the district sub-commissary of taxation as chairman, four elected commissioners, and an overseer as executive officer of the Board who was appointed by the governor. Real power, however, resided in the central government which could incorporate any village, make estimates of work required, issue loans for village improvement whether sought or not, assess property, and impose and collect rates recoverable by summary execution. The elected commissioners were reduced to mere rubber stamps who were consulted monthly as a courtesy on the conduct of affairs. They had no power of their own, and could merely submit their objections to any works or expenditure to the colonial legislature for consideration.[27]

The resulting improvements in drainage thus achieved encouraged the governor further. Critical of the land tenure system in the villages, he contemplated the establishment of model villages under government control in which lots of a "convenient" size would be laid out near the house of each proprietor with proper facilities for drainage, access, churches, schools, hospitals and dispensary. To this end he not only procured a loan fund of $60,000 (£12,500) from the Combined Court, but also appointed a five-man commission to examine and report on the whole question of village administration.[28] Two separate reports emerged from this commission which differed sharply on the question of government control of village administration. Hincks, naturally enough, embraced the report which endorsed his bias in favour of a highly centralized system of village administration.[29]

The resulting ordinance No.1/1866 by which the new system was set up effectively removed any vestiges of self-management from the villages and subjected them to the absolute control of the government. A Central Board of Villages was established consisting of the governor and the Court of Policy, and such other persons appointed by the governor. It was entrusted with the general management and supervision of the several local boards and officers. The villages were classified either as incorporated or unincorporated, and power was reserved to the legislature to incorporate any village under the regulations framed by the Central Board.[30]

Considerable powers were vested in the Central Board, and in the governor who, as president, was entrusted with custodial authority of the board when it was not in session. It was empowered to partition villages, to issue loans for village improvement from the fund of $60,000, and to impose special rates for their repayment. The board could also authorise any works regardless of the opinion of the villagers who had to pay for them, and it could enter into agreement on behalf of a village with the proprietor of a neighbouring plantation to drain the village for a term of years at an annual rate guaranteed by the colony. Finally, subject only to the legislature, it was authorised to make regulations for improving the sanitary condition of the villages and for defining and regulating the powers and duties of local superintendents and village overseers.[31]

The main effects of this new system was thus to remove any semblance of self-management by the black villagers, and to subject them to the direct control of the central government and of the colonial executive itself. Even the Colonial Office entertained grave reservations on the propriety of the governor being a member of the Central Board which removed the exercise of local functions and duties from the responsibility of local authorities.[32] Apart from the powerless elected commissioners of the local boards, the governor, through the Central Board, made all appointments down to the village overseer without consulting the villagers.[33] For all practical purposes, therefore, the 1866 ordinance effectively undertook to force the political subordination of the black villagers to the absolute authority of the central government.

While critical of the financial burden which was imposed on the villages and which in their view made the new system unworkable, some scholars[34] argue that at least in its administrative centralization this legislation was defensible given the villagers' so-called "lack of experience in the affairs of local government".[35] Indeed bearing in mind that in Britain itself, despite the passage of a Municipal Corporation Act in 1835 and other related legislation during the 1840s, it was not until the 1850s that significant administrative powers were transferred to the larger cities,[36] it can be argued that the idea of centralization was 'handed down' to the colonies. But the fact is that while in the metropolis greater powers were being extended to the local authorities, in Guyana the reverse was the case. Hence colony and metropolis were moving in opposite directions so far as local government was concerned, and the racial factor seems to have played a crucial role in explaining this difference.

It might also be argued that it is unrealistic to expect that the colonial state would finance public works in the villages without assuming political control over them if only to ensure that these works were properly carried out. In other words, 'he who pays the piper calls the tune'. This unfortunately has always been the prescription for authoritarian rule in Guyana ever since the colonial period. But it is important to bear in mind that it was the villages, and not the colony, which were meeting the full costs of such works through the rates on property, at least until 1884. By the same token, one might ask why the colonial government, which financed up to 70% of the cost of immigration (and which was not recoverable by any taxes on the planters, the sole beneficiaries), did not take control over the plantations. One cannot have it both ways, although ironically that is precisely what the planter-dominated government did.

Adamson is no doubt correct in asserting that the legislation of the 1860s was well intentioned[37] in so far as it aimed to effect physical improvements in the villages. But it did not require the 'enlightened paternalism' of the colonial administration to achieve this. The same end probably could have been attained far less painfully and far more effectively by the villagers themselves had they been vested with appropriate municipal power and organization, and granted financial support from the central government as was the plantation sector. In this case, the government need merely have performed an advisory function. Instead the 1866 legislation imposed the heavy-handed control of the central government on the villages and burdened them with oppressive taxes. From a theoretical standpoint, this signified a decisive abrogation of the role of the village as a sectional political institution. Hereafter the villagers were subjected to an extreme form of incorporation in the colonial polity characterized by their total subordination to the white dominated state. This subordination was symbolized by their forced payment of burdensome rates.

Governor Hincks wasted no time in putting the system into operation. By March 1866, over 160 villages had been brought under the control of the Central Board.[38] But this gross deprivation of their rights, privileges and freedom did not go unprotested by the black villagers who embarked on a campaign of resistance.[39] In 1863–64, the villagers of Friendship and Buxton had refused to pay the rates despite levies on the properties of their leaders, and mounted protests and petitions. They had even sent two representatives to elicit the support of the black Barbadian newspaper, the *Liberal*, which published a long statement by the leaders of the protest.[40] When the system became general after 1866, further disturbances occurred at Ithaca in Berbice, Agricola and Bagotstown on the east bank of Demerara, and again at Friendship, requiring in several instances armed police to suppress the irate villagers.[41]

Adamson claims that fear of high rates was the main reason of this "rates war". This is only partially correct. It is true that the new rates were considered burdensome (as indeed they were) and that they were perceived as an infringement of property rights.[42] But Young reminds us that the proprietors of the old incorporated villages were not unaccustomed to paying rates. The main difference was that while previously the rates 'had been fixed by themselves through their chosen representatives on the all-elected village councils', 'now they were being called upon to pay a rate that was to be fixed by Councillors nominated by the Governor'.[43] It was fundamentally this loss of local self-government about which the villagers were protesting. It was clear that the payment of rates imposed by agents of the central government implied an acceptance of the political subjugation of the black villagers to the direct control of the dominant white minority.

This was very clearly articulated on their behalf by an independent minister in Victoria village, Rev. Westley, who protested against the expensive, pressing and arbitrary action of 'an ordinance by which they would be at once bereft of all their village rights, privileges, and freedom of action, as if forfeited ... to the individual will of the Chief Ruler of the

Province'. But he, like many others, was not averse to sacrificing principle on the altar of personal gain when offered the post of village superintendent by Hincks.[44] Likewise other missionaries were called upon to use their influence to persuade the villagers to acquiesce to the new system.[45]

The loss of local autonomy, therefore, was the root cause of the people's resistance; and it is important to note that that resistance was not confined to the persons who were liable to pay the rates i.e. property holders, but involved the village populations as a whole. This "rates war" assumed the significance of a political struggle by the black villagers against the undisguised efforts of the white colonial government to subjugate them, and to prevent their developing the organizational structure and leadership which would constitute a politically viable corporate group.

No system of administration could hope to succeed in the face of strong opposition from the people it was designed to govern. Moreover, the local superintendents and overseers appointed by the governor not only possessed imperfect knowledge of local conditions, but were so autocratic that they did not bother to consult the elected commissioners, and overruled their objections. The result was costly and improperly done projects which burdened the black villagers with excessive taxation,[46] and occasionally caused more physical damage and loss of stock and produce than improvement, as was the case in Buxton in 1872.[47] Thus, Hincks' scheme ultimately failed; and by the end of the sixties, only 23 villages had received any credit at all.[48]

The establishment of village councils in 1873, consisting of the district commissary of taxation and three elected councillors, was a partial attempt to revert to the pre-Hincks system. This change, however, proved to be purely cosmetic and a mere pretence at self-management, since the Central Board was retained with powers to act above the heads of the village councils in undertaking public works and imposing rates.[49] The system also maintained its top-heavy and cumbersome bureaucratic structure resulting in bungling inefficiency, the cost of which had to be borne by the villagers who naturally resented it enormously.[50]

Further tinkering with the system in 1878 simply added to an already unwieldy bureaucratic superstructure by the creation of a Central Board of Health. This Board was responsible for the sanitary condition of the colony which was divided into town, country and village districts.⁵¹ The problem, however, was that the villages were now subject to two superior state authorities — the Central Boards of Villages and of Health — whose areas of responsibility were not sufficiently differentiated. The villages increasingly became the victims of over-centralization with the result that hardly any improvements were made to their physical or sanitary condition.

Yet on account of strong racial prejudices among government officials, it was the villagers who were held culpable for the deplorable state of the villages and, ironically, the solution was seen in even greater government control. The inspector of villages in 1881 argued that still too much power remained with the villagers who were insufficiently civilized to govern themselves. He further asserted that they required to be forced by a gentle pressure into the ways of civilized men, and that it was necessary to guide them in almost every action of their lives by rules of law — the white man's burden! He thus called for legislation to empower him to force the proprietors to work on village lands, sea dams, drains and roads, or to provide the means for having these works done, under pain of imprisonment.⁵² Governor Irving, too, shared the view that the black villagers were incapable of governing themselves, and that the innocuous village councils should be dissolved in favour of the absolute control of the central government.⁵³ Thus race remained a powerful factor in rationalizing the political subordination of the black villagers.

At the same time, however, Irving recognized that the system of financing village works through loans and local rates was totally inadequate and unsuitable, since loans became bad debts and the rates, being improperly collected, were largely absorbed in the cost of collection and management. He proposed the overhaul of the entire system of village administration by repealing the special village legislation, and by administering the drainage and sanitary affairs under the general law of the colony. His plan was to ask the Combined Court to write off the debts owed by the villages to the government, and to vest in the Public Works Department (P.W.D.) the engines and other drainage works for which those debts had been incurred. Expenditure on village empolders would form part of the annual budget, and the works would be executed by the P.W.D.[54]

This plan constituted a radically new approach in government policy towards the villages. For the first time it was recognised that the financing of public works in the villages should be met, not from special rates on the villages (which were in effect the imposition of an additional tax), but from the general public revenues to which the villagers already contributed very substantially in the form of licences and indirect taxes. But the determination to intensify the control of the central government over the villages, ostensibly to ensure the prompt and efficient execution of public works of prime necessity, resulted in Irving's plan being partly reactionary.[55]

Not surprisingly, because of these two divergent aspects of the plan, it satisfied neither the villagers nor the planters. On the one hand, it threatened to remove the last vestiges, however nominal they had been, of the villagers' participation in the conduct of local affairs, and to subject them to the absolute authority of the government. On the other hand, the planters were hardly enthused by the proposal to write off village debts and add village works to the colonial budget. They refused to recognise any distinction between the polder of a plantation and that of a village, arguing that it was the obligation of the respective occupants to maintain it. The Combined Court was thus only induced to grant money from colonial revenues for village works on condition that the rates were retained. Hence only $25,000 (£5,208) were provided, leaving the remainder of the estimated $48,000 (£10,000) needed for village works to be raised from the rates.[56]

In the final analysis, therefore, the black villagers remained burdened with an additional tax for village works, while they were totally deprived of a voice in local government. The 1883 ordinance (no.4) repealed the previous village laws, discarded the old Central Board of Villages, and vested the lands and property theretofore held by village corporations in the P.W.D. This was tantamount to expropriation of village lands without compensation. Each previously incorporated village was made a sanitary district, and the P.W.D. assumed sole responsibility for the main drainage works and roads. Rates were payable to the government, and were fixed by the

Central Board of Health at two percent on the appraised value of property.[57]

Both the rate-paying system and the centralization of village administration, however, continued to impose severe limitations on the effectiveness of the system. The retention of local rates meant that works could only be undertaken in the old incorporated villages (comprising about 80,000 people), which were geared for rate collection. The other villages, totalling about 87,000 inhabitants, received no aid whatsoever. Besides, the autocratic manner in which business was conducted generated considerable ill-feeling and discontent among the black villagers, who were never informed about the amount of revenue collected in rates or how it was spent.[58] There were also allegations of mismanagement directed at the P.W.D. whose overseers and engineers were accused of paying insufficient attention to the needs of individual villages.[59] The disastrous floods at Plaisance and Golden Grove on the east coast in 1887 lent credibility to these charges.[60] These shortcomings led to new demands from some villagers for the restoration of the village councils with corporate municipal powers.[61]

The climate of political change at the state level in the late eighties and early nineties, influenced and accompanied by the recession of the race factor in colonial politics, together provided the much needed impetus to the idea of devolving power back to the black villages, and according their inhabitants an effective voice in the administration of their own affairs.[62] It would have been absurd to contend that black and coloured people were not capable of managing themselves at the local level when they had begun to participate in the exercise of power at the state level. Thus in 1892 a change was implemented in the system of village government which parallelled that which was occurring in the colonial government between 1891–96.

Accordingly, corporate village councils were established with an elective majority of three to each member nominated by the Central Board of Health, which in turn retained responsibility for the overall supervision of local government.[63] Nevertheless, these local councils were vested with substantial administrative powers which ensured a considerable degree of self-management, and they provided the black villagers with the institutional framework for developing the type of corporate organisation and leadership from the "grassroots" which could constitute them into truly cohesive local communities, capable of effective collective activity directed at improving their political and social status. Although far from ideal, this structure was clearly an improvement on the previous system. The Central Board of Health still retained considerable power, including the power to dissolve any council for not performing its duties adequately,[64] while the system of rate payment was retained. And it might have worked if sufficient funds had been made available by the central government for village improvement schemes. But, as Adamson has shown, this was precisely what was in short supply during the 1890s, with the result that most villages remained in as poor condition as before the changes of the 1890s.[65]

Not unlike the situation at the state level such political change at the local level was possible only as a result of the gradual, ofttime imperceptible recession of the prominence of race as a determinant of socio-political status. For the issue of race had always been the underlying basis for denying the black villagers an effective voice in the conduct of local affairs, and thus for imposing the direct and absolute control of the central government over the villages. This highly centralized system of local administration was thus instrumental to the political subordination of the black villages, and by corollary to the maintenance of white minority dominance.

The weakening of the central importance of race as an independent criterion of social and political status facilitated the political changes of the 1890s. Not only were the black villagers granted the power to manage their own affairs; but it was even possible for white planters to sit as nominated members on the new councils alongside the elected black villagers, and to contribute to the better management of village affairs.[66] The political changes at the local level, parallel to those at the state level, thus reflected the structural change which had occurred within the colonial society, i.e., a gradual breakdown of the racial barrier between white and black in the public domain.

In theoretical terms, the political changes of the 1890s at the local level meant that the villages could once again perform the institutional role of providing sectional or ethnic group organization. But they went beyond the limited function of serving as alternative sectional political institutions to become important broker institutions which facilitated the political integration of the black and coloured section into the public domain on a basis of equality without regard to race, and complemented the reformed political institutions at the colonial state level. The differential incorporation of the black and coloured section, therefore, gave way to a more universalistic incorporation within the colonial polity both at the local and state levels.

CHAPTER 6

SECOND CLASS SUBJECTS: THE SOCIO-ECONOMIC STATUS OF THE BLACKS AND COLOUREDS

The concentration of state power in the hands of the small white minority, in particular the plantocracy, so characteristic of plural and plantation-dominated societies, was designed not only to perpetuate the social and political dominance of that minority, but also to deny the other ethnic sections political rights or the opportunities to organize themselves as corporate groups. This applied both to the blacks and coloureds and to the immigrants. M.G. Smith notes that though forming a majority of the population, such subordinated people are not citizens but subjects.[1] In colonial society, however, all members are legally "subjects" of the imperial Crown: hence the distinction between subject and citizen is not quite appropriate. Rather one has to distinguish between different classes or categories of colonial subjects. Here we shall treat the socially and politically subordinated blacks and coloureds as "second-class subjects".

The theoretical issue here, and for each succeeding chapter relating to the other subordinate ethnic groups, is whether this subordination implied simply differences of class status, or a manifestation of structural pluralism. Class status is alterable over time through mobility criteria such as educational and professional/occupational achievement, material wealth, and acculturation to the dominant norm or tradition. Structural pluralism, however, implies subordination enforcable by law or custom, and entailing institutionalized inequalities of ethnic group status accompanied by sectionalization along racial and cultural lines. In the context of

Guyana, one needs to ascertain whether the social mobility of individuals implies a breaking-down of sectional boundaries, thus significantly altering the basic structure of the society or whether such cases of individuation occur without any fundamental changes in ethnic group status, in which case the sectional boundaries and consequently the basic structure of the society remain unaltered. These are questions which this chapter will address.

In chapter 2, it was pointed out that the black and coloured section consisted of local and West Indian Creoles and Africans. Although derived from the Spanish term *criollo* meaning local-born, the term "creole" was almost exclusively used in post-emancipation Guyana to refer to the native blacks and coloureds; and accordingly it has thus been used in this study (except when referring to the three-tier traditional biracial host society carried over from the slave period in which case it has been italicized).

As a result of miscegenation with the white "master class" over generations, the Creoles were of almost every conceivable colour gradation, ranging from the *fustee* who were nearly white, through the *mustee* who were a "shade" darker, the *mulatto* with woolly hair and decidedly negroid features, and the *cob* of still darker hue, to the *Negro*, some of whom were nearly jet black, but the majority of a dark brown complexion. Other categorizations included *octoroon* and *quadroon* — one-eighth and one-quarter black respectively.[2] It is evident that many of these categorizations were not very precise, although they had great social significance especially within the Creole section itself.

The local Creoles were the largest category among the black and coloured section, and increased from 65,319 in 1841 to an estimated 120,161 in 1891. The West Indians likewise increased in number from 9,899 in 1841 to 21,025 by 1891. But with the termination of African immigration in 1865, that category gradually diminished from 4,384 in 1841 to 3,433 in 1891. Together, however, the black and coloured section formed the vast majority of the population at emancipation (92.9 percent in 1841). This was greatly changed with the influx of Indian and Chinese immigrants in the ensuing decades, and the Creole proportion of the society diminished to just 52 percent in 1891. However, their actual numbers increased from 91,074 in

1841 to an estimated 144,619 in 1891.³

Differences, particularly of origin and colour, divided the black and coloured section. The coloureds allegedly looked down on the blacks and tried to avoid forming associations with them, even though they, in turn, were spurned by the whites.⁴ The work "nigger" was reputedly the most common and offensive term of abuse within the Creole section.⁵ One could not insult a Creole more than by calling him/her a "nigger". Hyper-sensitivity over such racist abuse could on occasion inadvertently lead to embarrassing misunderstandings — as, for instance, when a white minister of religion outraged his Creole congregation by referring to the collection taken as "a niggardly one".⁶ Although they seemed fairly well disposed towards the Africans whom they married and counselled,⁷ the local Creoles were generally antagonistic to other black immigrants, particularly the Barbadians, and this occasionally resulted in communal violence.⁸

In the post-emancipation society, the preservation of white dominance was seen to depend simply on the subjugation of the black and coloured majority as an ethnic group. Within the context of a plantation-dominated society, this meant their subjection to the plantation regime, as Thompson and Beckford point out.⁹ Particularly in Guyana, this was effected socially and economically in three ways: firstly, restricting black settlement to the plantation belt; secondly, by the imposition of high taxation to subjugate the blacks and coloureds, forcing them to depend on the plantation system for economic survival; and thirdly, by hindering the growth of an independent peasant sector as a viable economic alternative to the plantation system.

It is crucial, therefore, to examine the pattern of creole settlement after emancipation, and the efforts of the colonial government to restrict it. For the first decade thereafter, creole settlement was voluntarily confined to the plantation belt, even though the cost of private land averaged £50 per acre, whereas the upset price for Crown lands in the interior of the colony was only £1 ($4.80) per acre. But the former had the advantage of contiguity to markets, churches, schools, and so on, whereas the Crown lands were isolated, not easily accessible, and suffered from poor drainage. Hence, by 1848, only 1,387 acres of Crown land had been purchased by the ex-slaves.¹⁰

A dramatic change occurred, however, after the economic depression and unsuccessful labour strike of 1847–48. Thereafter many Creoles drifted from the plantation belt into the remoter interior. The village population declined by almost ten percent between December 1848 and June 1849, while the Creole labour force on hire to the estates declined by 18.75 percent. By 1850, hundreds of Creoles had settled for miles along the banks of the main rivers, where previously there had been no settlements.[11]

The spectre of black bush settlements beyond the control of the colonial authorities was alarming both to them[12] and to their imperial overlords. Considering it an evil of great magnitude, Secretary of State Grey urged that the vagrancy laws should be vigorously enforced by the police against vagrants and squatters, and that the Amerindians be used to ferret out Creole settlers in the remote interior. At the same time, he advocated the development of social facilities to encourage the Creoles to establish a stable, civilized life within the plantation belt, and to assist them to acquire smallholdings on secure and permanent tenures near the plantations.[13] But the colonial government found that the most effective way to restrict Creole settlement to the plantation belt was by imposing stringent regulations governing the granting and usage of Crown lands and, if necessary, by increasing their price.[14]

Even before the final emancipation, Secretary of State Glenelg had suggested making the availability of Crown lands difficult by applying the Wakefield system of selling in minimum parcels of 100 acres at a predetermined upset price in order to forestall any probable desire by the slaves to purchase land when freed.[15] This proposal was duly implemented in 1839 by Governor Light, who fixed the upset price at £1 ($4.80) per acre and increased the cost of five-year licences of occupancy to prevent 'persons without capital' from engaging in woodcutting.[16] A further attempt in 1845 by the planters to impose more stringent regulations on the granting and usage of Crown lands was, however, rejected by Secretary of State Stanley expressly because they were clearly intended to operate exclusively against the Creoles.[17]

The mood shifted in 1849 when the colonial government was placed in the hands of Henry Barkly who had been a leading member of an absentee planter lobby advocating more stringent Crown lands regulations in 1845.[18] Not surprisingly, therefore, he vigorously pressed this issue during his governorship. To impede the Creoles from engaging in woodcutting he not only proposed that the minimum grant of occupancy should be half an acre, and the annual rent per acre be increased from eight pence (16 cents) to one shilling (24 cents), but also that a competent security for the payment of the five years' rent should be required beforehand. As regards the sale of Crown lands, he proposed that the upset price should be raised to as high as £5 ($24) per acre except for extensions of existing holdings i.e., plantations, in which case it should remain at £1 per acre. Again the entire purchase money was to be paid before the land was taken possession of. Not only were these proposals designed to bar the Creoles from buying Crown lands, but they were biased in favour of the plantations. Consequently these proposals failed to gain the approval of the imperial government.[19]

Despite Barkly's failure to implement his blatantly discriminatory proposals, the Crown lands regulations continued to be employed as a major instrument of policy to hinder Creole settlement in the remote interior. In 1861 the upset price per acre was doubled to $10, while the cost of licences of occupancy was increased to thirty cents per acre per annum.[20] Not only was the sale price *per se* an effective deterrent,[21] but the gross disparity between it and the cost of licences was clearly intended to discourage the Creoles from purchasing and settling on Crown lands. It was clearly uneconomical to pay $1000 for 100 acres when one could lease the same acreage for $30 a year renewable indefinitely.[22] Since the licencing authorities could exercise greater scrutiny and control over the issue of licences, this was an effective way of limiting the number and *type* of persons who would be permitted to establish independent enterprises, whether in agriculture, forestry, or later on, prospecting in the interior.

The objective of restricting Creole settlement to the plantation belt remained a major feature of government policy for the rest of the century. In 1872, Governor Scott did not hide his opinion that the movement of Creoles into the remote interior beyond the reach of "civilising" influences was objectionable;[23] and, in the following year, he had the Crown lands regulations revised to discourage any such development.[24] Similarly, in 1884, Governor Irving refused to consider a reduction in the sale price of Crown lands, arguing that it was the object of the government to seek to bring back into cultivation the uncultivated lands on the coast.[25] This was evidently designed to restrict the Creoles to the plantation belt in order to provide a sufficient supply of cheap labour to assist the recovery of the plantation system suffering from the acute economic depression of the 1880s.

However, the increased demand for land at that time, occasioned mainly by the gradual settlement of Indian immigrants as free residents, forced a change of the Crown lands regulations making more land available for sale, but without fundamentally altering the policy of preventing independent settlement inland. Thus in 1887, the upset price was reduced to $5 per acre, except for land more than ten miles from a public road, in which case it retained the old price of $10 per acre.[26] The desired effect of restricting non-white settlers to the plantation belt was by these means achieved; and even there the reduced price of Crown lands was still higher than that for abandoned estates which hardly sold for more than $1 per acre.[27] Accordingly the price of $10 per acre for virgin forest land in the interior was an effective deterrent to settlement inland.

The successful restriction of the Creoles to the plantation belt was only the first facet of a grand design to exercise effective control over them and to reduce them to a state of economic dependence on the plantation system. The second facet of this scheme was the imposition of discriminatory taxation. As colonial taxation was in the hands of the planter majority in the Combined Court, its incidence was intended to be borne primarily by the Creole and immigrant workers. Hence taxation was generally indirect — on foodstuff, consumer durables, clothing and luxuries.

The planters held that high taxation on consumer and other imported commodities in general demand would compel the Creoles to continue working regularly on the plantations in order to earn sufficient cash with which to buy those goods. This policy was evident in the first tax ordinance after emancipation, wherein the duties on bottled wine and wheat flour were increased by 50 percent, tobacco by 200 percent, spirits by 100 percent, and horses by 40 percent. New *al valorem* taxes were imposed on tea and mules, and a new tax levied on cigars. At the same time, however, the tax on plantation produce was reduced from 1⅞ percent to 1½ percent. Thus, while the Creoles were being burdened with increased taxes, the planters reduced their own tax burden.[28]

It was soon evident that this discriminatory tax system was oppressive to the Creoles,[29] who in 1846, mainly with the assistance of the L.M.S. missionaries, petitioned against it. They complained that the tax on flour stood at 42 percent, cornmeal 30 percent, prime beef 52½ percent, prime pork 32 percent, codfish between 20 and 25 percent, tobacco leaf 245 percent and manufactured tobacco 207 percent. In fact, two-thirds of the entire colonial revenue of $550,000 was raised from taxes on essential commodities, while the tax on plantation produce yielded only $40,000 (7 percent).[30] In 1847 an import duty of 4 percent *ad valorem* was imposed, thereby nullifying whatever relief might have resulted from the repeal of the Crown duties.[31] In 1850 the import duties on foodstuff and other consumer goods were so greatly increased that those on flour, rice, fish and pork alone yielded $230,000 or more than a moiety of the revenues from import duties.[32]

In response to a suggestion by Secretary of State Grey to reduce indirect taxes, in 1851 Governor Barkly persuaded the planter majority in the Combined Court to make small reductions on a number of commodities.[33] These reductions, however, were purely cosmetic. For instance, although the duty on flour was lowered from $1.75 to $1 per barrel, it was still between 20 and 25 percent of the commodity's value; and likewise the salt-beef duty, reduced from $2.75 to $1.50, remained not much less than its actual value.[34] Simultaneously, however, the planters took the opportunity to abolish their own income tax, while the tax on plantation produce was converted into an export tax thereby exempting that portion consumed within the colony.[35]

Yet even these token tax cuts were shortlived. The Combined Court in 1853 doubled the duty on rice, and raised those on Indian corn and other grain by 60 percent. Likewise, the duties on cloth fabrics and hardware were increased from 4 to 10 percent *ad valorem*.[36] These tax increases were followed in 1855 by the doubling of duties on pickled beef and pork, dried fish, beer and soap; increases on tobacco of between 20 and 30 percent; and the duties on confectionary, salt and tobacco pipes were changed from 10 percent *ad valorem* to rateable duties of 15½ cents per pound on the first two, and $1 per gross on the third. At the same time, the excise duty on rum consumed in the colony was increased by 12½ percent.[37].

Taken together, the tax increases of 1853 and 1855 symbolized the use of fiscal policy as an instrument of repression. They were evidently intended to suppress and subjugate the Creole people and to force them into economic dependence on the plantations. Guyana enjoyed the dubious distinction of having the highest tax burden per capita ($9.81) in the British Caribbean.[38] In 1858 import duties alone produced about $1,275,000 from a population of 130,000; and by 1867, out of a total revenue of $1,323,214.67, no less than 94½ percent was raised by taxes on consumption.[39] At the same time, after 1862 most plantation supplies including coal, bricks, machinery, manures, lime, hay, staves, steam-draining engines and steam ploughs were exempted from taxation, while the duties on others varied from 2 to 5 percent, and yielded only $42,853 or 3.2 percent of the total revenue in 1867.[40]

Not surprisingly, this policy of discriminatory taxation caused considerable financial and economic distress among the Creole people, some of whom in 1871 felt compelled to remonstrate against it and to demand relief even if it required political change.[41] Coming at a time of general unrest among the indentured immigrants on the plantations, the imperial government thought it prudent to urge a reduction of taxation on essential goods. The Combined Court obliged in 1872 by abolishing the duty on rice, and reducing those on flour and dried fish by 90 percent, tallow candles by 83 percent, pepper by 80 percent, and lard and soap by 50 percent. The import duties on luxuries such as cigars, tobacco and wines, however, were significantly increased.[42]

These tax reductions, taken together were merely sop to appease the discontented masses by offering temporary relief. In the very next year, the duties on dried fish and flour were restored to their previous levels, though the *ad valorem* duty on merchandise was lowered from 10 to 5 percent, and rice remained free of duty.[43] That did not last long however: in 1877 a tax of 25 cents per 100 pounds was imposed on rice,[44] and in 1882 the 10 percent *ad valorem* duty was reimposed,[45] though it was lowered again the following year to 5 percent.[46] The somewhat more enlightened fiscal policy of Governor Irving which, as we have already seen, led to a reduction in village rates, also brought positive benefits in taxation levels in the depression years of the mid-1880s. In 1884 he for the first time procured from the Combined Court a quinquennial tax ordinance in which the duties on pickled beef and pork, and on lard, were removed, while those on coal and luxuries such as spirits and wines, tobacco and pistols were increased.[47]

This measure of tax relief should not be construed as indicative of a change of attitude on the part of the planters who remained wedded to the idea that the Creoles and immigrants should bear the brunt of taxation. Not surprisingly, in 1885 they reverted to annual tax ordinances which enabled them to exercise full control over fiscal policy; and in 1888, shortly after Irving's departure, they restored the onerous duties on pickled pork and beef, and on lard.[48] High indirect taxation thus remained a major instrument in suppressing the Creole population and in perpetuating their dependence on the plantation system.

The use of taxation against the interests of the Creole people also assumed the form of licences. Licences were required for porters, hucksters, and shopkeepers; and, as the following chapter demonstates, this system operated in favour of the Portuguese immigrants who were facilitated in establishing their dominance in the lucrative retail trade. Similarly, boat operators were required to have licences. There again these regulations discriminated against the Creole peasants and woodcutters living in the river districts since no licences were required for vessels employed by the plantations along the coasts and creeks.[49] Similarly, whereas the proprietors of cabs, mule-carts and donkey carts were required to pay for a licence 12 months in advance, the horses, mules and carts in the service of the plantations were exempt.[50]

By far the most oppressive tax to which the Creole community was subjected was the registration or poll tax imposed in 1856 to recover the cost of suppressing the riots against the Portuguese immigrants (chapter 7), and to compensate them for losses. Though payable by the whole adult population of the colony, its incidence was admittedly calculated to bear most heavily on the Creole people as a punitive measure.[51] This tax was a levy of $2 per annum for males (equivalent to 2 months wages at an average of 24 cents per week) and $1 per annum for females for five years. Coinciding with the ravages of a cholera outbreak, it bore mercilessly on the

Creoles, particularly the aged and infirm. Non-payment was punishable by fine or imprisonment with hard labour; and as the registrars stood to gain one-third of the fine, this led to personal harassment and the invasion of homes to enforce the tax.[52] The oppressive nature of the tax not only generated widespread hostility among the Creoles, but also the determined opposition of some influential whites including the redoubtable Peter Rose, and the L.M.S. missionaries. Further afield the British Anti-Slavery Society lent its support to the campaign for its repeal.[53] This was finally accomplished in 1858,[54] but not before the Creoles had vented their anger towards Governor Wodehouse, the chief architect of the tax, by stoning him on his way to the wharf when departing the colony on vacation leave in July 1857.[55]

The third facet of the process of subordinating the Creole section in social and economic terms was by hindering the growth of an economically independent peasant and small farming sector as a viable alternative to the plantation system. The very problems which facilitated the intervention of the central government in village affairs and its eventual exercise of absolute control over village administration formed the basis of the economic decay of the villages, viz., the land tenure system and poor drainage. The practice of dividing an estate by allotting several small plots to each part-proprietor in different parts of the estate, in addition to the subsequent subdivisions without proper legal titles, ultimately led to the fragmentation of village lands into uneconomic units. Adamson shows that the majority of village landholders owned less than one acre[55a] which could hardly sustain subsistence agriculture. This parcellization of land contributed to the drainage problems since it was difficult to persuade the owner of a small unprofitable plot to maintain his drainage canals and dams so necessary to the rest of the village. Thus for want of the financial resources to raise the £5,000 ($24,000) required to purchase steam-draining engines,[56] the villages literally sank beneath the floodwaters to become inhabited swamps in which both crops and livestock were invariably lost.

Despite their assistance to neighbouring plantations in distress, the villagers generally found the plantations unwilling to reciprocate and assist in draining village lands.[57] Similarly, the commercial sector and banks were only prepared to make loans to the villages for drainage equipment at the ruinous interest rates of 40–50 percent.[58] And as was noted in the last chapter, far from making grants for public works to the villages, the central government was content only to make loans repayable by onerous rates in exchange for assuming political control over the villages; and in any case very few villages received such improvement loans. In sum, the growth of a peasant/smallfarming sector was effectively stifled for want of adequate financial aid from either the public or private sector as both were under the influence of the plantation system which, in turn, was fundamentally unsympathetic to the creation of a viable, independent minifundia.

The result was, as noted before, that by the 1860s some villagers found it more profitable to rent drained plantation lands at £5 ($24) per acre than to cultivate their own.[59] This signified the final demise of the independent village economy as the Creole peasants themselves became dependent on the plantations for survival. This development represents one of the classic features of plantation systems identified by Thompson.[60]

The reduction of the peasant/small-farming sector to a state of dependency made it possible for the planters to operate paternalistically. Thus in 1866 they actually thwarted a move by Governor Hincks aimed at preventing the villagers of Beterverwagting from purchasing Plantation Triumph to conduct an experiment in cooperative agriculture.[61] With the guidance of the London Missionaries, this venture worked well for a few years before disintegrating in 1871.[62] Similarly, in 1872, the proprietor of Plantation La Bonne Intention, William Russell, encouraged the villagers of Beterverwagting to cultivate sugar on their farms, which he undertook to purchase at a price based on the sucrose content of the canes.[63] The initial success of this experiment[64] encouraged other villagers to enter similar agreements with neighbouring plantations, and cane farming not only became fairly widespread[65] but reasonably lucrative as well. The Beterverwagting farmers, for instance, earned $42,271 between 1873 and 1884.[66]

The plantation owners were not acting altruistically since cane farming was conducted within a framework of dependency on the plantation system. This was vividly demonstrated in 1881–82 when a dispute over the method of pricing between the Beterverwagting farmers and Russell culminated in the latter's refusal to buy the farmers' canes. Eventually the farmers were obliged to accept Russell's terms in order to have their canes crushed.[67] Subsequent attempts by individuals and groups of villagers to erect their own mills in order to lessen their dependence on the plantations proved too small-scale and uneconomic to displace the plantations.[68] Moreover, the colonial legislature once more refused to grant financial aid to the Creole farmers to assist them in purchasing and erecting machinery for sugar manufacture[69] — understandably so since the legislature consisted of planters who stood to lose. Thus the success of small-farming in the villages remained inexorably dependent on the perceived benefit of the planters.

Hence by a systematic policy of restricting Creole settlement to the plantation belt, high taxation, and hindering the growth of an economically independent small-farming sector, the ruling white minority were able to subjugate the Creole population, and to reduce them to a state of parlous dependency on the plantation system for sheer survival. Although many tried to escape the pervasive domination of the plantations after 1848, there were in 1850 some 19,939 Creoles resident on them, while more than half the 42,755 villagers continued to hire their services to the estates.[70] By 1871 there were still at least 20,000 hired Creole workers out of a village population of 67,719 working on the estates, in addition to 17,808 Creoles resident thereon.[71]

Not that this dependence assured them a livelihood. The large-scale influx of immigrant workers, particularly after 1850, not only caused a decline in wages, but rendered employment uncertain for hired Creole labour.[72] Under the indentureship system, the plantations were bound by law to provide five full days' work per week for the immigrants before extra labour could be hired.[73] This regulation most affected the hired Creole workers during periods of recession, floods, or droughts, as it was they who bore the brunt of retrenchment or reduced wages.[74] Indeed, as both Adamson and Rodney have noted, by the late 19th century not only did the continuous influx of immigrant workers cause chronic under- and unemployment among the Creole labour force, but in fact even some of the heavier and better paid tasks preferred by, and previously reserved for, the Creoles were by then being done by the immigrants.[75] This suggests that although by 1891 the number of Creoles resident on the estates remained roughly equal to the 1871 figure, they represented only 19.6 percent of the 90,000 full-time estate labour force.[76] Furthermore, the number of non-resident, Creole hired workers almost certainly would have declined during the depression of the 1880s. In effect, therefore, by 1891 the Creoles were becoming increasingly marginal to the production system of the dominant economic institution in the colony.[77]

As we have seen, many Creoles attempted to escape the pervasive domination of the plantation system particularly after 1848, and this trend accelerated during the sixties. Several migrated up the banks of the main rivers where private lands could still be purchased at reasonable prices, and engaged in woodcutting and small-farming.[78] Others migrated to the sparsely settled Pomeroon district in Essequibo. The population of the Pomeroon thus increased from just 150 in 1861 to 2,116 by 1871.[79] Still others went to the Corentyne coast of Berbice,[80] and even across the river border into the Dutch colony of Surinam where, after the abolition of slavery in 1863, there was a demand for plantation labour.[81] But not surprisingly, this emigration was frowned on by the local government which instituted legal and other obstacles to try to restrict it.[82]

Those Creoles who could not buy private lands up-river were, of course, prevented from settling inland by the restrictive Crown lands regulations: before they could obtain a licence, they had to borrow money at ruinous rates of interest to make the required outlay with the government and to start operations on the tract.[83] Thus, if they wished to engage in forestry, balata-bleeding, gold and diamond prospecting, or any other occupation in the interior they were constrained to become the hired employees of grantholders who were invariably white, including Portuguese. Although these workers did earn considerable sums of money when lucky in these occupations,[84] they remained economically dependent on the white dominated economy.

From the moment of emancipation, some rural Creoles began to move to the towns in search of economic and social advancement. In 1841 about 22 percent of the total black and coloured population were resident in Georgetown and New

Amsterdam. The rural-urban population movement continued throughout the 19th century, so that by 1891 it is estimated that the urban component comprised about 35 percent of the total black and coloured population. In absolute terms, this represented an increase of over 30,000 from the 19,962 urban Creoles of 1841. This means that the Creoles comprised about 80 percent of the total urban population in 1891.[85]

In the towns, the Creoles worked as porters, stevedores, domestics, hucksters, handicraftsmen, carters, warehousemen, mechanics, masons, carpenters, smiths, coopers, tailors, shoemakers, clerks, painters, tram-drivers and conductors, railwaymen, printers, schoolteachers, dispensers, policemen and parsons.[86] Skilled and white-collar jobs were held at a premium. It was the ambition of parents to make artisans and teachers of their children since farming and unskilled labour offered little prospect for social and economic improvement.[87] Many people thus claimed to be skilled tradesmen whether competent or not, and those occupations soon became over-crowded.[88] Between 1851 and 1891, the number of artisans increased by 136.4 percent from 5,983 to 14,146,[89] the vast majority of these being Creole. While they all aspired to be independent, however, many still remained dependent on nearby estates for employment.[90]

Although a competent and reliable tradesman could earn a reasonably good living, white-collar jobs were the most socially desirable among the educated Creole youth.[91] Many parents longed for the day when their sons might become the proud messengers of lawyers' offices or cash-boys of dry-goods stores.[92] These jobs, however, were not that readily available to the majority of urban Creole youth. For some considerable time after emancipation, the commercial firms preferred to introduce white clerical staff from abroad on a contractual basis rather than to employ Creoles.[93] As late as the 1860s, Creole clerks were a rarity and, as H.V.P. Bronkhurst put it, 'in a walk along [Water] street one could almost have counted on the ten fingers the number of them employed in the various stores, English or Portuguese'.[94]

Whether as a result of the high costs engendered to maintain staff in this way or an insufficient supply of prospective recruits, the practice gradually declined in the later 19th century and Creole youths began to be employed in growing numbers. By the 1880s, the majority of the 1,521 clerks in business establishments were Creoles, and an oversupply of candidates soon meant that such jobs became increasingly difficult to obtain. In 1891 there were 2,505 clerks and shop assistants of whom 213 were female.[95] Even so, they represented a very small (and despite their low wages) socially privileged category of the urban Creole population.

By far the most desirable and prestigious job, however, was an appointment in the colonial Civil Service, unless, of course, one could afford to train for one of the liberal professions i.e. law, medicine or the clergy, Yet perhaps no other area of employment generated so much frustration and discontent among the Creoles as the Civil Service on account of alleged race and colour discrimination attending appointments, promotions, benefits and dismissals. Shortly after emancipation, Creoles had begun to agitate for fairer distribution of government jobs on the basis of merit without regard to race or colour. In 1842 a group of them formed the British Guiana African Association (B.G.A.A.) which, together with its organ the *Freeman's Sentinel*, attacked the colonial adminstration on its allegedly discriminatory employment policy.[96]

The leading members of this group were an educated black teacher, L.M.S. catechist and journalist named MacFarlane; a Surinamese medical practitioner, druggist and shopkeeper named Vries; a schoolmaster and ex-police inspector by name of Oudkirk; and a journalist, ex-postholder and ex-schoolmaster named Belgrave. The latter three were coloured. The Association enjoyed the support of the L.M.S. missionaries who, as we have seen, were very active in colonial politics during the 1840s.[97] Allegations of racial discrimination in the public service were made repeatedly throughout the 19th century; and black newspapers like the *Creole* and the *Echo* lost no opportunity to highlight this problem much to the embarrassment of colonial governors.

Instances of alleged discrimination on racial grounds are thus not difficult to pinpoint. Some of the very leaders of the B.G.A.A. apparently were victims of such discrimination. Oudkirk, the youngest of three police inspectors in the early 1840s, was made redundant because of alleged incompetence. Belgrave was reportedly peeved about not being offered a more senior and lucrative position in 1841 than postholder on the Demerara river. Whether these two men were "not fit" by way of "station" or "ability" to hold responsible office, as Governor Light claimed, is difficult to verify.[98]

It would, however, be a twist of irony if the Oudkerk (notwithstanding the difference of spelling which could be an error), a coloured chief clerk of 20 years experience, but who was superceded in 1857 for the post of financial accountant by a white man from Barbados, was related to the ex-inspector of similar name. It was indeed the father of the younger man who filed the application on his son's behalf with the governor only to have it turned down on the grounds of the applicant's lack of 'influence with the merchants' and 'for the good of the public service'.[99] How a complete stranger could, except on purely racial grounds, be expected to have more "influence" with the merchants than a local man with experience is mystifying. Such instances of racial discrimination in the public service were by no means isolated during the 19th century.[100]

The problem was that matters of appointment, promotion, etc. in the public service were conducted largely through patronage, family connections and social standing. This meant that Creoles had very little chance. E.N. McDavid, a prominent Creole, claimed that 'merit, if associated with a sable complexion, is not recognized, or, if called into play at all, is made to fulfil the drudgery, while the lucrative positions are bestowed upon others'.[101] According to the *Echo*, the senior ranks of the Civil Service were virtually 'monopolized by certain families of the community sharing between them a large sum of money'.[102] Duff observed that

> instead of men brought up in the service and thereby trained to its duties [getting promotions], a large proportion of them [in senior positions] are men who, having spent the best of their days in some private employment, and at last failed in it, have, by their connection with some member of the Legislature, obtained a Government appointment, the duties of which, although put over the heads of competent men who have grown grey in the service, they have yet to learn.[103]

Bronkhurst further noted that in many cases such incompetent and inexperienced men had to be taught or get the work done for them by the very men whom they superseded.[104] What rankled the most was when white youths not long out of Queen's College, the leading grammar school, were found well-paid, responsible positions after very short service, regardless of their educational attainments or ability, in preference to experienced and suitably qualified coloured men.[105]

This system of patronage and racial discrimination not only held out little prospect for advancement to Creoles in the junior ranks of the Civil Service, but it also deprived them of benefits for long service. There were essentially two basic categories of officer in the Civil Service: (a) staff officers on the permanent establishment (mainly white) who were provided salaries in addition to ancillary benefits such as pensions and leave of absence, and were required to contribute four percent of their salary to the Widows and Orphans Fund from which their dependents would receive a pension after the death of the officer; (b) supernumerary officers who were also paid salaries, in some cases as much as staff officers, but who were not entitled to the ancillary benefits enjoyed by the latter. They held their positions on a year to year basis, thus lacking job security, and in very many cases were never promoted to staff positions. Many of these Creole officers, after several years of dedicated public service, retired without a pension or died leaving their widows and orphans without economic security.[106]

Throughout the post-emancipation 19th century, however, successive governors were at pains to deny the existence of such racial discrimination in the public service. Official Colonial Office policy was supposed to adhere to the principle that 'wherever coloureds qualified for jobs, they should be employed. But it is their responsibility to educate themselves to justify appointment'.[107] Herein, however, lay the loophole which permitted colonial administrations to pay only lip-service to the idea of equal opportunity, and to make only cosmetic or token appointments while in other ways thumbing their noses at the established principle. The excuse was repeatedly made that the coloureds were aspiring to positions for which they were not qualified or competent. They were generally regarded as semi-educated upstarts who were seldom satisfied with their lot, and who were prone to suffer from the delusion that jobs were withheld from them solely on account of their colour.[108]

At the same time, it is evident that public pressure exerted by the Creoles, especially through the press, forced the governors on the defensive and obliged them to appoint some token coloureds and blacks to public office.[109] But such gestures evidently did not go very far towards redressing the racial imbalance in the senior Civil Service and satisfying Creole discontent.

The priesthood was regarded by many Creoles as one of the liberal professions which offered greater scope for social mobility than the ordinary white-collar jobs in the private and public sectors. But, the various churches in Guyana were not without blemishes on the race issue. By far the most liberal was the London Missionary Society which shortly after emancipation took steps to encourage Creoles to assume leadership positions,[110] a process which led to the emergence of native pastors. This is not surprising given the positive political and moral support which they lent to the emancipated people during and after the 1840s. What is surprising is the fact that within that body the Creole pastors had, in Rodney's words to 'fight for respect' in order to have a voice in the running of the local church. The Wesleyan Methodist Missionary Society was in all spheres, religious and secular, much more conservative and more closely controlled by the parent society than the L.M.S. They were consequently slower in nativizing the local church; and even then Creole pastors encountered discrimination especially with respect to prestigious appointments in urban churches, which seemed to bear the same hallmarks of racism as the Civil Service.[111]

So far as the Anglican church was concerned, the race question raised its head in an indirect way soon after emancipation in respect to the training of coloured priests at Codrington College in Barbados. Because the coloureds were then generally the "illegitimate" or "bastard" progeny of "illicit" sexual unions between white men and black/brown women during slavery, they were disqualified from training for the priesthood.[112] Although the problem was one of Euro-Christian morality, it was perceived by a hypersensitive Creole population as a racial one. In this case the myth became reality. Even after Creoles began to enter the Anglican priesthood, they encountered racial discrimination, and had to settle for junior positions in rural parishes.[113]

It was the prevalence of racial discrimination in every walk of colonial life which pushed Creoles into the independent professions of law and medicine. In 1842, there were no coloured lawyers and only four coloured doctors in the colony.¹¹⁴ Fifty years later the American consul observed that most of the lawyers and doctors in the colony were coloured men 'and certainly they will compare favourably with many, and excel some of their brethren of the white race'.¹¹⁵ McDavid similarly stated in 1900 that

> the learned professions have more than a fair share of men of local birth, and coloured parentage, and their "limitations" in these spheres, where talent and inherent worth are in request, do not manifest themselves anywhere ... We have creole clergymen, doctors, lawyers, mostly if not all, men of sound ability filling with credit their chosen professions.¹¹⁶

This avenue, however, was not open to the vast majority of Creoles because it involved specialized tertiary education overseas at considerable expense. Thus only the wealthier Creoles could afford such training abroad which helps to explain the predominance of coloureds in these professions.

The almost prohibitive costs of higher education to qualify for the independent professions, the closed nature of the senior Civil Service ranks, over-crowding in white-collar and skilled manual occupations, growing unemployment in unskilled estate jobs as a result of the inflow of immigrant workers, low wages, stagnation of the small-farming and peasant village sector, restricted occupational opportunities in the hinterland, and severely limited participation in the retail trade because of the Portuguese quasi-monopoly — all these factors combined to reduce the great majority of Creoles to a very depressed economic and social condition characterized by chronic poverty, high un- and under-employment, and increasing social and political disaffection. In short, in the 19th century, the majority of Creoles had not only been reduced to the status of second-class subjects, but were facing the prospect of being increasingly marginalized socially, politically and economically. Such conditions were conducive to crime. Bronkhurst opined:

> How the hundreds of young fellows employed in the minor stores in Water Street and other parts of the town contrive to subsist on the miserable pittances they receive, is one of the mysteries which only an occasional exposé in the Police Court serves to elucidate.¹¹⁷

As unemployment increased, so did crime. By the 1860s instances of burglary, street robbery, shoplifting, and crimes of violence had become prevalent.[118] Vagrant youths prowled the streets and loitered on the wharves earning their living by stealing. They became a nuisance and menace to the merchants and businessmen whose backstores were natural targets for these predators. Juvenile delinquents congregated in gangs on the streets betting on illegal dog races, and not infrequently engaging in street brawls; and the use of ribald and indecent language became commonplace among Creole males and females alike.[119] The criminal statistics show that convictions for "offences against the person" numbered 4,407 by 1871, peaked at 7,215 in 1877, but declined thereafter to just 1,623 by 1891; while those for "offences against property" stood at 2,524 in 1871, peaked in 1876 at 4,390, and declined to 2,264 in 1891.[120] Of course these figures are applicable to the whole population and not just to the Creoles; indeed it is quite likely that the significant increase in crime during the 1870s was related to the spate of industrial unrest among the Indian immigrants on the plantations which subsided late in that decade (see chapter 8).

Crime was not confined to the urban centres. Theft of provisions, plantains, and livestock from peasant farmers in the villages as well as from estates increased considerably. Although the Chinese immigrants were notorious for their nocturnal foragings, such praedial larceny was quite common among the Creoles as well.[121] Convictions for this offence numbered 101 in 1871, peaked at 1,879 in 1875 and exceeded 1000 between 1878 and 1880 and again in 1885. In 1891, the figure stood at 844.[122] The vagrancy law, stringent as it was,[123] had little effect on this spate of lawlessness. The press urged a greater use of the "cat-o-nine tails" against hardened criminals and called for the erection of a reformatory for juvenile offenders. Yet it was doubtful whether corporal punishment had any remedial effect on the incidence of crime.[124] In 1868, however, a law was passed for the establishment of industrial and reformatory schools for juvenile delinquents,[125] the first of which was finally completed nine years later at Onderneeming in Essequibo.[126]

For most of the half century after slavery, the Creoles were ascribed a status of second-class subjects in the land of their birth. While the act of emancipation accorded legal equality to the ex-slaves at least in theory, it could not remove the prejudices of race and colour long endemic in the society. The freed people encountered racism at every turn despite the bland assertions of most whites that racial and colour prejudice had evaporated after emancipation or was confined to the Creoles.[127]

A contemporary observer, M.F. Milliroux, simplistically argued that the abolition of slavery destroyed two main causes of colour prejudice. Firstly, the former master could not despise the ex-slave when he theoretically might attain a social rank as high as the master's; nor did the latter have any more reason to fear the ex-slave since he had no motive for resorting to violence to improve his lot. Secondly, even if the ex-master were still inclined to hate the freedman, the latter had no occasion to bother about this powerless hatred.[128]

Milliroux was obviously wrong on both counts. It was the apprehension of legal equality being translated into social, economic and political equality after emancipation which crystallized the racial prejudices of the dominant whites; and that race hatred, once aroused, was by no means powerless. Racist attitudes of whites towards Creoles were based on pre-slavery notions of inherent black inferiority, and reinforced during the later 19th century by the spread of popular pseudo-scientific race theories (e.g. social Darwinism) from Britain. This became more pronounced as steam-powered ships brought colony and metropolis into closer and more frequent contact, and as most white administrators and management staff in the private sector came to the colonies with preconceived racist notions about non-white people. As already pointed out, these ideas were vividly expressed in the historical works of James Rodway.

However, such rabid racism was not confined to the history books, but permeated even the corridors of "justice". For instance in 1885 Acting Sheriff and Stipendiary Magistrate Hewick of Essequibo, in delivering sentence on a black worker convicted of loitering on Plantation La Belle Alliance after refusing work at the rate offered, engaged in a tirade of racial abuse against the Creole people. According to him, blacks would neither work nor starve; instead

> they stole someone's plantains and lay in the sun everyday after eating them. The heads of the blacks were so thick, it was no use telling them anything, and it was useless doing

them a good turn; the only way to make the black man work was by use of the lash ... If the black man wished to be their own lords and masters, let them go to Hayti ... They seemed to think that white people only lived to put food in their (the blacks') mouths. He had no hestitation in saying that as a race, the blacks were the laziest on the face of the earth, and were there no white men they would soon starve; and they did not appreciate acts of kindness shown to them, and were most ungrateful ... [129]

(It is astonishing to note the attitude of this magistrate half a century after the abolition!)

Such racial stereotypes of the Creoles were very prevalent during the post-emancipation period. "Quashie" was the typical black who displayed certain personality characteristics considered peculiar to his race. He was thought to be lazy, lacking determination, drive, independence and self-reliance. Like an over-grown, querulous, excitable child, he was supposed to be fond of change and easily distracted by trifles and amusements. Although vain and deficient in pride, he was nonetheless civil and polite, hospitable, faithful and humorous, and fond of music and dance, according to this extremely pejorative stereotype.[130]

The pervasiveness of such stereotypes and racist ideas reflected itself in the various forms of discrimination already observed in the public and private sectors of the colony. They also, quite naturally, had a profound impact on social relations between white and black. Although it appears that shortly after emancipation a few white men married their coloured "concubines" with whom they had cohabited for years,[131] that did not signify for the Creoles access to, and acceptance in, white social circles. At the same time that many whites were professing the disappearance of racial prejudice, Richard Schomburgk, a very keen observer, noted that the Creoles were barred from every entrance into the "pure-blood" white aristocracy. According to him,

> Life in all its bitterness spurns them with frigid callousness, contempt dodges their every step, and scorn is meted out to those who strive to force their way through these cold and inhuman barriers ... If in isolated cases the European disregards these prejudices and still marries a coloured woman upon whose reputation even the most stinging envy can find no stain, the blot of birth indelibly remains: all the aristocratic

circles are open to the husband, but to the wife they are impenetrably closed.[132]

In fact, it appears that as travel between Britain and the colony became more frequent and rapid in the second half of the century, more white men were inclined to go home to get married, and return to the colony with their wives. This increased presence of white women led to the creation of a more exclusive and self-contained white social "enclave", and the old "tradition" of forming "establishments" with Creole women was increasingly regarded with disfavour until it more or less disappeared. Social distance between white and black thus increased, and, as Kirke noted, there was a growing 'objection to the negro taint, the "touch of the tar brush" as it is locally called ...'[133] This tendency has also been observed in Jamaica by Philip Curtin.[134]

Despite the persistence of such deep-seated racist attitudes, a minority of individual Creoles did manage to achieve a significant measure of social and economic mobility by the 1880s. According to Bronkhurst,

> There is no denying the fact ... that during the last fifty years ... the black and coloured Creoles of the Colony have struggled hard (and they still have to struggle hard, and perhaps harder), through honour and dishonour, through evil report and good report, through caste prejudice and non-caste prejudice, to maintain their ground and raise themselves to their present position.[135]

That very significant social progress had been made by the Creoles was noted by almost all contemporary commentators. Indeed the evidence was there for all to see: parsons, lawyers, doctors, teachers, schoolmasters, etc. — in fact, most of the 1,419 persons in this category of professionals in 1891 were Creoles, and these included 509 females. In addition, there was a "middle" middle-class of clerks, bookkeepers and shop assistants numbering 2,505 in 1891, and a "lower" middle-class of skilled mechanics and artisans amounting to 13,693 individuals, including 3,749 females many of whom were probably seamstresses.[136] Most of the people in these occupational categories were Creoles.

In addition, coloureds had entered the town councils ever since the 1840s and had become mayors.[137] Even though the very high landed and income qualifications were aimed at excluding the Creoles from the state institutions, we have seen that a few were still able to enter the two colleges during the 1880s, though entry into the legislature remained closed until after the 1891 reforms.

This does not necessarily signify a decline in white race prejudice as Bronkhurst claimed:[138] the Hewicks and Rodways of the day attested to its retention in virulent form among some whites. The social mobility of the educated and acculturated coloured elite was in no way dependent on white acceptance. The weight of historical evidence indicates that they effectively and successfully challenged and broke through the socio-racial barriers by their own individual efforts. Many of them, however, felt the need or desirability to inculcate white cultural values, beliefs and mores in the process in order to prove that, despite differences in pigmentation, they were the social equals of the whites. It was a quest for social equality at the price of cultural self-denial. Some of these educated coloureds imbibed so much of the "superior" airs and graces of their white peers as to attract the label of "conceited and affected". Acculturation for these in some cases went so far as to regard Britain as "home" and to talk about their family traditions, sports crests, coats-of-arms, etc.[139]

It is evident that the racial boundaries between white and black in post-emancipation Guyana never resembled the "apartheid-like" system of segregation in the southern United States under "Jim Crow". The existence of very strong racial prejudices among, and discrimination by, the dominant whites did not entail legal segregation; nor did it preclude social mobility by the Creoles based on such universalistic-achievement criteria as education, accumulated wealth, and acculturation to the norms of the dominant culture. Lastly, it did not preclude inter-racial sexual and marital relations although such instances, few to begin with, apparently diminished to insignificance in the early decades of the second half of the century.[140]

This situation changed somewhat in the 1880s and 1890s when instances of inter-racial marriage, mainly between white men and coloured/quadroon women, became more noticeable. What is significant is that these women, unlike their predecessors in the 1840s, were apparently not excluded from some white circles, but seem to have been accorded the prestige and status that went along with having a white husband in colonial society.[141] Although the actual number may well have been small, this trend is nevertheless notably different from the Trinidadian situation described by Brereton.[142] The reason for this may perhaps be related to the greater political prominence of the Guyanese coloureds as a class at this time in collaboration with the white middle-class, which made the former (or rather the women) appear more desirable and acceptable as marriage partners. The documentary silence about marriages between Creole men and white women suggests that when they did occur they were, as in Trinidad, cases of educated Creoles returning with women whom they had married abroad perhaps while studying.[143] The difference in attitude towards the sexes could be explained by the greater sensitivity which has always been associated with the need to "protect" white women from the stereotyped sexual libido of black and coloured men.

The fact that only a small minority of Creoles actually achieved any notable degree of social advancement, while the majority remained socially and politically disadvantaged, raises the theoretical issue of the importance of individual mobility in effecting structural change in a composite society. Indeed this was an issue that did not pass unnoticed by the Creoles themselves. In 1889 the *Echo*, while applauding the advancement of individual Creoles, pointed to the lack of unity which pervaded that social section and warned that

> individual effort cannot do when the progress of a race is in consideration; they tend to lessen sympathy and encourage a state of selfishness; they form exceptions rather than the rule to the rise of the people. United efforts, therefore, are what are required in a rising race.[144]

While the *Echo* recognized the significance of the social change brought about by the social mobility of individual Creoles, this exhortation was clearly intended to encourage these elites to relate their own status and identity to those of the whole ethnic group.

Although the data presented here seems to give credence to the view of M.G. Smith that social identity is ascriptive and corporate in base and significance and is not determined by individual qualities, it does not support his discounting the importance of individual mobility as a determinant of social change. He argues that 'the maintenance and modification of intersectional boundaries and relations depend primarily on collective social action rather than on cultural assimilation'.[145] But while the *Echo* and its readers might have desired such collective action, the reality of individual mobility could not be denied.

The case of the Creoles in post-slavery Guyana seems to indicate that individuation was a significant determinant of social change, though by no means monumental in its proportions. It is true that for a considerable time after emancipation social identity was indeed ascriptive and corporate in base. But this had been premised on race and colour, and to a lesser extent on culture, as determinants of sectional differentiation and status. The breaking down of the racial barrier by individual Creoles and their assimilation of white culture, therefore, resulted in the integration of the white and Creole sections around a common system of values based on the superiority of white culture — a condition which was to a large extent promoted by the spread of English education, morals, values, and religion (as will be described in chapter 9). Since such social and cultural mobility is considered one of the mechanisms for the reduction of both social and cultural pluralism,[146] the case of the Creoles signifies that Guyanese society underwent significant structural modification during the half century after slavery.

In sum, there was social change from a structure in which the Creoles, as an ethnically distinct section, were differentially incorporated to one in which they were integrated with the white section by a system of shared values (which ironically emphasized the inferiority of their African cultural tradition and heritage). At the same time, the majority of Creoles occupied an inferior class status. This social change, as we have seen, was complemented in the political sphere by parallel changes both at the colonial state and local levels.

It is important not to overstate the extent of these changes in the colonial society and polity. In the first place, the changes had *practical* significance only for the Creole elites; and in the second place, they occurred against a background of continued economic dependence on the plantation system. The vast majority of Creoles thus remained politically disfranchised, socially disadvantaged, and economically dependent and impoverished. Their status as second-class subjects thus remained basically unaltered, although the principal criterion for determining this status underwent a change in emphasis from race and ethnic differences to class distinctions.

THE INCORPORATION OF IMMIGRANTS

CHAPTER 7

SECONDARY COLONISTS: THE RISE OF THE PORTUGUESE IMMIGRANTS

One notable feature of many composite colonial societies is the presence of an ethnically distinct category which forms a social buffer between the dominant colonialist section and the native subordinate population. According to John Rex, this social category constitutes "secondary colonists", and they perform certain economic roles which are considered morally dubious. Consequently, they form a pariah element in the societies of which they are a part, and in times of trouble and difficulty might serve as a scapegoat both to the ruling colonialist element and to the local working population.[1]

In South-east Asia, and to a lesser extent in Jamaica and Trinidad as well, the Chinese assumed this role of secondary colonists; whereas in East Africa, Indians and in West Africa, Levantines did likewise. In post-slavery Guyana, however, it was the Portuguese immigrants who acceded to this title. Although they never totalled more than 6.4 percent of the whole population, their increase from 2,619 persons in 1841 to 12,166 in 1891[2] was a significant numerical boost to the white population — a factor which M.G. Smith considers important for the structural stability of a plural society.[3]

Nonetheless, the Portuguese, although phenotypically white, constituted a separate ethnic category in colonial Guyanese society, differentiated from the dominant whites by class origin, nationality and culture. Indeed the latter regarded them in the same way as they did lower-class Irish peasants[4] on account of their humble socio-economic background and their general state of illiteracy, even in the Portuguese language.[5] They were even more sharply differentiated from the Creole section not only by culture, but also by race;

and soon differences of economic status arose as well. In theoretical terms, therefore, the Portuguese are a special case forming a clearly defined social class in relation to the dominant whites, but at the same time forming a distinct and separate racial and cultural section in relation to the Creoles. The theoretical issues which arise, therefore, are to determine firstly how socially mobile they were during the course of the 19th century, and secondly whether the racial and cultural boundaries which separated them as a group from the Creoles were transcended during that period.

From the outset Portuguese immigration was encouraged on essentially racial grounds. Successive governors not only admitted the importance of their numerical contribution to the white population and to the preservation of white interests in the colony, but also considered them a guarantee against the colony ever relapsing into barbarism through Creole ascendancy.[6] Hence despite high mortality among new arrivals owing to yellow fever, malaria, malnutrition, and over-exhaustion in the tropical heat, Portuguese immigration was vigorously promoted both by the Colonial government and the planters.[7].

The irony was that even though the Portuguese used every conceivable means of evading and escaping indenture and of avoiding paying a monthly tax in lieu of such contractual service to the plantations,[8] the planters nevertheless continued to support this immigration. This was vividly demonstrated when, in 1856, the government determined that the Portuguese should be indentured on the plantations for three years.[9] The consequent refusal of Portuguese to emigrate to the colony under those conditions was so disturbing that the planters not only decided to waive the indenture obligation altogether in relation to the Portuguese, but furthermore to provide $35,000 of public money to finance their re-introduction.[10] Although a two-year indenture was subsequently instituted in 1859, the Portuguese were permitted to commute their service after only six months.[11] The Portuguese were thus the only immigrant category which was practically free of any compulsory obligation to indentureship on the plantations.

The result of this partiality towards the Portuguese was that those who became indentured were able to withdraw from plantation employment within a very short period, while a great many never ever worked on the plantations at all. Already by 1850 not more than one-third of the Portuguese population was still employed on the plantations;[12] and, by 1862 there were just 477 Portuguese plantation workers.[13] The significance of this was that of all the subordinate groups in the society only the Portuguese were able to become "independent" of the plantation system in so far as that was possible in a plantation-dominated society. This enabled them to assume the socio-economic role of secondary colonists.

Several Portuguese returned to Madeira or went elsewhere after accumulating some wealth.[14] Some, however, remained in agriculture as small farmers, particularly in the Canals region of the Demerara river;[15] and after 1870 some settled in the Pomeroon district of Essequibo where they cultivated a variety of crops for subsistence and the local market, e.g., cocoa, Indian corn, plantains and ground provisions, on land leased from the Crown. The historical records, however, do not give any indication about the number of Portuguese who became small farmers. With a view to enhancing their political influence, some Portuguese during the 1870s contemplated forming an agricultural company to purchase plantations and to encourage wealthy individual Portuguese to become large landholders.[17] It is not clear if anything concrete materialized from this idea.

It was primarily in the retail trade as hucksters, peddlars, grocers, druggists, butchers and spirit dealers, however, that the Portuguese established the economic base which promoted their rise as secondary colonists. The emancipation of the slaves suddenly created a lucrative market for retailers[18] which the old rudimentary internal trade consisting of servants selling a few goods for their employers could not adequately satisfy.[19] The Portuguese immigrants thus seized this golden opportunity to fill the vacuum and rapidly took command of all aspects of the retail trade, outpacing their Creole rivals in the process.[20] Portuguese shops rapidly sprang up not only in Georgetown, but throughout the rural districts,[21] and the Portuguese huckster became ubiquitous. Their boats, fitted up as shops, plied up and down the rivers calling at every hamlet.[22]

By the end of the 1840s they had established an effective dominance over the retail trade, which was further entrenched in the ensuing decades. Some became wealthy merchants forming an intermediary link between the large import firms and the retail shops,[23] and some even rivalled the major white wholesale merchants.[24] As early as 1851, Portuguese held over 67 percent of the retail spirit licences in Demerara and Essequibo, almost 70 percent of store licences, over 45 percent of hucksters' licences, and 55 percent of hire cart licences.[25] In 1871, just before Chinese and Indians began to mount a serious challenge to their commercial dominance, the Portuguese held about 64 percent of all shop and store licences in the whole colony, about half the drug shop licences, about 61 percent of butcher shop licences, and about 43 percent of licences for hire carts and carriages.[26] They also formed the vast majority of licensed hucksters;[27] while in the lucrative retail spirit trade, they enjoyed a virtual monopoly.[28]

Thrift and frugality, sheer hard work and shrewd business acumen all contributed to the success and rapid domination of the retail trade by the Portuguese.[29] Their initial willingness to accept small profits enabled them to undersell their competitors,[30] while their zealous industry generated a quick turnover of stock which further endeared them to the major white importers whose own wealth was augmented in the process.[31] This success, coupled with prompt repayments in ready cash, encouraged these white merchants to advance credit on relatively easy terms to the Portuguese retailers, whereas they either refused credit to the Creoles or granted them only on very stringent and ruinous terms.[32] Thus the Portuguese were actually assisted in outcompeting their Creole rivals.

Another very important factor which promoted the rapid accession of the Portuguese immigrants to a dominant position in the retail trade was the licence system. The huckster and shop licences constituted a tax which, like the imposition of other licences and forms of taxation, was calculated to hinder the Creoles from establishing an economic base independent of the plantations.[33] Unlike the Portuguese immigrant whose sole ambition was to acquire sufficient money to buy a licence, stock a pack, and turn itinerant peddlar,[34] the Creole (perhaps with a family to support) seeking to accumulate enough funds to achieve his prime goal of purchasing a plot of land, was hardly in a financial position to outlay $10 or $20 in advance (about 6–12 weeks' wages) for a huckster or shop licence respectively,[35] and to buy stock without credit. This indicates sharp differences of circumstances and orientation between the Creoles and the Portuguese.

Successive governors recognized that the retail trade licences discriminated against the Creoles in favour of Portuguese dominance,[36] while simultaneously imposing an additional tax burden on the consumer to whom the cost of the licence was invariably passed in the price of the goods.[37] Consequently there was a tendency to lower or remove these licences in time of tension between the discontented Creoles and the Portuguese retailers, as for example, between 1856–59 and in 1862.[38] The Portuguese themselves were fully conscious of the discriminatory effects of the licences in their favour. Thus, for instance, when the planters refused to raise taxes during the political crisis of 1848–49, the Portuguese actually petitioned the Combined Court for the reimposition of the licences.[39] The fact that the same policy of discriminatory taxation/licences which buttressed the socio-economic supremacy of the plantocracy was employed to promote the rise of the Portuguese economically through their domination of the retail trade, serves to emphasize the importance attached to their performing the socio-economic function of secondary colonists.

There is evidence that the Portuguese immigrants in other British Caribbean colonies also gravitated to the retail trade with similar success[40] though their general impact might have been less pronounced than in Guyana because of their considerably smaller numbers. But it is important to stress that this success had nothing to do with the idea that they were inherently racially and/or culturally superior, and thus more industrious, than the Creoles as contemporary whites would have us believe. In Bermuda, for instance, where Portuguese also migrated in the late 19th century, no such dramatic success was achieved. The reason for this stark difference in their fortunes must lie in the differences of socio-economic environment.

Unlike Guyana, plantations never achieved any importance in Bermuda; instead when agriculture was developed during the 19th century, it took the form of settler farming. There was never, therefore, the large ex-slave population which could provide a viable internal market as in the

Caribbean colonies. Nevertheless, since this agricultural development was geared to producing vegetables and arrowroot for the American market, the white farmers increasingly felt the need for additional labour. This is where the Portuguese immigrants from Madeira and the Azores came into the picture, and a few thousand were imported in the late 19th and early 20th centuries. Although noted for the same qualities of thrift and hard work as their counterparts in Guyana, they remained employed in agriculture and never experienced the commercial success as those in Guyana and other Caribbean colonies.[41] What this demonstrates is that if the market opportunities were lacking and there was no encouragement and assistance from the dominant whites, the Portuguese could do no better than the Creoles in the Caribbean.

There was no intrinsic racial or cultural superiority which enabled the Portuguese to achieve success in Guyana. Apart from the artificial advantages which they enjoyed through the assistance of the dominant whites, their success was essentially due to their familiarity with the functioning of a competitive capitalist money economy into which the great mass of ex-slaves were for the first time fully immersed after emancipation. Laurence argues that the Portuguese were more familiar with figures and arithmetic, with the attitudes needed for independent success in business and with general business methods than were the ex-slaves.[42] This familiarity with the handling of money, borrowing loans, repaying with interest and so on has also been considered by Freedman to be a key factor in accounting for the success of overseas Chinese performing similar roles as did the Portuguese in Guyana.[43]

There was nothing, therefore, unique about the Portuguese in this context. They constituted a socio-economic type whose growth is typical in composite colonial societies worldwide, and whose very presence and success are partially dependent on the favours of the dominant colonial section in return for the role which they play of keeping the native population dependent on wage labour whether on plantations, mines or in other European-owned enterprises — hence the application of the term "secondary colonists" to them.

John Rex notes that the economic roles which such social categories perform can be construed as morally dubious.[44] It is not that the specific fields of economic activity in which they engage are intrinsically shady or underworldly; it is rather the manner in which they conduct business which gives rise to doubts about the moral and even legal basis of their operations. As Brereton has noted these immigrant minorities are able with the encouragement and often the support of the colonizer to carve out and exploit a special niche in the colonial economy, usually in commerce; and since they operate outside the value system of the wider society, they can ignore pressures to conform to an "acceptable" way of life[45] and economic behaviour. Thus in Guyana, once the Portuguese had established effective dominance over the retail trade, some of them exercised that power ruthlessly and with scant regard for the consumer.[46] They reportedly established a syndicate or cartel which fixed prices and uniform quantities of goods to be sold,[47] and in 1867 even threatened to deal collectively with any wholesale merchant who refused them three months' credit instead of six weeks'.[48] They also successfully exploited the chronic shortage of small coinage[49] by refusing to sell anything in quantities smaller than half a bitt (four cents).[50] Generally they used the bitt (eight cents) to measure the value of articles e.g. one pint of rice or one pound of flour, salt fish or biscuits, etc.;[51] and as a rule refused to give change for it, citing the shortage of small coins.[52] Similarly, they valued a dollar at twelve bitts (96 cents), which meant that for each transaction under a dollar the purchaser lost the additional four cents.[53] The price-fixing system was clearly designed to ensure that profit margins were substantial. Thus in 1862 the profit on one pint of rice priced at one bitt was 205 percent after tax, on salt-fish and flour 60 percent, and on pork 52.4 percent.[54]

This strong profit-making drive among the Portuguese retailers encouraged many to engage in a variety of openly illegal and fraudulent activities. The least unethical was their general disregard of the law prohibiting Sunday trading.[55] It was the prevalence of blatantly dishonest trading, however, which aroused widespread suspicion and hostility towards the Portuguese immigrants as a group. There was reputedly hardly a district where the consumers got full measure and weight for their money. Some traders used lead in the scale to cheat their customers;[56] others used false weights, and in some cases the two-ounce weight was found to be as light as half an ounce.[57] Retailers also used false-bottom cup measures for selling rice, flour and so on. In one instance, this enabled the rogue to cheat customers of about one-fifth on every transaction.[58] Convictions and fines of between $10–20 were hardly sufficiently stringent to curb such widespread fraud.[59]

Portuguese shopkeepers also made money by providing rudimentary banking and pawnbroking services. In the absence of a general banking system, indentured immigrants on the plantations often deposited their savings with Portuguese shopkeepers; but it was not rare for some of the latter to decamp with these deposits, and in one notable case, the scamp absconded from the colony with nearly $5,000 in immigrant deposits.[60] Likewise both immigrants and Creoles generally took their small valuables to Portuguese shops as pawns or collateral for loans of about half their intrinsic value. If the loan were not repaid within a given period, the pawn was forfeited. The percentage of pawns confiscated provided by itself a large profit for the moneylenders which was further augmented as the entire loan was generally spent on the same shopkeeper's overpriced goods.[61] The gross corruption perpetuated by this practice eventually forced the government to introduce legislation in 1884 designed to regulate the system of pawnbroking;[62] (although there was no move towards "nationalization" of these pawnshops as the Dutch would later do in Indonesia with respect to simialr Chinese pawnbroking enterprises.)[63]

Lucrative though the retail trade was, it was also highly speculative and risky,[64] and thus always susceptible to business failures. Bankruptcies were not infrequent even for the wealthiest of entrepreneurs, and were most prevalent during periods when the plantation economy faced recession.[65] This demonstrates that, although relatively "independent" of the plantations, the retail trade nonetheless formed an integral part of a colonial economy whose fortunes were determined by those of the plantation system. This is important as it demonstrates that the economy was one of the elements which integrated the differentiated socio-economic groups in the colonial society.

Some Portuguese traders, however, found ingenious means to convert business failure into financial gain. In some cases, they allegedly set aside small sums daily over the course of a few years before declaring themselves insolvent. Since they were generally illiterate and kept no accounts, it was virtually impossible to detect their fraud. This money was reputedly either remitted to Madeira or, after a lapse of sufficient time, reinvested in new business on a larger scale.[66] Others, on finding themselves in difficulty, quietly transferred their licences, premises and stock-in-trade to other parties. Wholesalers, unaware of the change, would continue to supply goods to the original licencee only to find when the crash came that the shop was owned by someone else. This type of fraud became so prevalent that in 1885 the licence laws had to be amended to compel persons parting with their business licences and stock to give public notice so that wholesalers could be forewarned.[67] Some Portuguese dealers even resorted to arson to recover their business losses from the insurance companies. This was particularly evident during the economic recession of the mid-sixties, and several Portuguese were actually arrested and charged with this offence.[68]

By far the most lucrative branch of the retail trade was the sale of spirits, on which the very high licence fees[69] enabled the Portuguese to establish a virtual monopoly. However, unlike the other retail licences, the spirit licensing system was designed not merely to restrict participation to a certain category of people, but also as a major source of public revenue.[70] These objectives affected the Portuguese traders in two ways. Firstly, the number of dealers who were allowed to engage in this trade was strictly controlled by the licensing authorities; and, secondly, these licences bore on the dealers as a heavy tax burden.

Not surprisingly, the Portuguese were vehement in their protests against the system, but to no avail.[71] In this case the licence was a double-edged sword. On one hand, it served to promote the Portuguese monopoly of the retail spirit trade; but on the other hand, it was used by the white ruling authorities to restrain the independent growth of Portuguese economic power and wealth, and to underline their subordinate status.

Notwithstanding the high licence fees, the spirit trade was nevertheless a highly lucrative venture in which a position was highly prized by the Portuguese dealers, and avidly sought by those traders not in it.[72] To offset the high cost of the licences, however, many dealers resorted to illegal activities such as smuggling from Surinam, stealing from plantation stores or from puncheons when in bond or being exported; and they also engaged in various forms of illegal trading.[73] They also capitalized on loopholes in the licence regulations which enabled them to evade the duties and quotas on rum sales.[74] In short, the Portuguese spirit dealers did whatever was necessary, regardless of legal or moral considerations, to maximize profits.

Levy[75] and Johnson[76] note that the similarly positioned Chinese traders in Jamaica provided a valuable service not only as retailers of goods in small quantities to meet the needs and pockets of their working class consumers, but also as suppliers of credit; hence they had a symbiotic rather than competitive relationship with the Creoles. In many respects, this observation is equally applicable to the Portuguese in Guyana. But it needs to be set in proper perspective. There was unquestionably fierce competition during the 1840s before the Portuguese established their dominance over the retail trade — a competition which Laurence partially attributes to the development of racial antagonism between the Portuguese and Creoles.[77] The fact, however, that the Portuguese were able to bring goods literally to the doorsteps of consumers and sell them in small quantities at low prices, and even offer credit in the bargain, went a far way to helping them achieve dominance in that sphere. These were undoubtedly very valuable services. But it was that dominance which once achieved, soured the symbiosis of which Johnson speaks as it enabled many Portuguese traders to exploit their customers (who in fact had no alternative but to buy and borrow from them) in a ruthless and immoral manner. Whatever valuable service was provided by the Portuguese traders was, therefore, offset by the rapacity and exploitativeness of their business dealings.

Some Portuguese sought to engage in forestry (woodcutting) and charcoal manufacture in the hinterland. But the Crown lands regulations and licences, designed to prevent Creole settlement inland, were so generally restrictive that they served to restrict the number of Portuguese who could operate in the interior. At the same time such laws clearly favoured the wealthy white commercial interests who consequently dominated the timber trade.[78] As a result, Portuguese participation in this sphere accounted for only about one-third of the licences granted.[79] Here again licences were used to keep the Portuguese economically subordinate to the dominant whites.

Despite these areas of grievance, the Portuguese business community amassed a considerable amount of wealth,[80] much of which was repatriated to Madeira. But they also invested in real estate throughout the colony, and by 1881 in Georgetown they alone owned 22.4 percent of the freehold property valued at almost $1.5 million.[81] One, however, needs to avoid creating the impression that *all* Portuguese immigrants prospered in Guyana. The historical evidence, incomplete as it is, shows that the failures and disappointments were many, particularly in commerce. Furthermore, many shopkeepers and hucksters were no more than lowly-paid employees of the wealthier Portuguese merchants. The complaints of Portuguese grantholders also suggest that many of them experienced great difficulty in making ends meet in their ventures, while several of the workers on those grants were lowly-paid Portuguese. It is doubtful whether those Portuguese who bought or leased small plots of land and became small farmers were any more successful than their Creole counterparts.

Thus there was evidently a fairly substantial "under-class" of not-so-well-off Portuguese who did not share in the prosperity of their more fortunate countrymen. Indeed the establishment of the Portuguese Benevolent Society (P.B.S.) and the Society of St. Vincent de Paul to provide relief to poor Portuguese is evidence of their plight. Between its inception in 1872 and its demise in 1886 the P.B.S., for instance, disbursed $137,352 in relief to poor and old Portuguese.[82]

The Portuguese as an ethnic category, however, remained a group apart: as one writer put it, 'like oil in water: among us, but not of us'.[83] They were differentiated by language, religion and culture from the host society. Although by 1891, 58 percent of the Portuguese were local-born, the vast majority also retained Portuguese citizenship.[84] Of course, they enjoyed certain advantages from this alien status such as exemption from military and fire service under the terms of an 1842 Anglo-Portuguese treaty,[85] while they could still own and devise property in the colony, own and operate British ships, and serve on juries;[86] and the local-born could vote when qualified.[87] The foreign-born, however, were disfranchised unless naturalized as British subjects; but on the other hand, as Portuguese subjects, they could call on the Portuguese government to represent their interests through the diplomatic channel. Moreover until 1882 when public-financed immigration from Madeira was discontinued, Portuguese immigrants also enjoyed the privilege of having their passages paid by the local taxpayer without the obligation to serve long-term indentures as were other categories of (non-white) immigrants.[88]

Many of them, therefore, enjoyed the best of two worlds — privilege, wealth and status in the colony without full commitment, plus whatever benefits accrued from the retention of their Portuguese nationality. But it was precisely these advantages which attracted both the envy and animosity of the less privileged social categories. Rex notes that in time of difficulty secondary colonists serve as scapegoats both to the dominant group and to the subordinate population.[89] The Portuguese in Guyana fitted this bill perfectly. On one hand, the employment of indirect taxation by the ruling white minority as the prime instrument of subjugating the Creole majority succeeded in directing the latter's discontent and hostility away from them towards the Portuguese as a group. The latter thus served as a protective buffer for the dominant whites. On the other hand, subjected daily to the avarice and fraud of many Portuguese retailers, the Creoles regarded them as agents of oppression and collaborators of the white power structure, whose wealth and privileged position were created through their own exploitation and impoverishment, and against whose very presence they felt the need to take action if they were to experience any material improvement in their economic and social condition.[90]

Thus the Portuguese found themselves the objects of physical attack or the threat of such attack at a communal level on five occasions in just over 50 years since their arrival in Guyana: 1848, 1856, 1862, 1889, and 1891. On each occasion high retail prices caused both by high indirect taxation and gross profiteering by many Portuguese traders, as well as general economic recession, figured prominently in generating hostility towards the Portuguese. As noted earlier, between 1847 and 1850 the colonial economy sank into a deep depression as the price of sugar slumped on the British market, and credit and investment capital dried up. The planters' determination to reduce wages was successful despite a two month work stoppage by Creole labour which left many of the latter virtually penniless. Yet the prices of essential commodities were maintained at a high level as a result of the imposition of a four percent *ad valorem* duty on imported goods in 1847 as well as the profit motive of the Portuguese traders. This combination of economic circumstances contributed to the outbreak of anti-Portuguese riots in March 1848 on the east bank of the Berbice river.[91]

High prices similarly contributed to the disturbances of 1856. In chapter six it was shown that between 1853 and 1855 enormous tax increases were reimposed on the necessities of life and ushered in a period of fiscal oppression and an inflationary cost of living precisely when the peasant economy was rapidly disintegrating and the influx of indentured immigrants were beginning to force down wages. It is by no means inconceivable that the alleged instigator of the 1856 riots, John Sayers Orr, might have been permitted by the colonial authorities to conduct his public agitation against the Portuguese traders unimpeded for two full months[92] in order to divert Creole attention from the key source of their distress i.e. high taxation. Certainly the Portuguese were made to bear the full blame for the high prices, and in retaliation the Creoles tried to set up cooperative shops to break the Portuguese dominance of the retail trade and to lower prices through competition. In defence of his own narrow-minded policies and actions, Governor Wodehouse alleged that these plans were subverted by Orr into a scheme for the general destruction of Portuguese property and the establishment of Creole shops on their ruins.[93] Not surprisingly, he could not provide evidence to substantiate this allegation.

The riots, of course, solved nothing. Prices remained very high both on account of high taxation and the excessive profiteering of the Portuguese traders. When in 1862 this was combined with a general economic recession occasioned by low sugar prices, resulting, in turn, in reduced plantation wages and increased unemployment, the economic plight of the Creoles became virtually insufferable.[94] As before (and not without good reason), the Portuguese were held accountable and the Creoles petitioned for their repatriation to Madeira,[95] and threatened to attack their shops again.[96] The government was thus obliged to remove the hucksters' and rural shop licences temporarily in order to appear to encourage Creole competition in the retail trade presumably with a view to reducing prices.[97]

Similarly in March 1889 when the colonial economy was still suffering from the effects of one of the worst depressions since emancipation, riots broke out in Georgetown. Once again artificially high prices had been charged by many Portuguese retailers in the midst of widespread unemployment and depressed wages. It was in these circumstances that a Creole youth, either deliberately or in error, took a penny loaf of bread instead of a cent loaf for which he had paid, and was severely punished with a brutal mauling by the Portuguese vendor. The beating left him unconscious and led to the outbreak of rioting by the Creoles.[98] Similar disagreements between Portuguese traders and Creole youths almost led to fresh outbreaks of communal violence in 1891.[99]

These economic considerations were superimposed on more deep-seated racial prejudices which had existed from the first encounters between these two groups and perdured for the rest of the century. The Creoles despised the Portuguese as pariahs — "white niggers", "nasty, good-for-nothing buckra"[100] — largely on account of the allegedly unhygienic habits of the early Portuguese immigrants and the menial estate and higglering jobs which they at first performed. On the other hand, 19th century Portuguese emigrants, however illiterate, were no less impregnated with preconceived notions of white racial and cultural superiority over blacks than other Europeans, as the behaviour of settlers in Portuguese Africa and Brazil bears testimony.[101] These mutually strong racial prejudices provided the basis of the almost permanent antagonism which characterized relations between these two groups. Moreover, the undisguised partiality of the dominant whites towards the Portuguese further fuelled Creole hostility to the latter.[102]

The economic conditions thus provided the necessary climate in which the more deeply rooted racial prejudices and passions could grow to a feverish pitch, ultimately resulting in physical violence. This was vividly demonstrated in 1856. John Sayers Orr (alias 'the Angel Gabriel'), a known anti-Catholic fanatic and agitator, commenced his crusade against the Portuguese in December, 1855. He skilfully blended his anti-papism with an assault on Portuguese economic activity and called for their repatriation.[103] His argument touched the pulse of the Creole section by its simple solution and triggered their most primal racist feelings and hatred of the Portuguese. In strict economic terms, Orr seemed to make sense, although he failed to identify the real source of the Creoles' distress i.e. the white colonial dominance. Not surprisingly the authorities permitted him to continue his anti-Portuguese campaign until February 15 when he was arrested for inciting a crowd five days earlier by displaying a life preserver and dagger.[104]

His arrest and indictment served as the immediate pretexts for the disturbances of 1856 as the Creoles considered them further evidence of official partiality towards the Portuguese on account of their racial affinity. That it should have taken as long as five days after the alleged offence to order Orr's arrest, particularly after a personal appeal to the governor by the Catholic bishop, smelled of collusion between the colonial authorities and the Catholic-Portuguese interests to remove the threat posed by Orr's effective leadership and mobilization of the Creoles. The latter also considered a proclamation issued by the governor forbidding public meetings as a serious infringement of their right of assembly. Moreover the fact that during the indictment the prosecutor completely ignored a threat to Orr's life by a group of Catholic-Portuguese agitators led by John Taggart, which in fact had caused Orr to carry the very weapons for which he was charged, incensed his supporters. The final straw came when the court refused to accept bail tendered by Orr's guarantor, a respectable propertied Creole, on legal technicalities.[105]

The remanding into custody of Orr appeared indicative of a racist conspiracy between the ruling whites and Portuguese against Creole interests.[106] Consequently the Creoles decided to defend those interests by attacking Portuguese *property* in the vain hope that this would force them to leave the colony permanently. The riots spread in all directions from Georgetown to engulf the east and west coasts of Demerara, the west coast of Berbice, the Essequibo coast and islands, and the banks of the Demerara and Essequibo rivers. Everywhere Portuguese shops were attacked and sacked; and altogether the Portuguese suffered losses assessed at $267,204, though with a view to profiting from the tragedy their claims were substantially higher.[107]

The racial factor was likewise the principal element in

fomenting the 1889 disturbances. Racial tension between these two groups began to mount to a feverish pitch following the cold-blooded murder of a coloured woman, Julia Chase, by her Portuguese lover, Manoel Gonsalves, in November 1888.[108] This case aroused keen interest throughout the colony since it revolved around the fundamental issue of race and, moreover, involved a white person as the defendant. It was commonly said that Portuguese could not be executed because they were white.[109] In fact, only two Portuguese had ever been convicted for murder in the colony; one was actually hanged in 1875, and the other had his sentence commuted the following year.[110] But none of these cases involved victims of a different race. In a different case involving the murder of a coloured man by a white Barbadian, however, the latter had been executed despite a recommendation for mercy by the jury; and in virtually the reverse situation to the Gonsalves case, a young coloured man had been hanged for killing his Portuguese wife.[111]

Gonsalves was duly tried and sentenced to death, but on the submission of a petition for mercy by the jury, the acting governor commuted his sentence.[112] This revived Creole animosity towards the Portuguese in all its original intensity. While Creoles and Indian immigrants were invariably executed for murder, it seemed that a different law operated for the benefit of the Portuguese, or that they could buy themselves out of justice.[113] This notion achieved further credibility by the circulation of a Lisbon newspaper containing the text of telegrams from the Portuguese king to the British queen, purporting to be an appeal on behalf of Gonsalves. Hence the Portuguese went about boasting that their king would not allow any of his subjects to be executed.[114]

The Creoles thus determined that since the Portuguese could apparently kill black people with impunity, they would adopt other means to protect themselves.[115] Then in March 1889 the brutal beating of the black boy by the Portuguese trader provided the spark to set Creole passions and anger ablaze. The news got around that the unconscious boy had in fact been killed; and that furthermore the market clerk had not only ordered the release of the Portuguese assailant, but also demanded that 'the damn nigger' should be thrown onto the street. The Creoles, inflamed with this story attacked Portuguese shops and properties in Georgetown and its environs,[116] causing damage to the assessed amount of $39,453 (though again their claims were considerably higher).[117]

Race relations between these two ethnic sections remained sour after the riots and even threatened to erupt in fresh violence in 1891 following the murder of an Indian immigrant by a Portuguese man named Antonio D'Agrella. The acting governor was again confronted with a delicate problem compounded by a petition for mercy by a number of Portuguese, as well as an appeal for commutation of the death sentence by the Portuguese government conveyed through the diplomatic channel. But it was evident that to reprieve D'Agrella would have provoked renewed race riots against the Portuguese, no doubt also involving the Indians. Hence he was duly executed in July 1891.[118]

Racial tension, however, remained high amidst rumours of planned attacks against the Portuguese, and ominous collisions between Portuguese traders and young Creoles.[119] After the experience of March 1889, some Portuguese adopted drastic means to defend themselves. One Portuguese man even began to manufacture bombs, consisting of about four ounces of powder in a bottle securely fastened and laced with tarred rope, for sale to his fellow shopkeepers.[120] As yet a further sign of the persistently poor race relations, a black man was murdered by a Portuguese in August 1891 which once again brought Creole passions to boiling point.[121]

Thus towards the end of the century, the Portuguese found that in spite of their enormous success, wealth and economic independence (as far as this was possible in a plantation-dominated economy), they were nevertheless treated as social pariahs which rendered them extremely insecure and vulnerable. There is no doubt that they were treated as scapegoats both by the ruling white minority and by the Creole majority. On one hand, they were subtly manipulated by the dominant whites who promoted their rise to a position of secondary colonists. In this role they served as agents of oppression of the Creole majority, and simultaneously formed a social buffer between the dominant white and the subordinate Creole sections. On the other hand, the Creoles regarded them as the main cause of their economic deprivation, and consequently singled them out as the prime targets of attack in order to alleviate their chronic distress.

It was the factor of race, however, which for all practical purposes determined the fate of the Portuguese in Guyanese society. Their initial introduction was heavily influenced by the consideration of their potential contribution to the numerical strength of the white population. Then when the issue of compulsory indenture threatened to put a complete stop to their immigration, the preservation of white racial interests took precedence even above the economic demand for labour by the plantations, and the Portuguese were exempted from such obligations in order enhance the colony's attractiveness. Racial considerations likewise motivated the dominant whites to encourage the rapid accession of the Portuguese to a position of dominance in the lucrative retail trade by means of easy credit and a discriminatory licensing system. This facilitated their attainment of the necessary economic base to support their role and status of secondary colonists 'betwixt the earthy grovelling of the more uncultured races and the heavenly exaltation of the other Europeans';[122] and at the same time generated enormous hatred towards them among the Creoles in particular.

The high level of racial tension and antagonism, and sharp cultural and economic differentiation contributed to the persistently poor race relations between the Portuguese and the Creoles. Even language interceded to hinder the growth of amicable interpersonal relations, as the anecdote about the efforts of a Portuguese lad to woo a Creole maiden illustrates. Standing below her window, in mellifluous tones he serenaded her with the only English words he knew — 'son of a beech, son of a beech' — only to be astounded by the violent response of the outraged damsel.[123] There evidently were a few instances of cohabitation and even marriage between Portuguese and Creole individuals; but, as we have seen, at least two of these ended tragically.

Inter-racial unions between members of these two ethnic sections were evidently limited for two very good reasons. Firstly, the high degree of racial animosity between the rank and file of both communities was an effective inhibition. The few who sought to defy familial and communal proscriptions were on occasion forced to elope secretly.[124] Secondly, there was the self-contained and apparently self-perpetuating character of the Portuguese community. Laurence notes that from the early 1840s Portuguese immigration into Guyana was characterized by a high proportion of women and children which in fact made it 'unique in [the] annals of nineteenth century West Indian immigration'. This is suggestive of whole families migrating 'which produced a settled community surprisingly quickly'.[125] The ratio of females to males was always high, and improved from 1:1.5 in 1851 to 1:1 by 1891.[126] Portuguese men, therefore, did not not need to seek sexual or marital partners outside of their ethnic group, though that did not prevent a few from doing so. For the most part, however, relations between the two groups were confined to the "market-place" i.e. the Portuguese shop. Thus in Furnivall's words, they mixed but did not combine.

The sole exception to this portrait is perhaps in the political sphere where, as seen in chapter 3, some of the leading Portuguese businessmen had supported the biracial middle-class demands for political reform ever since the 1840s. This was indicative of a recognition by the Portuguese and Creole elites that as a "class" (Weberian-Marxist sense) they shared similar political interests and were disadvantaged by common political disabilities. On the other hand, given the sharp racial and cultural differences between the two groups (especially among the rank and file), it appears that they stood in a structural relationship with each other signifying the condition that M.G. Smith labels "segmental pluralism". This indicates a growing complexity in the structure of the total society.

Still other perspectives emerge when the relationship between the Portuguese and the dominant whites is examined. Although they were not subordinated in the same manner as the Creoles and Asian immigrants, the Portuguese were on arrival nevertheless sufficiently differentiated from the British whites socially and culturally to have to deal with the issues of integration and assimilation. But in spite of the great socio-economic mobility achieved by the wealthier Portuguese, they remained culturally distinct from the British, retaining a strong preference for in-group socio-cultural activity and "associations".

This tendency was made possible by a number of factors. Firstly, the balance between the sexes favoured endogamy. Secondly, their common adherence to Roman Catholicism helped to promote group cohesion and ethnic unity, and thus to perpetuate their differentiation from the British whites.

Roman Catholicism, much to the dismay of the English Catholics in the colony, virtually became a Portuguese ethnic religion. By 1858, 5,000 out of the estimated 6,000 Catholics in Georgetown, most of the 800 Catholics in New Amsterdam, and indeed most of those in the rural areas, were Portuguese.[127]

During the 1850s Italian Jesuits had to be specially recruited, in the absence of available Portuguese clergy, to conduct services in the Portuguese language. The most notable of these was Benedict Schembri whose fierce pro-Portuguese stance in the church brought the underlying cleavages between the English and Portuguese Catholics into the open and ultimately resulted in the erection of the first separate Portuguese church in Georgetown (the Sacred Heart) in 1861. During the seventies and eighties, the Portuguese pressed even further to promote a distinct ethnic religious identity by calling for the erection of a new church to be staffed by priests of their own nationality. They complained that the Italian Jesuits, who spoke "grammatical" Portuguese, could not communicate effectively with them (since they spoke a Madeiran dialect, and many were illiterate in Portuguese). Eventually, on the representation of the Portuguese government, the Vatican conceded and authorized the recruitment of three Portuguese priests from the order of St. Peter in 1883.[128]

Apart from the fact that most Portuguese cultural festivities were associated with Catholic religious festivals, the church also played a very important role in the organization of Portuguese social clubs e.g., the Catholic Glee Club, the Catholic Reading and Recreation Club, the Portuguese Union Club, the St. Joseph's Society, the Portuguese Philharmonic Club, and even a Portuguese cricket club.[129]

From the foregoing it is evident that the Portuguese language was considered very important in moulding a distinct identity in the colony. This formed the third cornerstone in differentiating the Portuguese from the British, and they went to great pain to preserve its use. When they sent their children to school (many Portuguese did not in fact see the value of schooling since they argued that they could get rich without it), it was generally not to Catholic schools where instruction was in English, but to small private Portuguese language schools which mushroomed all over Georgetown in particular. It was only after the passage of the 1876 compulsory education law, when these schools proved incapable of absorbing the great influx of Portuguese children, that many found their way to the Catholic schools. This access to English schooling led to a decline in the use of Portuguese among the young and in the 1870s and 1880s, there was a mushrooming of Portuguese language newspapers in order to help to keep the language alive. The leading Portuguese also campaigned vigorously for Portuguese nationals to replace the Italian Jesuits in the church[130] for just this reason.

The fourth linchpin in the preservation of Portuguese ethnic identity was their primary identification with the "motherland". Virtually all the first generation Portuguese immigrants retained their Portuguese nationality; and even those born in the colony appear to have been taught to pay primary allegiance to Portugal as evidenced by the learning of the Portuguese national anthem, etc. in the private Portuguese schools.[131] For all practical purposes, these local-born Portuguese enjoyed dual nationality; and as shown earlier, they were not averse to calling on the "protection" and "intervention" of the Portuguese government for various things such as exemption from military and fire service, securing political rights, seeking reprieve from capital punishment for murder, and even procuring Portuguese priests to service their religious needs.

Thus despite their socio-economic advancement during the 19th century, the Portuguese remained very distinctly differentiated culturally from the British whites. Although by the 1890s the wealthier Portuguese occupied a socio-economic position approximating that of the middle-status British, their structural relationship to the latter was indicative of the condition which M.G. Smith calls "cultural pluralism". But in addition to their cultural differences, they continued to be socially subordinate to the planter class.

In the context of the debate addressed in this study, therefore, the case of the Portuguese is extremely complex, and clearly indicates that neither the theory of stratification nor of pluralism suffices to explain the changes which occurred between the Portuguese on one hand and the constituent groups of the host society on the other. The evidence shows that, in structural terms, the position of the Portuguese by 1890 varied in relation to the different classes in the host society, even though the latter were integrated by a core of common values. This seems to suggest that as composite societies undergo structural change they are likely to develop a variety of hybrid and complex permutations of the features of both class stratification and pluralism which are not predictable and thus make every case unique.

CHAPTER 8

THE SUBJUGATION OF THE INDIAN AND CHINESE IMMIGRANTS

Wolf and Mintz have noted that one of the important conditions necessary for the establishment and continued operation of the plantation system is a regular or seasonal oversupply of cheap labour.[1] Thompson further observes that whenever the plantation established its own regimen as the dominant socio-economic system, it imported vast numbers of unfree labourers to fulfil its labour requirements. According to him, therefore, 'it is actually the introduction of such an industrial army of occupation that gives the plantation its character.'[2]

After slavery in Guyana such an "army" of unfree labourers was formed by the introduction of indentured immigrants, mainly from India and China. Between 1838 and 1890, some 164,465 Indians migrated to the colony,[3] while 12,832 Chinese were introduced between 1853 and 1879.[4] The Chinese thus formed a small minority, never constituting more than 3.5 percent of the total population; and by 1891 their number (3,714) had declined by 46 percent from a peak of 6,880 in 1871. The Indians, on the other hand, increased considerably to 105,463 individuals or 37.9 percent of the total population by 1891.[5]

Both Indian and Chinese immigration was characterized by an acute shortage of females. It was most marked among the Chinese; at the height of their immigration in 1863, the proportion of females per hundred males was only 13.64.[6] Although this figure improved to 25.7 by 1880, it was hardly an adequate ratio.[7] Among the Indians, the proportion of females arriving in the colony varied from as low as 11.3 per hundred men in 1851 to 61.5 in 1858;[8] but the imperial government attempted to stabilize the proportion of females by stipulating a minimum of 33 per hundred males in 1856, and 40 per hundred men in 1868.[9] Together with the high proportion of females born on the plantations (80 per hundred men),[10] the overall proportion of Indian females resident on the plantations improved from 27.33 per hundred males in 1851 to 58 in 1891.[11]

The initial shortage of females among both the Chinese and the Indian immigrants was largely due to the suspicion with which emigration to Guyana was regarded in both countries where, it was generally believed, the women would be reduced to prostitution.[12] Indian women were further dissuaded by the automatic loss of caste which accompanied emigration.[13] The recruitment policies were also telling, and as the agents tried to attract workers suited to the rigorous conditions on the plantations, little effort was made to recruit females who were considered a liability.[14] Generally both the Chinese and Indians (male and female) who emigrated were either the poor seeking to make money quickly and return to their homelands, or social out-casts seeking to escape ostracism of one form or another in their home countries.[15] In the case of the Chinese, there was the additional push factor caused by the T'ai P'ing Rebellion, which produced a body of refugees eager to emigrate.[16]

Raymond Smith has observed that 85.6 percent of the Indian immigrants originated from the provinces of Agrah, Oudh and Bihar in northern India. They were subdivided by differences of caste and religion. According to Smith's estimates, 13.6 percent were of Brahmin and other high castes, 30.1 percent were of agricultural castes, 8.7 percent of artisan castes, and 31.1 percent of low castes or outcasts. In addition, 16.3 percent were Muslims, and 0.1 percent Christians.[17] These differences were sufficiently deep-seated to create friction among the several categories which sometimes resulted in violent clashes.[18]

The important theoretical consideration here is determining the method and manner by which the Indian and Chinese immigrants were incorporated into Guyanese society. If this incorporation took the form of free settlement as equal members of society devoid of any restrictions as to residence, occupation or physical mobility, and was accompanied by an ease of social interaction with members and groups within the host society which facilitated socio-cultural assimilation, then the basic conditions favouring their integration into the colonial society existed with only differences of class serving to differentiate one person from another regardless of whether he/she was an immigrant or a native.

If, on the other hand, the Indian and Chinese immigrants were incorporated into a subordinate socio-economic position as dependent or bonded labour, and were disadvantaged by social, political and legal disabilities, then this would constitute a condition of differential incorporation. While M.G. Smith regards this as an important indicator of hierarchical pluralism, it does not necessarily signify pluralism at all, but might just as well be an indicator of a rigid form of stratification or, in Rex's terms, of an "estate" system. The crucial factor would be whether the incorporation was accompanied by sufficiently sharp racial and cultural (or "institutional") differences to promote ethnic compartmentalization; in which case it could be identified as structural pluralism.

It must be noted that Indian and Chinese immigrants were introduced into Guyana during the 19th century for the sole purpose of satisfying the demand for labour by the plantations. Their principal role in the colonial economic system was thus construed as simply the production of plantation staples for profit. Every effort, legal, political and otherwise, was made to ensure that their whole existence was inextricably bound to the production regimen of the plantation system. This has led some writers to argue that the plantation constituted a "total institution" in which all aspects and phases of the immigrant worker's life were acted out. Raymond Smith, for instance, asserts that 'the individuals who comprise the group live out all aspects of their lives within the institution and all activities are tightly scheduled in terms of a single rational plan designed to fulfil the official aim of the institution'.[19] This notion of a "total institution" is supported by the words of a 19th century observer, Edward Jenkins:

> Take a large factory in Manchester or Birmingham, or Belfast, build a wall around it, shut in its work-people from all intercourse save at rare intervals with the outside world, keep them in absolute heathen ignorance, and get all the work you can out of them, treat them not unkindly, leave their social habits and relationships to themselves as matters not concerning you who make money from their labour, and you would

have constituted a little community resembling in no small degree a sugar estate village in British Guiana.[20]

This concept of the plantation as a "total institution" has dominated the plantation society theory as advanced by Beckford, *et al*, yet at the same time it has been its major weakness. In reference to the immigrants after emancipation, the notion of "totality" reduces them to the status of production robots who could not evolve an existence of their own within the context of the plantation world. The evidence, however, contradicts this assumption,[21] as the immigrants, even while under indenture, were able within the constraints of the oppressive plantation environment to create their own ethos incorporating key elements of their traditional cultures. The scope to do so was considerably enlarged after the expiration of their indentures even if they chose to remain resident on the estates.

The system of indenture was the *modus operandi* employed to isolate and separate the immigrant workers on the plantations, and to regulate and regiment their labour. This was not simply a means of organizing the immigrants into a disciplined and reliable work force in order to extract the maximum labour from them, but was also an effective method of systematically subjugating them to the absolute authority of the planters on individual plantations as well as within the wider society. From a theoretical angle, M.G. Smith identifies indenture as a form of individual domination, which in turn signifies differential incorporation.[22]

Indenture was, therefore, not just a labour system designed to maintain the primacy and prosperity of the plantation system, but also a mechanism of social control aimed at preserving the dominance of the white minority. Race was an important factor in determining that only the Portuguese of all the immigrants were permitted to evade their obligations or to commute them after a very short period.

Because of the paternalistic attitude of the imperial government towards potential African and Indian immigrants, aimed at preventing their oppression by the planters,[23] it was a full decade after emancipation before any system of indenture was formally established; and then only for one year on a compulsory basis, while Indians could enter voluntary three-year contracts.[24] However the serious threat posed by the economic crisis of the late forties overcame good intentions and the planters were able to convince the imperial authorities that the whole future of the plantation system, indeed of "civilization" in the colony, depended on an assured and abundant supply of cheap contract labour. This not only resulted in imperial government approval of compulsory three-year contracts,[25] but in the establishment of a comprehensive system of indentureship by which five years' labour on a plantation (the so-called "industrial residence") was made the prerequisite for a return passage to India.[26]

Despite this obvious attempt to compel the immigrants to work for five years on the plantations, many refused to work beyond their three-year indenture. Thus in 1853 the planters decided to impose five years' compulsory indenture, and further to extend industrial residence to ten years.[27] This so clearly threatened to violate the personal liberty of the immigrants by subjecting them for such a prolonged period to the absolute will of the planters, that the imperial government felt obliged to disallow it. Yet it was the suggestion of Secretary of State Newcastle that on the expiration of the initial three-year indenture the immigrants might be required to reindenture for two further yearly periods, or commute those at a cost of $12 per annum which, when adopted in 1854, paved the way for five-year indentures for both Indian and Chinese immigrants.[28]

Some immigrants nonetheless successfully withdrew from plantation labour by commuting their service. In 1859 they paid $1,822 for commutation, and this figure increased considerably in the ensuing years.[29] This practice naturally represented a drain on the supply of labour to the plantations, especially as the value of the immigrant's labour appreciated considerably in his fourth and fifth years of residence, after being fully acclimatized and conditioned to the production regimen of the plantation. Thus the planters avidly sought imperial approval for the imposition of five years' compulsory indenture, and finally succeeded in obtaining it with respect to the Indian immigrants in 1862, and to the Chinese in 1864.[30]

The planters were also keen to secure the labour of the immigrants for as long as possible *beyond* their period of compulsory indenture. Their object was thus to coerce or entice the immigrants to reindenture. Hence in 1851, those who did not reindenture after their initial three-year indenture were required to pay a penalty of $1.50 per month (more than one week's statutory wages) over the remaining two years of their industrial residence.[31] This penalty, however, proved difficult to enforce, and was abandoned after having filled the prisons with defaulters and spending nearly $9,000 in collecting a mere $604.68.[32] In 1854 reindenture became automatic if the immigrant could not afford to commute the rest of his industrial residence. Moreover, the immigrant was required to pay the whole cost of his return passage to India after completing just five years of industrial residence or commuting a portion thereof, or to contribute $35 towards the cost after a further five years of non-industrial residence. In other words, if the immigrant were to be entitled to a free return passage, he was required to reindenture for a second five-year period.[33]

The disinclination of the Indians to emigrate to the colony under the liability of contributing to their return passage signalled the failure of this scheme, which was finally abandoned in 1859.[34] In the meantime, however, the planters began to entice the immigrants to reindenture by offering them a bounty of $50 for another five-year stint, with the right to change employers or commute their services after three years.[35] Reindenture thus became an integral feature of the contract labour system[36] and, as many immigrants went so far as to commute their first term and reindenture in order to get the bounty,[37] its propaganda value in support of the entire system was enormous. As reindenture was ostensibly voluntary, it was argued that no immigrant would re-engage his services to a plantation if he were dissatisfied.[38] But representing almost 42 weeks' statutory wages, the $50 bounty was a powerful enticement which few of the underpaid and impoverished immigrants could have foregone.

The reindenture statistics were convincing enough. In 1865, for instance, $219,800 were paid to 5,920 Indian and Chinese workers as bounty;[39] and between 1865 and 1870, 20,914 Indians were paid $1,032,400 to reindenture, and another $317,375 were paid to 6,359 Chinese. By 1870 about 44 percent of the 40,227 immigrants under indenture had reindentured, and some were in their fourth, fifth and even sixth term.[40] A further 10,957 immigrants reindentured between 1871 and May 1875 when the practice was discontinued.⁴¹

The payment of $50, therefore, was certainly a tempting inducement to reindenture, since at the very least it enabled the immigrant to buy a cow, and thus make some more money by selling milk and calves.⁴² This was particularly important in a colony where there were few economic opportunities for the immigrants except as agricultural workers.⁴³ The retail trade was dominated by the Portuguese (though in the late 19th century both the Indians and in particular the Chinese were gradually able to break that dominance) and land was not readily available for immigrant settlement before the seventies on account of high prices, poor drainage, and the restrictive Crown lands regulations. Small wonder that several immigrants complained about the loss of the one boon that contract labour seemed to offer, when the reindenture system was priced out of existence in the mid-seventies. Off the plantations many fared badly and turned vagrants and beggars, while others continued to depend on the plantations for employment.⁴⁵ The system of indenture and reindenture thus functioned as a process for reducing the immigrants to a state of total dependence for their very existence.

But perhaps the most compelling reason for the high rate of reindenture was the iron rigidity of the system of law which governed the indentureship system.⁴⁶ A commission appointed in 1870 to examine the treatment of the immigrants observed that 'a harsh system of law has been kept up, not so much for use, as that condonation for offences under it, might be bartered against reindenture'.⁴⁷ Between 1866 and 1870, for instance, there were 31,900 cases under the labour laws which resulted in 16,222 convictions (50.8 percent) while the rest were either dismissed or withdrawn. The practice of withdrawing charges operated as an effective lever for coercing the immigrants to reindenture, since it left them under a permanent threat of prosecution at a subsequent time if their employers were in any way offended.⁴⁸

These labour laws regulated every aspect of an immigrant's working life under indenture — the amount the work required, regular attendance at work, conduct during work, and so on. Most importantly, breaches of contract were treated as criminal offences punishable by fines and/or imprisonment with or without hard labour. The indentured immigrants were thus governed 'not by kindness and good treatment, but through fear of the severity of the laws',[49] which they quite naturally regarded 'as a mere instrument wielded by the manager for their chastisement, and not as an intelligent arbitration between them and him'.[50] But this harsh system of law was justified on the grounds that:

> where you have to deal with men, by nature little disposed to labour, and able to subsist with very trifling exertion, who have, with their own consent, been introduced at heavy cost, with the express object of obtaining labour from them, it is impossible to dispose altogether with the means of compelling them to fulfil their agreements.[51]

It is significant that this kind of argument was never used in relation to the Portuguese who were likewise introduced at public expense.

All field work was performed by task, which was fixed at seven hours' labour per day;[52] and each adult was required to perform five days' labour or five tasks per week.[53] Task-work, however, was vaguely measured by comparing it to the amount of work done by free workers which was nowhere defined in law.[54] This consequently placed enormous power in the hands of the planter who could manipulate the system to pay less than the actual value of the work done, and to extract more labour from his workers.[55] Although the ill-defined measurement of task-work was nullified by a judicial decision in 1867,[56] and the value of a task was subsequently fixed at one shilling,[57] it still offered the planters great scope to manipulate the immigrants. Not surprisingly, before 1870, convictions for failure to perform the required five tasks per week accounted for 23.7 percent of the total convictions under the labour laws. Since it was an acknowledged fact that less than half the immigrants (44 percent) could actually perform the statutory number of tasks and earn the required five shillings per week, the planters held a permanent threat of punishment over more than half the immigrants which they could inflict at any time.[58]

There were numerous offences for which the indentured immigrant could be convicted and fined $24 (20 weeks' wages) and/or sentenced to one month's imprisonment with hard labour. These included the failure to attend the daily roll-call by which desertion was checked, or to begin or finish work, absence without leave, drunkenness at work, the use of abusive or threatening language to plantation staff, or committing any nuisance on or near any dam or public thoroughfare on a plantation.[59] Twelve percent of the convictions of indentured immigrants between 1866 and 1870 were for neglect or refusal to work i.e., to commence or finish work. This charge was brought in cases of idleness, but more particularly to enforce discipline in the factory where work was measured by time.[60] After 1868, this offence was further punishable by stopping wages, which practically placed the power of enforcing the penalty in the hands of the planters. Hence they took it upon themselves to stop wages illegally for all kinds of reasons e.g., absence without leave, damage of tools, deferred payments, repayments for victuals supplied by the manager on credit or of money advanced, insubordination and other disciplinary reasons, and neglect of duty.[61]

The great majority of convictions between 1866 and 1870 (59.9 percent) was for absence from work without leave. An immigrant could be so indicted for any type of work, particularly in the factory, where a task measure was not required. The free resort to this charge lent enormous credibility to the claim that 'the immigrants on some estates are bound to be always, during the hours of work, either actually at work, or in hospital, or in jail'.[62]

The immigrants were further disadvantaged by their inferior status before the law. As justices of the peace, planters were permitted to remain on the judicial bench even during the trial of their own cases.[63] This was justified on the racial grounds that

> it is carrying a little too far the doctrine that all men are equal before the law, to object to any customary arrangement whereby in a crowded and ill-ventilated courtroom, under a tropical sun, the few Europeans present are exempted from the necessity of standing close packed among a crowd of Asiatics, whose very cleanliness consists in the free use of oil.[64]

This inequality became even more damaging when the immigrants were confronted with a phalanx of "evidence" produced by the planters. The immigrants were rarely able to induce fellow workers to testify on their behalf against a planter for fear of victimization; hence they often felt obliged to distort the facts to give weight to their case, a move which often proved counter-productive. Very often an indentured immigrant was convicted on the sole evidence of a planter or his subordinate.[65]

The impartiality of the magistrates was also questionable. Having risen from lowly positions and long resident in the colony, they too inculcated a feeling of awe for the powerful planters whose disfavour they did not wish to incur as they depended on them for social intercourse and physical comforts on their daily rounds.[66] Furthermore, their unfamiliarity with any of the languages used by the immigrants added to the disadvantage of the latter who had to depend on interpreters whose reliability was not beyond doubt.[67]

Following the investigation and report of the 1870 commission of inquiry, an attempt was made to ameliorate the indenture system. It has already been shown that by May 1875, reindenture was priced out of existence. In the following year a provision was made to add to the indentureship period the number of days lost through absence from work without leave or wilful indolence.[68] Although this was a step towards treating breaches of the indentureship contract as a civil matter, they were still punishable as criminal offences under the 1873 immigration law.[69] So indentured immigrants continued to be prosecuted and imprisoned even after a further amendment in 1876. In 1877, for instance, 137 immigrants were convicted for absence without leave, and 809 for refusal or neglect to begin or finish work.[70]

Gradually, however, less use was made of the labour laws to coerce the indentured workers. In 1880, for example, the managers of 43 plantations were reportedly conducting their business on a basis very nearly approximating a system of free labour; and in 1881 only ten employers bothered even to make use of the provisions of the 1876 law for absenteeism. The occasional absence of the industrious worker could be disregarded, while it was considered a disadvantage to retain the services of a "lazy" worker. Many planters came to the view that the legal procedure was troublesome and disruptive of plantation work since it entailed the loss of a day's labour for all immigrants against whom charges were made, as well as the time of overseers.[71] Thus the number of legal complaints against immigrants declined from 13,725 (35.56 per 100) in 1874 to just 3,732 (24 per 100) in 1889; while convictions decreased from 10,354 to 2,075 in the same period. Nevertheless, the system remained weighted against them, as evidenced by the low number of legal proceedings against employers which fell from 118 with 58 convictions in 1874, to a mere eleven with three convictions in 1890.[72]

Not surprisingly, there was no question of abolishing the indentureship system by which the planters achieved total domination and absolute power over the indentured immigrants, who were thus subjected to a variety of insults and abuses. In 1860, for instance, in order to intimidate a Chinese task gang, one member was forcibly taken behind the closed doors and windows of the factory, bound, and had his hair or "pigtail" cut on the manager's orders — a most provocative offence to a Chinese.[73] Even more serious was the systematic whipping and kicking of immigrants, particularly those just discharged in a convalescent state from hospital, by the manager of Plantations Versailles and Malgre Tout, for which he was actually fined $250 in 1863.[74] In another incident at Plantation Schoon Ord, an overseer defiantly told the court that he had long promised to give an old Indian man 'a damned good beating' and showed the magistrate the buck-rope walking-stick with which he had administered the beating.[75] Such physical assaults were by no means infrequent and in isolated instances might even lead to the murder of immigrants as the case of the Chinese, Low-a-si, on Plantation Annandale in May 1868 demonstrated.[76] Nor was the greatly resented practice by plantation managers and overseers of cohabiting with the wives and daughters of immigrants an infrequent occurrence.[77]

The immigrants adopted many techniques to alleviate or escape from the harshness of this system of domination.[78] Since the indenture is seen here as an integral part of the total system of white (planter) hegemony, then these methods of resistance employed by the indentured immigrants cannot be interpreted solely as industrial action, but as acts of political resistance. The simplest and least hazardous method was to feign illness, in which case it was 'impossible to use coercion by way of application to the stipendiary magistrate' under the labour laws. Another technique was to flock to the magistrate's office for the most trifling reasons thereby causing a loss of time and labour.[79] But commutation was the only legitimate means of escaping indenture, and considerable use was made of it when available although many immigrants did so only to reindenture for the $50 bounty. In eleven years from 1855, $101,880 were paid for this right;[80] and when this provision was reinstituted, 1,905 immigrants commuted their indentures between 1872 and 1890.[81]

Even imprisonment was viewed as a form of escape by some immigrants. Hard labour sentences held no terror for men bound to labour in any event and the loss of wages was partially compensated by being sustained at public expense while in prison. In recognition of this, the colonial legislature in 1864 legalized the employment of convicted immigrants in gangs on plantations; in 1868, two district gaols for immigrants were opened to put this plan into effect.[82]

Many indentured immigrants, however, tried to desert altogether from the plantations. Several became vagrants, wandering aimlessly about the countryside and towns, begging, some crippled or ulcerated with sores, walking skeletons, dying from disease and sheer starvation.[83] Some, especially the Chinese, decamped to neighbouring territories of Venezuela, Surinam, Trinidad and Cayenne.[84] Others went inland either to live and work among the native Amerindians,[85] or, incredibly, to seek an overland route back to India.[86] The Chinese, however, were particularly adept at absconding after receiving their bounty of $50 for reindenturing.[87] Between 1865 and 1869 alone, 4,258 immigrants deserted;[88] while another 9,728 did so between 1874 and 1890, during which period the percentage of deserters actually increased from 2.6 to 3.32.[89]

With a view to curbing desertion and vagrancy, after 1850 the indentured immigrant was prohibited by law from travelling more than two miles from his plantation without a pass issued by the manager. The power to arrest vagrants was not only vested in the police, but also in managers and overseers. Still the deserters enjoyed considerable latitude in the country districts, unlike the capital where police pickets were placed at strategic points of entry to hinder their access, though not with much effectiveness except as a source of harassment to those immigrants with legitimate business in the city.[90]

For a few immigrants the harsh reality of the indentureship system proved overwhelmingly unbearable and in abject despair several Chinese took overdoses of opium. Hanging and drowning were also common methods of immigrant suicide.[91] Between July 1865 and June 1870, there were 70 suicides among the immigrants, while 96 more were recorded between 1872 and 1881, and another 28 from 1886 to 1890.[92]

The immigrants, however, did not merely seek means of escaping the indenture system; they often felt compelled to strike back against this systematic process of subjugation and exploitation, even to the point of violence. Work stoppages were quite common. For instance in six weeks between July–August 1873, there were 14 strikes, and from 1886 to 1889, no less than 100 were recorded.[93] These stoppages were often accompanied by incendiarism of canefields and megass logies,[94] assaults of plantation managers, overseers and drivers, and sometimes open rioting.[96] Labour relations seemed to deteriorate further during periods of economic recession (for example, between 1869 and 1874, and again during the severe depression of the 1880s). In 1888 alone, nine cases of riot and assault of plantation personnel reached the courts.[97] The most serious disturbances, however, occurred at Plantation Leonora in August 1869 when both armed police and military detachments were required to restore order[98] and at Plantation Devonshire Castle in September 1872 in which five Indians were shot dead by the police.[99]

As a system of domination, indenture was an effective means of subjugating the immigrant population by reducing them to a state of total dependence on the plantations for their very survival, and by severely restricting their access to economic opportunities outside of plantation labour. The most that the indentured immigrants could hope for was either to save enough money to buy a cow and thus improve their earning capacity from the sale of milk, as was popular among the Indians;[100] and/or to cultivate their gardens and provision grounds with cash vegetables as the Chinese especially did.[101] Yet in several cases the plantation managers imposed restrictions by not providing either any or enough facilities for these activities primarily because it made the immigrants less dependent on wage labour and, particularly in the tending of cattle and collecting and selling of milk, diverted them from their routine plantation work in the mornings.[102] Some only allowed cattle-rearing as a privilege to well-behaved and industrious immigrants; while others permitted it on condition that a small sum be collected weekly by the cattle owners to pay for cattle-minders to prevent the cattle from straying.[103] Similarly, in 1870 more than half the plantations on which over 2,000 of the 5,000 Chinese indentured immigrants were located had no gardens at all, while on the rest a total of 248 acres were shared between the remaining 3,000 indentured and free Chinese (110 acres were on two plantations alone).[114] By 1891, restrictions were eased and indentured immigrants were allowed to own 17,084 head of cattle and 4,469 sheep.[105]

It was the severe economic depression of the 1880s, however, that ultimately force the plantation owners to make more land available for farming to the immigrants. By 1887, about 4,000 acres were cultivated with vegetables, plantains, rice and provisions.[106] In addition, Crown lands in the savannahs behind the plantations were opened for use by free immigrants on a yearly licence of $1.00.[107] Between 1887–1890, 29 such tracts varying from five to fifty acres were granted.[108]

At no time, however, did the indentureship system permit the immigrant workers to accumulate any real wealth — since economic independence was incompatible with a system of domination/subjugation. The rationale behind granting more land for livestock rearing and farming was to make the plantations themselves more self-sufficient in meeting the needs of the indentured population rather than to increase the latter's earning capacity. The immigrants thus found that, particularly after the end of reindenture, their only chance of accumulating significant wealth was outside of plantation labour despite the greater financial risks involved. To do so, of course, meant breaking down the Portuguese dominance over the licensed trades e.g. shopkeeping, huckstering, transport (carts, cabs, boats, etc.). Toward that end the Indians also introduced a rival spirit trade in the manufacture and sale of coconut toddy[109] (an Indian alcoholic beverage made from the sap extracted from the flower bud of the coconut tree), while the Chinese engaged considerably in illegal spirit trading.[110]

By 1870 many plantations had small shops owned by Indians or Chinese,[111] and the latter effectively began to challenge the long-held Portuguese domination of the total retail trade. Commencing on a cooperative basis during the 1860s[112] (as they had to if they were to counter the cartel tactics of the Portuguese), they began to make significant inroads in this sphere. By the late 1870s one Chinese firm, Messrs. Kwong-san-Lung & Co., was already engaged in the import trade, obtaining most of its merchandise directly from China.[113] In fact, the participation of Indians and Chinese in all branches of the licensed occupations and trades increased considerably during and after the 1870s, which coincides with the disappearance of the system of reindenture. In 1870, both groups held 300 licences for provision shops, 90 for carts, horses or donkeys, 3 for hire carriages, and a few for retailing opium and coconut toddy[114]

By 1891 both groups shared 784 provision shop licences almost evenly (50.6% Chinese), and held 320 licences for the sale of spirits, wines and malts (89.3% Chinese), 1,587 hucksters' licences (98.5% Indians), 953 for carts and carriages for hire (77.6% Indians), 354 for batteaux (70.1% Indians), and 107 for the sale of opium and marijuana/ganga (73.8% Chinese).[115] But not unlike the Portuguese traders, some of these Indian and Chinese traders exploited new and poorer immigrants by operating a form of truck system and selling goods and lending money at high rates.[116]

By the 1890s, the Chinese were well on their way to breaking the Portuguese stranglehold of the retail trade, and had established commercial bases in the Lombard Street area of Georgetown and along Main Street in New Amsterdam,[117] quite apart from the numerous shops and stores scattered in the villages and plantations. These laid the foundation for the dramatic Chinese commercial expansion which took place after the turn of the century with the rise of chain-shop enterprises such as Ho A-Shoo Ltd., Hing Cheong & Co., and the vast empire of Evan Wong, who by 1915 not only owned a vast chain of shops and stores, but also several plantations of rubber, cocoa, coffee and coconuts, balata and goldmining grants including the rich Omai gold mines in Essequibo, sawmills, and shares in several companies in Georgetown.[118]

A few Chinese immigrants also engaged as barbers and hair-dressers, and as skilled moulders and engravers of jewellery,[119] of whom the most famous was M.U. Hing.[120] Others established a settlement up the Demerara river where they reared pigs, cultivated rice and provisions, and did lumbering, shingle splitting and charcoal manufacture.[121] Indians became barbers, fishermen, milksellers, mechanics, domestics, grass-sellers, watchmen, trench-diggers, weeders, porters, etc. A small number also found jobs in the Civil

Service, Police Force, and the hospitals.[122] Even though considerable wealth could be accumulated in some of these occupations (particularly the licensed trades, which offered a measure of social mobility), only a very small minority of Indian and Chinese immigrants actually participated in them since indenture (and until its cessation, reindenture) was designed to prevent any substantial movement of immigrants away from plantation labour, thus hindering their economic and social advancement.

But the increasing signs of unrest and disaffection generated by the indenture system during the late sixties and early seventies forced the planters, colonial and imperial authorities to contemplate new schemes to placate the immigrants, about 30,000 of whom were by then eligible for free return passages having completed their ten years of industrial residence. Thus the idea was discussed of granting them land as had been done in Trinidad, Jamaica and St. Lucia provided that they waived their right to a return passage.[124]

A successful experiment had already been undertaken in 1865 of establishing an immigrant settlement of Chinese up the Demerara River on a grant of Crown land. With the aid of a government loan of £600 ($2,880), the land was drained and soon supported a thriving community engaged in agriculture, livestock rearing, woodcutting, and shingles and charcoal manufacture. In fact, within two years, 40 charcoal ovens had been constructed and the Chinese were producing a better grade of charcoal at 30 percent less than the Portuguese, which effectively broke the latter's monopoly in that field.[125]

In 1872 the government purchased Plantation Nooten Zuill on the east coast of Demerara for an experiment in settling 225 Indian immigrants in lieu of return passages.[126] But no immigrant took any land.[127] They felt that the grant of three acres of land for house, provision ground and cattle pasture, in addition to another acre and a half for wives, was too small and observed that as it was impossible to get extensions, it imposed unacceptable restrictions on cattle rearing. Many were also unhappy about having to settle far from old friends and acquaintances. Furthermore, the settlement was to be subject to the same vexatious village laws about which the Creole villagers so loudly complained, and the Indians were not prepared to place themselves in the same dilemma.[128]

But the pressure to find suitable land settlements for immigrants who had completed their indentures continued to mount since by 1880, many of the estimated 60,000 immigrants eligible for return passages worth about £400,000 were claiming them.[129] A scheme proposed in that year to make 100 acres on the Mahaica river available for settlement was, however, aborted due to Colonial Office reservations about the terms of granting the lands.[130] But in 1881 the Combined Court resolved to provide $100,000 for purchasing, draining and improving lands on which to settle immigrants in lieu of return passages.[131]

In that same year, the adjoined plantations of Huis t' Dieren and Middlesex in Essequibo were laid out, and each adult immigrant was offered 2¼ acres for cultivation and residence, while children between 10–15 years old received two acres, and those between 1–10 years got half an acre. Grazing pasture was common to all villagers for as many head of livestock as the *Zemindar*, appointed by the immigration agent general as supervisor, allowed.[132] But only 69 immigrants waived their return passages to settle there,[133] and in 1883 Governor Irving, considering it unwise to offer free grants, sanctioned the sale of 2½ acre parcels for house lots and cultivation. The price of $24 (£5) per acre, however, was uncompetitive, since private land was available at $5 per acre on the Essequibo islands, and at $4 per acre in Mahaicony on the east coast of Demerara.[134] Although the scheme was reorganized in 1887 to make larger plots available,[135] by 1890 only 153 Indians had bought 384¾ acres at Huis t' Dieren and Middlesex worth $10,260. Similar government sales of land at Plns. Cotton Tree, Brighton, Letter Kenny, Dead Tree Farm and Massiah in Berbice, and at Maria's Lodge in Essequibo only resulted in 61 Indian buyers of 3,398½ acres valued at $6,425.[136]

It was not simply the uncompetitive prices of government lands which made them unattractive to the immigrants. The fact was that the Indians preferred to choose their own land and to be free of any interference or intervention by the government.[137] They had evidently taken good note of the effects of government overrule in the Creole villages. Thus while eschewing the purchase of government lands, they were quite prepared to buy private lands. By 1876, after the end of reindenture, Indian villages began to spring up in several parts of the colony, and this continued with a fervour reminiscent of the land purchases by the ex-slaves after emancipation. In Essequibo, settlement spread along the coast into the North-West District bordering Venezuela.[139] Indian and Chinese settlements sprang up along the coasts and banks of Demerara;[140] but their most spectacular development was in Berbice, particularly on the Corentyne coast.[141] A *few* immigrants also settled in the old Creole villages, while some migrated to the capital to form small Chinese and Indian enclaves in separate sections of the town in the midst of otherwise Creole areas.[142] By 1890 Indians possessed houses and land valued at $102,543 in the 25 old incorporated villages, $91,530 in Georgetown, and $37,535 in New Amsterdam. It is estimated that between 1873–1890, they spent over $320,000 on the purchase of land throughout the colony.[143]

The indentureship system clearly posed a fundamental obstacle to Indian settlement in the colony but once the practice of reindenturing ceased, such settlements began to mushroom. The settlement of the immigrants signified their desire to be incorporated into the colonial society as full members, rather than remain in the position of marginality which they held while under indenture.

The extent of their integration into the host society, however, was decidedly limited by the race factor. It is by no means surprising that these immigrants should have encountered the full impact of race and racism in a society which had become increasingly obsessed with this issue after emancipation. From the very outset, the fact that the Creoles had to bear high taxation to pay a third of the cost of introducing Indian and Chinese immigrants who, through the indentureship system, gradually supplanted the former in the labour market and reduced their wages, created an atmosphere of suspicion and animosity between these ethnic sections.[144] Thus Bronkhurst commented that

> there is no denying the fact that there exists an uncalled-for bitter feeling between the native Creole and the Indian immigrant towards each other. The native looks upon the heathen Indian as an intruder or interloper, whilst the Indian looks down upon the native black as being inferior to him in a social aspect.[145]

For the Creole, the Indians were semi-savages or semi-civilized barbarians — an ignorant, illiterate people from a barbarous country. They were simply "coolies" or "motiyon", porters, day labourers, burden-carriers. An Indian was addressed 'you sammy', 'you coolie'.[146] Creoles would not even contribute to religious charities which benefitted Indians. One contemporaneous anecdote related that on hearing of the tragic drowning of six Indians, a christian Creole woman simply dismissed it thus: '"Coolies! Only coolies! Tchups! I thought you were speaking of people!"'[147]

In turn the Indians were equally prejudiced towards the Creoles whom they despised and considered less civilized.[148] They spurned any association with the "caffair";[149] and as an Indian witness told a black prisoner in court, 'me no keep company with black men'.[150] In another instance, Indian prisoners objected to black jurors in their criminal trial.[151] This is not surprising when one takes into account the fact that the Indian immigrants retained modified notions of their traditional caste system in which dark skin-colour was associated with low-caste or pariah status. When transferred to Caribbean society, it was the blacks who were perceived as fitting this status.[152] The Chinese were no less prejudiced, and a strong feeling was said to exist between them and the Creoles.[153] They were so averse to mixing with Creoles in their initial period in the colony that in 1861 the acting governor was obliged to advise plantation managers against placing them under black sub-overseers or drivers.[154]

The indentureship system contributed in no small way to the manifestation of racism by its isolation and separation of the Indian and Chinese immigrants on the plantations. Thus each ethnic category occupied separate living quarters and, with the probable exception of the driver, more often than not worked in racially homogeneous gangs. Even the children were generally prevented from mixing with Creole children since special "coolie" schools were set up on the estates, while Creole children attended village schools. Besides, many Indian parents preferred not to encourage racial intermingling by their children, and in some cases did not wish to have them taught and disciplined by Creole school-masters.[155]

Racial separation was further entrenched by the pattern of government-encouraged free immigrant settlement off the plantations. Adamson claims that there is little sign that the Indians attempted to segregate themselves, or that they were rejected by the Creoles in the countryside, and that there were no exclusively Indian villages in the beginning.[156] Whatever is "the beginning" is not clear. But except for the *few* immigrants who went to live in Creole villages (and Adamson himself admits that they were few),[157] most immigrant settlements were ethnically exclusive — from the 1870s onwards. Moreover, the government land schemes were also designed for settlement along racial lines. The establishment of the Chinese settlement of Hopetown led to the displacement of Creoles who had previously lived on wood grants there.[158] The ill-fated Nooten Zuill project was approved although part of the estate had already been leased to Creole and Portuguese farmers who were consequently displaced.[159] At L'Amitie in 1880, it was the government's intention to ensure that allotments remained perpetually in Indian hands which aroused Colonial Office reservations. The Crown surveyor had proposed that rather than give the settlers transports, grants should be made by the governor so that safeguards could be built into future transfers to prevent any possible alienation from the Indian settlers.[160] Likewise, the government undertook in 1881 to eject 200 Creole squatters from Huis t' Dieren to make room for Indian settlers.[161]

It is extremely doubtful whether the Creoles cared to have Asians settling amidst them, and that no doubt partially accounts for the paucity of immigrant settlers in the Creole villages. Perhaps the most extreme case of Creole rejection of Indian proximity was in 1874 when an entire black village in the Canje district uprooted itself to move 25 miles and establish a new settlement at Nurnay on the Corentyne coast, 'literally in order that they might keep themselves to themselves, and above all be far away from the coolies whose notions ... of "meum and tuum" are very broad'.[162]

The result, of course, was that there was very little social interaction between the Indians, Chinese and the Creoles. It is true that Creoles participated in immigrant festivals, particularly the Muslim Mohurrum festivities and the Chinese New Year celebrations. For instance, they joined the Indians in procession, helped to carry the *tazzias*, 'beat their breasts in the same manner, uttered ... the same words and helped to swell the demonlike yells of these poor idolatrous'.[163] During the 1870s the Creoles even organized their own "tadjas",[164] so much so that it was feared that the festival would lose its ethnic religious identity and become a truly national cultural phenomenon.[165] Indeed it was this very apprehension which aroused the disapproval of many Indians and motivated their withdrawal from the festivities,[166] while simultaneously inducing the white colonial authorities to discourage what appeared to be the moulding of interracial understanding and cooperation between the two sections.[167] Similarly, Creole participation in Chinese gambling activities, particularly the *chefa* lottery, was discouraged by the authorities ostensibly on the ground that the dubious manner in which the Chinese operated might lead to violent friction between the two categories as in Trinidad.[168]

During the seventies and eighties the Anglican church tried to encourage racial intermingling between the Asians and Creoles by organising annual school picnics in Demerara where children of all races from several schools in the region assembled and played together evidently with their parents' approval; and in fact, few problems were encountered in those few cases where interracial schooling was conducted.[169] Similarly, blacks and Asians were occasionally regaled together by the management of some plantations on festive occasions such as Christmas;[170] and both the Indians and the Chinese were noted to have adopted the Creole practice of obeah.[171]

Such sectional interaction, however, was decidedly limited and confined to the peripheral areas of cultural activity. At a more fundamental and private level, there was very little interaction. As Wood and Brereton found for Trinidad,[172] so too in Guyana, interracial marriage and miscegenation were rare,[173] particularly between Indians and Chinese on one hand and Creoles on the other.[174] Nevertheless, as early as 1841, some Indians were found to cohabit with Creole women on Plantation Bellevue, while the first legal marriage of this sort took place at Plantation Wales.[175] Two other such marriages were reported in 1842 at Plantations Highbury and Waterloo on either bank of the Berbice River. But most of the Indians on those two estates expressed a desire to go back home and bring wives.[176] Similarly, in 1861 the first two marriages between Chinese men and Creole women were observed, though in one case the woman was soon "sent away".[177] Even the Chinese missionary founder of the Hopetown settlement, Wu-Tai-Kam, fell to the charms of a coloured woman whose consequent pregnancy forced him to disappear to Trinidad in disgrace since he had previously been married and had a family in Singapore.[178] It appears, however, that cohabitation between Chinese men and Indian women was less rare, and in a few instances the women accompanied their reputed husbands to China.[179] The general rarity of intermarriage and miscegenation meant, of course, that there was very little dissolution of the biological purity of the Indians and Chinese for the duration of the century.[180]

The lack of partners of the same ethnic background prompted different sexual solutions among these two categories of immigrants. Indians adopted flexible mating patterns, including polyandry, to alleviate the problem. But that "solution" was by no means stable as the high incidence of "wife murders" testifies.[181] How the Chinese dealt with the matter is uncertain, but the choices were few: celibacy, homosexuality, or clandestine sexual relations with Creole and Indian women. In the absence of tangible evidence in the form of mixed progeny, one has to adhere to the position that inter-racial sexual relationships involving Chinese men were indeed rare (unless of course they practised a very effective method of birth control).

With this background of racial separation and animosity, it is not surprising that as in Trinidad,[182] intersectional relations were somewhat frictional. To unemployed Creoles who attributed their misfortune to the presence of immigrants, the custom of Indian women to wear their jewellery in a gaudy display all over their person was, in too many cases, an irresistible temptation. This thus gave rise to muggings by Creole delinquents from which not even Indian men were exempt.[183] Equally unsavoury was the Creole habit of bullying, abusing and assaulting both Indians and Chinese. Insults and missiles were tossed at these immigrants on the public streets, regardless of age or sex, for amusement. In many instances, black policemen who witnessed such scenes would not intervene and arrest the culprits.[184]

For their part, however, the Creole villagers suffered terribly from the nocturnal depredations of their provision grounds and stock yards by Asian immigrants, particularly the Chinese who moved in gangs of between twenty and fifty armed with cutlasses fastened to long sticks. During the sixties and seventies these marauding plunderers constituted a terror despite legislation to deter them by public floggings.[185] Several deaths occurred on both sides in clashes between the Chinese gangs and black watchmen;[186] and on one occasion the discovery of a hut in a canefield where the Chinese stored their stolen booty resulted in a full-scale racial clash between Chinese and Creoles on Plantation Zeelandia in 1863.[187] Indian immigrants were also engaged in such nocturnal thefts but were by no means as dangerous as the Chinese.[188] Of course, the need of the Asian immigrants to resort to such drastic action to procure food was a grave indictment of the deficiencies of the indentureship system.

If, as in Trinidad,[189] violent communal confrontations were not large-scale, it was not for want of opportunities. A dispute over property boundaries in 1881 between 200 Indians and 25 blacks in Wakenaam, Essequibo, might easily have degenerated into racial conflict.[190] So too might have the "discovery" of extensive fields of rice on Crown lands behind the estates on the east coast of Demerara in 1885 which resulted in the reaping of this bonanza by the neighbouring villagers. As it turned out the rice had been planted, albeit illegally, by Indian immigrants on the plantations who were thus deprived of the fruit of their labour by the Creoles.[191].

As Brereton found in Trinidad, racial conflict was very prevalent at an individual level and on a small localised scale.[192] It was not uncommon for both individual and small groups of Creoles to attack and beat Indians and Chinese.[193] The Barbadians seemed particularly prone to such racial aggression, especially towards the Indians.[194] But this behaviour was not confined to the lower strata of Creoles. In 1875, for instance, a black doctor at a Berbice hospital reportedly flogged a male Indian nurse severely for refusing to clear the spittoons and basins.[195] Nor were the Asian immigrants themselves too timid to launch severe attacks on the Creoles, some of which were particularly savage.[196] Similarly, although the Indians and Chinese occasionally combined in disputes with the management of plantations,[197] race relations between them were generally no more cordial than with the Creoles. Indians, too, were victims of nocturnal Chinese attacks in which several lives were lost;[198] and violent communal clashes occurred between these two categories on a number of occasions.[199]

In contrast to the evidence presented here, Walter Rodney

considered these incidents to be 'piddling', 'brief and usually without fatalities'. In fact he overtly de-emphasized their racial character and preferred to see them 'as contradictions among the people springing from the inability of the colonial economy to satisfy the demands of the majority of the producers.'[200] Whatever racism existed between the Indians and the Creoles, Rodney was prepared to attribute largely to the ideological impact of planter propaganda aimed at preventing

> the maturing of working class unity by offering an explanation of exploitation and oppression that seemed reasonably consistent with aspects of people's life experience.[201]

Thus he argued that the Creoles were not intrinsically antagonistic to Indians; and that although anti-immigration, they were not anti-Indian.[202] In addition, he placed great stress on the process of creolization or the 'indigenizing experience' of labour on the estate in moulding common responses to capital at the point of production by both Indians and Creoles.[203]

In face of the overwhelming evidence to the contrary, it is difficult to see how Rodney could have reduced the conflict between the Indians and Creoles to "piddling" proportions. He was evidently misled by the relative absence of communal conflict on a scale akin to that which occurred on several occasions between the Creoles and the Portuguese.[204] But this did not mean an absence of serious conflict particularly at a localized and individual level, as we have already seen.[205]

The fact is that the incidence of communal conflict was kept to a minimum[206] by the high degree of physical separatism which characterized the coexistence of these two large differentiated ethnic groups, but which at the same time accentuated and perpetuated their social and cultural differences. And while both groups did see themselves in a protracted struggle against capital or at least the representatives of capital, they also saw themselves in a growing conflict of interest in which they were pitted against each other in their competition for scarce resources, a situation which was reflected essentially in racial terms.

There was nothing contradictory about this: such racial competition and conflict were perfectly natural and rational in a society preoccupied and indeed obsessed by considerations of race. Considerations of racial differences were a key aspect of everyday reality in 19th century Guyana facing all groups if they were to survive, let alone advance in a racist society. If there is any contradiction it lies in the fact that the recognition of differences based on race and culture was actually one of the values held *in common* by all the constituent ethnic groups in the colonial society. In short, the common idea of racial difference was one of the few things which seemed to unite them. This was one of the most important consequences of their socialization on the plantations: it was an integral part of that 'indigenizing experience' of which Rodney spoke.

That this common perception of racial difference was manipulated by the white minority to exacerbate divisions among the subordinate groups and to perpetuate their dominance, there can be no doubt. But even if the source of racism could be placed wholly or largely at their feet, the point remains that it formed an essential part of the social reality because it was inculcated and acted out by the subordinate socio-racial groups.

As to such fine intellectual distinctions between "anti-immigration" and "anti-immigrant", these were certainly made by educated Creole leaders and by liberal whites. But for the great mass of functionally illiterate Creoles, anti-immigration meant anti-Indian, anti-Portuguese, anti-Chinese, or even in some cases anti-Barbadian. These people were neither interested in nor, in some cases, capable of making such fine distinctions — a fact with which Rodney was forced to come to terms though he preferred to attribute it to the frustration of their claims by the dominant white minority.[207] However plausible an explanation that might be, the fact still remains that racist sentiment was very strong and deep-seated among the Creoles and indeed the Indians, and was very often acted out when individuals of the two groups came into contact with one another.

Finally with respect to the creolization process through the shared experience on the estates, I have already pointed out that the inculcation of the idea of racial difference was an integral aspect of that experience. Rodney, however, laid great stress on the similarity of response by Creoles and Indians to the common work experience.[208] That is not surprising given the fact that they were both exploited and oppressed in similar ways by the same economic institution.

We have established that the "economy" is one of the few integrating forces even in the most highly segmented society. But two points need to be made about these similar economic responses to common exploitation. The first is that they were related almost entirely to the work-place situation. In that sense, both groups shared the same "work culture" which in fact influenced their attitudes to estate work.[209]

But having said that, it is important to stress the second point, which is that that "work culture" did not help to make common cause of the separate struggles of the two groups against white planter hegemony. Thus though similar, their actions were separate, along racial lines. Even Rodney was forced to acknowledge that 'there were in effect two semi-autonomous sets of working class struggles against the domination of capital.'[210]

Rodney also emphasized cross-cultural transferences or interculturation, most of which have been treated above, as evidence of some measure of cultural integration.[211] It is important to observe here, however, that those integrative cross-cultural transferences were peripheral to the core of the cultures of the two groups. Even the Creole participation in Indian religious festivals was confined only to the public processions and did not entail conversion to Islam or Hinduism.[212] With respect to language, it is not correct to argue as some scholars have done informally that the adoption of the Creole language by the Indians was indicative of socio-cultural integration with the Creoles. The Creole patois was the "lingua franca" of the work/market place where the immigrants came into contact with membes of the other ethnic groups. So long as fresh immigrants kept on being imported in large numbers, the Creole patois not only had to coexist with Hindi in particular, and to a lesser extent Tamil and Urdu in the case of the Indians, and Hakka and Punti in the case of the Chinese, but its use was for a long time likely to remain essentially confined to the work and market situations and not employed in the home and in socio-cultural gatherings of the immigrants. Thus in that context, even the language acquisition could be considered "peripheral" on account of the restricted purposes for which it was used.

Rodney argues that there was no strict coincidence of '*absolute* cultural differences' [my emphasis] and race in so far as the Indians and Creoles were concerned, *but* it is extremely doubtful, to say the least, that one can seriously talk about 'aspects of cultural convergence' since these were so few and peripheral. Nor is it realistic to attempt to reduce the differences between these two groups to 'cultural differences' as does Adamson[213] since race was no less important in socially differentiating the one group from the other. For all practical and analytical purposes, the boundaries of race and culture between them were well nigh coterminous.

In so far as the wider theoretical debate is concerned, the historical evidence clearly demonstrates that the Indian and Chinese immigrants were differentially incorporated into the colonial society through a system of individual domination in the form of indenture. Not until the late 1860s and 1870s was there any semblance of the idea of encouraging the free settlement of these immigrants, and even so this was only after they had served their indenture period. Within the indentureship system itself the degree of absolute domination was relaxed somewhat after 1870, although the essential features remained unaltered. Thus as a system for maintaining a section of the Asian population in subjection, it was retained beyond the turn of the century.

Those who found themselves within its bounds thus continued to be subordinated in an extreme way to the dominance of individual planters and/or their agents. The mere existence of the indentureship system was a fundamental obstacle to the development of a fully free society based on the universalistic ideal of equality of opportunity.

Nevertheless its existence did not preclude social mobility for those who could legitimately escape its control and domination. In this regard, the mere act of terminating one's indenture entailed a significant adjustment in one's social status. To be sure, it did not remove the ex-indentured worker from the pervasive influence of white minority dominance. But it opened up new opportunities, at least in theory, for social and economic advancement either through small farming, retail trading or other jobs off the estates, or through the acquisition of a western (British) education (see chapter 9).

Thus the fact that by 1881 only 17,339 adult Indians out of a total Indian population of 105,463 (16.4%) were still indentured signifies an important adjustment in the social position of the group. However, this adjustment did not lead to their integration into the host society for they remained very sharply differentiated racially and culturally from the constituent members/groups of that society with whom, apart from holding similar attitudes to estate work, they shared no common beliefs, values, mores, customs, actions, etc. Right up to the end of the 19th century, they remained isolated and insulated behind racial and cultural boundaries, reinforced and fostered by their residential separation both on and off the estates.

The Indian and Chinese immigrants thus formed very distinct ethnic sections within 19th century Guyanese society. Their cases come as close as one can expect to approximating the kind of sectionalization characteristic of the plural society model. While under indenture their differential incorporation at the very bottom of the society (below the Creoles) was consistent with the condition of structural or hierarchial pluralism. After the cessation of the practice of reindenture, when they began to settle freely on their own lands and to achieve some measure of economic mobility, there was a structural adjustment in their social position. While still differentially incorporated in relation to the dominant white section, they were now juxtaposed alongside (parallel to) the lower classes of Creoles from whom they continued to be sharply differentiated racially and culturally — i.e. a condition of segmental pluralism obtained. Thus instead of a straightforward situation of hierarchial pluralism, this structural adjustment in the position of the Indians and Chinese towards the end of the century produced the coexistence of both hierarchial and segmental pluralism in the colonial social structure. This naturally has very important theoretical implications.

THE ORGANIZATION AND STRUCTURE OF THE TOTAL SOCIETY

CHAPTER 9

THE STABILITY AND UNITY OF THE SOCIETY: CONSENSUS OR COERCION

The stabilisation of composite societies lies at the very heart of the debate between the advocates of the rival theories of pluralism and stratification. M.G. Smith argues that the monopolization of political power by a social and cultural minority and the institutionalised inequalities characteristic of the plural society render it inherently unstable. Hence, there is a great dependence on the employment of the means of force to maintain the stability and unity of the total society.[1] While agreeing that coercion forms a major element in stabilizing plural societies, however, Pierre van den Berghe considers it notoriously unreliable on its own, and emphasizes economic interdependence in combination with coercion for holding together the widely differentiated sections.[2]

In contrast, Lloyd Braithwaite asserts that the emphasis which the pluralists place on coercion is the result of their having ignored the shared values and ties of common sentiment which every society must have in order to preserve its unity;[3] although, because of differences in racial identity which he recognizes, he more recently seems to have had some doubt whether in countries like Trinidad and Guyana with large Indian populations there is that degree of unity and consensus which he previously presumed.[4] Likewise R.T. Smith stresses the view that Caribbean societies are integrated around a common value system based on the acceptance of white cultural superiority, which can include the use of force as a unifying factor.[5] For him, as well as for Hall and Edward Brathwaite, this common value system is created by the process of "creolization". Harmannus Hoetink emphasizes the factor of biological race, and argues that based on the somatic norm image of the constituent social categories, biological-cum-cultural mingling leads to the integration of the society (and ultimately to its racial and cultural homogenization) most likely around the practices and values of the dominant group.[6] This chapter examines the extent to which integration was promoted by value consensus in the case of Guyana and which of these theoretical positions is consequently most applicable.

In Guyana after slavery, white minority dominance was effected by their monopoly of political power which enabled them to employ the state apparatus to institutionalize social and political inequalities, and thereby to subjugate the subordinate majority. This systematic programme of repression was a major source of social instability as witnessed by the perennial unrest generated by the high indirect taxation, high village rates, and the harsh indenture system. But this instability was further exacerbated by the racial factor. One recalls that this served as the rationale and justification for preserving white dominance, and the propagation of the myth of white superiority was an important aspect of that process.

White racism thus complemented and buttressed white social and political dominance.[7] As H.V.P. Bronkhurst observed, 'the whites, considering themselves to be a highly superior race, look down upon both the coloured and black people with scorn and derision.' If the white newcomer was "colour-blind" and indifferent to the question of race, within a few months,

> you see him in nine cases out of ten, distorting his body in all forms, and keeping his head high in the air and set upon a neck as stiff as a crowbar — he has been innoculated with the prevailing poison of prejudice, and can no longer feel at ease near a black man ...[8]

This element of race and racism further served as an agent of destabilization within the society by promoting a high degree of social segmentation along ethnic lines. It was primarily the racial factor, reinforced by cultural differences, which accounted for the isolation and insulation of the several ethnic categories behind firm sectional boundaries. This segmentation proved inherently unstable as the permanent state of racial disharmony and conflict which resulted demonstrates. Moreover, it was always liable to be exploited by the white ruling minority to maintain their own dominance, thereby contributing further to social instability.

A policy of divide and rule was thus made possible by the high degree of segmentation based on race. Throughout the post-emancipation 19th century, white planters and officials felt that in face of the overwhelming majority of non-white people, their security could be enhanced by playing one group off against another. During the 1848 strike, an estate manager opined that 'the safety of the whites depends very much upon the want of union in the different races.'[9] Similarly, in 1851, the Administrator-General observed that 'our population consists of various races, with conflicting feelings and prejudices, without a common bond of union, and herein lies ... one great element of [white] security.'[10] This view was re-echoed by the 1870 commissioners who stated that 'there will never be much danger of seditious disturbances among the East Indian immigrants ... so long as large numbers of negroes continue to be employed with them.'[11] Thus an important aspect of policy was to play one ethnic section against another, and even at times to pit them physically against one another.[12] It did not escape the attention of the white authorities, for instance, that the predominantly black Police Force would be particularly effective in putting down immigrant disturbances, especially as there were no predilections of race to impair their efficiency.[13]

At the same time, however, they fully recognized that because of its built-in instability, this policy was tenuous. The police inspector-general noted in 1882 that while the Creoles and Asian immigrants might never unite against the dominant white minority, no one category could be totally depended upon for assistance in the event of a general uprising by the other. In his view, the most likely scenario was for the category not immediately involved to remain neutral so long as the authorities appeared capable of suppressing the revolt. But if the reverse occurred, they would probably join the uprising against the white government.[14] Thus, it was recognised that the exploitation of racial differences to preserve white minority dominance (divide and rule) was fraught with danger, and was likely to contribute to social instability.

In general terms, it is evident that the factor of race, whatever its manifestation, was an agent of destabilisation in colonial society. The stability and unity of the society thus depended on the extent to which this divisive racial factor could be transcended by integrative forces whether economic, biological and/or cultural. The alternative was the employment of coercion, perhaps in combination with one or more of the other elements.

The economic factor will be considered first. Not only van den Berghe, but Rex, Furnivall and van Lier consider(ed) the economic factor to be a major integrative element in the composite colonial society. According to Furnivall, 'the highest common factor is the economic factor, and the only test that applies in common is the test of cheapness'.[15] Van Lier further noted that 'social processes are controlled by the economic motive. Social values originate, but only in so far as these may be economically advantageous'.[16] Rex, however, adds the caveat that if the differentiated segments are united through the "economy", then they must have some of the characteristics of classes in the Marxist sense.[17] But each of these writers indicates that there is occupational specialization or a division of economic roles along racial lines.[18]

In post-emancipation Guyana, it was the plantation economic system which provided the common economic factor. All subordinate social categories, even some of the favoured Portuguese, were initially introduced to work on the plantations. Rodney, as we have seen, made much of this shared work experience to advance his argument for the creation of common working class interests and responses to planter dominance and exploitation.[19] But notwithstanding certain similarities in the economic behaviour of the subordinate working people (what we have termed a "shared work culture"), there was generally no unity of action which transcended racial boundaries. Rather each ethnic section pursued its own economic activities and took its own action in defence or promotion of its group interests quite independently and without the active support of the other subordinate sections. Thus despite undergoing the same process of socialization within the plantation milieu, no generally united inter-racial response was produced to counter or combat common economic exploitation.

Nevertheless to the extent that all sections were in some

degree, directly or indirectly, dependent on the plantation economy for their well-being, it served as an integrative factor. When it was in recession, all sections experienced economic hardship; when it encountered circumstances of relative prosperity, they all to varying degrees enjoyed the benefits which trickled down. However, the conditions of socio-economic development in the post-emancipation period promoted economic segmentation along ethnic lines. Thus in broad terms, the superordinate whites controlled the government and churches, and held top managerial and professional occupations; Creoles were engaged as hired agricultural labourers specializing in certain tasks, small peasant farmers, skilled and semi-skilled artisans, junior white-collar workers, and later on as professionals and priests; the Portuguese immigrants operated mainly as retail traders and other forms of entrepreneurs, although some were also small farmers; and the Indian and Chinese immigrants worked as indentured plantation labourers, and later as small farmers and shopkeepers. Such occupational specialization along ethnic lines, though not rigid, naturally reinforced the tendency towards separate and independent action in pursuit of sectional economic interests. But on the other side of the argument, it promoted a high degree of economic interdependence among the several sections, albeit asymmetrical and in many circumstances exploitative, which fostered a certain measure of inter-ethnic cooperation for mutual economic gain.

Yet even such intersectional economic cooperation was liable to breakdown into racial instability as a result of competition for scarce resources, insufferable exploitaion and general economic recession. Thus competition between the white planters and the Creole peasantry for labour in the forties, between the Creoles and the Portuguese in the early retail trade, and between the Creoles and the Indian and Chinese immigrants for plantation jobs, all resulted in racial confrontation. Again the Portuguese exploitation of their dominance of the retail trade through gross profiteering and sometimes unfair and illegal practices generated conflict with the Creoles and did little to eliminate racial tension while in periods of economic recession the resulting severe hardships both for the Creoles, Indians and Chinese often led to racial conflict of one form or another. The important point, therefore, is that the economic factor (interdependence) was not sufficient on its own to stabilize and unite the differentiated ethnic sections.

The biological factor has been advanced primarily by Hoetink as an integrative element. Despite the racial barrier which existed between white and black, there had always been a certain amount of interracial sexual relations ever since the period of slavery which produced a mixed population. According to the 1827 census in Berbice, there were 1,161 free coloureds out of a population of 22,493; and by the 1829 census for Demerara and Essequibo, there were 6,360 free coloureds in a population of 69,467. Taken together, the free coloureds comprised 8.1 percent of the total population of the three provinces, and these statistics exclude coloured slaves. Only two censuses during the remainder of the century provided any details on the size of the mixed population. In 1851 they numbered 14,754 or 10.8 percent, and in 1891 they stood at 29,376 or 10.5 percent.[20] This suggests that the proportion of mixed people remained virtually static for most of the century, from which one might conclude that the biological factor was not very significant as an integrative element. In other words, the somatic norm images of the constituent social groups did not seem to favour the idea of ultimate racial homogenization as a desirable ideal.

It is, of course, the cultural factor through which the value consensus capable of stabilizing and uniting a society is created. Religion played a very crucial role in this regard in Guyana. We have already seen that in the case of the Portuguese, in spite of their racial affinity and shared Euro-christian tradition with the British whites, they remained ethnically distinct for the whole of the post-emancipation 19th century, and in fact firmly resisted assimilation by practising their own ethnic brand of Roman Catholicism, by preserving the use of the Portuguese language, and by retaining Portuguese nationality. Such consensus as existed between them and the British whites centered largely on the fundamental issue of the day — race — which enabled them to serve as collaborating agents of the latter in restricting Creole economic advancement. For this reason, we have treated their problems of acculturation separately since Portuguese resistance to British culture was not construed as a threat to "civilization" or to white power in the colony.

As far as Creoles, Indians and Chinese were concerned, the effort to promote value consensus was undertaken mainly by the missionaries through a systematic process of indoctrination in church and school. The association of freedom with the activities of the missionaries created the necessary pyschological conditions among the ex-slaves for such indoctrination, and they were predisposed to accept the missionaries as friends and mentors. Hence after emancipation, they demonstrated their gratitude by financing the erection of churches, chapels and schools which they and their children frequented in great numbers.[21]

The techniques of the clergy of the state churches and of the Wesleyan Methodist missionaries were calculated to bolster the stability of the established socio-political order by firstly, inculcating in the ex-slaves a sense of deference to white authority and, secondly, fostering acceptance of their subordinate position in society. They were also designed to encourage industrious habits with a view to rendering the freed blacks and coloureds into a disciplined and reliable work force suitable for the regimentation of plantation labour, given the absence of the whip in a free society.[22] Thus after the 1856 disturbances, for instance, the Methodist superintendent proposed employing the missionaries directly in subduing 'the heathen population of the villages' by bringing them under more efficient moral control. His idea of cultivating 'these moral wilds' by intensive house to house missionary work, and compelling parents to send 'their wild, vicious and untaught children' to school was well received by the imperial government which appreciated the social benefits of such a missionary role in 'redeeming the rising generation from barbarism'.[23]

For their part, the independent missionaries of the London Missionary Society adopted a more liberal socio-political approach, although their teaching stressed white cultural superiority. Far from promoting the subjugation of the ex-slaves, they encouraged them to be self-reliant, to insist on their civil rights, and to resist political oppression.[24] This explains their involvement in the campaigns for political reform, their forceful opposition to the immigration policy, their advice to the Creoles to resist attempts aimed at forcing them to work for low wages on the plantations, their struggle in support of efforts to enfranchise the Creole smallholders during the

1840s, and their assistance in establishing cooperative agricultural and commercial enterprise in the 1860s. At the same time, however, they sought to 'improve their moral character',[25] which in effect meant deprecating their African cultural heritage as "barbarous heathenism" and instilling in them the beliefs, practices and values of white Anglo-Saxon Protestant civilization.[26]

Missionary indoctrination seemed highly successful during the first decade after emancipation. But the attitude of the ex-slaves changed after the 1848 strike which the missionaries openly opposed. Impoverished by the sharp reduction of wages, their attendance at both church and school declined markedly, ostensibly for want of money to pay church dues and school fees.[27] Children were kept from school to assist in the provision grounds, or to work on the plantations to boost the family incomes.[28] Furthermore, the migration of many Creoles inland and their reversion to traditional Afro-Creole religious and cultural beliefs and practices was nothing short of alarming to the white missionaries.[29]

The result was that the 8,958 registered school pupils in 1848 was a 23 percent reduction on the 1838 figure, and of these only 57.5 percent actually attended shcool.[30] In 1863 the 12,455 registered pupils were less than 39 percent of the children between ages 5–15;[31] while the average attendance in 1864 and 1865 accounted for less than half the registered number.[32] Even after the introduciton of compulsory schooling in 1876, attendance remained irregular for want of enforcement particularly in the rural districts. Hence in that year the average attendance of 10,224 was just 59 percent of the total number of registered pupils, and this only increased to 16,766 by 1890.[33] Similarly, by 1853 it was estimated that 75 percent of the rural Creole population no longer attended church or chapel.[34] However, the 1860s witnessed a dramatic revival in church attendance among the Creoles, which parallelled that in Jamaica. Whether it was Africanized in the same way as the Jamaican phenomenon is difficult to say.[35]

The results of schooling and religious proselytization in instilling the superiority of white culture, religion and values among the Creole population were at best ambiguous. Amidst signs of intense religiosity and behavioural changes,[36] they retained strong Afro-Creole beliefs and practices such as the *cumfo* worship of the river god, reverence of ancestral and other spirits (*jumbi*), and belief in magic and witchcraft (*obeah*); while the Creole common law marriages (so-called "concubinage") and the matrifocal family deviated from the white Anglo-Christian norm and ideal.[37] The missionaries themselves recognized the existence of these phenomena as evidence of the limitations of their indoctrination process,[38] though they naturally attributed them to the transition of the Creoles from a state of semi-barbarism to civilization.[39] This seems to endorse Brathwaite's idea of "incomplete creolization",[40] because the white norms and ideals were in fact creolized versions of the British standard.

Far less effort was expended on indoctrinating the Indian and Chinese immigrants, no doubt because they were generally considered as transient residents. Besides, the planters were highly suspicious about the schooling and religious conversion of the immigrants. Rather than stabilizing them, the planters thought that these processes contributed to unrest, conceit and hypocrisy, and did more harm than good to the character of the indentured workers.[41] Furthermore, the schooling of immigrant children meant a loss of a valuable source of cheap labour.[42]

Thus planter opposition imposed severe constraints on missionary activity. Although the Anglican body opened an infant school for Indians in Georgetown in 1850, it was another decade before they made grants to seven "coolie" schools on estates in Berbice;[43] and it was only in 1862, 17 years after large-scale immigration from India had begun, that they appointed their first missionary to the Indians.[44] During the 1870s, however, they increased their efforts, and in conjunction with the proprietor of Plantation Bel Air in Demerara, they established a "coolie" mission there to convert both Indians and Chinese, and to train some as catechists and interpreters.[45] The Anglicans seemed to be more active among the Chinese largely on account of the tireless work of the Chinese missionary, Wu-Tai-Kam (1864–67). It was in fact on the recommendation of the Anglican bishop that the legislature granted the Chinese immigrants the land for settlement up the Demerara River in 1865.[46] Similarly, it was on a grant of land from the Anglican body on which the first Chinese church was erected in 1874–75 in Georgetown.[47]

The only other missionary body which made any real effort to work among these immigrants before 1890 was the

Wesleyan Methodists.[48] In fact, they were the first to appoint a special missionary to the Indians as early as 1852.[49] His untimely death three years later created a vacuum which was not adequately filled until the appointment of another full time missionary in 1860.[50] Nevertheless, such a one-man approach generally adopted towards the task of missionary work among the immigrants was hopelessly inadequate for promoting value consensus especially in face of an ever-increasing influx of fresh Indians.

This was most vividly demonstrated in the area of schooling. In 1860 the inspector of schools noted that the vast majority of immigrant children were totally without schooling.[51] Although in 1870 the planters claimed that there were 50 "coolie" schools on the estates, albeit attended by only 1,053 Indian and 63 Chinese children, while another 192 immigrant children reputedly attended village schools; the Anglican missionary pointed to the existence of only 19 immigrant schools in operation.[52] Certainly the 1870 commission of inquiry was highly critical of the patent neglect of schooling for immigrant children.[53] Consequently the 1873 immigration ordinance prohibited the indenturing of children between ages 10–15 if the planter made no arrangements for their schooling.[54] The 1876 compulsory education ordinance furthermore required plantation managers to obtain a proficiency certificate from the teacher indicating regular attendance at school before employing a minor between 10–12 years old; it also prohibited the employment of children under nine.[55]

Still the effect on the schooling of immigrant children was minimal. In fact, the introduction of compulsory schooling enraged the planters who stood to lose valuable labour, and they argued that it would break down all habits of industry among the children.[56] Not surprisingly, therefore, no serious attempt was made to enforce the law on the estates.[57] Thus in 1890, as many as 43 of the 102 plantations still had no school, and in several cases where a schoolroom was provided, the necessary machinery for conducting a proper school simply did not exist.[58]

Even without planter opposition, the Indians were themselves either indifferent or opposed to schooling. Many feared that their children would be indoctrinated with Christian dogma.[59] Others considered it pointless to have their children schooled in English since they entertained intentions of returning to rural India where it would not be of much use.[60] Some, however, were pragmatic, considering that there was no harm in the children learning to read and write, provided the estate manager permitted them to go to school and it did not affect their earning capacity. If, however, the child was not earning his bitt, parents were less inclined to send him to school.[61] Hence the parents too were enraged by the 1876 compulsory schooling law.[62]

As many parents feared, the process of schooling did threaten to "de-Indianize" their children. According to Bronkhurst,

> The children in our public schools make good use of the opportunity afforded to them; they are not idle scholars, they have an aptitude for learning which is astonishing ... they see how people live. They watch them narrowly. Though they do not try to ape as some people do, they strive to imitate them in their dress and manners, desire to do what is right, and try to be respectable in their own way, as far as means will allow them to do ... they see how their parents live and act; they feel ashamed of their heathenish ways, and yet they lack moral courage and strength to break away from their influence.[63]

The effect of this assimilation of the dominant white culture, however, was unquestionably minimal since only a minute minority of Indians was exposed to the process of indoctrination in school.

Indian immigrants proved highly resistant to missionary proselytization as well. Their general reaction varied from cold indifference to hostile opposition.[64] The Muslim would hardly even condescend to listen to a Christian missionary,[65] and for the Hindu, conversion meant an automatic loss of caste and ostracism by his friends and relatives.[66] Although the regular missionaries to the Indians were conversant in Hindi and Tamil, the multitude of Indian languages or dialects posed a serious obstacle to easy communication.[67] Too few to cope adequately with the great mass of Indian immigrants, the missionaries also had to compete against the Brahmin and Muslim clerics who exercised enormous influence over their followers.[68] The result, therefore, was that the Indian section remained culturally distinct and differentiated from the host society with which they shared precious little in terms of values, beliefs or cultural practices. This might appear to endorse Brathwaite's idea of "incomplete creolization"; but in reality the case of the Indians seems to be more indicative of creolization hardly begun rather than incomplete.

Nevertheless, considerable success appears to have been achieved among the Chinese. Several of them had apparently been converted Christians even before their arrival in the colony.[69] Besides, the fact that Wu-Tai-Kam was ethnically Chinese and was conversant in their languages was a decided advantage.[70] Even after his departure in 1867, several Chinese were converted[71] and during the 1870s they established a number of Chinese language churches in different parts of the colony.[72] Similarly, in spite of the very limited schooling facilities on the plantations, the Chinese evinced a keen desire for education both in English and Chinese, and reportedly made very good progress.[73] Although the Chinese immigrants were, therefore, receptive to both Christian proselytization and schooling, their efforts to confine their involvement within an ethnically exclusive environment (e.g. separate churches) and by the medium of the Chinese language, suggests that very definite limits were imposed on the implanting and acceptance of the idea of white cultural superiority. Thus if one can stretch Brathwaite's *creole* concept, the case of the Chinese suggests that creolization was not just incomplete but minimal.

It is evident, therefore, that the cultural factor did not prove highly effective as an integrative element among the Indians and Chinese sections, though one might claim some success among the Creoles. It is thus difficult to make a claim for the stabilizing and uniting of the total society around a common set of shared values. Certainly the planters and several senior colonial officials were not convinced of the likelihood of achieving this, and were not prepared to rely on the cultural factor to preserve white dominance. Rather these "hard-nosed" realists were more inclined to place emphasis on the coercive power of the state.[74] Thus, as Adamson has noted, expenditure on education never exceeded 7.5 percent of the total annual expenditure, whereas that on the police and judiciary varied from 14 to 25 percent,[75] without taking into account expenditure on the local armed forces and the imperial troops stationed in the colony.

Above all, white authorities placed great emphasis on coercion — the show and actual use of armed force — to promote social stability by instilling fear and awe of white power in the minds of the subordinate population. They never equivocated about the absolute need for military force to keep these subordinates in submission to the lawful authority of the ruling white minority.[76] On paper, the forces at their disposal were formidable indeed. They consisted of the Colonial Militia, the Police Force, the Estates Armed Force, the Volunteer Force, and the imperial troops comprised of both white regiments from Britain and the black West India Regiments.

The Militia had been in existence since 1825 and had been composed of every free adult male, which meant that it was predominantly white. As emancipation would have radically altered this composition unless a racially discriminating process of selection was employed,[77] the Militia was suspended from active service in 1838 but could be called out by proclamation whenever necessary.[78] However, the desire among the whites to have an active local military force led successive governors to seek to establish a volunteer corps through which greater selectivity could be exercised over its membership.[79] It was thus precisely to avert the obvious racial prejudices implicit in these suggestions that the imperial government recommended the adoption of financial qualifications for membership of any such force.[80]

Thus when the need for re-embodiment of the Militia arose as a result of the 1856 riots, property qualifications equivalent to those for the electoral franchise, and an income qualification of $240 per annum, were set for membership. But since the latter qualification admitted Creole mechanics and artisans to the Militia,[81] it was raised in 1857 to $350 per annum specifically to "exempt" them.[82] Amidst growing resentment of the white rank and file to the regular military drills, this "exemption" of master tradesmen was subsequently lifted in 1858.[83] Nevertheless, the Militia remained a predominantly white force.

Notwithstanding efforts to increase its strength and efficiency in 1859,[84] the Militia rapidly became defunct because of its unpopularity particularly among those whites liable to serve, as well as the business community who stood to lose the services of their clerks for drills and parades twice per week.[85] Moreover, as wealthy whites could commute their service by paying a fixed sum,[86] and the Portuguese were exempt from all military service by the 1842 Anglo-Portuguese treaty,[87] it was the less well-off whites and coloureds who bore the brunt of militia service.[88] Hence courts martial for defaulting were frequent and opposition to the Militia mounted.[89]

The result was that by 1864 active enrolment and drilling had ceased, while the corps were simultaneously depleted by the deaths and absence of some of their members from the colony. Yet the Militia still remained technically in existence, with a staff and a band supported from the public revenues.[90] Subsequent attempts to resurrect it in 1871–72 proved unsuccessful in the face of general public opposition.[91] Although legally reconstituted in 1872,[92] the Militia was never actually re-embodied.[93] Still with seven companies of 528 men in 1872,[94] and a well-equipped armoury of 530 rifles of different types and eight artillery field pieces,[95] the fact that the Militia could be called out at any time rendered it a very formidable force for suppressing the subordinate population in the event of civil disorder.

The Estates' Armed Force, established in 1856 in the wake of the disturbances, suffered a similar fate to the Militia. Composed of a list of persons hand-picked by the planters and rubber-stamped by the governor, this force likewise consisted mainly of whites drawn from among the estate managers and overseers, with a few trusted Creole master tradesmen and other employees or estate residents.[96] Here again, because of the dislike of the white rank and file for regular drills, this force was practically defunct by 1861. But it nevertheless resulted in strengthening the security and coercive power of the planters on individual estates by placing at their disposal a small armoury on each plantation[97] which could be used to 'pop down fellows who may be shying stones at us from the other side of the trench'.[98]

The virtual disappearance of the Estates' Armed Force and the Militia by the 1870s meant that there was no local white military force in the colony precisely at a time when the immigrant population was showing disturbing signs of restlessness. The emphasis placed on coercion by the dominant whites to maintain stability thus led to their establishment of a Volunteer Force in 1878.[99] By the mid-1880s this force numbered 264 members in Georgetown and New Amsterdam,[100] and although it declined after 1885,[101] it was sufficiently strong in 1889 to assist in the suppression of the riots in Georgetown.[102]

Despite their dependence on coercion and the show of force to maintain stability, the white minority was never sufficiently powerful by itself to guarantee its own security. Instead, whites were forced to rely for tranquility both on the military support of the imperial power as well as, ironically, on the very subordinate population whom they sought to coerce and subjugate. Thus it was the Police Force, established in 1839,[103] and transformed into an armed quasi-military body in 1845,[104] which formed the only permanently operational local force whites could turn to for protection. This body steadily increased in strength to 763 men in 1891, of whom 80 percent were black and coloured.[105] It was supported in its civil duties by a Rural Constabulary, established in 1849, which was recruited from among the Creoles.[106]

Although predominantly black, the white authorities had full control over the recruitment, training, disciplining and deployment of the Police Force, and consequently stored great confidence in its loyalty, reliability and efficiency as a coercive body. This control over and confidence in the Police Force was underlined by the fact that for the most part the officer corps was white, under the command of an inspector-general. As late as 1887 it was made up exclusively of ten white officers; the other 20 whites (inclusive of four Portuguese) in the rank and file were greatly outnumbered by an overwhelming, though not homogeneous, black and coloured majority. It was indeed noticeable that the 249 Barbadians and 52 other West Indians comprised the majority (48.1 percent) of the force's strength, while the local Creoles numbered 204 (32.6 percent). Indian policemen numbered only 67 (10.7 percent at a time when the Indian population was about 38 percent of the total).[107]

It was also very revealing that the greatest increases to the numerical strength of the police were made during periods of social instability such as the "rates war" in the villages during the 1860s, and the Indian unrest on the plantations in the 1870s. Not surprisingly, expenditure on the police which stood at £19,363 in 1850 rose to £33,554 by 1868, and was further boosted in the troubled 1870s by about 50 percent to over £50,000 per year.[108] Such expenditure permitted the police to be armed up to 70 percent of their strength by 1887[109] and, as one attorney-general noted, almost turned them into a standing army.[110]

The need to instil a feeling of awe in the subordinate population necessitated the arming and organising of the police as a military force. For at least two years after in the 1856 riots, for instance, armed policemen could be seen at all hours in Georgetown as if martial law had been declared.[111] Similarly, they were used to suppress the disturbances in the villages during the sixties;[112] and they were the main force employed to suppress the Indian disturbances on the plantations, leading in 1872 to the killing of five Indians at Plantation Devonshire Castle in Essequibo.[113] By 1880 the armed police were considered the only local force capable of dealing with the 80,000 Indian immigrants who, with their agricultural implements, were regarded as a fearsome armed group.[114]

The arming of the police was thus considered crucial to the preservation of social stability. It was as much intended as a deterrent as an active means of suppression.[115] As the inspector-general stated in 1882: 'the mere fact of an armed police force putting in an appearance in a district which is in a disturbed state is now sufficient of itself to restore order, while the appearance of an unarmed force under similar circumstances would be a signal for increased disorder ...'[116] Hence, the mere show of force was an integral aspect of this coercive approach. Jenkins thus wrote in 1870:

> They used frequently to be turned out to parade in the Georgetown streets, dressed in a neat uniform, their white pugeries framing their faces, a band of Fifers preceding them; ... and at the head of his men, on a necessarily capacious steed, the stalwart Inspector-General. As I used to watch this strange procession, and saw the fiery sun gleaming along the polished barrels of the rifles, I could not resist an uncomfortable questioning whether the system really required this sort of argument to adapt to the reasons of those whom it chiefly concerned.[117]

The white colonists also enjoyed the protection of the imperial troops consisting both of British regiments and the West India regiments. But the great distrust which they evinced towards the latter was in stark contrast to their confidence in the Police Force, though both were predominantly black under white command. The difference lay in the fact that they exercised no control whatever over the recruitment and disciplining of the West India regiments which, after 1844, were composed increasingly of West Indian Creoles as opposed to Africans as before. They argued that the local recruits from the Caribbean colonies were the most idle, dissolute, worthless and least intelligent of their class who preferred military service to steady industry in agriculture and other occupational pursuits.[118]

Whites believed that the discipline of these black troops depended entirely on the direct personal influence of individual commanding officers, and could therefore break down at any moment. Repeated violent clashes with the police merely underlined this view of the basic lack of discipline of the black troops, and it was feared that certain "ruffian" elements in the local Creole population might take advantage of these fights between the police and the troops to foment disorder. In addition, the close fraternization between the black troops and the Creole population, particularly the women, was cause for great anxiety and apprehension among the whites. They feared that in the probable absence of white forces, the disaffected elements of the Creole population, particularly the press, would attempt to politicize the black soldiers and make them fully aware of the power in their hands, and thus induce them to mutiny.[119]

Not surprisingly, therefore, the whites were very troubled over the presence of the black West India regiments, especially if there were no white troops to keep them in check. In 1852, the withdrawal of white troops from the colony on account of a yellow fever epidemic led to demands for the withdrawal of the black troops as well.[120] But this pre-existing racial distrust and apprehension[121] turned into morbid fear and trepidation after the mutiny of Sepoy troops in India in 1857. Although the black troops had been welcomed and admittedly performed commendably in suppressing the 1856 disturbances which had led to their being retained in the colony,[122] by 1858 there were strident demands for their immediate replacement by white soldiers.[123] Governor Wodehouse even warned of a very fearful catastrophe if the lives and property of the whites were made to depend entirely on the protection of the blacks and coloureds.[124]

The white authorities consistently adhered to the principle that either the black troops should be totally replaced by white troops or, at least be counterbalanced by an equal number of the latter.[125] To withdraw only white troops, whatever the reason, was considered tantamount to leaving the white colonists 'at the mercy of the blacks'.[126] Many influential whites even preferred the withdrawal of all troops, thus leaving the colony entirely to its own military resources, rather than being left with only the black troops.[127]

Governor Wodehouse admitted in 1855 that the presence of the white troops 'is really of much consequence, politically and socially'.[128] This view was shared by successive governors and colonial officials[129] who agreed that no arrangement made by the colonial government could fully compensate for the want of "moral influence" which the mere presence of a body of European troops exercised over the mass of the population. It was feared that as soon as the white troops were withdrawn, the nascent feeling among the black and coloured majority that the colony was theirs, and that the whites must be driven out, would assert itself in acts of violence and outrage. It was again Governor Wodehouse who, in 1859, demonstrated the vital importance of the coercive influence of the white troops to the stability of the colonial society when he asserted:

> If all military protection is to be withdrawn, how ... is the administration of the governments of these colonies to be carried on in subordination to that of England. How is the governor to enforce obedience to his authority or to the laws, whenever they may be opposed to the wishes of the people for the time being. And without such obedience in what would consist their allegiance to the Queen. Not one of these West Indian colonies could stand alone.[130]

By the end of the 19th century the social conditions which necessitated the security arrangements described above had been significantly modified. Perhaps the most important change was that the racial factor was now less of a deterrent to the entry of the Creoles into the colony's elite. This meant that the issue of security and stability was considered more along lines of class interest than along purely racial lines. The presence of white forces, therefore, ceased to be a matter of sheer social and political necessity, though the continued emphasis on coercion to hold the differentiated social sections together led to a demand for the maintenance of an imperial military presence.[131] This explains why the colonial authorities moved to retain at least one company of the black West Indian regiment, even to the extent of paying the full cost of supporting it.[132] But the unwavering decision of the imperial government to station the troops in St. Lucia and Jamaica[133] eventually forced the colonial government to rely entirely on local forces after 1891.[134]

The persistence of rigid lines of social segmentation particularly between the Creoles and the differentiated categories of Indians and Chinese, the perpetuation of social and political inequalities both along class and racial lines, and continued racial conflict, all combined to preserve the emphasis on coercion as a principal instrument of social stability and unity resulting in the reorganization of the local military forces in 1891[135] to replace the imperial troops. The armed Police were constituted as the main security force; and by more rigorous drilling and training, it was intended to make them a more efficient *military* body.[136] The strength of this force was increased by a third from 575 in 1890 to 763 in 1891, while expenditure on it increased from £47,131 to £51,141 in the same period.[137] The Rural Constabulary was brought more directly under the control of the police high command, and were better trained and disciplined in order to make them an efficient auxiliary to the police in the performance of ordinary duties, as well as in assuming normal police duties in time of civil disorder.[138]

As an additional deterrent, a Volunteer Militia Force was established to serve as a military auxiliary to the police in suppressing civil disturbances.[139] Consisting of an artillery unit, a battalion of seven infantry companies, and a band of musicians, the active force was comprised of 266 men in 1891. But there was also a reserve consisting of all persons liable to serve who were not in the active force. The qualifications for membership were equated with those for the elective franchise under the 1891 political reform law.[140] This meant that the principle of equating political with military power was preserved; and the biracial middle-class interests which acceded to political power during the 1890s were expected to rally in defence of that class-determined power position. No longer, therefore, was social stability perceived solely in terms of the preservation of the dominance of any single racial section, but increasingly in terms of the defence of certain broader class interests without regard to race. This situation more or less conformed to the idea which Secretary of State Lytton had advocated ever since 1858,[141] but which the dominant whites were not ready to contemplate. Still the fact that considerable emphasis continued to be placed on coercion to ensure stability despite the changing socio-political situation points to a persistent absence of value consensus among the differentiated subordinate "classes" or "segments" to integrate the whole society.

Thus, if any one factor can be identified as the primary element of social stability and unity in 19th century Guyanese society, it is that of coercion. Far greater emphasis was placed on it by the ruling white minority than on any other factor for the preservation of the *status quo*, and the perpetuation of white dominance. Nevertheless, the economic, cultural and biological factors did perform integrative functions in the society with varying degrees of effectiveness particularly between black and white. The accession of Creoles to professional and other white-collar and skilled occupations eventually led to the development of common economic class interests with the whites. Similarly their gradual assimilation of white culture, albeit with varying degrees of perfection, created a consensus of values, symbols and ideals between these two sections. Finally, biological mixing was promoted by a gradual increase of interracial marriages between white men and Creole women especially in the last decades of the century, although the actual number may not have been large.

The integrative effects of these three factors, however, were limited mainly to the white and Creole sections. The Indian and Chinese generally remained racially and culturally differentiated from the rest of the society, while the Portuguese remained a distinct social and cultural section as well. The total society remained both highly segmented along racial lines and (consequently) inherently unstable, with a positive value placed on coercion in order to hold it together.

The continued reliance on coercion in determining power and status in the colonial society despite the clear shift from purely racial to class considerations tends to favour the analysis of Raymond Smith who has viewed the use of force as supportive of cultural integration or creolization. But on the other hand, it could be argued that coercion continued to be emphasized precisely because the society remained highly sectionalized along racial and cultural lines; and furthermore that the incorporation of the acculturated Creole elites into the upper societal levels merely broadened the racial base of the dominant cultural minority section. Hence the subordinate masses (Creoles, Chinese and Indians) remained sharply differentiated culturally and institutionally from the new dominant biracial cultural section. This would signify a persistence of the type of social and cultural pluralism defined by M.G. Smith.

Yet it must also be recalled that the subordinate Creole masses imbibed European religious and cultural values, and practices, even though their assimilation of these was by no means complete (they became somewhat culturally ambivalent). Nevertheless a Euro-African *creole* cultural continuum could be said to have developed, which permitted the permeation of shared values from those who occupied one pole (the whites and Creole elites) to those at the other pole (the rural Creole peasants.) Outside of that framework lay the immigrants, particularly the Indians, who remained very distinctly differentiated racially and culturally from the rest of the society. One concludes, therefore, that the total society appeared to exhibit simultaneously very clearly distinguishable features of both class stratification, as well as racial and cultural segmentation signifying structural and segmental pluralism.

CHAPTER 10

CONCLUSION: RACE, POWER AND SOCIAL SEGMENTATION

This study has focussed not only on a number of events and issues pertaining to 19th century Guyanese society, but also on the wider theoretical implications relating to form, structure, and development of composite colonial societies in general, and to the theoretical debate on social stratification versus pluralism in particular.

It has been shown that the principal social effect of emancipation in Guyana was the ethnic diversification of the society. The yearning of the ex-slaves for social and economic advancement and independence, and the availability of land, led to a significant decline and a growing irregularity in their supply of labour to the plantations. To preserve the primacy and profitability of the plantation system, therefore, it was found necessary to import immigrant labour from available sources — whether West Africa, the Caribbean, Europe and the Mediterranean, India, or China. The resulting multi-racialism in the colonial society was thus a direct consequence of the continued predominance of the plantations after emancipation.

What was striking about this new societal development was the fact that it was accompanied by a high degree of social segmentation. For most of the post-emancipation 19th century, the constituent social categories were sharply differentiated by race and culture. There was also a strong tendency towards residential separation along racial lines on the plantations, in racially exclusive villages, or in different sections or "street enclaves" of the towns. This is not suggestive of forced segregation as in the United States or South Africa, since there were no laws stipulating that division in Guyana. In contrast, there was always a fair degree of contiguity in the towns where literally just around the corner from a mainly white residential street, one might find a predominantly Creole street. Thus none of the main areas of white residence in Georgetown e.g. Kingston, Cummingsburg, and along the Brickdam in Stabroek, was segregated.[1] Similarly the Chinese and Indian urban enclaves were centred on, but not confined to, one street e.g., Lombard Street in Charlestown (Chinese), and Alexander Street in the Lacytown/Bourda area (Indian). Both of these were located in the midst of otherwise Creole districts.[2] Thus there was racial separation, but not mandated segregation.

Similarly, it has been demonstrated that there was a tendency for economic activity to take on the appearance of occupational specialization along racial lines. Whites generally held leading positions in government and the Civil Service, in plantation and commercial management, the professions and the church; blacks and coloureds worked as hired agricultural and other unskilled workers, peasant farmers, domestic servants and artisans, and in junior white collar jobs; Portuguese immigrants were essentially retail traders and shopkeepers; and Indian and Chinese immigrants were mainly indentured agricultural workers and small-farmers. This pattern, however, became far less clearcut towards the end of the century particularly as coloureds and blacks entered the professions, church and government, and as Indians and Chinese entered commerce.

The historical evidence is thus overwhelming in support of the hypothesis that race was the primary factor of social segmentation in post-emancipation Guyana, and that it was mainly responsible for the isolation and insulation of the several social groups behind ethnic boundaries, across which there was very little social interaction. Consequently, interracial marriages and miscegenation were rare, while other forms of social and cultural interaction were restricted to peripheral activities such as the public celebration of ethnic festivals. Intersectional cooperation, however, occurred in the economic sphere where a high degree of inter-dependence and symbiosis was inevitable given the occupational "specialization". While competition did arise (for example, between Creoles and Asian immigrants in the plantation labour market, and between the former and

Portuguese immigrants in the retail trade) nevertheless the quest for economic gain was the only factor which applied in common to all the constituent social categories. Beyond that there was no common social will or value system shared by *all* segments of the society. Even though at emancipation the Creoles were arguably already in the process of assimilating white culture through the powerful religious and cultural influence of the white missionaries, there was no shared system of values which integrated the new immigrant groups into the colonial society.

One of the most critical features of the social order was the domination of the political system by the small white minority. In the context of a colonial (and) plantation society, the exercise of real political power was monopolized by the planter class and the imperial government represented by appointed officials. The attitude and role of the imperial government was critical in preserving white social and political dominance in the colonial society. Racial considerations were also vital in determining both the political pre-eminence of the white planters and in retaining the supreme legislative power of the imperial Crown since the Creole majority was not considered sufficiently intelligent or civilized to exercise political power. The dominant white plantocracy were thus allowed to exercise state power, subject only to the authority of the Crown, to perpetuate their own hegemony by seeking to deny the non-white subordinate categories political rights and privileges as equal colonial subjects i.e., the vote and membership in the colonial political institutions. Likewise, the latter were denied the opportunities to organize themselves as corporate groups with competent leadership capable of effective political action, as their aborted efforts at local village administration demonstrated.

The ruling white minority moreover employed the apparatus of the colonial state in a systematically repressive manner to subjugate the non-white subordinate majority. Thus the Crown lands' laws and regulations were designed to confine the Creoles and Indians to the plantation belt and so limit their economic opportunities; the village laws and rate system imposed a stultifying economic burden on the peasant/small-farming sector, and subjected the Creole villagers to the direct political control of the white colonial government; high taxation was calculated to suppress the Creoles economically, and to force them to depend on plantation labour for survival; and the harsh indentureship system was intended to subjugate the Indian and Chinese immigrants and to entrench their dependence on the plantations.

Subject only to the authority of the imperial Crown, the state became the expression of the political will of the planter class through which they were able to institutionalize social and political inequalities designed to preserve and perpetuate their dominance in the colonial society. An important element of their continued domination was the maintenance of the numerical proportion of the whites within the total population. This was done by the introduction of Portuguese immigrants either free of or with minimal contractual obligations, largely on racial grounds, and the assistance given to them by way of discriminatory licences and easy credit to attain dominance in the retail trade. The Portuguese thereby achieved rapid economic and social mobility which enabled them to perform a role of secondary colonists, but which also singled them out as a distinct social and cultural section, often the object of scorn by the less favoured.

This study has also demonstrated that both racial segmentation and the structural inequalities which underlined the system of white domination were conducive to social instability and conflict. These were perennial problems in the society both at an individual and collective level, and these often assumed violent forms. Because of the general absence of societal consensus embracing all the constituent social groups, great emphasis was placed on coercion to stabilize and unite the total society. Economic interdependence was to a lesser degree a contributing factor to cohesion, while towards the end of the century the gradual development of value consensus between white and black moved Guyana a step further toward unity.

Racially determined social segmentation, economic "specialization" along ethnic lines, political dominance by a small racial or cultural minority (bolstered by the imperial power), differential incorporation of the racially differentiated subordinate majority, emphasis on coercion for societal stability — all these are symptomatic of structural pluralism. But it would be premature to classify 19th century Guyanese society as plural without taking full account of the indicators of social change and integration which crystallized in the political reforms of the 1890s. Despite racial discrimination, blacks and coloureds were able through education and technical training to enter high status professions and occupations by which they achieved considerable social mobility. At the same time, this process accelerated their assimilation of creolized white culture which, in turn, gained limited acceptance into white social circles for some.

The gradual breakdown of the racial barrier by individual black and coloured elites, further demonstrated by the increase in white-coloured marriages, facilitated their incorporation into the more privileged sectors of the colonial society on a basis of equality; and this was accorded full recognition by the political changes of the nineties. By this time less emphasis was placed on particularistic-ascriptive criteria such as race and colour for determining social status, and more importance was attached to universalistic-achievement criteria such as education, occupation, wealth and culture. This indicated a process of structural and organisational change in the social and political framework from an essentially white dominated, racially segmented system towards an integrated stratified order based on shared economic and social class interests and cultural values.

This is *not* to suggest or suppose that race ceased to be an important independent factor of social differentiation or that the structural inequalities were removed. Certainly the Creole elite formed only a very small minority of the Creole section, the vast majority of which remained socially, politically and economically disprivileged and disadvantaged. In addition, while the settlement of Indian and Chinese immigrants from the 1870s onwards signified their desire to be incorporated as full members of the colonial society, and a tiny minority began to achieve a modicum of socio-economic mobility by acquiring wealth as traders, they too were subjected to similar structural inequalities. But more significantly perhaps, they remained as sharply differentiated racially and culturally from the other ethnic groups as when they first arrived in the colony over a half century before, a condition further accentuated by their pattern of settlement into racially exclusive villages. Thus they continued to form distinct social sections behind firm racial and cultural boundaries. In this context, therefore, the total society remained ethnically segmented to a considerable degree.

This conclusion is somewhat at variance with that of Walter Rodney who emphasized the similarities in experiences and responses of the subordinate population to the exploitation of the planters. In stressing the shared work experience on the plantations and the process of "creolization" (defined as an "indigenizing experience"),[3] he tended to minimize the degree of ethnic segmentation among these social sections. Clearly interculturation occurred, but as this study demonstrates, it is rather doubtful that by the end of the 19th century, the creolization of Indian immigrants was as advanced as Rodney suggested. On the contrary, it is apparent from the data presented here that such interculturation as there was among the subordinate sections was restricted to the peripheral aspects of cultural life, for example, the public celebration of ethnic festivals, dress, food, and so on. It did *not* extend to the core culture of each ethnic section, for example, religious beliefs, marriage and family, ideas and values. Rodney himself was obliged to recognize the social reality of ethnic segmentation among the subordinate population, although he chose to deal with it as the consequence of insufficient cultural convergence (which if successful would transcend racial boundaries and thus lead to the development of a common working class consciousness[4]), rather than as a racially (and culturally) determined social divergence.

Rodney is not alone in downplaying race as a key factor in explaining socio-political developments in 19th century Guyana. Adamson refers to the traditional colour-class correlates in the structure of Caribbean society, but admits that they are not homologous and that the social matrix is further complicated by the presence of large Indian populations especially in Guyana and Trinidad.[5] However, he treats the differences between the Indians and the constituent groups of the host society as cultural rather than racial in base,[6] and thus sees 'a society in which ethnic difference superimposed on class distinction set the subcultures of the oppressed at each others' throats'.[7]

Another important observation suggested by the evidence presented here is that it is unproductive to look statically at Guyana in the 19th century, as the society was constantly undergoing change. Toward the end of the century, Guyana exhibited structural and organizational features which were not exclusively characteristic of either plural or stratified societies, but a varied combination of different elements of both societal models. By the 1890s, the old biracial three-tier *creole* social matrix was clearly modified into a socio-cultural continuum by shared creolized values, mores, beliefs, etc. in which the more prestigious "Euro" forms were to be found at one pole (among the dominant whites and acculturated Creole elites), with the discredited "Afro" forms at the other pole (predominantly among the black rural villagers). This clearly approximates the class stratification theses advanced by Braithwaite, Brathwaite, Hall, R.T. Smith, *et al.* and does not correspond with the plural model.

On the other hand, when the immigrants, are added to that societal matrix, the application of a pure stratification model is questionable. Though white and from the same broad western European cultural tradition, the Portuguese were sufficiently differentiated from the dominant whites socially and culturally to be treated as a separate ethnic group. Social mobility was facilitated by their acquisition of wealth mainly from commerce. However, they exhibited a strong tendency to preserve in-group socio-cultural "associations" and activities, including endogamous marriage, ethnic clubs, poor relief societies and schools, and ethnic religio-cultural festivities, all centred around their "ethnic" Roman Catholic religion, the Portuguese language, and a strong primary identification with Portugal (i.e., Portuguese nationality).

Since the Portuguese, in racial and socio-economic terms, occupied a position approximating that of the middle status British whites, the relationship between these two groups approximated a condition of cultural pluralism, while simultaneously they stood in a position of a subordinate class in relation to the planters. In turn, they were sharply differentiated both racially and culturally from the Creole section with very little social interaction except literally in the "market-place" (the shop). In relation to the latter, therefore, a condition of segmental pluralism obtained, although as a group they enjoyed higher status than the Creoles on account of their racial affinity to the dominant whites. The complexity here lies in the fact that a single immigrant group had in effect different structural relationships with the racially differentiated "classes" within the integrated *creole* social matrix.

The analysis is further complicated by the inclusion into this schema of Indian and Chinese immigrants who were sharply differentiated racially and culturally from all the abovementioned groups, and thus constituted distinct ethnic sections. The legal requirement to serve a period of indenture signified their differential incorporation in an extreme way which, together with their racial and cultural differentiation, indicated the existence of a condition of structural or hierarchical pluralism. The termination of the reindenture process, however, brought about a gradual change in their status approximately parallel to that of the lower class of Creoles. Thus the label of segmental pluralism seems appropriate here, although in relation to the dominant whites the original characterization of hierarchical pluralism is more apt. Once again, therefore, one could speak of the coexistence of different structural relationships between an immigrant group and the different "classes" comprising the integrated *creole* matrix, as in the case of the Portuguese.

A number of theoretical considerations, therefore, emerge from this study of 19th century Guyanese society. The most obvious is that neither the theories of stratificaion nor of pluralism are sufficient to explain the changes which composite societies undergo over a significant time period: nor can they, for that matter, predict the myriad forms which (as in the case of Guyana) such changes may take. Indeed a plausible hypothesis based on the Guyanese experience would suggest that a plural society is "normally" liable to experience a gradual transition towards a more integrated class-based social order over a protracted period of time, based on the growth of shared values. But the modalities and forms of such change are likely to vary considerably from one society to the next depending on such variables as population composition, both in terms of numbers and ethnicity; the distribution and use of state power in creating and maintaining sectional inequalities; the existence of an ideology which favours racial and cultural integration or separation, and so on.

No exclusivity can be claimed, therefore, for either pluralism or stratification because combinations of the features and characteristics of both societal models may frequently be present. In fact the development of such unpredictable structural complexity is one of the hallmarks of social change in composite societies such as Guyana (and elsewhere in the Caribbean), and demonstrates that the two theoretical positions, different though they may be, are by no means incompatible with each other. The only analytical difficulty is that the variable and unpredictable combination of features manifested in such societies makes it difficult to formulate a comprehensive general theory to deal with them as they undergo structural change.

That does not mean that no theoretical generalizations are possible. The mere fact that one can posit a gradual progression in societal development from a plural to an integrated class structure under "normal" circumstances is suggestive of the fact that these two divergent societal models must be "ideal" types which coexist along a broad societal continuum. This perception, as used here, is markedly different from van den Berghe's notion of a continuum ranging from "maximal" to "minimal" pluralism which incorporates certain types of stratified societies.[8] The problem with that concept is that it renders the use of the term "plural" somewhat nebulous.

In the present conceptualization of a societal continuum, race would be a key independent factor in determining the structure and form of the societal type and its position along the continuum. (This differs greatly from M.G. Smith's plural model as he devalues the importance of the racial factor). Since most composite societies are likely to display various combinations of the features and characteristics of each broad societal type, each society must be examined separately to determine its classification and proper location along the continuum. Two major criteria are important here: (a) determining which features and characteristics are operative; and (b) establishing the size of the ethnically differentiated sections and the degree to which they fundamentally influence the overall form and structure of the total society. Thus, for instance, a biracial society with a small, yet differentiated (racially and culturally), subordinate minority may not be classified as "plural" because the influence of that minority is minimal on the overall social structure. On the other hand, a society with a similarly differentiated but larger subordinate minority (or majority) must certainly be classified as "plural". Of course, the greater the number of sharply differentiated ethnic groups, the more pluralistic the society would be.

Using these criteria, Guyanese society c.1890 can now be classified on the hypothetical societal continuum. It is clear that it displayed a complex combination of various features of both societal models. The host (*creole*) society, comprising British whites, coloureds and blacks, was integrated around a set of shared values, incomplete though that process undoubtedly was. Yet the immigrants, notably Portuguese, Indians, and Chinese, were variably differentiated from the *creole* matrix, culturally and/or racially. The result was the complex coexistence of different conditions of pluralism — structural, segmental, and cultural which was arrived at as consequence of the changes undergone in the social structure after emancipation. Taken together, however, these "immigrants" amounted to 43.6 percent of the total population — a very substantial minority. Thus one is dealing with a situation in which almost a moiety of the total population was sharply differentiated from the constituent groups within the integrated *creole* sector.

On that basis alone, Guyanese society c.1890 should be placed at the plural pole of our societal continuum, even though there was clear evidence of significant socio-cultural integration and the development of class stratification within the *creole* matrix. But a society that is so structurally divided, "in half" so to speak, cannot be regarded as integrated. This division was manifested in the persistent structural inequalities among the ethnic sections, continued social segmentation along racial lines especially with respect to the immigrants, the prevalence of racial tension and conflict both at the individual and collective levels, the continued emphasis and dependence on coercion to maintain social stability and unity, and a general absence of consensus among *all* ethnic sections within the total society. The persistence and salience of these pluralistic features signify that despite significant changes which occurred within the social system after emancipation, Guyanese society towards the end of the 19th century has to be classified as being closer to the plural model.

This, however, is not suggestive of a fixed situation. As Dale Bisnauth's analysis of the Indian community in the period up to 1930 implies,[9] the plural structure which existed at the end of the century underwent further significant change, with the gradual integration of the Indian section, moving it towards a more fully integrated class stratified social order. One suspects, however, that as for the 19th century, further historical analysis of the 20th century society would no doubt reveal similar admixtures of the features of both models, though perhaps favouring a greater degree of integration.

Finally, it is evident from this discussion on Guyana that social science theory can be successfully applied to a corpus of historical data with beneficial results. Not only does it allow for heuristic organization of the data, but it enables the historian to take a processual view of the development of a society. As Guyana's complex societal structure demonstrates, there is constant change in the historical past. Stepping out of the bounds of static analysis to describe that ongoing differentiation is immeasurably advanced by utilizing already existing theories explored by anthropologists and sociologists. Borrowing the tools of other disciplines does not detract from the "truth" of historical data; rather it allows us to view that data in fresh, new ways which may be a revelation (if not revolutionary).

NOTES

Abbreviations

AA	American Anthropologist
BECA	Bulletin of Eastern Caribbean Affairs
BELC	Boletin de Estudios Latinoamericanos y del Caribe
BG	Berbice Gazette
BJS	British Journal of Sociology
CA	Current Anthropology
CI	Caribbean Issues
CIS	Contributions to Indian Sociology
CO	Colonial Office papers. Great Britain
CQ	Caribbean Quarterly
CS	Caribbean Studies
CSSH	Comparative Studies in Society and History
(D)DC	(Demerara) Daily Chronicle
DT	Demerara Times
ERS	Ethnic and Racial Studies
GT	Guiana Times
IJCS	International Journal of Comparative Sociology
IM	Immigrants and Minorities
JAF	Journal of American Folklore
JCCP	Journal of Commonwealth and Comparative Politics
JCH	Journal of Caribbean History
JEH	Journal of Economic History
JHR	Jamaica Historical Review
JSH	Journal of Social History
LMS	London Missionary Society papers
MMS	(Wesleyan) Methodist Missionary Society papers
NW	New World
OG	Official Gazette, British Guiana
PA	Pacific Affairs
PP	Parliamentary Papers, Great Britain
PS	Population Studies
RG	Royal Gazette
SES	Social and Economic Studies
SJA	Southwestern Journal of Anthropology
SJ/BG	Society of Jesus papers on British Guiana
SPG	United Society for the Propagation of the Gospel papers
WIQ	West India Quarterly
WO	War Office papers. Great Britain

Introduction

1. B. Higman, 'Theory, Method and Technique in Caribbean Social History', *JCH*, 20 (1), 1985/1986.
2. D. Wood, *Trinidad in Transition* (Lond., 1968); B. Brereton, *Race Relations in Colonial Trinidad, 1870-1900* (Lond., 1979).
3. R.A.J. van Lier, *Frontier Society* (The Hague, 1972).
4. P. Curtin, *Two Jamaicas* (N.Y., 1971).
5. A.H. Adamson, *Sugar Without Slaves* (New Haven, 1972).
6. W. Rodney, *A History of the Guyanese Working People, 1881-1905* (Balt., 1981).
7. M.N. Menezes, *Scenes from the History of the Portuguese in Guyana* (Lond., 1986). Unfortunately thus book appeared too late to be treated in depth in this study.
8. J. Mandle, *The Plantation Economy: Population and Economic Change in Guyana, 1838-1960* (Philadelphia, 1973).
9. M. Shahabuddeen, *Constitutional Development in Guyana, 1621-1978* (Georgetown, 1978).
10. A. Young, *The Approaches to Local Self-Government in British Guiana* (Lond., 1958).
11. T. Ramnarine, 'The Growth of the East Indian Community in British Guiana, 1880-1920', D. Phil. thesis, Sussex University, 1977.
12. D Bisnauth, 'The East Indian Immigrant Society in British Guiana, 1891-1930', Ph.D. thesis, University of the West Indies, 1977.
13. L. Potter, 'Internal Migration and Resettlement of East Indians in Guyana, 1870-1920', Ph.D. dissertation, McGill University, 1975.
14. M. Wagner, 'Structural Pluralism and the Portuguese in Nineteenth Century British Guiana: A Study in Historical Geography', Ph.d. dissertation, McGill University, 1975.,
15. R.J. Moore, 'East Indians and Negroes in British Guiana, 1838-1880', D. Phil. thesis, Sussex University, 1970.
16. P.D. Fraser, 'Education and Social Values in British Guiana, 1870-1914', D. Phil. thesis, Sussex University, 1977.
17. Higman, *loc. cit.*
18. *Ibid.*
19. *Ibid.*
20. S. Hall, 'Pluralism, Race and Class in Caribbean Society', in *Race and Class in Post-Colonial Society*, (Paris, UNESCO, 1977); and his 'Race, Articulation and Societies Structured in Dominance', in *Sociological Theories: Race and Colonialism* (Paris, UNESCO, 1980).
21. R.T. Smith, 'Race, Class and Political Conflict in a Post-colonial Society', in *Small States and Segmented Societies*, S.G. Neuman (ed.), (N.Y., 1976); and his 'Race and Class in the Post-Emancipation Caribbean', in *Racism and Colonialism*, Robert Ross (ed.), (The Hague, 1982).
22. H. Hoetink, 'Resource Competition, Monopoly and Socio-racial Diversity', in *Ethnicity and Resource Competition in Plural Societies*, L. Despres (ed.), (The Hague, 1975); and his '"Race" and Colour in the Caribbean', in *Caribbean Contours*, S.W. Mintz and S. Price (eds.), (Balt., 1985).
23. L. Despres, 'Ethnicity and Ethnic Group Relations in Guyana', in *The New Ethnicity*, J.W. Bennett, (ed.), (N.Y., 1975); 'Ethnicity and Resource Competition in Guyana', and 'Toward a Theory of Ethnic Phenomena',

both in *Ethnicity and Resource Competition in Plural Societies, supra cit.*
24. C. Stone, *Stratification and Political Change in Trinidad and Jamaica* (Calif., 1972); and his *Class, Race and Political Behaviour in Urban Jamaica* (Kgn., 1973).
25. M. Cross, 'Colonialism and Ethnicity: A Theory and Comparative Case Study', *ERS*, 1 (1), 1978.
26. A. Kuper, *Changing Jamaica* (Lond., 1976); and his 'Race, Class and Culture in Jamaica', in *Race and Class in Post-Colonial Society, supra cit.*
27. P. Hintzen, 'Capitalism, Socialism and Socio-Political Confrontation in Multi-Racial Developing States: A Comparison of Guyana and Trinidad', Ph.D. thesis, Yale University, 1980.
28. M.G. Smith, *Culture, Race and Class in the Commonwealth Caribbean* (Kgn., 1984).

Chapter 1

1. Charles Wagley, 'Plantation America: A Culture Sphere', *Caribbean Studies: A Symposium*, Vera Rubin (ed.), (Seattle, 1960), pp. 5-7.
2. E. Padilla, 'Contemporary Social-Rural Types in the Caribbean', *loc. cit.*, p. 23.
3. Edgar Thompson, 'The Plantation as a Social System', *Plantation Systems of the New World*, Soc. Sc. Monographs VII, 1959, Pan American Union, Wash., D.C., pp. 31-32.
4. E.R. Wolf & S.W. Mintz, 'Haciendas and Plantations in Middle America and the Antilles', *SES*, Sept. 1957; also S.W. Mintz, 'The Plantation as a Socio-Cultural Type', *Plantation Systems of the New World, supra cit.*, pp. 44-47.
5. Thompson, *loc. cit.*, pp. 33-34.
6. George Beckford, *Persistent Poverty* (N.Y., 1972), pp. 73-79.
7. D.M. Benn, 'The Theory of Plantation Economy and Society: A Methodological Critique', *JCCP*, XII (3), 1974, pp. 256-258.
8. Wagley, *loc. cit.*, pp. 7-8.
9. Beckford, *op. cit.*, p. 56.
10. *Ibid.*
11. *Ibid.*, pp. 64-83.
12. Leo Kuper, 'Plural Societies: Perspectives and Problems', *Pluralism in Africa*, Leo Kuper and M.G. Smith (eds.), (Berkeley, 1971), pp. 7-11.
13. J.S. Furnivall, *Colonial Policy and Practice: A Comparative Study of Burma and Netherlands India* (Lond., 1948), p. 304.
14. *Ibid.*, pp. 123, 150, and 306-312; see also his *Netherlands India: A Study of Plural Economy* (Lond., 1939). pp. 446-459.
15. J.H. Boeke, *Economics and Economic Policy of Dual Societies* (N.Y. 1953), pp. 3-4.
16. R.A.J. van Lier, *The Development and Nature of Society in the West Indies* (Amsterdam, 1950), pp. 3-4; see also his *Frontier Society* (Den Haag, 1971).
17. M.G. Smith, *The Plural Society in the British West Indies* (Berkeley, 1965), pp. 79-82.
18. M.G. Smith, 'Institutional and Political Conditions of Pluralism', in *Pluralism in Africa, supra cit.*, pp. 34-35.

19. See note 6.
20. Smith, 'Institutional and Political Conditions', *Pluralism in Africa, supra cit.*, pp. 39-52.
21. M.G. Smith, 'Some Developments in the Analytic Framework of Pluralism', in *Pluralism in Africa, supra cit.*, pp. 434-447; also his *Culture, Race and Class in the Commonwealth Caribbean* (U.W.I., Mona, 1984), pp. 28-35.
22. *Ibid.*,
23. Leo A. Despres, 'The Implications of Nationalist Politics in British Guiana for the Development of Cultural Theory', *AA*, 66 (5), Oct. 1964, pp. 1051-77; also his *Cultural Pluralism and Nationalist Politics in British Guiana* (Chicago, 1967), pp. 13-27; and his 'Anthropology, Cultural Pluralism, and the Study of Complex Societies', *CA*, 9 (1), Feb. 1968, pp. 11-15.
24. *Ibid.*
25. *Ibid.* These concepts are further applied in some of his more recent work. See, for instance, his 'Ethnic and Resource Competition in Guyanese Society', and 'Toward a Theory of Ethnic Phenomena' in *Ethnicity and Resource Competition in Plural Societies*, Leo. A. Despres (ed.), (The Hague, 1975); and 'Ethnicity and Ethnic Group Relations in Guyana', in *The New Ethnicity: Perspectives from Ethnology*, John W. Bennett (ed.), (N.Y., 1975).
26. Malcolm Cross, 'Cultural Pluralism and Sociological Theory: A Critique and Re-evaluation', *SES*, 17 (4), 1968, pp. 381-97; also his 'On Conflict, Race Relations and the Theory of the Plural Society', *Race*, xii (4), 1971, pp. 477-93; and his 'Colonialism and Ethnicity: a Theory and Comparative Case Study', *ERS*, 1 (1), 1978, pp. 37-59; and John Rex, *Race Relations in Sociological Theory* (Lond., 1970) pp. 82-83.
27. L. Braithwaite, 'Social Stratification and Cultural Pluralism', *Social and Cultural Pluralism in the Caribbean*, Vera Rubin (ed.), Annals N.Y. Academy of Sciences, vol. 83, art. 5, (1960), pp. 819-822.
28. Stuart Hall, 'Pluralism, Race and Class in Caribbean Society', in *Race and Class in Post-Colonial Society* (Paris, 1977), p. 154.
29. *Ibid.*, pp. 154-158.
30. P.L. van den Berghe, 'Pluralism and the Polity: A Theoretical Exploration', *Pluralism in Africa, supra cit.*, pp. 67-68.
31. M.G. Smith, *the Plural Society . . ., supra cit.*, p. 86; and his 'Institutional and Political Conditions . . ., loc. cit.*, pp. 53-55.
32. Hall, *loc. cit.*, p. 158.
33. P. Van den Berghe, *Race and Racism* (N.Y., 1967), p. 139; and his 'Pluralism and the Polity', *loc. cit.*, p. 73.
34. Hall, *loc. cit.*, pp. 158-159.
35. See note 22.
36. Smith, *The Plural Society, supra cit.*, pp. 56-57.
37. *Ibid.*, p. 89.
38. Rex. *op. cit.*, pp. 21-22; H. Hoetink, 'The Concept of Pluralism as Envisaged by M.G. Smith', *Caribbean Studies* 7 (1), 1967, pp. 37-38; and his *Caribbean Race Relations* (Lond., 1967), pp.96-97.
39. J. Rex, 'Racism and the Structure of Colonial Societies', in *Racism and Colonialism*, Robert Ross (ed.), (The Hague, 1982), p. 218.
40. Smith, *Culture, supra cit.*
41. van den Berghe, *Race and Racism, supra cit.*, p. 135.

42. *Ibid.*, pp. 25-37, and 144-145.
43. *Ibid.*
44. M.G. Smith, *The Plural Society* ..., *supra cit.*, p. 91; and his 'Analytic Framework of Pluralism,' *loc. cit.*, pp. 434-443.
45. van den Berghe, 'Pluralism and the Polity', *loc. cit.* pp. 73-74 & 79.
46. Despres, *Cultural Pluralism* ..., *supra cit.*, pp. 26-29; also his *Protest and Change in Plural Societies*, Occas. Papers Sers. No. 2 (Montreal, McGill Univ. 1969); and his 'Differential Adaptation and Micro-Cultural Evolution in Guyana', *SJA*, 25 (1), 1969, pp. 14-44.
47. Braithwaite, *loc. cit.*
48. H.I. McKenzie 'The Plural Society Debate: Some Comments on a Recent Contribution', *SES*, 15 (1), 1966, pp. 53-60.
49. Braithwaite, *loc. cit*; also his 'Social Stratification in Trinidad', *SES*, 2 (2-3), 1953; R.T. Smith, 'People and Change', *NW*, May 1966, p. 51; his *British Guiana* (Lond., 1962), pp. 41-45; and his 'Race and Class in the Post-Emancipation Caribbean', in *Racism and Colonialism, supra cit.*, pp. 93-119.
50. *Ibid.*; Hall, *loc. cit.*
51. L. Braithwaite, 'Problems of Race and Colour in the Caribbean', *Caribbean Issues*, 1 (1), 1974, pp. 5-6.
52. E. Brathwaite, *Contradictory Omens: Cultural Diversity and Integration in the Caribbean* (Mona, 1974), p. 25.
53. *Ibid.*, pp. 50-54.
54. *Ibid.*, pp. 22 and 55.
55. *Ibid.*, pp. 64.
56. V. Rubin, 'Culture, Politics, and Race Relations', *SES*, 11 (4), 1961, pp. 433-455; see also, R.T. Smith, 'Social Stratification, Cultural Pluralism, and Integration in West Indian Societies', *Caribbean Integration*, S. Lewis and T. Mathews (eds.), (P.R., 1967), pp. 226-258; and D. Lowenthal, *West Indian Societies* (N.Y., 1972).
57. Hall, *loc. cit.*, pp. 161-165.
58. See note 45.
59. Hall, *loc. cit.*, pp. 165-172.
60. R.T. Smith, 'Social Stratification ...', *loc. cit.*, pp. 234-235.
61. Braithwaite, 'Stratification and Cultural Pluralism', *loc. cit.*, pp. 822-23.
62. *Ibid.*
63. Braithwaite, 'Problems', *loc. cit.*, p. 8.
64. M. Weber, *Essays in Sociology*, H.H. Gerth and C. Wright Mills (eds.), (Lond., 1946); see also Susan Craig, 'Sociological Theorizing in the English-Speaking Caribbean: A Review', in her *Contemporary Caribbean: A Sociological Reader*, vol. 2 (P.O.S., 1982), pp. 143-180.
65. K. Marx, *The Economic and Philosophical Manuscripts of 1844* (Moscow, 1967); see also Craig, *loc. cit.*
66. K. Post, *Arise Ye Starvelings* (The Hague, 1978); G. Beckford and M. Witter, *Small Garden ... Bitter Weed* (Morant Bay, 1982); W. Rodney, *A History of the Guyanese Working People, 1881-1905* (Balt., 1981); see also my 'Walter Rodney: His Contribution to Guyanese Historiography', *Bulletin of Eastern Caribbean Affairs*, 8 (2), 1982.
67. Rex, 'The Plural Society: The South African Case', *Race*, xii (4), 1971, pp. 401-3; and his *Race Relations* ..., *supra cit.*, pp. 72-75.
68. J. Rex, 'Racism', *loc. cit.*, p. 207.

69. *Ibid.*, p. 211.
70. *Ibid.*, pp. 208–211; and his 'A Working Paradigm for Race Relations Research', *ERS*, 4 (1), 1981, pp. 10–12.
71. M.G. Smith, *Culture*, *supra* cit., p. 135.
72. Rex, *Race Relations*, *supra* cit., pp. 75–78.
73. *Ibid.*
74. Hoetink, *Caribbean Race Relations*, *supra* cit., pp. 90–109.
75. *Ibid.*; see also his '"Race" and Color in the Caribbean', in *Caribbean Contours*, Sidney Mintz and Sally Price (eds.), (Balt., 1985), pp. 55–84.
76. Hoetink, *Caribbean Race Relations*, *supra* cit., pp. 150–51 and 161–190.
77. H. Hoetink, 'Resource Competition, Monopoly, and Socioracial Diversity', in *Ethnicity and Resource Competition*, *supra* cit., p. 16.
78. van den Berghe, *Race and Racism*, *supra* cit.

Chapter 2

1. J.F. Milliroux, *Demerara: The Transition from Slavery to Liberty* (Lond., 1877; translated by J.R. McFarlane), p. 17.
2. W.A. Green, *British Slave Emancipation* (Oxford, 1976), table 5, p. 193, and table 13, p. 246.
3. *Ibid.*, p. 193.
4. This assumes that one takes the total area of modern Guyana into account (83,000 square miles). But that is an unrealistic measurement because settlement has always (both before and after emancipation) been confined to the narrow coastal belt and along the banks of the main rivers, which Adamson correctly notes constitutes no more than four percent of the total land area i.e., about 3,300 square miles. Thus the density of population would have been about 27 per square mile, still clearly very low. (See A.H. Adamson, *Sugar Without Slaves*, New Haven, 1972).
5. First Annual Report of the Royal Agricultural and Commercial Society, encl'd in Light to Stanley, No. 107, 15 May 1845, C.O. 111/223; see also encl. in Light to Russell, No. 5, 11 Jan. 1841, C.O. 111/182.
6. Douglas Hall, *Free Jamaica, 1838–1865* (New Haven, 1959), appendix 2, p. 270.
7. Green, *op. cit.*, pp. 234–35; and B. Premium, *Eight Years in British Guiana* (Lond., 1850), p. 183.
8. Light to Grey, private, 18 Jan. 1848, C.O. 111/249; and his separate letter of 3 May 1848, C.O. 111/252.
9. Premium, *loc. cit.* In 1844, for instance, Pln. Thomas was sold for just £8,000, less than its value in 1831. One planter who had paid £5,000 for a plantation previously valued at £30,000 and thought he had a bargain, was forced to suspend payments within two years.
10. Light to Grey, 25 Mar. 1847, C.O. 111/242.
11. Walker to Grey, No. 146, 17 Nov. 1848, C.O. 111/258; and Barkly to Grey, No. 121, 15 Aug. 1850, C.O. 111/275.
12. Green, *op. cit.*, p. 235.
13. Hall, *op. cit.*, table 10, p. 82.
14. Light to Grey, 25 Mar. 1847, C.O. 111/242; and encl. 4, Barkly to Grey, No. 12, 25 Jan. 1851, P.P. 1851. XXXIX.

15. R. Farley, 'The Rise of Village Settlements in British Guiana', *CQ*, 3 (2), 1953, pp. 53-54.
16. W.E. Riviere, 'Labour Shortage in the British West Indies after Emancipation', *JCH*, 4, 1972, pp. 15-16.
17. Encl. in Light to Russell, No. 75, 4 June 1840, C.O. 111/171; sub. encl. in No. 10, 26 Jan. 1841, C.O. 111/177; report for District I, encl. in Light to Stanley, No. 31, 10 Feb. 1844, C.O. 111/208.
18. Light to Russell, No. 48, 9 Apr. 1840, C.O. 111/171; and No. 4, 7 Jan. 1841, C.O. 111/177. This figure excludes the purchase of Plns. New Orange Nassau and Victoria in Demerara.
19. Light to Stanley, No. 75, 19 May 1843, C.O. 111/200.
20. See the stipendiary magistrates' reports, encl. in Walker to Grey, No. 79, 18 Aug. 1848, C.O. 111/256.
21. Encl. 3 in Barkly to Grey, No. 121, 15 Aug. 1850, P.P. 1851. XXXIX. For detailed information on the establishment of villages in Guiana, see the governors' correspondence for the period 1838-1852 in C.O. 111/166-291.
22. Encl. in Light to Stanley, No. 233, 31 Oct. 1845, C.O. 111/225; encl. in Light to Gladstone, No. 163, 12 Aug. 1846, C.O. 111/235; Barkly to Grey, No. 26, 9 Feb. 1850, C.O. 111/272, and No. 121 (encl. 2), 15 Aug., 1850, C.O. 111/275.
23. O. Nigel Bolland, 'Systems of Domination after Slavery: The Control of Land and Labor in the British West Indies after 1838', *CSSH*, 23, 1981, pp. 591-619; and his 'Reply to William A. Green's "The Perils of Comparative History"', *CSSH*, 26, 1984, pp. 120-125.
24. William A. Green, 'The Perils of Comparative History: Belize and the British Sugar Colonies after slavery', *CSSH*, 26, 1984, pp. 112-119.
25. Light Glenelg, No. 46, 4 Sept. 1838, C.O. 111/155; Light to Russell, separate, 21 Dec. 1840, C.O. 111/173; also Light to Stanley, No. 54, 14 Mar. 1844, C.O. 111/209; No. 255, 12 Dec. 1844, C.O. 111/215; and No. 70, 7 Apr. 1845, C.O. 111/227.
26. See note 25. By the mid-forties, however, more children were sent to do light work on the plantations in Guiana though not foregoing basic schooling.
27. Riviere, *loc. cit.*, pp. 10-11.
28. Light to Glenelg, No. 74, 15 Oct. 1838, C.O. 111/156; and Premium, *op. cit.*, p. 36. One planter noted in 1840 that although his work force numbered over 500 and there should have been a daily average of about 150 in the field, the actual number at work was no more than a third of that.
29. Milliroux, *op. cit.*, p. 20; and Light to Glenelg, No. 49, 6 Sept. 1838, C.O. 111/155.
30. Light to Russell, No. 48, 9 Apr. 1840, C.O. 111/171.
31. Light to Stanley, No. 54, 14 Mar. 1844, C.O. 111/209; and No. 255, 12 Dec. 1844, C.O. 111/215.
32. W.K. Marshall, 'Metayage in the Sugar Industry of the British Windward Islands, 1838-1865', *JHR*, 5 (1), 1965, pp. 28-29.
33. Green, *British Slave Emancipation, supra cit.*, p. 255.
34. For the métairie system in Jamaica, see Hall, *op. cit.*, pp. 190-92.
35. There is a considerable amount of historical data on the métairie system in Guyana, particularly in the governor's correspondence and the

stipendiary magistrates' reports, which can be found in C.O. 111/194–272 and C.O. 116/167–169. The London Missionaries also made occasional reference to it. See, for instance, L.M.S. 7/9 (Demerara).
36. Premium, *op. cit.*, p. 17.
37. Light to Russell, separate, 21 Dec. 1840, C.O. 111/173.
38. Light to Normanby, No. 103, 24 June 1839, C.O. 111/164.
39. Riviere, *loc. cit.*, p. 5.
40. *Ibid.*, pp. 6–8.
41. Light to Russell, No. 97, 11 July 1840, C.O. 111/172.
42. Coleman to Wolseley, 15 Jan. 1842, encl. in Light to Stanley, No. 12, 19 Jan. 1842, C.O. 111/189.
43. Report of a Planters' Meeting held on 6 Nov. 1841, encl. in Light to Stanley, No. 166, 4 Dec. 1841, C.O. 111/183; and encls. A & C in Light to Stanley, No. 4, 6 Jan. 1842, C.O. 111/189; see also Donald Wood, *Trinidad in Transition* (Lond., 1968), p. 54. According to Wood, in Trinidad the planters agreed to stop allowances of rum and salt fish from January 1, 1842. They also attempted to lower wages in 1841 and 1842, but failed as did their Guyanese counterparts for want of cohesion. It was not until 1844 that they were able to enforce a general wage reduction.
44. See note 50.
45. Premium, *op. cit.*, pp. 95–96; also encl. in Light to Stanley, No. 6, 7 Jan. 1842; encl. 4 in No. 9, 13 Jan. 1842; and encl. 1 in No. 33, 2 Feb. 1842, C.O. 111/189.
46. Light to Stanley, No. 9, 13 Jan. 1842; No. 5, 7 Jan. 1842; No. 42, 11 Feb. 1842; No. 43, 16 Feb. 1842; and No. 49, 28 Feb. 1842, C.O. 111/189.
47. Wood, *loc. cit.*
48. Ord. No. 30/1846, C.O. 113/2; petition of the London Missionaries to Lord Grey, 14 Dec. 1846, encl. in Light to Grey, No. 254, 18 Dec. 1846, C.O. 111/237; and Arrindell to Light, 1 Jan. 1847, encl. in Light to Grey, No. 1, 2 Jan. 1847, C.O. 111/241.
49. Light to Grey, No. 224, 31 Dec. 1847; and Grey to Light, No. 293, 12 Feb. 1848, C.O. 111/246; also Light to Grey, private, 18 Jan. 1848, C.O. 111/249.
50. Stipendiary magistrates' reports, encl. in Light to Grey, No. 61, 4 Apr. 1848, C.O. 111/252; and Walker to Grey, No. 124, 9 Oct. 1848, C.O. 111/258.
51. Light to Grey, private, 18 Jan. 1848, C.O. 111/249; Walker to Grey, No. 86, 31 Aug. 1848, C.O. 111/256; No. 131, 1 Nov. 1848, C.O. 111/259; and No. 159, 18 Dec. 1848, C.O. 111/260; also Barkly to Grey, No. 53, 21 Mar. 1849, C.O. 111/264.
52. Light to Grey, No. 35, 14 Feb. 1848, and encl., C.O. 111/249.
53. Light to Grey, No. 60, 4 Apr. 1848, C.O. 111/252.
54. Hall, *op. cit.*, pp. 21–22; Green, *British Slave Emancipation, supra cit.*, p. 263; V. Daly, *A Short History of the Guyanese People* (Georgetown, 1966), pp. 146–47; K.O. Laurence, *Immigration into the West Indies in the 19th Century* (Barbados, 1971), p. 12.
55. Laurence, *op. cit.*, p. 17.
56. Report of the [1870] Commissioners (ms), sec. 4, C.O. 111/379.
57. K.O. Laurence, 'The Establishment of the Portuguese Community in British Guiana', *JHR*, 5 (2), 1965, pp. 58–59.

58. Return of Immigrants, P.P. 1873, L; and Blue Books of Statistics, 1870–1881.
59. Laurence, *Immigration, supra cit.*, p. 18.
60. *Ibid.*, pp. 12–14; Green, *British Slave Emancipation, supra cit.*, pp. 265–72; and Return of Free Immigrants, 1835–49, P.P. 1851. XXXIX.
61. Green, *British Slave Emancipation, supra cit.*, pp. 272–73; Laurence, *Immigration, supra cit.*, p. 14.
62. Return of Immigrants, P.P. 1868–69. XLIII.
63. Laurence, *Immigration, supra cit.*, p. 15.
64. Report of the [1870] Commissioners (ms), sec. 4, *supra cit.*
65. Wood, *op. cit.*, pp. 67–68.
66. Report of the [1870] Commissioners, sec. 4, *supra cit.*
67. Light to Stanley, No. 229, 30 Oct. 1845, C.O. 111/225; and Return of Immigrants, P.P. 1868–69, XLIII.
68. Wood, *op. cit.*, pp. 65–66.
69. Blue Books of Statistics, 1864–85.
70. Report of the Immigration Agent General for 1891, C.O. 114/53.
71. Laurence, *Immigration, supra. cit.*, p. 11.
72. *Ibid.*, pp. 19–21; Green, *British Slave Emancipation, supra cit.*, pp. 276–78.
73. Laurence, *Immigration, supra cit.*, pp. 21–26.
74. Report of the [1870] Commissioners (ms), sec. 4, *loc. cit.*
75. Return of Immigrants, P.P. 1868–69. XLIII; Laurence, *Immigration, supra cit.*, p. 36; Hall, *op. cit.*, appendix 3D, p. 272.
76. Laurence, *Immigration, supra cit.*, p. 37.
77. Colonial Land & Emigration Commissioners (C.L. & E.C.) to Herbert, 22 & 24 Mar. 1873, C.O. 318/271.
78. Kortright to Hicks Beach, No. 13, 19 Jan. 1880, C.O. 384/128.
79. Alan Adamson, *op. cit.*, chapter 5, pp. 166ff; Walter Rodney, *A History of the Guyanese Working People, 1881–1905* (Lond., 1981), pp. 19–30, and table 4, p. 226.
80. Bridget Brereton, *A History of Modern Trinidad, 1783–1962* (Lond., 1981), pp. 82–88; Eric Williams, *From Columbus to Castro* (Lond, 1970), p. 366.
81. Hall, *op. cit.*, appendix 2, p. 270; Green, *British Slave Emancipation, supra cit.*, table 13, p. 246; Williams, *loc. cit.*
82. Even before the abolition of slavery in the Dutch colony of Surinam in 1863, efforts were made to introduce immigrant workers under contract from Java and China. In addition, Madeirans were also introduced. During and after the 1870s, substantial amounts of Indians were also imported into that colony (see Laurence, *Immigration*, pp. 43–45). In so far as the form of the society is concerned, M.G. Smith considers the numerical size of the new racially and culturally differentiated immigrant groups to be important. So although Jamaica and the Windward Islands imported Indian and other immigrants, they were numerically too small in his view to alter the basic biracial *creole* social structure. But he does recognize the new multiracialism of Guyana, Trinidad and Surinam (see M.G. Smith, *Culture, Race and Class in the Commonwealth Caribbean*, U.W.I., 1984, pp. 37–45).

Chapter 3

1. A.G. Keller, *Colonisation and Colonies*, (Boston, 1908) pp. 4ff; F. Knight, *The Caribbean* (N.Y. 1978), pp. 50–66; C.H. Haring, *The Spanish Empire in America* (N.Y., 1975 ed.) pp. 27–31; Leonard Thompson, 'Historical Perspectives of Pluralism in Africa', *Pluralism in Africa*, Kuper & Smith (eds.), (Berkeley, 1971), pp. 351–54.
2. H. Kirke, *Twenty-five Years in British Guiana* (Lond., 1898), p. 42; Richard Schomburgk, *Travels in British Guiana, 1840-44*, vol. 2 (G'town, 1922 edit.), p. 28; J. Heatley, *A Visit to the West Indies* (Lond., 1981), p. 42. In 1840, there were only 45 Dutch residents in Demerara and Essequibo, and 26 in Berbice (see Light to Russell, No. 160, 24 Dec. 1840, and encls., C.O. 111/173).
3. See censuses, 1841–1891.
4. Schomburgk, *op. cit.*, p. 40; and E. Jenkins, *The Coolie: His Rights and Wrongs* (Lond., 1871), p. 76.
5. *Report of the Commissioners Appointed to Inquire into the Treatment of Immigrants in British Guiana* (G'town, 1871), pp. 78–81; J.G. Pearson (ed.), *New Overseer's Manual* (G'town, 1890), pp. 33–34.
6. See notes 4 and 5 in chapter 1.
7. A Trollope, *The West Indies and the Spanish Main* (Lond., 1859), p. 170; G.W. DesVoeux, *Experiences of a Demerara Magistrate* (G'town, 1948), p. 88; J. Beaumont, *The New Slavery* (Lond., 1871), p. 8.
8. Encl. G. in J. Stephen to the Law Officers, 9 Sept. 1840, C.O. 111/187; also, Minutes of the Berbice Council of Govt. and Criminal Justice, 1802–03, vol. 29.
9. Bathurst to D'Urban, private, July 1825, C.O. 111/98.
10. *Ibid.*; also Wodehouse to Molesworth, No. 131, 19 Sept., 1855, C.O. 111/306.
11. Royal Instructions (art. 4), 5 Mar. 1831, in *Minutes of the C.P. for 1831*, vol. 2; also, Light to Glenelg, No. 3, 30 June 1838 and No. 10, 16 July 1838, C.O. 111/155; see also note 9 above.
12. Bathurst to D'Urban, private, July 1825, C.O. 111/98.
13. Encls. in Stephen to Law Officers, 9 Sept., 1840, C.O. 111/187; and Proclamation of 21 July 1831, in 1832 *Local Guide of British Guiana*, p. 169.
14. Carmichael to Bathurst, 8 Sept. and 12 Oct. 1812, C.O. 111/13; Minutes of the C.P., 7 Sept. 1812; Bathurst to Carmichael, 25 Nov. 1812, C.O. 112/4; and Royal Instructions (art. 4), 5 Mar. 1831, *loc. cit.*
15. Ord. No. 86/1836, C.O. 113/1.
16. Minute of Sir G. Grey, 6 Sept. 1838 (appended to No. 10), C.O. 111/155.
17. For the several proposals made regarding the extending of the franchise, see Light to Normanby, No. 96, 13 June 1839, and Russell to Light, No. 52, 10 Feb. 1840, C.O. 111/164; Minutes of H. Taylor, 12 Aug. 1839, J. Stephens, 18 Jan. 1840, and Vernon-Smith, 18 Jan. 1840, C.O. 111/186; Light to Stanley, No. 171, 7 Oct. 1842, C.O. 111/193; Light to Gladstone, No. 52, 1 Apr. 1846, C.O. 111/232; Light to Grey, sep. & priv., 11 Nov. 1847 and minute of Taylor, 18 Jan. 1848, C.O. 111/246.
18. Ord. No. 15/1849, C.O. 113/2.
19. *R.G.*, 12 June 1849.

20. Barkly to Grey, No. 146, 5 Oct. 1849, C.O. 111/269; and No. 164, 24 Nov., 1851, C.O. 111/284.
21. Barkly to Grey, No. 134, 23 Sept. 1850, C.O. 111/276; and No. 172, 29 Nov. 1849, C.O. 111/270; see also the Blue Book of Statistics for 1851, C.O. 116/220.
22. Light to Normanby, No. 96, 13 June 1839, C.O. 111/164.
23. Light to Russell, separate, 21 Dec. 1840, C.O. 111/173.
24. Shahabuddeen notes that women were granted the franchise in 1812 by Governor Carmichael on a basis of equality with men i.e., as persons paying tax on an annual income of 10,000 guilders. They retained that right to vote until 1849; and not until 1928 was it restored. See M. Shahabuddeen, *Constitutional Development in Guyana, 1621-1978* (Georgetown, 1978).
25. See note 23; also, Light to Stanley, No. 101, 17 July 1843, C.O. 111/201; Barkly to Grey, No. 39, 3 Mar. 1849, C.O. 111/264; and No. 134, 23 Sept., 1850, C.O. 111/276.
26. Minute of H. Taylor, 18 Jan. 1848, C.O. 111/246.
27. Barkly to Grey, No. 146, 5 Oct. 1849, C.O. 111/269.
28. D'Urban to Goderich, No. 32, 15 Oct. 1831, C.O. 111/117; Light to Glenelg, Nos. 3 & 10, 30 June and 16 July 1838, respectively, C.O. 111/155; Light to Russell, separ., 21 Dec. 1840, C.O. 111/173; No. 63, 10 May 1840, C.O. 111/171; Light to Stanley, No. 171, 7 Oct. 1842, C.O. 111/193; and Light to Normanby, No. 96, 13 June 1839, C.O. 111/164.
29. Minutes of H. Taylor, 12 Aug. 1839 and 16 Jan. 1840, and of Lord John Russell, 21 Jan. 1840, C.O. 111/186.
30. Barkly to Grey, No. 146, 5 Oct. 1849, C.O. 111/269; and ord. no. 15 of 1849, C.O. 113/2.
31. Ord. No. 15 of 1849, *loc. cit.*; Barkly to Grey, No. 134, 23 Sept. 1850, C.O. 111/276; Shahabuddeen, *op. cit.*
32. C. Clementi, *A Constitutional History of British Guiana* (Lond., 1937), p. 203.
33. *Ibid.*
34. *Ibid.*, p. 241.
35. Encl. C. in Barkly to Grey, No. 100, 16 June 1849, C.O. 111/266. The planters overcame the problem of the black and coloured vote by insisting on a literacy qualification.
36. Blue Book of Statistics for 1849, C.O. 116/218.
37. Ord. No. 15/1849.
38. *R.G.*, 12 June 1849.
39. Barkly to Grey, No. 172, 29 Nov. 1849, C.O. 111/270.
40. Hincks to Newcastle, No. 154, 22 Sept. 1863, C.O. 111/341; Hincks to Cardwell, 5 Aug. 1864, C.O. 111/347.
41. Hincks to Newcastle, No. 154, 22 Sept 1863, C.O. 111/341.
42. Encl. in Hincks to Newcastle, No. 7, 7 Jan. 1864, C.O. 111/344.
43. Hincks to Newcastle, No. 154, 22 Sept. 1863, C.O. 111/341.
44. Barkly to Pakington, No. 106, 8 June 1852, C.O. 111/290.
45. Pakington to Barkly, No. 81, 13 Nov. 1852, C.O. 112/32.
46. Wodehouse to Molesworth, No. 131, 19 Sept. 1855, C.O. 111/306. In 1855, four of the six elected members of the Financial College were planters.

47. Labouchere to Wodehouse, 16 Feb. 1856, C.O. 112/33.
48. Minutes of H. Taylor, 22 Oct., 1863 and Sir. F. Rogers, 6 Nov. 1863; Newcastle to Hincks, No. 753, 30 Nov. 1863, C.O. 111/341; also encl. in Hincks to Newcastle, No. 7, 7 Jan. 1864, C.O. 111/344. See also Ord. No. 16/1864.
49. *R.G.*, 12 June 1849 (statement of Hon. J. White in the Combined Court), and 20 June 1850 (editorial); also, Attorney-General's speech in the Court of Policy, 27 March 1850, encl'd in Barkly to Grey, No. 71, 2 May 1850, C.O. 111/274.
50. W. Rodney, *A History of the Guyuanese Working People, 1881–1905* (Balt., 1981), p. 125.
51. Beaumont, *op. cit.*, p. 9. Beaumont himself fell victim to the authoritarianism of Governor Hincks (see *Creole*, 8 Jan. 1866 and *Colonist*, 22 Aug. 1865).
52. Encl. D. in Walker to Grey, private & confidential, 19 Oct. 1848, C.O. 111/258. These planters included John Gordon, Henry Zuill, E. Bishop, William Ferguson and J.H. Albouy. Among the coloureds were William McPherson and James Spooner (merchants).
53. Light to Stanley, No. 171, 7 Oct. 1842, C.O. 111/193.
54. See note 52; also sub-encl. in Light to Grey, separate and private, 11 Nov. 1847, C.O. 111/246; encls. in Light to Gladstone, No. 52, 1 April 1846, C.O. 111/232. Apart from Haynes, the committee of the Reform Association included E.A. Wallbridge, J. Spooner, D. McLeod, J. Taggart, J.F. Obermuller and Messrs. MacFarlane and Henry.
55. *Ibid.*
56. Light to Gladstone, No. 52, *loc. cit.*
57. Barkly to Grey, No. 93, 14 June 1850, C.O. 111/274.
58. Barkly to Grey, No. 145, 9 Oct. 1850; and confid., 11 Nov. 1850, C.O. 111/276.
59. Encl. in Barkly to Grey, No. 100, 16 June 1849, C.O. 111/266; and No. 14, 12 Jan. 1850, C.O. 111/272. Rose headed a deputation of influential persons to the governor and presented a petition for political reform signed by 812 people. During the debate on this petition in the legislature in April, three of the five colonial members voiced their concern over the drift to mass politics and urged a more gradual approach towards representative government (Barkly to Grey, No. 71, 2 May 1850, C.O. 111/274).
60. Barkly to Grey, No. 93, 14 June 1850, C.O. 111/274.
61. Barkly to Grey, confidential, 11 Nov. 1850, C.O. 111/276.
62. Barkly to Grey, No. 145, 9 Oct. 1850, C.O. 111/276.
63. See note 61; also Barkly to Grey, No. 11, 22 Jan. 1851, and encl. 5, C.O. 111/280.
64. *Colonist*, 18 June 1851,
65. Barkly to Grey, No. 79, 10 June 1851, C.O. 111/280. This should not have come as a surprise because Rose had in 1849 stood by the planters in opposing even the very limited extension of the franchise embodied in the 1849 law (see Barkly to Grey, No. 100, 16 June 1849, C.O. 111/266).
66. *Colonist*, 13 and 16 June 1851.
67. *R.G.*, 14 June 1851.
68. *Colonist*, 1 Oct. 1851; Barkly to Grey, No. 149, 30 Oct. 1851, C.O.

NOTES

111/284; *Colonist*, 10 May 1852. By July 1851 the Association was so weakened that it was even prepared to compromise its position on representative institutions in favour of simply modifying the existing system. A petition to this effect, however, only mustered 843 signatures. The Association suffered a further setback by the forced, but shortlived retirement of Peter Rose from politics at the end of 1851 for health reasons. Maybe that was his way of extricating himself honourably from a dying cause (see Barkly to Grey, private, 28 Dec. 1851, C.O. 111/284.

69. *Colonist*, 10 May, 1852; Barkly to Pakington, No. 100, 22 May 1852, C.O. 111/289.
70. Hincks to Cardwell, No. 132, 5 Aug. 1864, and encls; No. 147, 7 Sept. 1864, and encls, both in C.O. 111/347; and No. 168, 8 Oct. 1864, C.O. 111/348; also, *Creole*, 11 March 1864. Over 200 of the signatories were mechanics and clerks in mercantile establishments, about 60 were property and landholders, and less than 50 were merchants and retail traders.
71. *Liberator*, 31 Oct. 1868.
72. Scott to Kimberley, No. 160, 7 Nov. 1871, and encl., C.O. 111/387. Although Governor Scott described the leaders as "coloured", it is very probable that they were blackmen. Certainly James Rodney was.
73. P.P. 1871. XLVII. 399: Correspondence arising out of complaints of Portuguese residents of British Guiana. See in particular No. 1 dated 30 Nov. 1870.
74. Between 1870 and 1890, no less than six Portuguese language newspapers were established. They were the *Watchman, O Portuguez, A Uniao Portugueza, O Lusitano, A Verdade*, and *A Liberdade*.
75. See the petitions of June 1849 encl'd in Barkly to Grey, No. 100, *loc. cit.*
76. See note 70.
77. *R.G.*, 31 March 1881.
78. *D.D.C.*, 3 July 1883.
79. See H.A. Will, *Constitutional Change in the British West Indies, 1880–1903*, (Oxford, 1970); and G. Knox, 'Political Change in Jamaica (1866–1906) and the Local Reaction to the Policies of the Crown Colony Government', in *The Caribbean in Transition*, F. Andic and T. Mathews (eds.), (Puerto Rico, 1965), pp. 141–162.
80. Encl. in Irving to Granville, No. 125, 12 May 1886, C.O. 111/435.
81. *Echo*, 5 Nov. 1887.
82. Rodney, *op. cit.*, pp. 141–142.
83. *DC*, 2 July 1886 (lecture by schoolmaster J.D. Fileen); *Echo*, 5 Nov. 1887, 24 Mar. 1888.
84. Blue Books of Statistics, 1886–1890, C.O. 114/46–50.
85. Clementi, *op. cit.*, Appendix Q, p. 542. The coloured members of the pre-reformed electoral college were D.W.A. McKinnon (merchant) and G.L. Davson (manager of the B.G. Bank). In the financial college there were two coloureds viz., D.M. Hutson and N.R. McKinnon (barristers), and one black viz, William Smith (merchant). Whites, however, were still in a majority in both of these institutions.
86. *R.G.*, 14 Sept. 1889.
87. Rodney, *op. cit.*, p. 143. The planter W. Howell Jones, was associated with this movement.

88. *Ibid.*
89. Encl. in Irving to Holland, No. 436, 11 Nov. 1887, C.O. 111/441. The mortality rate among the indentured immigrants for the first half of 1886 was 2.7%, higher than among the unindentured whose mortality rate was 1.6%.
90. Irving to Holland, No. 363, 28 Sept. 1887 and encl.; No. 368, 30 Sept. 1887; encl. in No. 371, 1 Oct. 1887; No. 395, 13 Oct. 1887 and encl.; No. 396, 14 Oct. 1887; and No. 400, 14 Oct. 1887 and encl., C.O. 111/440.
91. Irving to Harris, 13 Oct. 1887, and Irving to Holland, No. 407, 22 Oct. 1887, C.O. 111/440.
92. Minute of E. Wingfield, 12 Nov. 1887 (appended to No. 407), C.O. 111/440; Holland to Irving, No. 288, 2 Nov. 1887, C.O. 111/440; and Telegram from Sect. of State, 3 Nov. 1887 (appended to No. 427), C.O. 111/441.
93. *Echo*, 15, 22, 29 Oct., 5 Nov. 1887, and 24 March 1888. The *Echo* (and to a lesser extent the *Daily Chronicle*) blamed the unreformed legislature for the political crisis, and urged its readers to petition the imperial government for a dissolution of the Court of Policy, the abolition of the whole machinery that produced it, the institution of free representation, and an extension of the franchise. References to the reforms in Jamaica suggest that this paper and perhaps the reformers in general were influenced and encouraged by the political developments in that island. On the other hand, the *Royal Gazette* which represented planter opinion preferred full Crown colony government to any extension of political rights.
94. *Echo*, 5 Nov. 1887 and 24 March 1888; also Irving to Holland, No. 467, 9 Dec. 1887, C.O. 111/441.
95. Holland to Gormanston, Nos. 53 and 54, 8 Feb. 1888, C.O. 111/441.
96. Irving to Holland, No. 466, 9 Dec. 1887, C.O. 111/441.
97. *Echo*, 10 Aug., 1889; Gormanston to Knutsford, No. 292, 15 Aug. 1889, and No. 323, 13 Sept. 1889 and encls., C.O. 111/453.
98. See encl. in Gormanston to Knutsford, confidential, 20 May 1890, C.O. 111/456 which contains a table of estimated earnings for different categories of skilled estate workers.
99. Gormanston to Knutsford, No. 4, 3 Jan. 1890, and minute of E. Wingfield, 22 Mar. 1890, C.O. 111/455; also Gormanston to Knutsford, No. 173, 22 May 1890, C.O. 111/456.
100. Minute of Wingfield, 10 June 1890 and Knutsford to Gormanston, No. 132, 11 June 1890, C.O. 111/456. For amendments to and comments on the draft ordinance, see Gormanston to Knutsford, No. 207, 20 June 1890, and Knutsford's confidential reply of 14 Oct. 1890, C.O. 111/456.
101. *Echo*, 10 Aug. 1889; Gormanston to Knutsford, Nos. 292 and 323, 15 Aug. and 13 Sept. 1889, respectively and encls., C.O. 111/453.
102. Gormanston to Knutsford, No. 266, 30 July 1890, C.O. 111/457.
103. Ord. No. 1 of 1891.
104. Gormanston to Knutsford, No. 4, 3 Jan. 1890, C.O. 111/455.
105. *Ibid*; also minute of E. Wingfield, 10 June 1890, C.O. 111/455; Gormanston to Knutsford, confid., 3 and 5 Nov. 1890 and Knutsford to Gormanston, confid., 25 Nov. 1890, C.O. 111/457.

106. Minute of E. Wingfield, 22 Mar. 1890; Gormanston to Knustford, No. 4, 3 Jan. 1890, C.O. 111/455 and confid., 20 May 1890, C.O. 111/456.
107. See note 101.
108. See note 106.
109. *Ibid.*
110. Gormanston to Knutsford, confid., 23 May 1890, C.O. 111/455; see also note 100.
111. Blue Books for 1890 and 1891 (see C.O. 114/50 and 114/53).
112. Minute of C.A. Pearson, 26 Feb. 1896, C.O. 111/484.
113. Encl. in Boyle to Chamberlain, No. 49, 3 Feb. 1896, C.O. 111/484.
114. Clementi, *op. cit.*, pp. 313-14 and appendix Q, p. 543. Only one coloured gained entry into the Court of Policy as a result of the 1891 reforms viz., the lawyer, D.M. Hutson. The remaining 7 members were all wealthy white planters and merchants. Likewise, the 1892 elections returned only one coloured to the financial college viz., N.R McKinnon (lawyer). Two other coloureds, J.P. Farnum (storekeeper) and Patrick Dargan (lawyer), and two blacks, J.A. Murdoch and W.E. Lewis (both lawyers) contested the elections but lost.
115. Chamberlain to Hemming, Nos. 69 and 138, 10 Mar. and 19 May, 1896 respectively, C.O. 111/484; also Hemming to Chamberlain. No. 153, 27 Apr. 1896, C.O. 111/485; No. 198, 11 June, 1896, C.O. 111/486; and No. 282, 10 Sept. 1896, C.O. 111/487.
116. In the first election (1897) after the introduction of the secret ballot, the composition of the elective institutions was significantly changed. Although the only coloured to enter the financial college was the Barbadian lawyer, W.M. Payne, three coloureds and one black were returned to the Court of Policy viz., A.B. Brown (black lawyer), Patrick Dargan, D.M. Hutson, and D.A.P. Ouckama (a coloured businessman). See Hemming to Chamberlain, confidential, 17 Feb 1897, and his private despatch of 4 Feb. 1897, C.O. 111/492.
117. Kirke, *op. cit.*, p. 22.

Chapter 4

1. See Leo Kuper, 'Ethnic and Racial Pluralism: Some Aspects of Polarization and Depluralization', *Pluralism in Africa*, Kuper and Smith (eds.), (Berkeley, 1971), pp. 462-63.
2. Office minute on the B.G. Finance and Constitution, 6 Aug. 1840, C.O. 884/1 (W.I. No. xviii); and minute of H. Taylor, 11 Aug. 1846 C.O. 111/233.
3. Minute of H. Taylor, 11 June 1840, C.O. 111/186. The socio-political role of the coloureds in Jamaica is disputed by Campbell and Heuman in particular. Generally speaking, the former tends to support Taylor's view; but Heuman's careful analysis of their activities both in and out of the assembly has produced a far more sophisticated picture of their role which shows that they manoeuvred very astutely in pursuit of their own interests as a class which might at different times coincide with either those of the dominant white minority or the subordinate black majority. See M. Campbell, *The Dynamics of Change in a Slave Society: A*

Socio-Political History of the Free Coloureds in Jamaica 1800–1865 (N.J., 1976); and G. Heuman. *Between Black and White: Race, Politics, and the Free Coloureds in Jamaica, 1792–1865* (Westport, 1981).
4. Taylor's minutes of 1840 and 1846, *loc. cit.*
5. Minute of Earl Grey, 12 June 1850, C.O. 111/274.
6. Minute of Lord John Russell, 31 Dec. 1839, C.O. 111/186; and Taylor to Merivale, 6 June, 1850, C.O. 111/274.
7. *Ibid*; also Taylor's minute (1846), *loc. cit.*
8. Office minute (1840), *loc. cit.*
9. Aberdeen to Smith, No. 29, 1 March 1835, C.O. 112/18.
10. Office minute (1840), *loc. cit.*
11. See. P. Curtin, *The Image of Africa: British Ideas and Action, 1780–1850* (Lond., 1965), pp. 28–57; H.A. Cairns, *Prelude to Imperialism* (Lond., 1965), pp. 73–101; C. Bolt, *Victorian Attitudes to Race* (Lond., 1971), pp. 75–156, and 206–218.
12. E. Long, *History of Jamaica*, 3 vols. (Lond., 1774).
13. J. Gratus, *The Great White Lie: Slavery, Emancipation, and Changing Racial Attitudes* (N.Y. 1973).
14. T. Carlyle, *Occasional Discourse on the Nigger Question* (Lond., 1849).
15. A. Trollope, *The West Indies and the Spanish Main* (Lond., 1860).
16. C. Kingsley, *His Letters and Memoirs* (Lond., 1877). For a brief analysis of Kingley's racial philosophy, see Michael Banton's *The Idea of Race* (Lond., 1977), pp. 63–88. Kingsley visited the Caribbean in 1869–70 out of which emerged the book *At last: A Christmas in the West Indies* (Lond., 1872).
17. Bolt, *op. cit.*, pp. 75–108; E. Williams, *British Historians and the West Indies* (Lond., 1966), pp. 127–153.
18. See Banton, *op. cit.*, pp. 27–61 and 89–100; Bolt, *op. cit.*, pp. 1–27.
19. J. Froude, *The English in the West Indies* (Lond., 1888).
20. J. Rodway, *History of British Guiana*, 3 vols. (Georgetown, 1891–94).
21. Bolt, *op. cit.*, pp. 99, 102, 108; B. Brereton, *Race Relations in Colonial Trinidad, 1870–1900* (Lond., 1979), pp. 196–197; Williams, *op. cit.* These racist notions of Haiti being representative of barbarism and the inability of blacks of rule themselves also permeated white society in Guyana. See for instance, the statement of the Hon. James White in the Combined Court (reported in the *Royal Gazette* of 12 June 1849), the attorney-general's speech in the Court of Policy on 27 March 1850 (in Barkly to Grey, No. 71, 2 May 1850, C.O. 111/274); the *Royal Gazette*'s editorial of 20 June 1850; and the judicial judgement of Magistrate Hewick reported in the *Royal Gazette* of 18 April 1885.
22. See note 17.
23. F.R. Augier, 'Before and After 1865', *New World Quarterly*, 2(2), 1966, pp. 26–27.
24. *Ibid.*, pp. 35–37.
25. Stephen to Law Officers, 9 Sept. 1849, C.O. 111/187.
26. Ibid; also, Bathurst to D'Urban, July 1825, C.O. 111/98.
27. Stephen to Law Officers (1849), *loc. cit.*
28. Stephen to Wilmot Horton, 5 Dec. 1826, C.O. 111/98; D'Urban to Bathurst, priv., 5 Mar. 1827, C.O. 111/104; Aberdeen to Smith, No. 28, 1 Mar. 1835, C.O. 112/18.
29. Aberdeen to Smith, No. 28. *supra cit.*

NOTES 241

30. *Ibid.*
31. Stanley to Smyth, No. 61, 22 Feb. 1834; and Aberdeen to Smith, No. 29, 1 Mar. 1835, C.O. 112/18.
32. Smith to Glenelg, 7 July 1835, C.O. 111/141.
33. Aberdeen to Smith, No. 29, 1 Mar. 1835, C.O. 112/18; minute of Taylor, 1 Nov. 1855, C.O. 111/306; Longden to Carnarvon, No. 229, 2 Nov. 1875; Carnarvon to Longden, No. 143 and No. 9, 13 Sept. 1875 and 14 Jan. 1876, respectively, C.O. 111/406; Longden to Carnarvon, No. 136, 24 June 1876 and encl., C.O. 111/408. After the crisis of 1848–49, the civil list was renewed septennially without much difficulty except in 1875 when the Colonial Office renewed its attempt to procure a permanent civil list which, of course, the planters refused. The Colonial Office were thus obliged to revert to the old compromise with a duration of seven years.
34. Barkly to Pakington, No. 183, 24 Dec. 1852, C.O. 111/291; Longden to Carnarvon, No. 229, 2 Nov. 1875, C.O. 111/406; and No. 136, 24 June 1876, C.O. 111/408.
35. Smith to Glenelg, 7 July 1835, C.O. 111/141; and Light to Stanley, No. 104, 18 June 1842, C.O. 111/191.
36. Light to Russell, priv, 16 Apr. 1840; No. 54, 29 Apr. 1840; and No. 68, 19 May 1840, C.O. 111/171; also Russell to Light, No. 121, 14 Sept. 1840, C.O. 111/173. As in 1835, this dispute between the planters and the colonial government was so deadlocked that it required the mediation of an outsider, on this occasion the governor of Trinidad Sir Henry MacLeod, to break it. He worked out a compromise not too dissimilar from that of 1835, but also permitting the Combined Court to raise a loan of $100,000 to finance immigration.
37. Light to Grey, No. 1, 1 Jan. 1848, C.O. 111/249; No. 36, 3 Mar. 1848 and priv. & confid., 18 Mar. 1848, C.O. 111/251; No. 65, 13 Apr. 1848 and No. 71, 28 Apr. 1848, C.O. 111/252; and Walker to Grey, No. 57, 20 July 1848, C.O. 111/255.
38. Encl. in Irving to Holland, No. 371, 1 Oct. 1887; and No. 396, 14 Oct. 1887, C.O. 111/440.
39. Wodehouse to Molesworth, No. 131, 19 Sept. 1855, C.O. 111/306.
40. Minute of Taylor, 10 Sept. 1852, C.O. 111/290.
41. Barkly to Grey, No. 145, 9 Oct. 1850, C.O. 111/276.
42. *Colonist*, 11 June 1851; Barkly to Grey, No. 79, 10 June 1851, C.O. 111/282.
43. Barkly to Grey, priv. & confid. and No. 129, 27 Aug. 1851, C.O. 111/283.
44. Wodehouse to Molesworth, No. 131, 19 Sept. 1855, C.O. 111/306.
45. Minutes of B. Hawes, n.d., H. Merivale, 15 Nov. 1850, and Lord Grey, 18 Nov., 1850, C.O. 111/276.
46. Minute of H. Taylor, 17 July, 1852; and Pakington to Barkly, No. 81, and confid, 13 Nov. 1852, C.O. 111/290.
47. Minutes of Taylor, 14 Nov. 1850, C.O. 111/276; 14 July 1851, C.O. 111/282; and 17 July 1852, C.O. 111/290.
48. Minute of Taylor, 1 Nov. 1855, C.O. 111/306.
49. Minute of Taylor, 4 Oct. 1851, C.O. 111/183.
50. Minute of Taylor, 1 Nov. 1855, C.O. 111/306.
51. Light to Normanby, No. 77, 1 May 1839 and encl.; and Normanby to

Light, No. 56, 4 July 1839, C.O. 111/163.
52. Minutes of Merivale, 15 Nov. 1850, and Hawes, n.d., C.O. 111/276.
53. Minute of Taylor, 10 Sept. 1852, C.O. 111/290.

Chapter 5

1. G. Beckford, *Persistent Poverty* (Lond., 1972), pp. 73–79.
2. M.G. Smith, 'Institutional and Political Conditions of Pluralism', *Pluralism in Africa*, Kuper and Smith (eds.), (Berkeley, 1971), pp. 32, 53–54.
3. C. Wagley, 'Plantation America: A Culture Sphere', *Caribbean Studies: A Symposium*, Vera Rubin (ed.), (Seattle, 1960), p. 8; see also his 'Recent Studies of Caribbean Local Societies', *The Caribbean: Natural Resources*, Curtis Wilgus (ed.), (Gainsville, 1959), p. 199.
4. L. Despres, *Cultural Pluralism and Nationlist Politics in British Guiana* (Chic., 1967).
5. Smith, *loc. cit.*
6. J.G. Cruickchank, 'The Beginnings of our Villages', *Timehri*, vol. 7, 3rd ser., 1921, pp. 20–21; J.B. Cropper, 'Our Villages and Countryparts', *Timehri*, 2 (2), 1912, p. 253.
7. Report of the Inspector of Villages, 28 Mar. 1882, C.O. 114/32.
8. Adamson has dealt with this problem in some detail and notes that the majority of villagers owned an acre or less land by the 1850s. Together with the acute problem of drainage, this meant that such "microculture", as he calls it, made the peasant economy unviable. See A. Adamson, *Sugar Without Slaves* (New Haven, 1972), pp. 63–66.
9. Hadfield to Young, 17 Dec. 1844, appendix to No. 3, Light to Stanley, (Jan.) 1845, P.P. 1847–48. XXIII. Pt. II; Encl. in Barkly to Grey, No. 53, 21 Mar. 1849, C.O. 111/264; and encl. in No. 46, 11 Apr. 1851, C.O. 111/281.
10. Barkly to Grey, No. 26, 10 Feb. 1852, C.O. 111/288.
11. Encl. in Hincks to Newcastle, No. 149, 11 Aug. 1862, C.O. 111/336.
12. H. Dalton, *A History of British Guiana*, vol. 2 (Lond., 1855), pp. 7–8; D. Comins, *Note on Emigration from India to British Guiana* (Calcutta, 1893), p. 7; R. Duff, *British Guiana* (Glas., 1866), p. 302; A. Young, *Approaches to Local Self Government in British Guiana* (Lond., 1958), p. 26; *Creole*, 17 May 1862.
13. Encl. in Light to Russell, 9 Apr. 1840, C.O. 111/171; and encl. (Walker) in Light to Stanley, 16 Oct. 1845, C.O. 111/125.
14. See note 13 above; see also encl. (Ross) in Light to Gladstone, No. 143, 17 July 1846, C.O. 111/234; and Light to Grey, No. 253, 15 Dec. 1846, C.O. 111/237.
15. Encl. (Walker) in Barkly to Grey, No. 53, 21 Mar. 1849, C.O. 111/264.
16. Young, *op. cit.*, p. 44.
17. Walker to Newcastle, No. 102, 20 Oct. 1853, C.O. 111/297.
18. Young, *op. cit.* pp. 31–34; and encl. (Walker) in Barkly to Grey, No. 53, 21 Mar. 1849, C.O. 111/264.
19. Encl. in Barkly to Grey, No., 46, 11 Arp. 1851, C.O. 111/281.
20. *Ibid*; Young, *op. cit.*, pp. 45–47; Barkly to Grey, No. 26, 10 Feb. 1852, C.O. 111/288.
21. *Ibid*; Attorney-General's report, 9 Jan. 1857, encl. in Wodehouse to

Labouchere, No. 157, 24 Dec. 1856, C.O. 111/313; *R.G.* 15 Apr. 1854.
22. *R.G.*, 8 Apr. 1856; encl. in Wodehouse to Labouchere, No. 157, 24 Dec. 1856, C.O. 111/313.
23. Young, *op. cit.* pp. 50–56.
24. Wodehouse to Newcastle, No. 78, 3 Aug. 1859, C.O. 111/324.
25. Hincks to Newcastle, No. 140, 28 July 1862, C.O. 111/336.
26. Walker to Newcastle, No. 96, 31 Dec. 1861, C.O. 111/332; encl. in Hincks to Newcastle, No. 149, 11 Aug. 1862, C.O. 111/336.
27. *Ibid*; Young, *op. cit.* pp. 58–59; Hincks to Newcastle, No. 66, 20 Apr. 1863, C.O. 111/340.
28. Hincks to Cardwell, No. 171, 17 Oct. 1864, C.O. 111/348; No. 4, 3 Jan. 1866, C.O. 111/355; *Creole*, 31 May 1865; and Young, *op. cit*, p. 89.
29. *Creole*, 31 May 1865; encls. in Hincks to Cardwell, No. 4, 3 Jan. 1866, C.O. 111/355. The commission consisted of William Walker, government secretary as chairman, Ludovic Porter, a colonial legislator, J. Brummell, sheriff of Demerara, N. Cox, inspector-general of police, and V.J. Jeffrey, a former commissary of taxation. Walker and Porter left the colony before the commission completed its task, but the remaining members submitted two separate reports. Brummell's report stressed the need for a highly centralized system of local administration under direct government control in which the villagers were accorded little voice. The other report of Cox and Jeffrey, while concurring with the principle of overall government supervision, favoured local self-management by the villagers and a move away from the coercive imposition of the rate system implemented in 1862. Governor Hincks adopted the first report.
30. Encl. in Hincks to Cardwell, No. 25, 22 Jan. 1866, C.O. 111/355; and *Creole*, 20 Dec. 1865.
31. *Ibid*.
32. Minute of H. Taylor, 3 Feb. 1866, C.O. 111/355.
33. *Creole*, 20 Dec. 1865.
34. Throughout his book, Young's entire analysis is premised on the view that the villagers lacked the necessary capacity and skill to manage their own affairs, and that the take-over of village administration was absolutely necessary if any improvements were to take place. In fact, Young is effusive in his admiration of Governor Hincks for having broken "the longstanding and deep-rooted resistance of the Negro proprietors to the idea of a compulsory village rate". See Young, *op. cit.*, p. 96.
35. Adamson, *op. cit.*, pp. 76–77.
36. Roberta Delson, 'Land and Urban Planning: Aspects of Modernization in Early Nineteenth-Century Brazil', *Luso-Brazilian Review*, 16 (2), 1979, pp. 207–209.
37. Adamson, 'Monoculture and Village Decay in British Guiana, 1854–1872', *Journal of Social History*, 3 (4), 1970, p. 402.
38. Hincks to Cardwell, No. 46, 8 Mar. 1866, C.O. 111/356.
39. Hincks to Cardwell, No. 26, 22 Jan. 1866, C.O. 111/355.
40. *Creole*, 26 July 1862; 22, 24, 27, 29 Oct. 1862; 5, 10 Nov. 1862; 6 Feb. 1863; 1, 13 Apr. 1863; 6 May 1863; 11 Jan 1864; 8 June 1864; *Colonist*, 13 Jan. 1864; Hincks to Newcastle, Nos. 196 and 199, 22 Nov. and 3 Dec. 1862, respectively, and encls, C.O. 111/337. See also Hincks to Cardwell, No. 146, 6 Sept. 1864, P.P. 1865. XXXVII.
41. *Colonist*, 2, 4, 6, and 7 May 1867; *B.G.*, 4 May 1867; *Creole*, 8 May and 13

Nov. 1867; encl. in Hincks to Cardwell, No. 186, 23 Nov. 1865, C.O. 111/353; Hincks to Buckingham & Chandos, No. 159, 20 Dec. 1867, C.O. 111/364.
42. See notes 35 and 37.
43. Young, *op. cit.*, pp. 59–60.
44. Hincks to Cardwell, No. 46, *loc. cit.*
45. Encl. in Hincks to Cardwell, No. 47, 19 March 1866, C.O. 111/356.
46. Petitions from Craig Village, 17 Jan. 1871, and Plaisance Village, 10 Nov. 1871; *Watchman*, 11 Nov. 1871 (Letter from Robert Will).
47. *R.G.*, 23 July 1872; *Colonist*, 22, 29 July 1872; 4, 7, Nov. 1872; 2 Dec. 1872; and 26 Feb. 1873 (see letters to the editor).
48. Alan Adamson, *Sugar Without Slaves, supra cit.*, p. 78.
49. Encl. in Rushworth to Kimberley, No. 126, 7 August 1873, C.O. 111/398.
50. *Watchman*, 4 July 1873; *R.G.*, 29 May 1875.
51. Encl. in Kortright to Hicks Beach, No. 52, 24 Feb. 1879, C.O. 111/412.
52. Report of the Inspector of villages, 29 Mar. 1882, C.O. 114/32.
53. Irving to Kimberley, No. 285, 3 Oct. 1882, C.O. 111/425.
54. *Ibid.*
55. *Ibid.*
56. Irving to Kimberley, No. 4, 4 Jan. 1883, C.O. 111/427.
57. Irving to Derby, No. 125, 5 May 1883, C.O. 111/428; *R.G.* 6 Jan. 1883.
58. Encl. in Gormanston to Knutsford, No. 248, 28 July 1890, C.O. 111/457; Report of the Inspector of Villages, 28 Mar. 1888 in *Administration Reports* for 1888.
59. *Echo*, 17 Oct. 1888.
60. *Ibid*, 12 and 19 Feb. 1887
61. *Ibid*, 8 Dec. 1887.
62. Gormanston to Knutsford, No. 354, 19 Nov. 1890, C.O. 111/457.
63. Encl. in Gormanston to Ripon, No. 384, 25 Nov. 1892, C.O. 111/465.
64. Adamson, *Sugar, supra cit.*, p. 92.
65. *Ibid.*, pp. 92–93.
66. See note 63.

Chapter 6

1. M.G. Smith, *The Plural Society in the British West Indies* (Berkeley, 1965), p. 86; and his 'Institutional and Political Conditions of Pluralism', *Pluralism in Africa*, Kuper & Smith (eds.), (Berkeley, 1971), pp. 53–55.
2. *Argosy*, 15 Aug. 1884; J. Marrat, *In the Tropics* (Lond. 1881), pp. 131–32.
3. See Decennial Censuses for 1841–91. In 1903, Governor Swettenhan claimed that between 1831 and 1891, there was hardly any natural increase in the local black population. Using the census and registration figures for 1829 and 1831, and comparing them with the 1891 census statistics, he asserted that though the number of black people had increased by 22,687 in that period, that increase was more than cancelled out by the influx of 48,178 immigrants from Africa and the West Indies. He erred, however, in assuming that all those listed as slaves in 1829–31 were black, while he also ignored the coloured people from his

1891 figures. See Swettenham to Chamberlain, No. 4, 5 Jan. 1903, C.O. 111/536.
4. H.V.P. Bronkhurst, *The Colony of British Guiana and its Labouring Inhabitants* (Lond., 1883), p. 165; H. Kirke, *Twenty-five Years in British Guiana* (Lond., 1898), p. 194.
5. Richard Schomburgk, *Travels in British Guiana*, vol. 2, (G'town, 1922 edit), pp. 46–47; A. Hardy, *Life and Adventure in British Guiana* (Lond., 1913), p. 93.
6. Hardy, *op. cit.*, p. 73.
7. Light to Grey, No. 10, 11 Jan. 1848, C.O. 111/250; Barkly to Grey, No. 102, 20 June 1850, P.P. 1851. XXXIX.
8. *Colonist*, 27 May 1864, 17 Oct. 1866, 3 and 17 July 1867, 29 Aug. 1867, 25 Sept. 1871, and 1 May 1879; *Creole*, 27 Sept. and 9 Oct. 1871, and 18 July 1873; *R.G.*, 26 Sept. 1871, 26 Oct. 1872, 30 Dec. 1875, 26 June 1882; *D.T.*, 29 Dec. 1875.
9. Edgar Thompson, 'The Plantation as a Social System', *Plantation Systems of the New World*, Soc. Sc. Monographs vii, 1959, Pan American Union, Wash. D.C., pp. 31–32.
10. Encl. in Light to Stanley, No. 233, 31 Oct. 1845, C.O. 111/225; encl. in Light to Gladstone, No. 163, 12 Aug. 1846, C.O. 111/235; Barkly to Grey, No. 26, 9 Feb. 1850, C.O. 111/272; and encl. 2 in No. 121, 15 Aug. 1850, C.O. 111/273.
11. Light to Glenelg, No. 2, 4 Jan. 1839, C.O. 111/162; Light to Russell, No. 10, 22 Jan. 1840, C.O. 111/170; reports of the Stipendiary Magistrates, encl. in Walker to Grey, No. 77, 17 Aug. 1848, C.O. 111/256; and No. 124, 19 Oct. 1848, C.O. 111/258; Barkly to Grey, Nos. 60 and 136, 17 Apr. and 24 Sept. 1850 respectively, and encls., C.O. 111/273; Alan Adamson, *Sugar Without Slaves* (New Haven, 1972), table 2, p. 37.
12. Walker to Newcastle, No. 102, 20 Oct. 1853, C.O. 111/297.
13. Grey to Barkly, No. 96, 31 Sept. 1849, C.O. 111/267; No. 202, 15 June 1850, C.O. 112/31; Barkly to Grey, No. 121, 15 Aug. 1850, C.O. 111/275.
14. Barkly to Grey, No. 121, 15 Aug. 1850, C.O. 111/275; and No. 26, 9 Feb. 1850, C.O. 111/272.
15. Adamson, *op. cit.*, p. 35.
16. Light to Glenelg, Nos. 24 and 41, 27 July and 1 Sept. 1838, respectively; and minute of J. Stephen, 21 Sept. 1838, C.O. 111/155; also Light to Normanby, No. 161, 29 July 1839, C.O. 111/164.
17. Stanley to Light, No. 608, 21 July 1845, and encl., C.O. 111/235.
18. Light to Gladstone, No. 45, 17 Mar. 1845, C.O. 111/232.
19. Barkly to Grey, No. 26, 9 Feb. 1850, and Grey to Barkly, No. 180, 1 May 1850, C.O. 111/272; Wood and Rogers to Merivale, 12 Nov. 1850, C.O. 386/87.
20. *R.G.*, 5 Feb. 1863; *Creole*, 7 Apr. 1865; also Ord. No. 4/1861, C.O. 113/4.
21. Report of the Crown Surveyor, 28 Feb. 1882, *Administration Reports*, 1881.
22. Scott to Kimberley, No. 114, 30 Aug. 1872, C.O. 111/391; and encl. in Kortright to Kimberley, No. 258, 15 Nov. 1881, C.O. 111/420.
23. Scott to Kimberley, No. 114, 30 Aug. 1872, C.O. 111/391.
24. Ordinance No. 9/1873.

25. Irving to Derby, No. 54, 23 Feb. 1884, C.O. 111/430.
26. Report of the Government Land Dept., 28 Apr. 1888, C.O. 114/43.
27. *Ibid.*; also Report of the Crown Surveyor, 30 July 1891, *Administration Reports*, 1890–91.
28. Light to Normanby, No. 78, 2 May 1839, C.O. 111/163; Light to Russell, separ., 23 June 1841, C.O. 111/177.
29. Light to Russell, No. 78, 23 June 1841, C.O. 111/178.
30. Light to Gladstone, No. 129, 1 July 1846, C.O. 111/234.
31. Light to Grey, No. 133, 30 June 1847, C.O. 111/244.
32. Ord. No. 11/1850, encl.in Barkly to Grey, No. 173, 31 Dec. 1850, C.O. 111/277; *Colonist*, 26 Feb. 1851.
33. *Colonist*, 12 May 1851.
34. Barkly to Newcastle, No. 82, 9 May 1853, C.O. 111/294; and Foreman to Tidman, 23 Jan. 1855, L.M.S. 7/4 (Bce).
35. *Colonist*, 12 May 1851.
36. Barkly to Newcastle, No. 82, 9 May 1853, C.O. 111/294. Barkly argued that the high taxes on imported foodstuff provided protection for local produce. So, far from inducing the blacks to work for more wages on the plantations, high taxation promoted their withdrawal to establish their own farms to produce crops for the lcoal market.
37. Wodehouse to Russell, No. 98, 9 July 1855, C.O. 111/305.
38. *Creole*, 7 Apr. 1858. In Trinidad, the tax per capita was stated to be $7.01, while in Jamaica it was just $1.47.
39. Foreman to Tidman, 24 Sept. 1858, L.M.S. 8/2 (Bce).
40. J. Beaumont, *The New Slavery* (Lond., 1871), p. 10; see also ord. No. 11/1850, sec. 2, and subsequent tax ordinances for succeeding years; E. Jenkins, *The Coolie: His Rights and Wrongs* (Lond., 1871), pp. 84–85; and encl. in Hincks to Newcastle, No. 120, 7 July 1863, C.O. 111/341. By sec. 1 of ord. No. 9/1862, 'all machinery employed in the manufacture of exports of the colony' were exempted from duty. Owing to difficulties in determining precisely what kinds of machinery came within this category, ord. No. 9/1863 stated that 'all machinery employed in the manufacture or preparation of produce or raw materials of the colony intended for exportation' would be free of duty.
41. Scott to Kimberley, No. 160, 7 Nov. 1871, and encls., C.O. 111/387.
42. Scott to Kimberley, No. 89, 5 July 1872, C.O. 111/390.
43. Encl. in Rushworth to Kimberley, No. 126, 7 Aug. 1873, C.O. 111/398.
44. Young to Carnarvon, No. 146, 6 July 1877, C.O. 111/411.
45. Irving to Kimberley, No. 198, 3 July 1882, C.O. 111/424.
46. Irving to Derby, No. 213, 25 July 1883, C.O. 111/428.
47. Irving to Derby, No. 20, 18 Jan. 1884, C.O. 111/430.
48. Adamson, *op. cit.*, p. 251.
49. *R.G.*, 30 June 1853; *Creole*, 22 Aug. 1857.
50. *Creole*, 28 Apr.1865, and 13 Aug. 1873.
51. Wodehouse to Labouchere, No. 83, 23 June 1856, C.O. 111/311; *R.G.*, 18 Oct. 1856; *Creole*, 22 May 1858.
52. Wodehouse to Labouchere, No. 83, 23 June 1856, C.O. 111/311; *Creole*, 17 Jan., 14 and 21 Feb., and 25 July 1857; 20, 23, and 27 Jan., and 3 Mar. 1858.
53. Encl. 2 in Wodehouse to Labouchere, No. 140, 6 Nov. 1856, C.O. 111/317; No. 76, 24 June 1857, and encl. 1 and sub-encls.; also encl. 5

in Labouchere to Wodehouse, No. 260, 18 May 1857, P.P. 1857 (305. Sess. 2). XXVIII; encl. in Wodehouse to Labouchere, No. 101, 23 July 1857, C.O. 111/317; and Letter to the editor, *Creole*, 12 June 1858.
54. *Creole*, 22 May 1858; Wodehouse to Stanley, No. 68, 7 June 1858, C.O. 111/320. The registration tax was repealed on 18 May 1858.
55. *Creole*, 21 Feb., 25 July and 8 Aug. 1857; *R.G.*, 28 July 1857; *B.G.*, 30 July 1857.
56. Hincks to Newcastle, No. 149, 11 Aug. 1862, C.O. 111/336.
57. *Creole*, 17 May 1862 and 6 Sept. 1869.
58. Adamson, *op. cit.*, p. 63.
59. Hincks to Newcastle, No. 140, 28 July 1862, C.O. 111/336.
60. Thompson, *loc. cit.*
61. *Creole*, 19 and 26 Jan., 7 Feb., 16 and 23 Mar. 1866; *G.T.*, 6 Feb. and 17 Mar. 1866; and Rattray to Tidman, 7 Jan. 1866, L.M.S. 8b/5 (Dem.).
62. Warder to Tidman, 20 Feb. 1865, L.M.S. 8b/4 (Dem.); also letter to the editor of *The Monthly Messenger*, 1 May 1866; and Rattray to Tidman, 9 and 23 July 1866, L.M.S. 8b/5 (Dem.); first annual report of the Cooperative Land Company, 12 Mar. 1867; and Warder to Mullens, 20 Mar. 1867, L.M.S. 9/1 (Dem.); *Creole*, 12 Jan. 1866 and 7 June 1871; *The People*, 13 Jan. 1866; *Colonist*, 15 Jan. 1866 and 8 Nov. 1872; and Irving to Stanhope, No. 265, 1 Oct. 1866, and encls; and No. 340, 10 Dec. 1866, C.O. 111/436.
63. *Creole*, 3 May 1872.
64. *R.G.*, 11 June 1874; *Colonist*, 11 and 18 June 1874.
65. *Colonist*, 12 Sept. and 2 Nov. 1883; *Argosy*, 15 and 29 Mar. 1884; Report of the Inspector of Villages for 1885, C.O. 114/40.
66. Letter by William Russell, *Argosy*, 27 Nov. 1880; and *Argosy*, 22 Mar. 1884.
67. *R.G.*, 16 July 1881; *Creole*, 21 July 1882; *DDC.*, 13 Aug. 1882; encl. in Kortright to Kimberley, No. 140, 4 Aug. 1881, C.O. 111/419; Reports of the Inspector of Villages for 1881 and 1885, C.O. 114/32 and 40 respectively.
68. *R.G.*, 28 Nov. 1878; *(D) DC*, 31 May 1883, 11 June 1884, and 8 Mar. 1885; *Argosy*, 4 Dec. 1880, 22 Apr., 23 May and 25 Oct. 1884.
69. Report of the Inspector of villages for 1881, C.O. 114/32; *Colonist*, 5 June 1883; *Argosy*, 15 Mar. 1884.
70. Encl. in Barkly to Grey, No. 12, 25 Jan. 1851, C.O. 111/280; and Barkly to Pakington, No. 161, 22 Oct. 1852, C.O. 111/291.
71. Hincks to Buckingham & Chandos, No. 135, 31 Aug. 1868, C.O. 111/369; see also the census for 1871, C.O. 116/240.
72. Light to Gladstone, No. 153, 30 July 1846, C.O. 111/234; Light to Grey, 25 Mar. 1847, C.O. 111/242; Wallbridge to Tidman, 17 Feb. 1847, L.M.S. 7/2 (Dem.); report of stipendiary magistrate Carbery, 28 Nov. 1857, encl. 3 in Wodehouse to Lytton, No. 119, 30 Sept. 1858, P.P. 1859, XX; Henderson to Mullings, 18 Jan. 1867, L.M.S. 9/1 (Dem.); Report of the [1870] Commissioners (ms.), sec. 26, C.O. 111/380; Wallbridge to Whitehouse, 4 Feb. 1874, L.M.S. 9/5 (Dem.); Pettigrew to Whitehouse, 24 Feb. 1874, L.M.S. 10/2 (Bce).
73. *Ibid.*; and Munro to Mullens, 18 Jan. 1867, L.M.S. 10/1 (Bce).
74. Hamilton to Tidman, 21 Feb. 1863, L.M.S. 8b/2 (Dem.); *Creole*, 26 Nov. 1873; encls. in Rushworth to Kimberley, No. 210, 31 Dec. 1873,

C.O. 111/400; Thompson to Whitehouse, 31 Aug. 1879, L.M.S. 11/1 (Bce); *D.C.*, 6 Oct. 1885.
75. Adamson, *op. cit.*, p. 87; W. Rodney, *A History of the Guyanese Working People, 1881-1905* (Balt., 1981), pp. 58-59.
76. Decennial censuses 1871, 1881, 1891 and the Reports of the Immigration Agent General. The 1891 census gives a figure of 32,665 "Creoles" resident on the estates, but that figure included local born Indians and Chinese. This was one of the very rare instances when the term "creole" was used to include persons other than blacks and coloureds without explanation.
77. Despres notes that by 1911, the Creoles comprised only 10 percent of the full-time estate labour force. See L. Despres, 'Ethnicity and Resource Competition in Guyanese Society', in his *Ethnicity and Resource Competition in Plural Societies* (The Hague, 1975), p. 92.
78. Scott to Tidman, 18 Feb. 1865, L.M.S. 8b/4 (Dem.); Scott to Mullens, 8 Mar. 1867, L.M.S. 9/1 (Dem.).
79. See the censuses for 1861 and 1871.
80. Adamson, *op. cit.*, pp. 58-59.
81. Pettigrew to Mullens, 22 Feb. 1868; and Munro to Mullens, 21 Feb. 1870, L.M.S. 10/1 (Bce).
82. Hincks to Newcastle, No. 60, 18 Mar. 1864, C.O. 111/345; *Creole*, 19 Aug. 1868. By ord. No. 3/1864, it was enacted that no person should act as an agent for the removal of emigrants from the colony unless licensed by the governor subject to such rules and regulations as he might from time to time prescribe with the concurrence of the legislature.
83. Report of the Crown Surveyor, 7 Mar. 1890, *Administration Reports*, 1889.
84. Tanner to Hawkins, 18 Jan. 1862, S.P.G./E.10; Hincks to Newcastle, No. 84, 26 Apr. 1864, and encl., C.O. 111/345. By ord. No. 4/1864, the B.G. Gold Co. Ltd. was incorporated as a joint-stock enterprise with limited liability. It was organised by a number of wealthy whites to seek for gold and other precious stones, and had a capital stock of $75,000 divided into 1500 shares. See also, the Report on the Balata Industry (1885) by G.S. Jenman, C.O. 114/38; Reports of the Crown Surveyor, and of the Gold Commissioner for 1891, *Administration Reports*, 1890-91; *D.C.* 18 Apr. and 25 July 1886; and J.E. Hewick, 'Our people', *Timehri*, Vol. 1, 3rd. ser., 1911, p. 232.
85. These are estimates derived from the statistics in the decennial censuses which do not provide a clear breakdown of the population distribution according to race.
86. Light to Glenelg, No. 102, 12 Dec. 1838, C.O. 111/156; encl. 4 in Light to Stanley, No. 255, 12 Dec. 1844; and encls. in No. 70, 7 Apr. 1845, C.O. 111/227; M.F. Milliroux, *Demerara* (Lond., 1877), pp. 19-20; Schomburgk, *op. cit.*, p. 35; Report of the [1870] Commissioners (ms), sec. 13, C.O. 111/379; Hardy, *op. cit.*, p. 64 and J. Heatley, *A Visit to the West Indies* (Lond. 1891), p. 43.
87. A.A. Thorne, 'British Guiana: Progress and Limitations', *Timehri* II (2), 1919, pp. 379-80.
88. D. Comins, *Note on Emigration from India to British Guiana* (Calcutta, 1893), p. 7; Barkly to Grey, No. 89, 2 June 1849, C.O. 111/266; *R.G.*, 1 Apr. 1875 and 29 Nov. 1881.

NOTES

89. See the censuses for 1851–1891.
90. Report of the [1870] Commissioners (ms.), sec. 13, C.O. 111/379.
91. H.V.P. Bronkhurst, *Among the Hindus and Creoles in British Guiana* (Lond., 1888) pp. 24–25.
92. P. DeWever, 'Our Future Peasantry', *Timehri*, 7, 3rd. ser. 1921, p. 107; Bronkhurst, *The Colony, supra cit.*, p. 72.
93. E.N. McDavid, *The Future Prospects of the Creoles of the Colony* [pamphlet] (Georgetown, 1900); Bronkhurst, *The Colony, supra cit.*, p. 72.
94. [Bronkhurst] *ibid*.
95. *Ibid.*; Decennial censuses, 1881 and 1891.
96. Light to Stanley, private, 1 Nov. 1842, C.O. 111/193; and his private and confidential despatch, 13 March 1843, C.O. 111/200.
97. *Ibid*.
98. *Ibid*.
99. *Creole*, 18 and 22 July 1857.
100. See Rodney, *op. cit.*, p. 113.
101. McDavid, *loc. cit*.
102. *Echo*, 13 July 1889.
103. R. Duff. *British Guiana* (Glasgow, 1866), p. 315.
104. Bronkhurst, *Among the Hindus, supra cit.*, p. 191.
105. *Echo*, 13 July 1889.
106. *Ibid.*, 3 Aug. 1889.
107. This was laid down shortly after emancipation by Secretary of State Stanley. (See Stanley to Light, private, 24 Dec. 1842, C.O. 111/193; also Rodney, *op. cit.*, p. 113.)
108. See, for instance, Light's despatches of 1 Nov. 1842 and 13 March 1843, *loc. cit.*; also Wodehouse to Labouchere. No. 29, 24 Feb. 1857, C.O. 111/316; Kortright to Kimberley, No. 229, 21 July 1881, C.O. 111/419 and No. 173, 3 Sept. 1881, C.O. 111/420; and Irving to Holland, No. 76, 19 Feb. 1887, C.O. 111/438.
109. *Ibid*.
110. Light to Stanley, confidential, 10 June 1844, C.O. 111/211.
111. Rodney, *op. cit.*, 114–115.
112. Light to Stanley, priv., 1 Nov. 1842, C.O. 111/193.
113. Rodney, *loc. cit*.
114. Light to Stanley, private, 1 Nov. 1842, C.O. 111/193.
115. Quoted in Comins, *op. cit.*, p. 8.
116. McDavid, *loc. cit*.
117. Bronkhurst, *Among the Hindus, supra cit.*, pp. 24–25.
118. *Creole*, 17 July 1865.
119. *Ibid.*, 18 Feb. 1860, 8 June 1861, 25 Sept. 1863, 17 July 1865, 11 May 1866; *R.G.*, 4 June 1853, 8 May and 27 Nov. 1855, 6 April 1875, 25 Aug. 1881, 1 July 1882; *Colonist*, 10 Aug. 1867 and 7 Sept. 1883; *DDC*, 29 Aug. 1882; Wodehouse to Grey, No. 41, 21 July 1854, C.O. 111/301; Scott to Kimberley, No. 25, 23 Feb. 1871, C.O. 111/383; and No. 147, 14 Oct. 1871, C.O. 111/386; Encl. in Longden to Carnarvon, No. 188, 7 Oct. 1874, C.O. 384/103; Report of the Inspector-General of Police for 1888, C.O. 114/44.
120. Blue Books of Statistics, C.O. 114. No consolidated criminal statistics are available before 1871.
121. Light to Grey, separate, 3 May 1848, C.O. 111/252; Roome to Tidman,

30 Jan. 1850, L.M.S. 7/1 (Bce); P.P. 1851. XXXIX, No. 8, Barkly to Grey, 10 Jan. 1851 and encls.; *B.G.*, 17 Feb. 1864; *Colonist*, 26 Jan., 19 July and 5 Aug. 1867, and 19 May 1874; *R.G.*, 20 Feb. 1879.
122. See note 120.
123. Wodehouse to Labouchere, No. 107, 23 Aug. 1856, C.O. 111/312.
124. *Creole*, 8 June 1861 and 17 July 1865; *B.G.*, 20 Feb. 1864; *Colonist*, 11 and 31 July, 5 and 24 Aug. 1867, and 19 May 1874; *R.G.*, 20 Feb. 1879.
125. *Colonist*, 15 Oct. 1868. The provision was made by ord. no. 12/1868.
126. Young to Hicks Beach, No. 241, 4 Nov. 1879, C.O. 111/415. This reformatory was established by ord. no. 5/1879.
127. Light to Stanley, No. 70, 7 April 1845 and encls., and No. 83, 18 April 1845 and encls., C.O. 111/227; also Wodehouse, No. 29, *loc. cit.*
128. M.F. Milliroux, *Demerara: The Transition from Slavery to Liberty* (trans. ed., Lond., 1877), pp. 56–57.
129. *R.G.*, 18 April 1885.
130. Negro stereotypes proliferate in the contemporary works on the post-slavery 19th century. In addition to those by Marrat, Bronkhurst, Schomburgk, Comins, Heatley, Hardy, Kirke and Milliroux mentioned above, see also J. Brummell, *Demerara after fifteen years of Freedom* (Lond., 1853); H. Dalton, *A History of British Guiana*, 2 vols. (Lond., 1855). The extent to which these stereotypes were internalised by the Creoles can be gleaned from the book by the black Anglican priest, J.R. Moore, entitled *A Handbook of Causes of Non-Success and Degradation of the Negro Race in British Guiana* (Dem., 1874). This stands in stark contrast to the Trinidadian J.J. Thomas' *Froudacity* (Lond., 1889) which aimed at countering such racist stereotypes of blacks.
131. Encl. in Light to Stanley, No. 255, 12 Dec. 1844, C.O. 111/215.
132. Schomburgk, *op. cit.* pp. 45–46.
133. Kirke, *op. cit.*, pp. 45–46.
134. P.D. Curtin, *Two Jamaicas*, (N.Y., 1970), pp. 174–75.
135. Bronkhurst, *Among the Hindus*, supra cit., p. 202.
136. Kirke, *op. cit.*, pp. 208–211; Bronkhurst, *Among the Hindus*, supra cit., p. 198; Heatley, *op. cit.*, p. 44; 1891 Census statistics.
137. The Georgetown Town Council was established in 1837. It consisted of 11 Councillors (representing wards) from among whom a mayor was elected every year. In 1837 the franchise was granted to every adult, including women, in possession of a house or tenement in the city valued at 3,500 guilders ($1,200/£250), but that was reduced in 1860 to $250. Qualifications for membership of the council was fixed in 1837 at property valued at 8,000 guilders (about £570/$2,740); but that too was lowered in 1860 to $1,500. These comparatively low property qualifications made it possible for the Creole elites to enter the council and to become mayors, starting with Richard Haynes in 1846. See Clementi, *op. cit*, pp. 128–136; J. Rodway, *The Story of Georgetown* (G'town, 1920); also, Comins, *op. cit.*, p. 8; Hardy, *op. cit.*; Heatley, *op. cit.*; Kirke, *op. cit.*, p. 40.
138. Bronkhurst, *Among the Hindus*, supra cit., p. 198.
139. Kirke, *loc. cit.*
140. *Ibid.*, pp. 45–46.
141. *Ibid.*; also, Bronkhurst, *Among the Hindus*, supra cit., p. 203.

142. B. Brereton, *Race Relations in Colonial Trinidad, 1870–1900* (Lond., 1979), p. 205.
143. *Ibid.*
144. *Echo*, 3 Aug. 1889.
145. M.G. Smith, 'Institutional and Political Conditions ...' *loc. cit.*, p. 54.
146. P.L. van den Berghe, 'Pluralism and the Polity: A Theoretical Exploration', *Pluralism in Africa, supra cit.*, p. 72.

Chapter 7

1. John Rex, *Race Relations in Sociological Theory* (Lond., 1970), pp. 75–76.
2. See the censuses for 1841 to 1891.
3. M.G. Smith, 'Institutional and Political Conditions of Pluralism', *Pluralism in Africa*, Kuper and Smith (eds.), (Berkeley, 1971), p. 54.
4. P.P. 1847–48. XXIII. Pt. 1. 395, No. 5, Light to Grey, 16 July 1847.
5. G. DesVoeux, *Experiences of a Demerara Magistrate* (Georgetown, 1948), p. 147.
6. Light to Stanley, No. 245, 3 Dec. 1845, C.O. 111/226; Light to Grey, No. 180, 3 Sept. 1846, C.O. 111/235; Barkly to Grey, No. 101, 5 July 1850, C.O. 111/275; and Wodehouse to Labouchere, No. 69, 6 June 1857, C.O. 111/316.
7. Light to Gladstone, No. 158, 3 Aug. 1846, and encl., C.O. 111/235; encl. 4 in Light to Stanley, No. 255, 12 Dec. 1844; and encl. in No. 83, 18 Apr. 1845, C.O. 111/227; Light to Grey, No. 136, and encl. in No. 150, 3 and 16 July 1847, respectively, C.O. 111/244; also No. 10, 11 Jan. 1848, and encls., C.O. 111/250; encl. in Barkly to Grey, No. 147, 16 Oct., 1850, C.O. 111/275; encl. in Barkly to Newcastle, No. 69, 22 Apr. 1853, C.O. 111/294; encl. in Wodehouse to Grey, No. 41, 21 July, 1854, C.O. 111/301; B. Premium, *Eight Years in British Guiana* (Lond., 1850), p. 126; K. Laurence, 'The Establishment of the Portuguese Community in British Guiana', *JHR*, 5 (2) 1965, pp. 58–59.
8. *Colonist*, 3 Feb. 1851; Barkly to Grey, No. 26, 11 Mar. 1851, C.O. 111/280; Colonial Land and Emigration Commission to Merivale, 19 May, 1851, C.O. 318/190; Barkly to Pakington, No. 146, 22 Sept. 1852, C.O. 111/291; Walker to Newcastle, No. 28, 8 July 1853, C.O. 111/295. Ord. No. 13/1851 enjoined those Portuguese for whom a bounty was paid to enter a contract for one to three years, or alternatively to pay $1 for every month not contracted.
9. Wodehouse to Labouchere, No. 117, 6 Sept. 1856, C.O. 111/312; also No. 69, 6 June 1857, C.O. 111/316.
10. Wodehouse to Labouchere, No. 80, 2 May 1857, and encl., C.O. 111/317; Rogers to Merivale, 8 Aug. 1857, C.O. 318/215; see also note 9.
11. Wodehouse to Lytton, No. 63, 18 June 1859, and encl., C.O. 111/324.
12. Encl. in No. 102, Barkly to Grey, 20 June 1850, C.O. 111/275.
13. Hincks to Newcastle, No. 23, 14 Feb. 1863, C.O. 111/339. Governor Scott claimed that there were 823 Portuguese on the plantations in 1871 (see Scott to Kimberley, No. 66, 8 May 1872, C.O. 111/390); but the 1870 commissioners could locate very few of them (see their Report, sec. 13, C.O. 111/379).
14. Encl. in Barkly to Grey, No. 102, 20 June 1850, C.O. 111/275.

15. *R.G.*, 6 Sept. 1883.
16. Report of the crown surveyor for 1880, C.O. 114/30; Preliminary Report by E. Im Thurn on the Pomeroon Judicial District, 1887, C.O. 114/43; and Report of the Government Land Dept., 1888, C.O. 114/44. Most of these Pomeroon settlers, however, were grantholders on crown lands, workers on those grants, or shopkeepers.
17. *Watchman*, 25 July 1873.
18. Report of Stipendiary Magistrate Ball, encl. in Light to Stanley, No. 183, 28 Aug. 1844, C.O. 111/212.
19. Encl. in Light to Stanley, No. 70, 7 Apr. 1845, C.O. 111/227.
20. Light to Russell, separ., 21 Dec. 1840, C.O. 111/173; and stipendiary magistrates' reports for June 1841, encl. in No. 111, 12 Aug. 1841, C.O. 111/183; Light to Stanley, No. 97, 31 May 1842, C.O. 111/190; and stipendiary magistrates reports for June 1842, encl. in No. 151, 5 Aug. 1842, C.O. 111/192; also stipendiary magistrates reports for Dec. 1843, encl. in No. 31, 10 Feb. 1844, C.O. 111/208.
21. Light to Stanley, No. 54, 14 Mar. 1844, C.O. 111/209; *Creole*, 12 May 1860; see also note 20.
22. J. Jones, 'Mission of British Guiana', *Letters and Notices* (Society of Jesus), vol. 1, 1862.
23. *Colonist*, 5 Mar. 1852.
24. Letter to the editor, *Creole*, 29 Nov. 1856; Sherlock to Barrow, 25 May 1858, S.J./B.G/12.
25. *Official Gazette*, 10 Sept. 1851, C.O. 115/21.
26. *Ibid.*, 5 April 1871, C.O. 115/38.
27. *O.G.*, 1853.
28. *O.G.*, 1852; Hincks to Granville, No. 23, 19 Jan. 1869, and encl., C.O. 111/371; encl. 2 in Gormanston to Knutsford, No. 222, 5 July 1888, C.O. 111/445; report of the Chief Commissary (1891), C.O. 114/50.
29. H. Bronkhurst, *The Colony of British Guiana* (Lond., 1883), pp. 100 and 103; Richard Schomburgk, *Travels in British Guiana*, vol. 2 (Georgetown, 1922), p. 25.
30. Light to Stanley, No. 22, 24 Jan. 1842, C.O. 111/189; No. 31, 10 Feb. 1844, C.O. 111/208; encls. in No. 183, 28 Aug. 1844, C.O. 111/212; No. 215, 30 Nov. 1844, C.O. 111/215; separate, 8 Apr. 1845, C.O. 111/222; and encl. in No. 174, 2 Aug. 1845, C.O. 111/224.
31. Light to Stanley, separ., 7 Dec. 1841, C.O. 111/181; No. 54, 14 Mar. 1844, C.O. 111/209; encls. in No. 183, 28 Aug. 1844, C.O. 111/212; separ., 8 Apr. 1845, C.O. 111/222.
32. *R.G.*, 30 Oct. 1843.
33. Light to Stanley, No. 70, 7 Apr. 1845, C.O. 111/227. Governor Light suggested that without the licences, the Creoles would have engaged in irregular trade which would have hindered their progress in "civilisation". He preferred their confinement to agricultural labour.
34. Encl. 4 in Barkly to Grey, No. 12, 20 Jan. 1851, C.O. 111/280.
35. Light to Stanley, No. 130, 18 Aug. 1843, C.O. 111/202; Barkly to Grey, No. 173, 31 Dec. 1850, C.O. 111/227.
36. *Ibid.*; *Colonist*, 26 Feb. 1851; see also note 33.
37. *Creole*, 19 Feb. 1862; Hincks to Newcastle, No. 50, 5 Apr. 1862; minute of H. Taylor, 6 May 1862; and Newcastle to Hincks, No. 427, 19 May 1862, C.O. 111/334.

38. Encl. in Wodehouse to Lytton, 24 May 1859, C.O. 111/323; *Creole*, 28 May 1862; encl. in Hincks to Newcastle, No. 102, 21 June 1862, C.O. 111/335; and encl. in No. 120, 7 July 1863, C.O. 111/341.
39. *O.G.*, 1852; and report of Chief Commissary (1891), C.O. 114/50.
40. See Robert Ciski, 'The Vincentian Portuguese: A Study in Ethnic Group Adaptation', Ph.D Dissertation, University of Massachusetts, 1975; W.K. Marshall, '"Vox Populi": The St. Vincent Riots and Disturbances of 1862', in *Trade, Government and Society in Caribbean History, 1700-1920*, B.W. Higman (ed.), (Kgn. 1983); D. Wood, *Trinidad in Transition* (Lond., 1968), pp. 101-106.
41. T. Tucker, *Bermuda: Today and Yesterday, 1503-1973* (Lond., 1975), p. 132; H.C. Wilkinson, *Bermuda from Sail to Steam: The History of the Island from 1784 to 1901*, vol. 2 (Lond., 1973), p. 655; James Purves, 'The Portuguese in Bermuda', *Bermuda Historical Quarterly*, vol. 3, pt. 3, 1946.
42. Laurence, *loc. cit.*, p. 55.
43. M. Freedman, 'The Handling of Money: A Note on the Background to the Economic Sophistication of Overseas Chinese', *Man*, 59, 1959.
44. Rex, *loc. cit.*
45. This incisive comment was made by Bridget Brereton on an earlier draft of this chapter.
46. *R.G.*, 2 June 1866.
47. *Creole*, 12 May 1860 and 16 Apr. 1862.
48. *Colonist*, 19 June 1867.
49. Small coinage was in short supply for practically the whole post-emancipation 19th century. See Light to Stanley, No. 54, 14 Mar. 1844, C.O. 111/209; Light to Grey, No. 244, 3 Dec. 1846, and encl., C.O. 111/237; No. 133, 30 June 1847, C.O. 111/244; and No. 37, 4 Mar. 1848, C.O. 111/251; Light to Hawes, 13 July 1848, C.O. 111/253; Walker to Grey, No. 74, 17 Aug. 1848, C.O. 111/256; encl. in Barkly to Grey, No. 36, 7 Mar. 1850, C.O. 111/273; No. 96, 4 July 1850, C.O. 111/275; and No. 39, 11 Apr. 1851, C.O. 111/281; Wodehouse to Newcastle, No. 18, 7 Feb. 1860, C.O. 111/326; Hincks to Newcastle, No. 107, 2 July 1862, C.O. 111/335; and Longden to Carnarvon, No. 106, 22 June 1874, and encl., C.O. 111/402.
50. A. Adamson, 'Monoculture and village Decay in British Guiana', *JSH*, 3 (4), 1970, p. 395. See also note 49.
51. Hincks to Newcastle, No. 50, 5 Apr. 1862, C.O. 111/334.
52. Hincks to Newcastle, No. 107, 2 July 1862, C.O. 111/335.
53. Walker to Grey, No. 74, 17 Aug. 1848, C.O. 111/256; and Barkly to Grey, No. 96, 4 July 1850, C.O. 111/275.
54. See notes 51-52; also *Colonist*, 2 Apr. 1862.
55. Light to Grey, No. 181, 15 Sept. 1847, C.O. 111/245; and No. 49, 18 Mar. 1848, C.O. 111/251; *Colonist*, 5 May 1874; *Creole*, 21 Aug. 1871; *D.D.C*, 6 Sept. 1882.
56. *D.C.*, 27 Feb. 1889.
57. *R.G.*, 27 Mar. 1875.
58. *Colonist*, 25 Aug. 1875; *D.C.*, 21 Mar. 1885.
59. *R.G.*, 27 Mar. 1875 and *Colonist*, 2 Mar. 1875. In March 1875, 28 Portuguese and 7 Indian shopkeepers were arrested in one swoop by the police on the West Bank of Demerara. These arrests were not infrequent, but the fines were too small to prove an affective deterrent.

60. *R.G.*, 31 July 1875; *D.D.C.*, 7 Feb. 1882.
61. *Colonist*, 16 Aug. 1878.
62. Haynes Smith to Derby, No. 168, 4 June 1884, C.O. 111/430.
63. R. von Albertini, *European Colonial Rule, 1880-1940* (Oxford, 1982) pp. 172 and 179.
64. *R.G.*, 27 Mar. 1875; *D.D.C.*, 6 & 13 Jan. 1884, *Echo*, 27 July 1887.
65. *O.G.*, 1857; *D.D.C.*, 2 Dec. 1883; *Argosy*, 2 Feb. and 15 Aug., 1884; encl. in Irving to Derby, No. 112, 5 May 1885, C.O. 111/432.
66. *R.G.*, 27 Mar. 1875, 1 Apr. 1876; *Colonist*, 18 Oct. 1880; *D.D.C.*, 22 Jan. 1884.
67. *D.D.C*, 2 & 12 Dec. 1883; ord. No. 5/1885.
68. *Creole*, 15 & 25 Apr., 6 May, 6 and 8 July 1864; *Colonist*, 15 & 25 Apr. 1864; Mundy to Buckingham & Chandos, Nos. 112 and 115, 7 and 23 Aug. 1867, respectively, C.O. 111/363.
69. See ords. No. 16/1850, No. 25/1868, and No. 8/1870; also Hincks to Buckingham & Chandos, No. 160, 7 Nov. 1868, C.O. 111/369; and Scott to Granville, No. 85, 11 July 1870, C.O. 111/376. In 1850, five classes of spirit licences were established ranging from $200 to $1700 per annum. In 1868, a new system of 14 classes of licences was instituted ranging from $600 to $6000; and the next year two higher classes were added at $7200 and $8400 per year.
70. Encls. in Irving to Derby, No. 244, 2 Sept. 1885, C.O 111/433; encl. 2 in Gormanston to Knutsford, No. 222, 5 July 1888, C.O. 111/445; and Report of the Chief Commissary, 1890-91, C.O. 114/50.
71. Portuguese petition, 30 Nov. 1870, encl. in Scott to Kimberley, No. 61, 26 Apr. 1871, C.O. 111/383; see also note 70.
72. Hincks to Granville, No. 23, 19 Jan. 1869, C.O. 111/371; and encl. 2 in Gormanston to Knutsford, No. 222, 5 July 1888, C.O. 111/445.
73. Scott to Kimberley, No. 61, 26 Apr. 1871, C.O. 111/383; Longden to Carnarvon, No. 105, 20 June 1874, C.O. 111/402; and encl. in No. 123, 7 July 1874, C.O. 111/402; encl. in Young to Carnarvon, No. 146, 6 July 1877; and encl. in Kortright to Carnarvon, No. 178, 5 Sept. 1877, C.O. 111/411; encl. in Young to Hicks Beach, 4 June 1879, C.O. 111/414. See also ords. Nos. 4/1874, 2/1877, 4/1877, and 4/1879.
74. Encl. in Hincks to Buckingham & Chandos, No. 110, 27 July 1868, C.O. 111/368; and No. 160, 7 Nov. 1868, C.O. 111/369; encl. in Scott to Kimberley, No. 94, 7 June 1871, C.O. 111/386; encl. in Kortright to Kimberley, No. 184, 26 Aug. 1880, C.O. 111/416; Report of the Chief Commissary, 19 Jan. 1881, C.O. 114/30; and also encl. in Gormanston to Knutsford, No. 118, 24 Apr. 1890, C.O. 111/456.
75. J. Levy, 'The Economic Role of the Chinese in Jamaica: The Grocery Retail Trade', *JHR*, xv, 1986, pp. 45-46.
76. H. Johnson, 'The Anti-Chinese Riots of 1918 in Jamaica', *Immigrants and Minorities*, 2 (1), 1983, pp. 56-57.
77. Laurence, *loc. cit.*, p. 68.
78. Encl. in Scott to Kimberley, No. 61, 26 Apr. 1871, C.O. 111/383.
79. *Ibid.*
80. Longden to Carnarvon, No. 158, 31 July 1875, C.O. 111/405; encl. in Irving to Stanhope, No. 290, 27 Oct. 1886, C.O. 111/436; see also the Blue Books of Statistics. By 1891, there were 887 Portuguese with savings banks' deposits amounting to £42,805. In addition, the Portu-

guese Benevolent Society had accumulated assets of $180,852 between 1872 and 1886.
81. Hincks to Newcastle, No. 23, 14 Feb. 1863, C.O. 111/339; Kortright to Kimberley, secret, 30 Nov. 1881, and encl., C.O. 111/420.
82. Longden to Carnarvon, No. 158, 31 July 1875, C.O. 111/405; and encl. in Irving to Stanhope, No. 290, 27 Oct. 1886, C.O. 111/436.
83. Scott to Tidman, 19 May 1856, L.M.S. 8a/2 (Dem.).
84. See Census for 1891; also Kortright to Kimberley, secret, 30 Nov. 1881, C.O. 111/420; Gormanston to Knutsford, No. 4, 3 Jan. 1890, C.O. 111/455. Over the years since their first arrival, a small number of individual Portuguese had become naturalized British subjects. But since there was no general provision under the laws to make this process simple, it required a special ordinance every time someone sought naturalization. This inconvenience no doubt contributed to the disclination of the Portuguese to change their nationality. Eventually in 1891, an ordinance was passed to make the process of naturalization relatively simple. See encl. in Bruce to Knutsford, No. 153, 12 May 1891 (re. Ord. No. 7 of 1891), C.O. 111/460.
85. Kortright to Kimberley, secret, 30 Nov. 1881, C.O. 111/420.
86. *Creole*, 25 Nov. 1857.
87. Light to Stanley, No. 243, 28 Nov. 1845, C.O. 111/226.
88. Scott to Kimberley, No. 167, 22 Nov. 1871, C.O. 111/386.
89. Rex, *loc. cit.*
90. Encl. 3 in Wodehouse to Labouchere, No. 57, 9 May 1856, C.O. 111/311; and Scott to Tidman, 19 May 1856, L.M.S. 8a/2 (Dem.).
91. Light to Grey, No. 60, 4 Apr. 1848, and encls., C.O. 111/252. The March 1848 disturbances occurred at Plns. Mara and Ma Retraite, and in the Villages of Sisters, Light Town, Highbury, and L'Enterprise, on the east bank of the Berbice River.
92. Wodehouse to Labouchere, No. 16, 24 Feb. 1856, C.O. 111/309. Even the Colonial Office were astounded about this. See Merivale to Labouchere, 7 April 1856 and Labouchere to Wodehouse, No. 65, 16 April 1865, C.O. 111/310.
93. Wodehouse to Labourchere, No. 25, 10 Mar. 1856, C.O. 111/310.
94. See note 54; *Creole*, 19 Feb. 1862.
95. *Creole*, 8 Mar. 1862; *Colonist*, 21 Mar. 1862; Hincks to Newcastle, No. 40, 22 Mar. 1862, C.O. 111/334.
96. See note 54. Also *Colonist*, 24 Mar. and 7 Apr. 1862; *Creole*, 2 Apr. 1862; and Hincks to Newcastle, No. 60, 22 Apr. 1862, C.O. 111/334.
97. *Creole*, 28 May 1862; encl. in Hincks to Newcastle, No. 102, 21 June 1862, C.O. 111/335.
98. *D.G.*, 20 Mar. 1889; *Echo*, 23 Mar. 1889; *Argosy*, 23 Mar. 1889; Gormanston to Knutsford, No. 111, 30 Mar. 1889, C.O. 111/451.
99. Encl. in Bruce to Knutsford, confid., 29 July, 1891, C.O. 111/460.
100. Premium, *op. cit.*, pp. 91–92; Report of the Demerara district committee, 9 Feb. 1847, L.M.S. 7/2 (Dem); *R.G.*, 19 May 1853; H. Kirke, *Twenty-five Years in British Guiana* (Lond., 1898), p. 202.
101. M. Newitt, *Portugal in Africa* (Lond., 1981); J. Duffy, *Portugal in Africa* (Lond., 1962); R. Conrad, *The Destruction of Brazilian Slavery, 1850–1888* (Calif., 1972); Albertini, *op. cit.*
102. Hudson to Gen. Sect., No. 363, 24 Feb. 1856, M.M.S/W. iv/5; Rattray

to Tidman, 25 Feb. 1856; and Wallbridge to Tidman, 23 Feb. 1856, L.M.S. 8a/2 (Dem.).
103. *Ibid*; also, Wodehouse to Labouchere, No. 16, 24 Feb. 1856, C.O. 111/309; and encl. 3 in No. 57, 9 May 1856, C.O. 111/311.
104. Wodehouse to Labouchere, No. 16, 24 Feb, 1856, C.O. 111/309.
105. Wallbridge to Tidman, 23 Feb. 1856, L.M.S. 8a/2 (Dem.). Orr was eventually tried for unlawful assembly in April 1856 and sentenced to three years' hard labour.
106. Wodehouse to Labouchere, No. 25, 10 Mar. 1856, C.O. 111/310; and Scott to Tidman, 19 May 1856, L.M.S. 8a/2 (Dem.).
107. Sub-encl. in Wodehouse to Labouchere, No. 115, 6 Sept. 1856, C.O. 111/312.
108. *D.C.*, 31 Jan. 1889.
109. Encls. A & B in Bruce to Knutsford, No. 68, 14 Feb. 1889, C.O. 111/451.
110. Longden to Carnarvon, No. 50, 22 Mar. 1875, C.O. 111/404; Bruce to Knutsford, confid., 1 Mar. 1889, C.O. 111/451.
111. Encl. A in Bruce to Knutsford, No. 68, 14 Feb. 1889, C.O. 111/451.
112. Bruce to Knutsford, No. 66, 9 Feb. 1889, and encl., C.O. 111/451; *Argosy*, 2 and 16 Feb. 1889.
113. Encl. in Gormanston to Knutsford, No. 109, 29 Mar. 1889, C.O. 111/451.
114. *Echo*, 23 Mar. 1889; Gormanston to Knutsford, confid., 29 Mar. 1889, C.O. 111/451; and No. 252, 5 July 1889, C.O. 111/453.
115. *Argosy*, 23 Mar. 1889.
116. *Ibid*.; *D.C.*, 20 Mar. 1889; *Echo*, 23 Mar. 1889; Gormanston to Knutsford, No. 111, 30 Mar. 1889, C.O. 111/451.
117. Encl. in Gormanston to Knutsford, No. 296, 16 Aug. 1889, C.O. 111/453; *Echo*, 28 Sept. 1889; *D.C.*, 25, 30 Sept. 1889.
118. Bruce to Knutsford, confid., and No. 245, 29 July 1891, C.O. 111/460.
119. Encl. in Bruce to Knutsford, confid., and No. 245, 29 July 1891, C.O. 111/460.
120. *Ibid*.
121. Bruce to Knutsford, confid., 26 Aug. 1891, C.O. 111/460.
122. J. Heatley, *A Visit to the West Indies* (Lond., 1891), p. 42.
123. Kirke, *op. cit.*, p. 60.
124. *D.D.C.*, 3 July 1883.
125. Laurence, *loc. cit.*, pp. 72–73.
126. Decennial censuses, 1851–1891.
127. Sherlock to Barrow, 25 May 1858, S.J./B.G./12.
128. Brian L. Moore, 'Social and Cultural Complexity in British Guiana, 1850–1891', unpublished Ph.D. Thesis, U.W.I., 1973, pp. 290–295.
129. *Ibid.*, p. 304.
130. *Ibid.*, pp. 292 and 295–96.
131. *Ibid.*, p. 304.

Chapter 8

1. E.R. Wolf and S.W. Mintz, 'Haciendas and Plantations in Middle America and the Antilles', *SES*, Sept. 1957; S. Mintz, 'The Plantation

as a Socio-cultural type', *Plantation Systems of the New World*, Soc. Sc. Monographs, VII, 1959, pp. 44-47.
2. E. Thompson, 'The Plantation as a Social System', *Plantation Systems*, Soc. Sc. Monographs VII, 1959, pp. 31-32.
3. Return of immigrants, P.P. 1873, L; D. Comins, *Note on Emigration from India to British Guiana* (Calcutta, 1893), p. 44.
4. Return of immigrants, P.P. 1868-69, XLIII; Colonial Land & Emigration Commission to Herbert, 22 and 24 Mar. 1873, C.O. 318/271; and Kortright to Hicks Beach, No. 13, 19 Jan. 1880, C.O. 384/128.
5. See the censuses of 1841-1891.
6. Hincks to Newcastle, No. 89, 4 May 1864, C.O. 111/345.
7. Report of the Immigration Agent General (I.A.G.), 15 Oct., 1881, *Administration Reports*, 1880.
8. Sub-encl. in encl. 1, Hincks to Buckingham and Chandos, No. 178, 22 Dec. 1868, C.O. 111/369.
9. *Ibid.*; and Labouchere to Wodehouse, No. 94, 30 June 1856, C.O. 112/33.
10. Report of the I.A.G., 29 Oct. 1877, *Administration Reports*, 1876.
11. Encl. in Barkly to Pakington, No. 86, 21 Apr. 1852, P.P. 1852. XXXI; Scott to Kimberley, No. 65, 2 May 1871, C.O. 111/385; and Report of the I.A.G. for 1891, C.O. 114/53.
12. G.A. Grierson, *Report on Colonial Emigration from the Bengal Residency* (1883), p. 30; Barkly to Grey, No. 152, 31 Oct. 1851, P.P. 1852-53, LXVIII.
13. J.H. Hutton, *Caste in India* (Lond., 1961), p. 88.
14. H. Tinker, *A New System of Slavery* (Oxford, 1974); and J.A. Weller, *The East Indian Indenture in Trinidad* (P.R., 1968).
15. Sub-encl. in Newcastle to Wodehouse, No. 38, 12 June 1854, P.P. 1859. XVI; Wodehouse to Newcastle, No. 31, 25 Feb. 1860, C.O. 111/326; encl. 5 in Walker to Newcastle, No. 83, 19 Nov. 1861, C.O. 111/332.
16. C. Clementi, *The Chinese in British Guiana* (Georgetown, 1915), pp. 333-349.
17. R.T. Smith, 'Some Social Characteristics of Indian Immigrants to British Guiana', *PS.*, 13 (1), 1959, p. 39.
18. *Creole*, 12 May 1865, 19 Apr. 1867; *R.G.*, 28 Feb. and 3 Mar. 1874; *Colonist*, 29 Dec. 1869; H. Bronkhurst, *The Colony of British Guiana* (Lond., 1883), pp. 358-59. There was also one reported instance of a violent clash between Nepalese and "Calcuttans" on Pln. Nonpareil in 1888. See *D.C.*, 21 and 23 Nov. 1888.
19. R.T. Smith, 'Social Stratification, Cultural Pluralism and Integration in West Indian Societies', *Caribbean Integration*, S. Lewis and T. Mathews (eds.), (P.R., 1967), p. 230.
20. E. Jenkins, *The Coolie: His Rights and Wrongs* (Lond., 1871), p. 63.
21. Several theses have been written within the last decade and a half which clearly demonstrate that the plantation was by no means a total institution even while the immigrants were under indenture; and the fact that there was an increasingly large number of unindentured Indians both on and off the estates after 1870 meant that it became increasingly difficult for the plantations to exercise total control over all aspects of life among its inmates. See R.J. Moore, 'East Indians and Negroes in British Guiana, 1838-1880', D.Phil. Thesis, Sussex Univ.,

1970; B.L. Moore, 'Social and Cultural Complexity in British Guiana, 1850-1891', Ph.D. Thesis, U.W.I., 1973; L. Potter, 'Internal Migration and Resettlement of East Indians in Guyana, 1870-1920', Ph.D. dissertation, McGill Univ., 1975; T. Ramnarine, 'The Growth of the East Indian Community in British Guiana, 1880-1920', D.Phil. Thesis, Sussex Univ., 1977; and D. Bisnauth, 'The East Indian Immigrant Society in British Guiana, 1891-1930', Ph.D. thesis, U.W.I., 1977.

22. M.G. Smith, 'Institutional and Political Conditions of Pluralism', and 'Some Developments in the Analytic Framework of Pluralism', both in *Pluralism in Africa*, Kuper & Smith (eds.), (Berkeley, 1971), pp. 56-57, and 434-447, respectively.
23. Glenelg to Smyth, No. 124, 29 June 1836, C.O. 111/144; Order in Council, 30 July 1838, P.P. 1837-38. LII.; circular letter from Lord Glenelg, 30 July 1838, and Glenelg to Light, No. 86, 19 Dec. 1838, P.P. 1839. XXXV.; C.L. & E.C. to Stephen, 14 Oct. 1843, and encl., P.P. 1844. XXXV.; and Lyttelton to West India Committee, 28 Mar. 1846, P.P. 1846, XXVII.
24. Ords. Nos. 2 and 3 of 1848, encl. in Light to Grey, No. 39, 5 Mar. 1848, P.P. 1847-47. XLV.
25. Grey to Barkly, No. 212, 16 July 1850, P.P. 1851. XXXIX.
26. Barkly to Grey, No. 127, 27 Aug. 1850, C.O. 111/275; and No. 130, 11 Sept. 1850, C.O. 111/276.
27. Barkly to Newcastle, No. 21, 11 Feb. 1853, C.O. 111/293.
28. *R.G.*, 16 June 1853; Newcastle to Barkly, No. 48, 14 May 1853, C.O. 111/293; C.L. & E.C. to Merivale, 30 Sept. 1853, C.O. 318/203; Newcastle to Walker, No. 175, 16 Jan. 1854, P.P. 1859, Sess. 1 XVI.; Wodehouse to Newcastle, No. 21, 7 June 1854, C.O. 111/300; C.L. & E.C. to Merivale, 15 Aug. 1854, C.O. 318/207.
29. *Report of the [1870] Commissioners* (G'town, 1871), p. 69.
30. Murdoch to Rogers, 28 May 1863, C.O. 318/240. See also ords. No. 30/1862 and No. 4/1864, C.O. 113/4.
31. See note 26.
32. See note 29.
33. C.L. & E.C. to Merivale, 15 Aug. 1854, C.O. 318/207; and 6 Mar. 1856, C.O. 318/212.
34. *Ibid.*; also Wodehouse to Lytton, No. 59, 18 June 1859, C.O. 111/324.
35. *Ibid.*; and encl. in Wodehouse to Labouchere, No. 1, 6 Jan. 1857, C.O. 111/316; also C.L. & E.C. to Merivale, 17 Feb. 1857, C.O. 318/215.
36. See ord. No. 4/1864, C.O. 113/4; and Hincks to Newcastle, No. 90, 22 May 1863, C.O. 111/340.
37. Hincks to Newcastle, No. 115, 29 June 1863, C.O. 111/341; encl. in Hincks to Cardwell, No. 24, 20 Jan. 1866, C.O. 111/355; and encl. in Mundy to Cardwell, No. 44, 3 Sept. 1866, C.O. 111/360.
38. Hincks to Buckingham & Chandos, No. 135, 31 Aug. 1868, C.O. 111/369.
39. See note 37.
40. *Report of the [1870] Commissioners, supra cit.*, p. 69 and appendix F. iv; Jenkins, *op. cit.*, p. 240.
41. Comins, *op. cit.*, p. 30.
42. Scott to Kimberley, No. 133, 8 Oct. 1872, C.O. 111/392.
43. Report of the [1870] Commissioners (ms), sec. 24, C.O. 111/380.

44. Longden to Carnarvon, Nos. 26 and 161, 2 Feb. and 4 Aug. 1875, respectively, C.O. 384/106; Report of the I.A.G. for 1874, C.O. 114/26; Report of the I.A.G., 29 Oct. 1877, *Administration Reports*, 1876; *Colonist*, 1 Dec. 1873, and *R.G.*, 14 Sept. 1878. The bounty payable by the planters for reindenture was increased from $50 to $95, then to $120 in 1873, and finally to $200 in 1875. This had a prohibitive effect on the practice of reindenture.
45. *D.T.*, 19 Jan. 1876.
46. Jenkins, *op. cit.* p. 241.
47. *Report of the [1870] Commissioners, supra cit.* pp. 71-72.
48. *Ibid.*, pp. 105-106.
49. *Ibid.*, p. 25; G. DesVoeux, *Experiences of A Demerara Magistrate* (G'town 1948), p. 119.
50. *Report of the [1870] Commissioners, supra cit.*, p. 105.
51. Wodehouse to Lytton, No. 119, 30 Sept. 1859, P.P. 1859, XX.
52. See ord. No. 4/1864. Also Hincks to Cardwell, No. 168, 13 Oct. 1865, C.O. 111/353; and encl. in Hincks to Buckingham and Chandos, No. 143, 17 Oct. 1867, C.O. 111/364.
53. See Ords. 7/1854 and 4/1864.
54. *Ibid.*; and encl. 1 in Hincks to Buckingham and Chandos, No. 167, 7 Dec. 1867, C.O. 111/364.
55. *Report of the [1870] Commissioners, supra cit.*, p. 72.
56. See note 54.
57. See Ord. No. 9/1868, C.O. 113/5; and Hincks to Buckingham & Chandos, No. 85, 22 June 1868, C.O. 111/367.
58. *Report of the [1870] Commissioenrs, supra cit.*, pp. 76 and 105-106.
59. *Ibid.*, pp. 74-75; see also note 51.
60. *Report of the [1870] Commissioners, supra cit.*, pp. 106-107.
61. *Ibid.*, pp. 111-112; also ord. No. 9/1868 (sec. 11). The last part of section 11 required that the manager should call the immigrant's attention to bad or incomplete work and request him to finish it satisfactorily. Only if the immigrant refused and the manager was then forced to use other workers to complete the work was he legally authorised to stop the immigrant's wages. But the employer could bring charges against the immigrant under the first part of section 11 for a number of alleged offences which would subject the latter, if convicted, to a maximum fine of $24 or to two month's imprisonment with hard labour.
62. See note 60.
63. DesVoeux, *op. cit.*, p.123.
64. *Report of the [1870] Commissioners, supra cit.*, pp. 23-24.
65. *Ibid.*, pp. 101-103.
66. DesVoeux, *op. cit.*, pp. 118-20.
67. See note 65.
68. Longden to Carnarvon, No. 122, 3 June 1876, C.O. 384/110.
69. Rushworth to Kimberley, No. 23, 5 Feb. 1874; and Longden to Carnarvon, No. 86, 16 May 1874, C.O. 384/103.
70. Report of the I.A.G., 23 July, 1878, *Administration Reports*, 1877.
71. *Ibid.*; also reports of I.A.G., 15 Oct. 1881 and 4 Aug. 1882, *Administration Reports*, 1880 and 1881 respectively.
72. Report of the I.A.G. for 1881, *loc. cit.*

73. *Creole*, 7 Nov. 1860.
74. *Ibid.*, 6 Feb. 1863.
75. *Ibid.*, 8 Apr. 1863.
76. Because of ill-health and fatigue, Low-a-si was unable to work. As a result, he was severely beaten by the head overseer, Matheson, and the black driver, Baker, and died. Both assailants disappeared after the act, but no charges were preferred against Matheson — racism? Baker was subsequently apprehended in Trinidad where he had fled, and returned to the colony where he stood trial for manslaughter. He was eventually acquitted. See the printed *Report of the [1870] Commissioners, supra cit.*, p. 82.
77. *Ibid.*, pp. 86–87, and appendix C.
78. See also Ramnarine, *op. cit.*; and Bisnauth, *op. cit.*
79. See note 51.
80. *Report of the [1870] Commissioners, supra cit.*, p. 118.
81. Report of the I.A.G. for 1881, *loc. cit.*
82. See note 80.
83. The press was replete with instances of immigrants wandering about, begging, emaciated, and dying or dead from disease and starvation. See for instance, *R.G.*, 14 Dec. 1871, 6 June 1872 and 22 July 1876; *Watchman*, 13 Dec. 1871; *Emery's Journal*, 24 Feb. 1847; *Colonist*, 27 June 1865, 17 Nov. 1873, 19 June 1874, and 27 July, 20 Sept., and 3 Nov. 1876; *D.T.*, 22 Sept. and 16 Dec. 1875.
84. Light to Grey, No. 223, 2 Nov. 1846, C.O. 111/235; encl. in Kortright to Kimberley, No. 253, 9 Nov. 1881, C.O. 111/420; *Creole*, 16 and 27 June, and 12 Sept. 1873; *R.G.*, 4 June 1872; *D.D.C.*, 27 Aug. 1882.
85. Barkly to Grey, No. 63, 18 Apr. 1850, P.P. 1851. XXXIX.
86. D.C., 20 Sept, 6 and 11 Oct. 1885; Comins, *op. cit.*, pp. 50–52.
87. Report of the [1870] Commissioners (ms), sec. 13, C.O. 111/379.
88. *Ibid.* (printed edition), p. 116.
89. Report of the I.A.G. for 1881, *loc. cit.*; Report of the Inspector-General of Police for 1888, C.O. 114/44; Comins, *op. cit.*, p. 50.
90. *Report of the [1870] Commissioners, supra cit.*, pp. 116–117; C.L. & E.C. to Merivale, 28 Nov. 1850, C.O. 318/186; and 15 May 1851, C.O. 318/190; D. Nath, *A History of the Indians in British Guiana* (G'town, 1950), pp. 56–57.
91. *Creole*, 5 May, 7 and 18 July 1860; *Colonist*, 3 Oct. 1860, 22 Oct. 1864, 27 Sept. and 2 Oct. 1867; *B.G.*, 19 Aug. 1865; *D.T.*, 23 June, 20 Aug., and 6 Sept. 1875.
92. Report of the [1870] Commissioners (ms), sec. 22, C.O. 111/380; report of the I.A.G. for 1881, *loc. cit.*; Comins, *op. cit.*, p. 65.
93. *Ibid.*, p. 95; encl. in Rushworth to Kimberley, No. 149, 26 Sept. 1873, C.O. 111/398; *Colonist*, 2 Sept. 1869, 2 July 1870, 7 Oct. 1871; *R.G.*, 11 July 1874, 26 July 1883; *D.C.*, 2 Apr. 1887, and 28 Mar. 1888.
94. *Colonist*, 1 Nov. 1864, 30 Jan. 1866, and 19 June 1872; report of the [1870] Commissioners (ms), sec. 25, C.O. 111/380.
95. *Creole*, 22 Nov. 1869; *Colonist*, 12 Dec. 1866, 10 Mar. 1871; *R.G.*, 4 July 1872; *D.T.*, 16 June 1875; *D.C.*, 20 Oct. 1885 and 18 Aug. 1886.
96. *Colonist*, 3 Nov. 1866; 1 Apr. 1870, 8 Sept. 1873; *R.G.*, 7 June 1883; *D.C.*, 10 May 1885, 11 Oct. 1888; report of the [1870] Commissioners (ms), sec. 25, C.O. 111/380.

NOTES

97. Encl. in Bruce to Knutsford, No. 4, 2 Jan. 1889, C.O. 384/173.
98. *Colonist*, 5 and 10 Aug. 1869.
99. *R.G.*, 1 and 7 Oct. 1872; *Colonist*, 2 Oct. 1872; *Creole*, 2 and 4 Oct. 1872; Scott to Kimberley, No. 179, 7 Oct. 1872, and encls., C.O. 111/393.
100. E. Abrahams, 'The East Indian Coolie in British Guiana', *WIQ*, 2, 1886, pp. 400–401.
101. Encl. in Scott to Kimberley, No. 48, 4 Apr. 1873, C.O. 111/397; report of the [1870] Commissioners (ms), appendix C, C.O. 111/382.
102. *Ibid*, sec. 24, C.O. 111/380.
103. Scott to Kimberley, No. 114, 30 Aug. 1872, C.O. 111/391.
104. See note 102.
105. Report of the I.A.G. for 1891, C.O. 114/53.
106. Reports of the I.A.G. for 1885 and 1887, C.O. 114/40 & 43, respectively.
107. *O.G.*, 1887.
108. Reports of the Government Land Department for 1887–1889, C.O. 114/43–47; see also the Blue Books of Statistics for 1889–91, C.O. 116/258–60.
109. See note 102.
110. Longden to Carnarvon, No. 105, 20 June 1874, C.O. 111/402; see also ord. No. 2/1874.
111. Report of the [1870] Commissioners (ms), appendix C, C.O. 111/382; *Creole*, 12 Jan. 1866; *Colonist*, 16 Aug. 1877.
112. *Creole*, 12 Jan. 1866.
113. *Colonist*, 16 Aug. 1877.
114. Report of the [1870] Commissioners (ms), sec. 24, C.O. 111/380.
115. Report of the I.A.G. for 1891, C.O. 114/53.
116. Encl. in Wodehouse to Lytton, No. 49, 20 may 1859, C.O. 111/323; and Bronkhurst, *The Colony*, supra cit., p. 208.
117. *Colonist*, 16 Aug. 1877; J. Heatley, *A Visit to the West Indies* (Lond., 1891), p. 42; A. Hardy, *Life and Adventure in British Guiana* (Lond., 1913), p. 85; L. Crookall, *British Guiana* (Lond., 1898), pp. 104–105.
118. Clementi, *op. cit.*, pp. 333–349.
119. J. Heatley, *op. cit.*, p. 41.
120. Clementi, *loc. cit.*
121. *Argosy*, 5 Apr. 1884; report of the Crown Surveyor, 16 Feb. 1881, *Administration Reports*, 1880.
122. A. Hardy, *op. cit.*, pp. 80–81; J. van Sertima, *Scenes and Sketches of Demerara Life* (Dem., 1899), p. 66; Comins, *op. cit.*, p. 23 and appendix A; encl. in Longden to Carnarvon, No. 188, 7 Oct. 1874, C.O. 384/103; and see note 43.
123. Nath, *op. cit.*, pp. 215–16.
124. Minutes of the Combined Court, 17 May 1870; reports of T. Murdoch, 15 May 1871 and 21 Mar. 1872, encl. in Kimberley to Scott, No. 295, 16 May 1872, C.O. 111/391. See also, W. Rodney, *A History of the Guyanese Working People, 1880–1905* (Balt., 1981); Ramnarine, *op. cit.*; and Potter, *op. cit.*
125. Hincks to Cardwell, No. 27, 21 Feb. 1865, C.O. 111/350; also encl. in No. 155, 19 Sept. 1865; and No. 200, 18 Dec. 1865, C.O. 111/353; G.S. Jenman, 'Model Settlers: A Lesson in the Small Industries', *Timehri*, Vol. 2, 1883, pp. 99–101; *G.T.*, 1 Mar. 1866; see also note 43.

126. *Creole*, 5 June 1872; *Colonist*, 29 Aug. 1872; also note 124.
127. Longden to Carnarvon, No. 8, 16 Jan. 1875, C.O. 384/106.
128. Letter to the editor, *R.G.*, 16 Oct. 1875.
129. *Colonist*, 17 Mar. 1881; minute of J.B. Gill, 11 Dec. 1880, C.O. 384/128.
130. Kortright to Kimberley, No. 235, 4 Nov. 1880; minute of E. Wingfield, 23 Dec. 1880; and Kimberley to Kortright, 7 Jan. 1881, C.O. 384/128; report of the Crown Surveyor, 16 Feb. 1881, C.O. 114/30; Herbert to Kortright, 15 Oct. 1881, C.O. 384/133; *Colonist*, 17 Mar. 1881.
131. Resolution of the Combined Court, 29 June 1881, encl. in Kortright to Kimberley, No. 152, 15 Aug. 1881; No. 144, 5 Aug. 1881; and minute of J.B. Gill, 10 Sept. 1881, C.O. 384/133.
132. Report of the Crown Surveyor, 28 Feb. 1882, C.O. 114/32; *O.G.*, 1881; *D.D.C.*, 10 Nov. 1881.
133. Irving to Kimberley, No. 238, 24 July 1882, C.O. 384/139.
134. Irving to Kimberley, No. 121, 4 May 1883, C.O. 384/144; report of the I.A.G. for 1882, C.O. 114/34.
135. Reports of the Government Land Dept. for 1887–1889, C.O. 114/43-47; report of the Crown Surveyor, 30 July 1891, *Administration Reports*, 1890–91.
136. Comins, *op. cit.*, p. 75; see also note 134.
137. Alexander to Govt. Sect., 12 Jan. 1894, encl'd in Lees to Ripon, No. 139, 12 May 1894, C.O 284/189.
138. Callier to Perks, 30 Sept. 1876, M.M.S./W.v./2. See especially Leslie Potter's thesis, *op. cit.*, also Ramnarine, *op. cit.*, and Bisnauth, *op. cit.*
139. Encls. in Young to Hicks Beach, No. 203, 29 Aug. 1879, C.O. 384/123; and Comins, *op. cit.*, pp. 74–75.
140. Report of the I.A.G. for 1881, *loc. cit.; Colonist*, 7 May 1883.
141. See Plummer's report, encl. in Young to Hicks Beach, No. 203, 29 Aug. 1879, C.O. 384/123; Comins, *op. cit.*, p. 74; and *Colonist*, 14 Apr. 1881.
142. *Colonist*, 16 Aug. 1877; *R.G.*, 18 Aug. 1863; Bronkhurst to Gen. Sect., 30 Nov. 1877, M.M.S./W.v./2; Abrahams, *loc. cit.*, pp. 405–406.
143. Comins, *op. cit.*, p. 69; and reports of the I.A.G. for 1882–1891, C.O. 114/34–35.
144. The independent missionaries of the L.M.S. played an important role in politicizing the Creoles and in articulating their opposition to immigration. See Light to Stanley, No. 98, 27 Sept. 1844, C.O. 111/213; Nos. 203, 204, and 207, 4 Oct. 1844, and encls., C.O. 111/214; and encl. in No. 22, 1 Feb. 1845, C.O. 111/220; Light to Gladstone, No. 153, 30 July 1846, C.O. 111/234; Foreman to Tidman, 24 Sept. 1858, L.M.S. 8/2 (Bce); Bleby to Boyce, 22 Oct. 1868, M.M.S./W.v./2. 'See in particular Robert Moore's thesis on race relations between these two groups (*op. cit.*)
145. H. Bronkhurst, 'The Religion and Religious System of the East Indian Population', *Colonist*, 21 July 1887; Comins, *op. cit.*, p. 95.
146. Bronkhurst, *The Colony, supra cit.*, p. 268; *D.C.*, 29 Oct. 1885.
147. Bronkhurst, *Among the Hindus and Creoles of British Guiana* (Lond., 1888), pp. 22–23.
148. Report of the [1870] Commissioners (ms), sec. 13, C.O. 111/379.
149. Bronkhurst to Gen. Sect., 22 Aug. 1862, M.M.S./W.v/5.
150. H. Kirke, *Twenty-five Years in British Guiana* (Lond., 1898), p. 195.
151. *Argosy*, 23 Feb. 1889.

152. Brian L. Moore, 'The Retention of Caste Notions among the Indian Immigrants in British Guiana during the 19th Century', *CSSH*, 19 (1), 1977.
153. Bronkhurst, *The Colony, supra cit.*, p. 124.
154. Circular letter to estate managers, encl. in Walker to Newcastle, No. 83, 9 Nov. 1861, C.O. 111/332.
155. *Colonist*, 24 June 1873; *Creole*, 7 June 1872; see also note 149.
156. Adamson, op. cit., p. 94.
157. *Ibid.*, p. 98.
158. Trotman to Gen Sect., 1 May 1867, M.M.S./W.v./5.
159. L. Key, 'East Indians and Afro-Guyanese', Carib. Historians Assoc. conference paper, Jamaica, 1972, pp. 5-6.
160. Report of the I.A.G. for 1881, *loc. cit.*
161. *Ibid.*; and *D.D.C.*, 10 Nov. 1881.
162. Seifferty to Hawkins, 31 Dec. 1874, S.P.G./E.29.
163. *R.G.*, 11 Aug. 1860; Watson to Gen. Sect., n.d. (1862), M.M.S./W.v./5.
164. *R.G.*, 24 Jan. 1878; and Bronkhurst, *The Colony, supra cit.*, p. 362.
165. *Argosy*, 11 Dec. 1880.
166. *R.G.*, 10 May 1873 and 11 Dec. 1883; Bronkhurst, *Among the Hindus, supra cit.*, p. 63.
167. *R.G.*, 11 Aug. 1860.
168. *Argosy*, 4 Nov. 1882; *D.C.*, 11 and 30 May 1888. The *chefa* lottery consisted of 36 animal, fish, and other characters on a roll of canvas which was rolled up in a cylindrical container and hung aloft in mid-air, with one character pre-chosen as the winner. People then gambled on which of the 36 characters was the winning one.
169. *Colonist*, 16 Feb. 1876, 23 Apr. 1880; J. Bridger's report, 31 Dec. 1871, S.P.G./E.26.
170. *Creole*, 28 Dec. 1870.
171. *Ibid.*, 22 Sept. 1858.
172. D. Wood, *Trinidad in Transition* (Lond., 1968), pp. 137-138; and B. Brereton, *Race Relations in Colonial Trinidad* (Lond., 1979), pp. 188-189.
173. Bronkhurst, *The Colony, supra cit.*, p. 124; Report of the [1870] Commissioners (ms), sec. 25, C.O. 111/380.
174. Encl. 4 in Walker to Newcastle, No. 83, 9 Nov. 1861, C.O. 111/332; Hincks to Buckingham and Chandos, No. 177, 18 Dec. 1868, C.O. 111/369; Report of [1870] Commissioners (ms), sec. 13, C.O. 111/379; Scott to Kimberley, No. 106, 18 July 1871, C.O. 111/386.
175. Wolseley's journal, encl. in Light to Russell, No. 101, 11 Aug. 1841, C.O. 111/179.
176. Light to Stanley, No. 168, 3 Oct. 1842, C.O. 111/193.
177. Encl. 4 in Walker to Newcastle, No. 83, 9 Nov. 1861, C.O. 111/332.
178. *Colonist*, 9, 10, 12, and 17 July, 1867; encl. in Murdoch to Rogers, 10 Apr. 1865, C.O. 318/245; Mundy to Buckingham & Chandos, No. 113, 22 Aug. 1867, C.O. 111/363; Hincks to Buckingham & Chandos, No. 147, 29 Oct. 1867, C.O. 111/364.
179. Comins, *op. cit.*, p. 95; *R.G.*, 25 July, 1876.
180. Report of the [1870] Commissioners (ms), secs. 13 and 25, C.O. 111/379-80; Bronkhurst, 'The Religion', *loc. cit.*
181. Brian L. Moore, 'Sex and Marriage among Indian immigrants in British Guiana during the 19th century', presented at the Third Confer-

ence on East Indians in the Caribbean, Trinidad, 1984.
182. Brereton, *loc. cit.*
183. *Liberator*, 2 Oct. 1869; *R.G.*, 14 Mar. 1872, 22 Aug. 1879; *Colonist*, 25 Feb. 1879, 13 Jan. 1880; *Argosy*, 17 June 1882; *(D) DC*, 14 Sept. 1882, 7 Feb. 1889.
184. Kirke, *op. cit.*, pp. 194–95; *G.T.*, 28 July 1866; *R.G.*, 25 Aug. and 22 Nov. 1881, 10 June 1882, 22 Nov. 1884.
185. R. Duff, *British Guiana* (Glas., 1866), pp. 320–21; encl. in Hincks to Newcastle, No. 212, 16 Dec. 1862, C.O. 111/337; encl. in Hincks to Cardwell, No. 189, 1 Dec. 1865, C.O. 111/353; *Creole*, 6 Oct. 1862, 14 July 1865; *B.G.*, 8 Feb. 1865; *Colonist*, 11, 24, 26 July, and 12 Sept. 1866, 10 July 1867, 19 Jan. 1869, and 14 Aug. 1875.
186. *Creole*, 24 July 1865, 22 June 1866, 8 July 1868; *B.G.*, 25 July 1865; *G.T.*, 25 Nov. 1865.; *Colonist*, 1 Apr. and 22 July 1865, 19 Nov. 1866; *Liberator*, 3 Mar. 1869; *R.G.*, 20 Jan. 1874, and 26 Oct. 1875.
187. *R.G.*, 28 May 1863.
188. *Colonist*, 3, 11, 19 and 22 Mar. 1875, and 14 Sept. 1877.
189. Brereton, *loc. cit.*
190. Encl. in No. 158, Kortright to Kimberley, 20 Aug. 1881, C.O. 384/133.
191. *D.C.*, 20, 22 Sept., 3 Oct., 12, 19, 24 and 27 Nov. 1885, 7 Jan. and 1 May 1886. Similar problems arose between the Indians of Anna Regina and the people of Bush Lot and Henrietta, Essequibo. See *D.C.*, 3 Oct. 1885.
192. Brereton, *loc. cit.*; also R.J. Moore, *op. cit.*
193. *R.G.*, 19 Feb. 1866, 20 and 25 July, 26 Oct., 23 Nov., and 20 Dec. 1876, 21 Aug. 1879, 10 May 1881, 6 Jan. 1883; *Colonist*, 11 May 1874, 4 Oct. 1875, 24 Nov. and 23 Dec. 1876, 26 Oct. 1880, 15 Nov. 1881, 24 May 1882; *(D) D.C.*, 25 June 1882, 22 Aug. 1883, 16 & 17 Apr., and 8 Nov. 1885; also Longden to Carnarvon, No. 199, 16 Sept. 1876, C.O. 384/111.
194. *Colonist*, 26 Oct. 1872, 23, 24 and 25 Mar. 1875, 27 Dec. 1876, 19 May 1881, 15 June and 28 Sept. 1882; *R.G.*, 25 Mar. 1875, 22 June 1876.
195. Longden to Carnarvon, No. 70, 31 Feb. 1876, and encl., C.O. 111/407.
196. *Colonist*, 4 May 1860, 10 July 1867, 2 Oct. 1871, 12 Nov. 1873, 8 Feb. and 20 Sept. 1881; *R.G.*, 19 Feb. 1866, 4, 6, and 8 Jan. 1876, 14 Mar. 1882; *Creole*, 14 Dec. 1870, 4 Oct. 1871; *(D) D.C.*, 19 Apr. and 12 Aug. 1882, 17 Oct. 1885, 13 and 14 Sept. 1887.
197. *R.G.*, 5 Aug. and 9 Oct. 1869, 24 June 1871; *Colonist*, 3 Aug. 1869, 31 Oct. 1870; report of the [1870] Commissioners (ms), sec. 13, C.O. 111/379.
198. *Creole*, 8 Mar. 1862, 8 July 1868; *Colonist*, 18 July and 30 Nov. 1866, 3 June 1867, 6 Feb. 1868; *R.G.*, 21 July 1874, 4 Sept. 1875, 20 May 1876, 16 Jan. 1877; also encl. in Mundy to Buckingham & Chandos, No. 114, 22 Aug. 1867, C.O. 111/363.
199. *Colonist*, 4 May 1860, 2 Oct. 1871; *R.G.*, 19 Feb. 1866; *Creole*, 14 Dec. 1870, 4 Oct. 1871.
200. Rodney, *op. cit.*, pp. 184–185.
201. *Ibid.*, p. 181.
202. *Ibid.*, pp. 175–77.
203. *Ibid.*, pp. 178–79.
204. *Ibid.*, p. 188.

205. See notes 193–199. These several incidents are by no means the sum total of violent conflict among Creoles and Indians, much of which undoubtedly went unreported because of its largely individual nature. This makes it impossible to quantify the incidence of racial violence. But the savagery and intensity of those reported cases, and general (albeit perhaps biased) comments by contemporary observers certainly creates a distinct impression of considerably more conflict than either Rodney for Guiana or Brereton for Trinidad seem(ed) prepared to admit.
206. That "minimum" was, however, by no means "piddling".
207. Rodney, *op. cit.*, pp. 179–180.
208. *Ibid.*, p. 178.
209. See, for instance, Leo Despres, *Cultural Pluralism and Nationalist Politics in British Guiana* (Chicago, 1967), pp. 86–95.
210. Rodney, *op. cit.*, p. 179.
211. *Ibid.*
212. B.L. Moore, 'Social and Cultural Complexity' (Ph.D. Thesis), *supra cit.*, pp. 410–433.
213. Adamson, *op. cit.*, pp. 157–58.

Chapter 9

1. M.G. Smith, *The Plural Society in the British West Indies* (Berkeley, 1965) pp. 88–91; also his 'Institutional and Political Conditions of Pluralism', *Pluralism in Africa*, Kuper & Smith (eds.), (Berkeley, 1971), p. 32; and his *Culture, Race and Class in the Commonwealth Caribbean* (Kgn., 1984).
2. P. van den Berghe, *Race and Racism*, (N.Y., 1967), p. 139; also his 'Race and Ethnicity: A Sociological Perspective', *ERS*, 1 (4), 1978.
3. L. Braithwaite, 'Social Stratification and Cultural Pluralism', *Social and Cultural Pluralism in the Caribbean*, V. Rubin (ed.), Annals N.Y. Acad. Sci., Vol. 83, art. 5, pp. 819 and 822.
4. L. Braithwaite, 'Problems of Race and Colour in the Caribbean', *CI*, 1 (1), 1974.
5. R.T. Smith, 'Social Stratification, Cultural Pluralism, and Integration in West Indian Societies', *Caribbean Integration*, S. Lewis and T. Mathews (eds.), (P.R., 1967), p. 235.
6. H. Hoetink, *Caribbean Race Relations* (Lond., 1971), pp. 90–109, 150–51, and 161–90.
7. Richard Schomburgk, *Travels in British Guiana*, Vol. 2 (G'town, 1922), pp. 39–40.
8. H. Bronkhurst, *The Colony of British Guiana* (Lond., 1883), p. 165
9. Quoted in A. Adamson, 'The Impact of Indentured Immigration on the Political Economy of British Guiana', in *Indentured Labour in the British Empire*, Kay Saunders (ed.), (Lond., 1984), p. 49.
10. Memorandum of the Administrator-General, encl. in Wodehouse to Lytton, No. 4, 7 Jan. 1859, C.O. 111/323.
11. Report of the [1870] Commissioners (ms), sec. 13, C.O. 111/379.
12. H. Kirke, *Twenty-five Years in British Guiana* (Lond., 1898), pp. 194–95; *DDC*, 12 Aug. 1882; *Creole*, 11 Apr. 1866; Light to Russell, No. 97, 11

July 1840, C.O. 111/172; and encl. 6 in Wodehouse to Labouchere, No. 16, 24 Feb. 1856, C.O. 111/309.
13. See note 10; also minutes of H. Taylor, 2 Mar. 1859, C.O. 111/323; and 24 July 1862, C.O. 111/362.
14. Notes of Inspector-General Cox, encl. in Young to Kimberley, No. 113, 24 Apr. 1882, C.O. 111/423.
15. J. Furnivall, *Colonial Policy and Practice* (Lond., 1948), pp. 123, 150, 306–12; and his *Netherlands India* (Lond., 1939), pp. 446–59.
16. R. van Lier, *The Development and Nature of Society in the West Indies* (Amsterdam, 1950), pp. 3–4.
17. J. Rex, 'A Working Paradigm of Race Relations Research', *ERS*, 4 (1), 1981.
18. *Ibid.*; see also his 'Racism and the Structure of Colonial Societies', in *Racism and Colonialism*, Robert Ross (ed.), (The Hague, 1982); van den Berghe, *op. cit.*; and notes 15 and 16.
19. W. Rodney, *A History of the Guyanese Working People* (Lond., 1981), pp. 178–79.
20. For the censuses of 1827 and 1829, and the registration of slaves of 1828 and 1829, see P.P. 1845, XXXI; see also the 1851 census in Barkly to Grey, No. 170, 28 Nov. 1851, C.O. 111/284; and the 1891 census statistics in the report of the Registrar-General for 1891, C.O. 114/57.
21. Encls. in Light to Stanley, No. 83, 18 Apr. 1845, C.O. 111/227; encl. in Light to Gladstone, No. 56, 1 Apr. 1846, C.O. 111/232; encl. in Light to Grey, No. 176, 2 Sept. 1846, P.P. 1847. XXXIX; and No. 181, 15 Sept. 1847, C.O. 111/245; Barkly to Newcastle, No. 50, 28 Mar. 1853, C.O. 111/294; Scott to Tidman, 23 Feb. 1860, L.M.S. 8a/6 (Dem.).
22. Report (ms) of the Guiana Diocesan Church Society (1858), S.P.G./D.16; Fidler to Gen. Sect., 21 Aug. 1859. M.M.S./W.v/5; J. Marrat, *In the Tropics* (Lond., 1881), pp. 130–31. Robert Moore's thesis is also very useful for understanding the aims and objectives of the various missionary bodies. (See R.J. Moore, 'East Indians and Negroes in British Guiana, 1838–1880', D.Phil Thesis, Sussex University, 1970.)
23. Hudson to Walker, 7 Mar. 1856, encl. in Wodehouse to Labouchere, No. 25, 10 Mar. 1856; minutes of H. Taylor and H. Merivale appended to No. 25; and Labouchere to Wodehouse, No. 65, 16 Apr. 1856, C.O. 111/310.
24. Warder to Tidman, 5 Feb. 1866, L.M.S. 8b/5 (Dem.); Warder to Mullens, 20 Jan. 1871, L.M.S. 9/4 (Dem.).
25. Bowrey to Tidman, 14 Feb. 1850, L.M.S. 7/1 (Bce); and 8 Feb. 1853, L.M.S. 7/2 (Bce); Dagleish to Tidman, 7 Mar. 1861, L.M.S. 9/1 (Bce).
26. Ricards to Tidman, 22 Jan. 1866, L.M.S. 9/3 (Bce); and Henderson to Mullens, 18 Jan. 1867, L.M.S. 9/1 (Dem.).
27. Stipendiary Magistrates' (S.Ms) reports for June 1848, C.O. 116/167; Walker to Grey, No. 124, 9 Oct. 1848, C.O. 111/258; and encl. in No. 20, 13 June 1848, C.O. 111/253; Barkly to Grey, Nos. 60 & 136, 17 Apr. & 24 Sept. 1850, respectively, and encls., P.P. 1850. XXXIX; Heath to Hoole, 16 May 1850; and Cleaver to Gen. Sect., 27 Sept. 1851, M.M.S/W.iv/5; Rattray to Tidman, 27 Mar. 1851, L.M.S. 7/6 (Dem.); Pettigrew to Tidman, 22 Feb. 1860, L.M.S. 8/3 (Bce).
28. Encl. in Walker to Grey, No. 104, 16 Sept. 1848, C.O. 111/257; Barkly to Grey No. 159, 13 June 1849, P.P. 1850. XXXIX. The Creoles

NOTES   267

became very apathetic towards schooling since they could see no practical benefits to be derived in terms of jobs, income, etc. See also encl. in Cleaver to Hoole, 24 Jan. 1860; Hincks to Newcastle, No. 140, 28 July 1862, C.O. 111/335; Hincks to Buckingham & Chandos, No. 135, 31 Aug. 1868, C.O. 111/369; and Veness to Sect., 31 Mar. 1871, S.P.G./E.26.

29. Limmex to Gen Sect., 4 Feb. 1848, M.M.S./W.iv/5; Rattray to Tidman, 19 Feb. 1850, L.M.S. 7/5 (Dem.); and *Report of the G.D.C.S.* for 1853, p. 22.
30. Light to Grey, separ., 3 May 1848, C.O. 111/252; Barkly to Pakington, No. 86, 21 Apr. 1852, C.O. 111/289.
31. Hincks to Cardwell, No. 146, 6 Sept. 1864, P.P. 1865. XXXVII.
32. Mundy to Carnarvon, No. 73, 30 Nov. 1866, P.P. 1867. XLVIII.
33. Reports of the Inspector of Schools, 12 Dec. 1877 and 21 Mar. 1891, *Administration Reports*, 1876 and 1890, respectively. For a full analysis of the ideas and objectives behind colonial education policies on the late 19th and early 20th Centuries, see Peter D. Fraser, 'Education and Social Values in British Guiana, 1870–1914', D.Phil. Thesis, Sussex University, 1977.
34. Walker to Newcastle, No. 102, 20 Oct. 1853, C.O. 111/297.
35. Marrat, *op. cit.*, pp. 80–86; Shrewsbury to Hoole, 2 May 1862, M.M.S./W.v/5; Greathead to Boyce, 23 Jan. and 7 Apr. 1868; Bronkhurst to Gen. Sect., 22 Feb. 1868; Broadbent to Boyce, 23 Apr. 1868 and 22 Apr. 1869; and Swinnerton to Boyce, 22 Apr. 1868, M.M.S./W.v/2; P.D. Curtin, *Two Jamaicas* (N.Y. 1970), pp. 170–171.
36. Limmex to Gen. Sect., 14 Dec. 1849, M.M.S./W.iv/5; Henderson to Tidman, 18 Jan. 1854, L.M.S. 7/9 (Dem); Foreman to Tidman, 6 Feb. 1861, L.M.S. 9/1 (Bce); Henderson to Tidman, 22 Jan. 1862, L.M.S. 8b/1 (Dem); Foreman to Mullens, 31 Jan. 1877, L.M.S. 10/2 (Dem); Jones to Gen. Sect., 3 Jan. 1878, M.M.S./W.v./2.
37. B.L. Moore, 'Social and Cultural Complexity in British Guiana, 1850–1891', unpubl'd Ph.D. thesis, U.W.I., 1973, pp. 329–46.
38. Jansen to Tidman, 18 Jan. 1855, L.M.S. 7/4 (Bce); Callier to Sect., 23 Dec. 1869; and Swinnerton to Boyce, 22 July 1870, M.M.S./W.v./2.
39. Muskland to Tidman, 11 Feb. 1846, L.M.S. 7/1 (Dem.).
40. See E. Brathwaite, *Contradictory Omens* (Mona, 1974.)
41. Marrat, *op. cit.*, pp. 130–31; also, J. Jones, 'Mission of British Guiana', *Letters and Notices* (Society of Jesus), vol. 1, 1862–63, p. 152.
42. *R.G.*, 8 Feb. 1879; *Colonist*, 16 Sept. 1881.
43. *Report of the G.D.C.S.* for 1860, p. 13.
44. *Report of the [1870] Commissioners* (G'town, 1871), p. 193. He was the Rev. E.B. Bhose.
45. Hore to Sect., n.d., S.P.G./D.44. The proprietor of Pln. Bel Air was Quintin Hogg, and the missionary was Rev. S.C. Hore.
46. Encl. in Hincks to Cardwell, No. 27, 21 Feb. 1865, C.O. 111/350; Mundy to Cardwell, 3 Aug. 1866, No. 30, C.O. 111/360; Mundy to Buckingham & Chandos, No. 113, 22 Aug. 1867, C.O. 111/363; Hincks to Buckingham & Chandos, No. 147, 29 Oct. 1867, C.O. 111/364; and *Colonist*, 19 Nov. 1869. Wu-Tai-Kam arrived from Singapore in 1864 and immediately set to work among the Chinese immigrants. In August 1866, he was officially appointed missionary to the Chinese with a

government salary of £300 per annum; and he was largely instrumental in the establishment of the Chinese settlement of Hopetown on the Demerara river. In 1867, however, he suddenly quit the colony after having impregnated a coloured woman. He had previously been married and had a family in Singapore.
47. *Colonist*, 28 Jan. and 8 Aug. 1874; *R.G.*, 4 Dec. 1875; Longden to Carnarvon, No. 153, 15 Aug. 1874, C.O. 111/402; and No. 249, 4 Dec. 1875, C.O. 111/406. The actual site in Georgetown was granted by the Anglican church, and the original structure cost $3,408.
48. *R.G.*, 7 Mar. 1872. The Presbyterians only began work among the immigrants in 1870.
49. Williams to Gen. Sect., 27 Mar. 1852, M.M.S./W.iv./5. The first Methodist missionary to the Indians was Rev. A. Williams.
50. Shrewsbury to Gen. Sect., 21 Dec. 1858; and Bronkhurst to Hoole, 27 Dec. 1860, M.M.S./W.v/5. After Williams' death in 1855, the Rev. Shrewsbury tried to work among the Indians in Essequibo, but was defeated by the variety of languages which they spoke. Rev. H.V.P. Bronkhurst was the second full-time missionary to the Indian immigrants.
51. *Colonist*, 18 May 1860.
52. Report of the [1870] Commisionerss (ms), secs. 3 and 25, C.O. 111/379–80.
53. *Ibid.*
54. Ord. No. 7/1873, sec. 52, C.O. 113/5.
55. Ord. No. 14/1876, secs. 11 and 16, C.O. 113/6.
56. *R.G.*, 8 Feb. 1879; *Colonist*, 16 Sept. 1881.
57. Reports of the Inspector of Schools, 9 Feb. 1881 and 1 Feb. 1882, *Administration Reports* for 1880 and 1881, respectively; see also Fraser, *op. cit.*; and T. Ramnarine, 'The Growth of the East Indian Community in British Guiana, 1880–1920', D.Phil Thesis, Sussex University, 1977.
58. D. Comins, *Note on Emigration from India to British Guiana* (Calcutta, 1893), p. 60.
59. Harris to Sect., 31 Dec. 1866, S.P.G./E.22; *Colonist*, 24 June 1866 (letter).
60. Christian to the Committee, 4 Jan. 1865, S.P.G./E.16.
61. Report of the [1870] Commissioners (ms.), sec. 25, C.O. 111/380.
62. Report of the I.A.G., 25 Oct. 1881, *Adminisration Reports*, 1880.
63. H. Bronkhurst, *Among the Hindus and Creoles of British Guiana* (Lond., 1888), p. 50; Comins, *op. cit.*, p. 8.
64. Williams to Gen. Sect., 25 June 1852, M.M.S./W.iv/5; Bronkhurst to Gen. Sect., 28 Feb. and 6 June 1861, 22 Aug. 1862, 2 Apr. 1864, 23 Apr. 1867, M.M.S./W.v/5; and 26 Mar. 1872, and 31 Nov. 1887, M.M.S./W.v/2. See also R.J. Moore, *op. cit.*; Ramnarine, *op. cit.*; and D. Bisnauth, 'The East Indian Immigrant Society in British Guiana, 1891–1930', Ph.D. Thesis, U.W.I., 1977.
65. Comins, *op. cit.*, p. 61; Brett to Austin, 18 July 1852, S.P.G./D.16; Bhose to the Bishop, 25 Jan. 1864, encl. in *Report of the GDCS*, 1863; H. Bronkhurst, 'The Religion and Religious System of Our East Indian Population', *D.C.*, 28 July 1887.
66. Bronkhurst to Gen. Sect. 7 May 1861, 22 Apr. 1863, 22 Nov. 1866,

M.M.S./W.v./5; and 7 Nov. 1872, M.M.S./W.v/2; also *Report of the [1870] Commissioners, supra cit.*, p. 193.
67. *Report of the G.D.C.S.* for 1858; Shrewsbury to Sect., 5 July 1860, M.M.S./W.v./5; E. Sloman, 'Coolie Missions in British Guiana', *WIQ*, Vol. 2, 1887, p. 236.
68. Bronkhurst to Gen. Sect., 22 Aug. 1862, M.M.S./W.v./5; and 24 July 1875, M.M.S./W.v/2.; *D.D.C.*, 9 Jan. 1883.
69. Report of the [1870] Commissioners (ms.), sec. 24, C.O. 111/380.
70. Austin to Bulloch, 20 Aug. 1866, S.P.G./D.28.
71. *Colonist*, 19 Nov. 1869, 25 Apr. 1876; *R.G.*, 6 May 1879; Bridger to Sect., 30 Dec. 1873, S.P.G./E. 28; Josa to Sect., 31 Dec. 1887, S.P.G./E.42.
72. *Colonist*, 10 Feb. 1876; *R.G.*, 9 Feb. 1878; *(D). D.C.*, 13 June 1884, 16 Nov. 1886; *Argosy*, 5 July 1884. Apart from the church in Georgetown, the Chinese built churches at Pln. Meten-Meerzorg, west coast Demerara; at No. 78 or "Hong Kong", Corentyne coast, Berbice; Enmore, east coast Demerara; and Bagotville, east bank Demerara.
73. Report of the [1870] Commissioners (ms.), sec. 25, C.O. 111/380; May to Sect., 22 Jan. 1862, S.P.G./E.10; Veness to Hawkins, 13 Jan. 1862, and May to Sect., 15 Feb. 1864, S.P.G./E.14.
74. *Creole*, 1 May 1857.
75. A. Adamson, *Sugar Without Slaves*, (New Haven, 1972), table 32, p. 243.
76. Light to Grey, No. 60, 4 Apr. 1848, C.O. 111/252; Barkly to Grey, No. 92, 10 June 1850, C.O. 111/274; Hincks to Cardwell, No. 47, 17 Mar. 1865, C.O. 111/355; Irving to Granville, No. 144, 27 May 1886, C.O. 111/435.
77. Circular letter from the Sect. of State, 30 Nov. 1838, C.O. 111/162; encl. in Wodehouse to Labouchere, No. 95, 18 July 1857, C.O. 111/317.
78. Light to Glenelg, No. 14, 28 Jan. 1839, C.O. 111/162; Light to Gladstone, No. 110, 12 June 1846, W.O. 1/584.
79. *Ibid.*; also Light to Stanley, separ., 7 Feb. 1845, C.O. 111/220; Barkly to Newcastle, confid., 28 Mar. 1853, W.O. 1/591.
80. Stanley to Light, No. 10, 1 May 1845, C.O. 111/220; Grey to Light, No. 1, 29 July 1846, W.O. 1/584; minute of Vernon Smith, 4 May 1853, W.O. 1/591.
81. Wodehouse to Labouchere, No. 16, 24 Feb. 1856, and encl. 8, C.O. 111/309; and No. 71, 7 June 1856, C.O. 111/311; *R.G.*, 21 Feb. 1856.
82. Encl. in Wodehouse to Labouchere, No. 95, 18 July 1857, C.O. 111/317.
83. Wodehouse to Lytton, No. 108, 4 Sept. 1858, and encl., C.O. 111/321.
84. *R.G.*, 9 Apr. 1859; Wodehouse to Lytton, No. 65, 20 June 1859, and encl., C.O. 111/323; also Notice of 16 Dec. 1859, *O.G.* for 1859.
85. Wodehouse to Labouchere, Nos. 93 and 95, 15 and 18 July 1857, respectively, C.O. 111/317; *Creole*, 7 Mar., 18, 22 and 25 July, 1857; *R.G.*, 9, 12, and 14 Apr. 1859.
86. *R.G.*, 25 Apr. 1857; and Wodehouse to Labouchere, No. 95, 18 July 1857, C.O. 111/317.
87. Wodehouse to Labourchere, No. 71, 7 June 1856, C.O. 111/311.
88. *Creole*, 21 Mar. 1864.
89. *Ibid.*, 18 Nov. 1857 and 16 Jan. 1858.
90. Mundy to Carnarvon, No. 76, 7 Dec. 1866, C.O. 111/360.

91. *Creole*, 13 and 20 Jan. 1871, 15 and 26 Apr., and 25 Sept. 1872.
92. Encl. in Scott to Kimberley, No. 11, 21 Jan. 1873, C.O. 111/395.
93. Encl. in Irving to Stanley, No. 40, 15 Feb. 1886, C.O. 111/434.
94. See Ord. 22/1872.
95. Longden to Carnarvon, confid., 25 June 1874, C.O. 111/402.
96. Encl. 5 in Wodehouse to Labouchere, No. 25, 10 Mar. 1856, C.O. 111/310; and encl. in No. 145, 8 Nov. 1856, C.O. 111/313.
97. *Creole*, 23 Dec. 1857, 10 Aug. 1861; *R.G.*, 7 May 1859; Walker to Newcastle, No. 96, 31 Dec. 1861, C.O. 111/332.
98. *Creole*, 22 Aug. 1857.
99. Kortright to Hicks Beach, No. 44, 6 Mar. 1878, and encl., C.O. 111/412; and encl. in No. 51, 24 Feb. 1879, C.O. 111/414.
100. Gormanston to Knutsford, No. 111, 30 Mar. 1889, C.O. 111/451; also, Reports of the B.G.V.F. for 1881–87, C.O. 114/34–43.
101. Report of the B.G.V.F. for 1888, C.O. 114/44; Gormanston to Knutsford, No, 158, 9 May 1889, C.O. 111/452.
102. Irving to Derby, No. 256, 3 Sept. 1883, C.O. 111/428; and Gormanston to Knutsford, No. 111, 30 Mar. 1889, C.O. 111/451.
103. Light to Normanby, No. 114, 16 July 1839, C.O. 111/164.
104. Light to Stanley, separ., 7 Feb. 1845, C.O. 111/220; and No. 161, 18 July 1845, C.O. 111/224.
105. Irving to Holland, secret, 4 May 1887, C.O. 111/439.
106. Barkly to Grey, No. 46, 16 Mar. 1849, C.O. 111/264; and No. 92, 10 June 1850, C.O. 111/274.
107. See note 105.
108. See the Blue Books of Statistics, 1850–91; also, Scott to Granville No. 75, 20 June 1870, C.O. 111/376.
109. Irving to Holland, secret, 4 May 1887, C.O. 111/439.
110. Encl. 1 in Kortright to Kimberley, No. 200, 7 Sept. 1880, C.O. 111/417.
111. *Creole*, 26 June 1858.
112. *Creole*, 13 Apr. 1863, 8 May and 13 Nov. 1867; *Colonist*, 2, 4, and 7 May 1867.
113. Encl. in Scott to Kimberley, No. 179, 7 Dec. 1872, C.O. 111/393; *Creole*, 9 Feb. 1874.
114. Scott to Granville, No. 47, 22 Apr. 1870, C.O. 111/375; Minutes of the Combined Court, June 1870; Kortright to Kimberley, No. 200, 7 Sept. 1880, C.O. 111/417; and No. 69, 6 May 1881, C.O. 111/418.
115. Notes of Inspector-General Cox, encl. in Young to Kimberley, No. 113, 24 Apr. 1882, C.O. 111/423; Irving to Kimberley, No. 336, 24 Nov. 1882, C.O. 111/425; and encl. in Irving to Derby, 2 June 1883, C.O. 111/428.
116. Encl. in Young to Kimberley, No. 113, 24 Apr. 1882, C.O. 111/423.
117. E. Jenkins, *The Coolie: His Rights and Wrongs* (Lond., 1871), pp. 101–102.
118. Light to Stanley, No. 131, 17 June 1844, C.O. 111/211; Wodehouse to Lytton, No. 4, 7 Jan. 1859, and encls., C.O. 111/323; Longden to Carnarvon, confid., 24 Oct. 1876 & encl., C.O. 111/409.
119. *Ibid.*; also Mundy to Buckingham & Chandos, No. 71, 27 May 1867, C.O. 111/362; Longden to Carnarvon, No. 167, 5 Aug. 1876, C.O. 111/408; and Irving to Stanley, No. 338, 25 Dec. 1885, C.O. 111/433.
120. Barkly to Grey, No. 1, 5 Mar. 1852, W.O.1/590.

121. Light to Stanley, No. 131, 17 June 1844, C.O. 111/211; and separ., 7 Feb. 1845, C.O. 111/220; Barkly to Grey, No. 92, 10 June 1850, C.O. 111/274.
122. Wodehouse to Labouchere, Nos. 24 and 25, 9 and 10 Mar. 1856, respectively, C.O. 111/310; and Nos. 65 and 92, 24 May and 23 July 1856, respectively, C.O. 111/311.
123. Walker to Labouchere, No. 14, 9 Feb. 1858, C.O. 111/319; Wodehouse to Stanley, No. 63, 25 May 1858, C.O. 111/320.
124. Wodehouse to Lytton, No. 117, 24 Sept. 1858, C.O. 111/321.
125. Hincks to Newcastle, No. 40, 22 Feb. 1864, C.O. 111/344; Longden to Carnarvon, confid., 24 Oct. 1876 and encl., C.O. 111/409.
126. See note 116.
127. Wodehouse to Lytton, No. 4, 7 Jan. 1859, and encls., C.O. 111/323; Hincks to Newcastle, 7 Aug. 1862, C.O. 111/336; See also note 120.
128. Wodehouse to George Grey, No. 2, 4 Jan. 1855, C.O. 111/304.
129. Light to Gladstone, No. 110, 12 June 1846, W.O. 1/584; Barkly to Newcastle, confid., 28 Mar. 1853, W.O. 1/591; Wodehouse to Stanley, No. 63, 25 May 1858, C.O. 111/320; Wodehouse to Newcastle, No. 57, 20 Apr. 1860, C.O. 111/327; Scott to Kimberley, No. 141, 23 Dec. 1870, C.O. 111/377.
130. Wodehouse to Lytton, No. 4, 7 Jan. 1859, and encls., C.O. 111/323.
131. Irving to Kimberley, No. 28, 25 Jan. 1883, C.O. 111/427.
132. Irving to Stanley, No. 338, 25 Dec. 1885, C.O. 111/433; and No. 4, 7 Jan. 1886, and encl., C.O. 111/434; Irving to Granville, No. 144, 27 May 1886, C.O. 111/435; Irving to Stanhope, No. 342, 24 Dec. 1886, C.O. 111/436; Bruce to Knutsford, confid., 18 Jan 1889; and Knutsford to Bruce, confid., 19 Feb. 1889, C.O. 111/451.
133. Irving to Stanley, confid., 26 Aug. 1885, C.O. 111/432.
134. Bruce to Knutsford, No. 354, 6 Oct. 1891, C.O. 111/461.
135. Ords. Nos. 17, 18 and 19 of 1891, C.O. 113/8.
136. Bruce to Knutsford, No. 103, 8 Apr. 1891, C.O. 111/459; and encl. in No. 208, 27 June 1891, C.O. 111/460.
137. Bruce to Knutsford, No. 226, 14 July 1891, C.O. 111/460; and the Blue Books of Statistics for 1890 and 1891.
138. Encl. in Bruce to Knutsford, No. 209, 27 June 1891, C.O. 111/460.
139. Bruce to Knutsford, No. 103, 8 Apr. 1891, C.O. 111/459; and No. 228, 14 July 1891, C.O. 111/460.
140. Ord. No. 10/1891, C.O. 113/8; encl. in Bruce to Knutsford, No. 333, 23 Sept. 1891, C.O. 111/461.
141. Lytton to Wodehouse, No. 74, 1 Dec. 1858, C.O. 111/321.

Chapter 10

1. J.W. Boddam-Whetham, *Roraima and British Guiana* (Lond., 1879), pp. 12–13; L. Crookall, *British Guiana* (Lond., 1898), pp. 85–86; R. Schomburgk, *A Description of British Guiana*, vol. 2 (Lond., 1840), p. 28.
2. *Colonist*, 16 Aug. 1872; *R.G.*, 18 Aug., 1863; H.V.P. Bronkhurst to Gen. Sect., 30 Nov. 1877, M.M.S/W.v/2; E.A.V. Abraham, 'The East Indian Coolie in British Guiana', *WIQ*, 2, July 1886, pp. 405–406.

3. W. Rodney, *A History of the Guyanese Working People, 1881-1905* (Balt., 1981), p. 178.
4. *Ibid.*, p. 179.
5. A.H. Adamson, *Sugar Without Slaves* (New Haven, 1972), p. 12.
6. *Ibid.*, p. 158.
7. *Ibid.*, p. 266.
8. P. van den Berghe, *Race and Racism* (N.Y., 1967).
9. D. Bisnauth, 'The East Indian Immigrant Society in British Guiana, 1891-1930', unpublished Ph.D. thesis, U.W.I., 1977.

APPENDICES

APPENDIX I
Governors of British Guiana

1831–1833	Sir Benjamin D' Urban
1833–1838	Sir James Carmichael Smyth
1838–1848	Henry Light
1848–1854	Sir Henry Barkly
1854–1861	Sir Philip E. Wodehouse
1862–1868	Sir Francis Hincks
1869–1873	Sir John Scott
1874–1877	Sir J.R. Longden
1877–1881	C.H. Kortright
1882–1887	Sir Henry Irving
1888–1893	Viscount (Lord) Gormanston

APPENDIX II
Immigration Statistics, 1834–1890

Period	India	Madeira	Africa	China	West Indies	Other Private Schemes
1834–40	396	608	91	–	8,092	1,470
1841–45	–	5,601	5,829	–	4,378	568
1846–50	12,374	11,156	4,699	–	428	–
1851–55	9,981	6,544	994	647	–	–
1856–60	16,206	4,373	971	6,008	–	–
1861–65	15,654	226	1,476	5,975	6,848	–
1866–70	22,436	1,351	–	–	3,282	–
1871–75	24,355	1,120	–	388	8,827	–
1876–80	27,374	1,237	–	515	4,045	–
1881–85	20,500	–	–	–	4,143	–
1886–90	20,471	–	–	–	974	–
Total	169,747	32,216	14,060	13,533	41,017	2,038

Source: G.W. Roberts & M.A. Johnson, 'Factors Involved in Immigration and Movements in the Working Force of British Guiana in the Nineteenth Century', *SES*, 23(1), 1974.

APPENDIX III
Population Statistics, 1841–1891

Category	1841	1851	1861	1871	1881	1891
Whites	2,776	3,630	2,881	2,903	3,225	4,558
Blacks and Coloureds/ Mixed	91,074	108,438	110,216	122,862	143,319	144,619
Portuguese	2,619	7,928	9,859	12,029	11,926	12,164
Indians	343	7,682	22,081	48,363	79,929	105,463
Chinese	–	–	2,629	6,880	5,234	3,714
Aborigines	–	7,000	7,000	–	7,656	7,463
Others	1,321	1,316	1,241	454	1,829	347
Total	98,133	135,994	155,907	193,491	253,118	278,328

Source: Decennial censuses, 1841–1891.

Except for the censuses of 1851 and 1891, there is no accurate breakdown of statistics according to race which clearly distinguishes the white from the black and mixed population. The general tendency was merely to classify people according to their place of origin/birth. This meant that the locally born whites were invariably classified as "Natives of British Guiana", along with the local black and mixed population. This rendered the two groups statistically indistinguishable.

In order, therefore, to estimate the number of local whites, the figures provided in the 1851 and 1891 censuses were used as guidelines. In 1851, there was a total white population of 3,630 (excluding Portuguese immigrants) of which 2,088 were foreign born (European and North American). Hence, the 1,542 local whites constituted 42.5 percent of the total white population. Similarly, in 1891, there were 2,535 foreign born in a total white population of 4,558. Thus the 2,023 local whites formed 44.4 percent of the white population. From these statistics one can reasonably presume that the proportion of local to foreign born whites remained relatively stable throughout the post-emancipation period. The mean average of 43.5 percent of the total white population has, therefore, been used to estimate the number of local whites of the years 1861, 1871, and 1881. This serves, when added to the foreign born to provide a more accurate indication of the size of the total white population in that period. Thus the 1861 figure of 2,881 whites includes an estimated, 1,253 locals; the 2,903 whites given for 1871 include 1,263 locals; and the 3,225 for 1881 include 1,403 locals.

The statistics of the black and mixed population are derived by estimating the number of local born (calculated by subtracting the estimated number of local whites, as well as the children of Portuguese, Indian and Chinese immigrants from the figures for the "Native" population), plus the African and West Indian immigrants.

APPENDICES

The Portuguese, Indian and Chinese populations do not present a statistical problem since figures for both the immigrants and the locally born of each ethnic group are clearly provided in the decennial censuses. On the other hand, no pretention is made about the reliability of the statistics pertaining to the Amerindians (Aborigines) which were admittedly crude estimates. This was so because there was no way of collecting accurate data about these widely dispersed, semi-nomadic people in the remote interior. Lying outside the limits of the plantation belt, however, they do not form an integral part of this study.

APPENDIX IV
Political Franchise

Year	Population	Registered Voters	Percentage of Population
1851	135,994	967	0.71
1861	155,907	605	0.39
1871	193,491	784	0.41
1881	253,118	1,001	0.40
1891	278,328	2,046	0.74

Source: Blue Books of Statistics, C.O. 116; and Voters Lists in the Official Gazettes.
N.B. The political franchise was extended in 1849 and 1891.

APPENDIX V
(a) Police Force

Year	Strength	Expenditure
1850	237	£19,363
1856	313	26,679
1866	436	30,776
1871	569	51,122
1873	721	52,940
1876	749	52,014
1880	671	48,049
1890	575	47,132
1891	763	51,142

Source: Blue books of Statistics, C.O. 116.

(b) Public Expenditure: Police & Military vs. Education

Year	Police/Military	Education
1850	£57,403	£ 1,970
1860	45,088	11,516
1870	60,530	17,682
1880	66,038	29,483
1890	55,027	35,740
Total (1850–90)	£2,392,420	£768,718

Source: Blue Books of Statistics, C.O. 116.

BIBLIOGRAPHY

PRIMARY SOURCES
Colonial Office Records (P.R.O.)
C.O. 111   British Guiana: Original Correspondence.
C.O. 112   Letters from the Secretary of State.
C.O. 113   Acts.
C.O. 114   Sessional Papers and Administration Reports.
C.O. 115   The Official Gazette
C.O. 116   Vol. 165 — Memoir on the Constitution of Berbice and of British Guiana, 1804–1852.
             Vols. 166–169: Stipendiary Magistrates' returns, 1845–54.
             Vols. 170–312: Blue Books of Statistics.
C.O. 318   West Indies: Original Correspondence.
C.O. 384   Emigration: Original Correspondence.
C.O. 386   Emigration: Colonial Land and Emigration Commission.
C.O. 537   Colonies (general), Supplementary: Original Correspondence.

War Office Records (P.R.O.)
W.O. 1   West Indies: Original Correspondence.

Guyana National Archives
Administration Reports.
Minutes of the Court of Policy and Combined Court.
Immigration Certificates.
Miscellaneous Files and Petitions — unclassified.

Parliamentary Papers
1828. XXIII. 507   Second Report of the Commissioners of Inquiry into the Administration of

	Civil and Criminal Justice in the West Indies and South American Colonies.
1836. XI. 499	Report of Select Committee on disposal of lands in the British Colonies.
1839. XXXIX. 55	Correspondence relative to the condition of the Hill Coolies and other labourers who have been introduced into British Guiana.
1840. XXXIV. 121	Correspondence between the Secretary of State and the Governor on Immigration.
1840. XXXIV. 181	Reports from or Despatches to the Governor of British Guiana respecting the Hill Coolies introduced into that Colony.
1840. XXXIV. 237	Lord Aberdeen's Despatch to the Governor of British Guiana relating to the Civil List and Related Correspondence.
1847–48. XXIII. Pt.III.1	Despatches relative to the condition and prospects of the Colony.
1847–48. XLVI.1	Reports, Tables, etc., exhibiting the condition of the Colony.
1847–48. XLVI. 323	Correspondence respecting the Colony.
1849. XI.	Report of the Select Committee on Ceylon and British Guiana.
1847. XXXIX. 115	Correspondence relative to the Supply of Labour in British Guiana.
1847–48. XLV. 7	Laws in force in British Guiana for the regulation of labour between masters and labourers.
1847–48. XXIII. Pt.I.395	Documents relative to the present state and prospects of the cultivation of sugar and coffee' and the supply of labour.
1851. XXXIX. 1	Despatches relative to the state of the Colony, particularly with reference to the growth of sugar.
1851. XXXVI. 135	Correspondence between Governor Barkly and Secretary of State Grey on Constitutional Reform.

1852–53. LXVIII. 535 & 1854–55. XXXIX. 159	Correspondence relating to Chinese Immigrants introduced into the colonies of British Guiana and Trinidad.
1856. XLIV. 9	Correspondence on the Recent Disturbances.
1857. XXVIII. 355	Correspondence with resepct to the Ordinance passed by the Colonial Legislature imposing a Registration Tax.
1857–58. XLI. 629	Letters and Papers relating to Emigration from China to British Guiana and Trinidad.
1859. XX. Pt.I.1	Correspondence with respect to the condition of the labouring population and the supply of labour.
1871. XX. 483	Report of the Commissioners appointed to inquire into the treatment of immigrants in British Guiana.
1871. XX. 691, 751	Appendices to the Report, Pts. I, II.
1871. XLVII. 339	Correspondence arising out of complaints of Portuguese residents of British Guiana.
1872. XLIII. 1	Further Correspondence.
1873. XLIX. 935	Correspondence respecting a disturbance among the Indian Immigrants employed on the Devonshire Castle estate.

Wesleyan Methodist Missionary Society Papers

Stack W.iv/5	West Indies: Correspondence, 1848–1857.
Stack W.v/2	British Guiana and the Leewards, 1868–1891.
Stack W.v/5	St. Vincent and Demerara, 1858–1890

London Missionary Society Papers

Boxes 7–11	Demerara: Original Correspondence, 1846–1894.
Boxes 7–11	Berbice: Original Correspondence, 1850–1899.

Society of Jesus (English Province) Papers and Publications
B.G./8–20   British Guiana: Correspondence, 1857–1902.
Letters and Notices (Printed), vols. 1–25, 1862–1900.

United Society for the Propagation of the Gospel Papers
Class D   Letters received, vols. 16–99.
Class E   Missionary Reports, vols. 1–45.

SECONDARY SOURCES
Newspapers

Royal Gazette, 1838–1889
Berbice Gazette, 1838–1900

The Colonist, 1848–1884
The Creole, 1856–1882
Guiana Times, 1840–1848, 1866
Demerara Times, 1875–1876
The Echo, 1887–1899
Liberator, 1868–1869
The Penny Weekly, 1869
Emery's Journal, 1847
Working Man, 1872
Guiana Herald, 1842–1844, 1885
Watchman, 1871–1879

Guiana Chronicle, 1840–1845
Demerara Daily Chronicle, 1881–1884
Daily Chronicle, 1895–1900
The Argosy, 1881–1900

Daily Liberal, 1891–1894
Mining Gazette, 1890–1897
The Nugget, 1888–1890
The Reflector, 1889–1892
Guiana Reformer, 1840–1841
A Liburdade, 1879–1880
O Portuguez, 1880–1889
Lusitano, 1891
A Uniao Portugueza, 1889–1890

Contemporary Books, Articles, and Pamphlets

Abraham, E.A.V., 'The East Indian Coolie in British Guiana', *West Indian Quarterly*, 2, 1886.

Alexander, A.H., *Statistics and other Information prepared for Dr. Comins in Regard to Immigration from India* (Demerara, Official Publn., 1893).

Amos, Sheldon, *The Existing Laws of Demerara for the Regulation of Coolie Immigration* (London, Head, Hole & Co., 1871).

Amphlett, John, *Under a Tropical Sky: A Journal of First Impressions of the West Indies* (London, Sampson Low, Marston, Low & Searle, 1873).

Ashmore, A.M., *Memorandum on Village Administration from 1838–1902* [pamphlet] (Georgetown, 1903).

Beaumont, Joseph, *The New Slavery: An Account of the Indian and*

Chinese Immigrants in British Guiana (London, W. Ridgway, 1871).

Beckitt, J. Edgar, 'Some Home Truths', *Timehri*, VI, 3rd. series, 1919.

Bennett, George W., *A History of British Guiana* (Georgetown, L. McDermott, 1875).

Boddam-Whetham, J.W., *Roraima and British Guiana* (London, Hurst & Blackett, 1879).

Brett, W.H., *The Indian Tribes of Guiana: Their Condition and Habits* (London, Bell & Daldy, 1868).

Bronkhurst, H.V.P., *The Origin of the Guyanian Indians* (Demerara, Colonist, 1881).

—— *The Colony of British Guiana and its Labouring Inhabitants* (London, T, Woolmer, 1883).

——*The Ancestry or Origin of Our East Indian Immigrants: being an Ethnological and Philological Paper* (Georgetown, Argosy, 1886).

—— *Among the Hindus and Creoles of British Guiana* (London, T. Woolmer, 1888).

Brumell, J. [A Landowner], *Demerara after Fifteen Years of Freedom* (London, T. Bosworth, 1853).

Candler, John, Extract from Diary (edited by Prof. Boromé), *Caribbean Studies*, 4 (2), 1964.

Carlyle, Thomas, *Occasional Discourse on the Nigger Question* (London, T. Bosworth, 1853).

Comins, D.W.D., *Notes on Emigration from India to British Guiana* (Calcutta, Bengal Secretariat Press, 1893).

Crookall, Lawrence, *British Guiana: or Work and Wanderings among the Creoles and Coolies, the Africans and Indians of the Wild Country* (London, T. Fisher Unwin, 1898).

Cropper, J.B., 'Our Villages and Country Parts', *Timehri*, II (2), 1912.

Cruickshank, J.G., 'The Beginnings of Our Villages', *Timehri*, 7, 3rd series, 1921.

Dalton, Henry G., *The History of British Guiana*, 2 vols. (London, Longman, Brown, Green, & Longmans, 1855).

Dance, C.D., *Chapters from a Guianese Log-Book* (Demerara, Royal Gazette, 1881).

Davy, J., *The West Indies before and Since Slave Emancipation* (London, W. & F.G. Cash, 1854).

DesVoeux, George W., *My Colonial Service in British Guiana* (London, Murray, 1903).

—— *Experiences of a Demerara Magistrate, 1863-69* (V. Roth, ed., Georgetown, Daily Chrouicle, 1948).

DeWever, P.M., 'Our Future Peasantry', *Timehri*, 7, 3rd. series, 1921.

Duff, R., *British Guiana: Being Notes on a Few of the Natural Productions, Industrial Occupations and Social Institutions* (Glasgow, Thomas Murray & Sons, 1866).

Eves, Charles W., *The West Indies* (London, Sampson Low, Marston, Searle, & Rivington, 1889).

Farrar, Thomas, *Notes of the History of the Church in Guiana* (New Amsterdam, W. Macdonald, 1892).

Froude, James A., *The English in the West Indies* (London, Longmans, 1888).

Gerard, John, 'Inter-Guianese' (ms.), (Society of Jesus, 1899-1900).

Glaisher, Ernest H., *A Journey on the Berbice River and Wieronnie Creek* (Demerara, Argosy, 1885).

Grierson, George A., *Report on Colonial Emigration from the Bengal Residency* (Calcutta, Official Publication, 1883).

Hardy, Alfred, *Life and Adventure in British Guiana* (London, Epworth Press, 1913).

Hart, D., *Trinidad and the other West Indian Islands and Colonies* (Port-of-Spain, The Chronicle, 1866).

Hartsinck, J.J., *Beschryving van Guiana of de Wilde Kust, in Zuid America*, 2 vols. (Amsterdam, G. Tielenburg, 1770).

Heatley, J., *A Visit to the West Indies* (London, Alnwick, Northumberland, H.H. Blair, 1891).

Hewick, J.E., 'Our People', *Timehri*, I, 3rd. series, 1911.

Im Thurn, Everard F., 'Occasional Notes', *Timehri*, 1, 1882.

Ireland, Alleyne, *Demerariana* (Demerara, Balwin & Co., 1897).

Jenkins, Edward, *The Coolie: His Rights and Wrongs* (London, Strahan & Co., 1871).

Jenman, G.S., 'Model Settlers: A Lesson in the Small Industries', *Timehri*, 2, 1883.

Josa, F.P., 'The Hindus in the West Indies', *Timehri*, II (2), 1912.

—— *The Tale of a Roaming Catholic* (London, Faith Press, 1920).

Kingsley, Charles, *At Last: A Christmas in the West Indies*, (London, Macmillan, 1890).

Kirke, Henry, *Twenty-Five Years in British Guiana* (London,

Sampson Low & Co., 1898).

Lobscheid, W., *Chinese Emigration: A Trip through British Guiana* (Demerara, Royal Gazette, 1866).

Low, F.O., 'Hopetown Chinese Settlement', *Timehri*, VI, 3rd. ser., 1919.

Luard, E.C., 'Demerara Sugar Plantations and Life Thereon', *West Indian Quarterly*, 3, 1887.

Luckhoo, E.A., 'East Indians in British Guiana', *Timehri*, II (2), 1912.

MacArthur, J. Sidney, 'Our People' *Timehri*, II (1), 1912.

Marrat, J., *In the Tropics*, (London, Wesleyan Conference Office, 1881).

Marx, Karl, *The Economic and Philosophical Manuscripts of 1844* (Moscow, Foreign Languages Pub. House, 1967).

McDavid, E.N., *Future Prospects of the Creoles of the Colony* [pamphlet] (Demerara, 1900).

Merivale, H., *Lectures on Colonisation and Colonies*, 2 vols. (London, O.U.P., 1861).

Moore, J.R., *A Handbook of the Causes of Non-Success and Degradation of the Negro Race in British Guiana* (Demerara, A.C. Taylor, 1874).

Netscher, P.M., *History of the Colonies Essequibo, Demerara, and Berbice*, translated by W.E. Roth (Gravenhage, Provincial Utrecht Soc. of Arts & Sciences, 1888).

Pearson, J.G. (ed.), *New Overseer's Manual: or the reason why of Julius Jugler* (Georgetown, Argosy, 1890).

—— 'The Life History of an East Indian', *Timehri*, 10, 1897.

Premium, Barton, *Eight Years in British Guiana, 1840-48* (London, Longman, Brown, Green & Longmans, 1850).

Rankin, William, *Thoughts on British Guiana* [pamphlet] (Demerara, 1847).

Rodway, James, *History of British Guiana*, 3 Vols. (Georgetown, J. Thomson, 1891-94).

—— *The Story of Georgetown* (Georgetown, Argosy, 1920).

Ruhoman, Joseph, *India: Progress of Her People at Home and Abroad* (Demerara, 1894).

Schomburgk, Richard, *Travels in British Guiana, 1840-44*, 2 vols., translated by W.E. Roth (Georgetown, Daily Chronicle, 1922).

Schomburgk, Robert, *A Description of British Guiana* (London, 1840 reprt. London, Coss, 1970).

Scoble, John, *Hill Coolies. A Brief Exposition of the Deplorable*

Condition of the Hill Coolies in British Guiana and Mauritius (London, Harvey & Darton, 1840).

—— *British Guiana: Facts! Facts! Facts!* [pamphlet] (London, 1840).

Scoles, Ignatius, *Sketches of African and Indian Life in British Guiana* (Demerara, Argosy, 1885).

Sewell, W., *Ordeal of Free Labour in the British West Indies* (N.Y., Harper & Bros., 1861).

Sloman, E., 'Coolie Missions in British Guiana', *West Indian Quarterly*, 3, 1887.

Swinton, Capt. & Mrs., *Journal of a Voyage with Coolie Emigrants from Calcutta to Trinidad* (London, Alfred W. Bennett, 1859).

Thompson, Alfred A., 'Our Civil Service: Competition versus Nomination', *West Indian Quarterly*, 3, 1887.

Thorne, Alfred A., 'British Guiana: Progress and Limitations', *Timehri*, II (2), 1912.

Thorne, J.T., *Some Haphazard Notes of a Forty-Two Years' Residence in British Guiana* (Demerara, Argosy, 1899).

Trollope, Anthony, *The West Indies and the Spanish Main* (N.Y. 1860 reprt. London, Dawsons, 1968).

Van Sertima, J., *Scenes and Sketches of Demerara Life* (Georgetown, C.K. Jardine, 1899).

—— *Among the Common People of British Guiana* (Georgetown, C.K. Jardine, 1897).

Veness, W.T., *El Dorado: or British Guiana as a Field for Colonisation* (London, Cassell, Petter, & Galpin, 1867).

Wallbridge, J.S., 'Fifty Years Recollections of British Guiana', *Timehri*, I, 3rd. ser., 1911.

Wesleyan Methodist Missionary Society, *A Missionary Present about the Children in British Guiana* (London, Wesleyan Conference Office, n.d.).

Whitfield, Richard H., *The present position and future prospects of British Guiana Considered: Being a Letter ... to the Colonists Thereof* (London, British & Colonial Co., 1872).

—— *'Hints' on Villages* [pamphlet] (Demerara, 1873).

'X', 'Stray Notes on Obeah', *Timehri*, VI, 3rd. ser., 1919.

Modern Publications

Abrahams, Roger D., 'The Negro Stereotype', *Journal of American Folklore*, 83 (328), 1970.

Adamson, Alan H., 'Monoculture and Village Decay in Brit-

ish Guiana, 1854–1872', *Journal of Social History*, 3 (4), 1970.
—— *Sugar Without Slaves: The Political Economy of British Guiana, 1834–1904* (New Haven, Yale Univ. Press, 1972).
—— 'The Reconstruction of Plantation Labor after Emancipation: The case of British Guiana', *Race and Slavery in the Western Hemisphere: Quantitative Studies*, S. Engerman and E. Genovese (eds.), (Princeton, P.U.P., 1975).
—— 'The Impact of Indentured Immigration on the Political Economy of British Guiana', in *Indentured Labour in the British Empire, 1834–1920*, Kay Saunders (ed.), (London, Croom Helm, 1984).
Ankum-Houwink, J., 'Chinese Contract Migrants in Surinam', *Boletin de Estudios Latinoamericans y del Caribe*, No. 17, 1974.
Augier, F.R., 'Before and After 1865', *New World Quarterly*, 2 (2), 1966.
Bacchus, K.M., *Education and Socio-Cultural Integration in a 'Plural' Society* (McGill, Univ., Occasional Paper Series No. 6, 1970).
Balandier, G., 'The Colonial Situation: A Theoretical Approach', in *Social Change: The Colonial Situation*, I. Wallerstein (ed.), (N.Y., Wiley & Sons, 1966).
Banton, Michael, *Race Relations* (London, Tavistock Pblns., 1967).
——, *The Idea of Race* (London, Boulder, Westview Press, 1977).
Beachey, R.W., *The British West Indian Sugar Industry in the Late 19th Century* (Oxford, Blackwell, 1957).
Beckford, George L., 'Plantation Society', *Savacou*, 5, 1971.
—— *Persistent Poverty* (London, O.U.P., 1972).
Beckford, G., and Witter, M., *Small Garden ... Bitter Weed: Struggle and Change in Jamaica* (London, Zed Press, 1982).
Benedict, Burton, *Indians in a Plural Society* (London, H.M.S.O., 1961).
—— 'Stratification in Plural Societies', *American Anthropologist*, 64 (6), 1962.
—— *Mauritius: Problems of a Plural Society* (London, Pall Mall Press, 1965).
Benn, Denis M., 'The Theory of Plantation Economy and Society: A Methodological Critique', *Journal of Commonwealth and Comparative Politics*, xii (3), 1974.

Bennett, John W. (ed.) *The New Ethnicity: Perspectives from Ethnology* (St. Paul, West Pub. Co., 1975).

Bently, Gerald, *Some Preliminary Observations on the Chinese in Trinidad* (Montreal, McGill Univ., [Occas. Paper], 1967).

Berreman, Gerald D., 'Race, Caste, and Other Invidious Distinctions in Social Stratification', *Race*, XIII (4), 1972.

Boeke, J.H., *Economics and Economic Policy of Dual Societies* (Haarlem, H.D. Tjeenk Willink & Zoon, 1953),

Bolland, O. Nigel, 'Systems of Domination after Slavery: The Control of Land and Labor in British West Indies after 1838', *Comparative Studies in Society and History*, 23 (4), 1981.

——, 'Reply to William A. Green's "The Perils of Comparative History",' *Comparative Studies in Society and History*, 26, 1984.

Bolt, Christine, *Victorian Attitudes to Race* (London, Routledge & Kegan Paul, 1971).

Braithwaite, Lloyd, 'Social Stratification in Trinidad', *Social and Economic Studies*, 2 (2 & 3), 1953.

—— 'The Problem of Cultural Integration in Trinidad', *Social and Economic Studies*, 3, 1954.

—— 'Social Stratification and Cultural Pluralism', *Social and Cultural Pluralism in the Caribbean*, V. Rubin (ed.), (N.Y., Annals N.Y. Acad. of Sciences, 1960).

—— 'Problems of Race and Colour in the Caribbean', *Caribbean Issues*, 1 (1), 1974.

Brathwaite, Edward, *The Development of Creole Society in Jamaica, 1770-1820* (London, Oxford, Clarendon, 1971).

—— *Contradictory Omens: Cultural Diversity and Integration in the Caribbean* (Jamaica, Savacou, 1974).

Brereton, B., 'The Foundations of Prejudice: Indians and Africans in 19th Century Trinidad', *Caribbean Issues*, 1 (1), 1974.

—— *Race Relations in Colonial Trinidad, 1870-1900* (Cambridge, C.U.P., 1979).

—— *A History of Modern Trinidad, 1783-1962* (London, Heinemann, 1981).

Cairns, H. Alan, *Prelude to Imperialism* (London, Routledge & Kegan Paul, 1965).

Cameron, N.E., *The Evolution of the Negro*, 2 vols. (Georgetown, Argosy, 1929-34).

Chan, V.O., 'The Riots of 1856 in British Guiana', *Caribbean Quarterly*, 16 (1), 1970.

Clementi, Cecil, *The Chinese in British Guiana* (Georgetown, Argosy, 1915).
—— *A Constitutional History of British Guiana* (London, Macmillan, 1937).
Conrad, R., *The Destruction of Brazilian Slavery, 1850–1888*, (Calif., Univ. of Calif. Press, 1972).
Cox, O.C., *Caste, Class, and Race* (N.Y., Doubleday, 1948).
—— 'The Question of Pluralism', *Race*, XII (4), 1971.
Craig, Susan, 'Sociological Theorizing in the English-Speaking Caribbean: A Review', in *Contemporary Caribbean: A Sociological Reader*, vol. 2, S. Craig (ed.), (P.O.S., the author, 1982).
Cross, Malcolm, 'Cultural Pluralism and Sociological Theory: A Critique and Reevaluation', *Social and Economic Studies*, 17 (4), 1968.
—— 'One Conflict, Race Relations, and the Theory of the Plural Society', *Race*, II (4), 1971.
—— *The East Indians of Guyana and Trinidad* (London, Minority Rights Group, 1972).
—— 'Colonialism and Ethnicity: A Theory and Comparative Case Study', *Ethnic and Racial Studies*, 1 (1), 1978.
Crowley, D.J., 'Plural and Differential Acculturation in Trinidad', *American Anthropologist*, 59 (5), 1957.
—— 'Cultural Assimilation in a Multi-Racial Society', *Social and Cultural Pluralism in the Caribbean*, V. Rubin (ed.), (N.Y., Annals N.Y. Acad. Sci., 1960).
Cumper, George, *Social Structure of the British Caribbean* (Jamaica, U.C.W.I. 1949).
Cumpston, I.M., *Indians Overseas in British Territories, 1834–54* (London, O.U.P., 1953).
—— 'A Survey of Indian Immigration to British Tropical Colonies to 1910', *Population Studies*, 10 (2), 1956.
Curtin, P.D., *Two Jamaicas: The Role of Ideas in a Tropical Colony, 1830–1865* (Cambridge, Harvard Univ. Press, 1955).
—— *The Image of Africa: British Ideas and Action, 1780–1850* (London, Macmillan, 1965).
Daly, Vere, *A Short History of the Guianese People* (London, Macmillan, 1975).
Deerr, Noel, *The History of Sugar*, 2 vols. (London, Chapman & Hall, 1949–50).
Delson, Roberta M. 'Land and Urban Planning: Aspects of Modernization in Early Nineteenth-Century Brazil', *Luso-*

Brazilian Review, 16 (2), 1979.

Despres, Leo A, 'The Implication of Nationalist Politics in British Guiana for the Development of Cultural Theory', *American Anthropologist*, 66 (5), 1964.

—— *Cultural Pluralism and Nationalist Politics in British Guiana* (Chicago, Rand McNally, 1967).

—— 'Anthropology, Cultural Pluralism, and the Study of Complex Societies', *Current Anthropology*, 9 (1), 1968.

—— 'Differential Adaptations and Mico-Cultural Evolution in Guyana', *Southwestern Journal of Anthropology*, 25, 1969.

—— *Protest and Change in Plural Societies* (Montreal, Occas. Paper No. 2, McGill Univ., 1969).

—— (ed.) *Ethnicity and Resource Competition in Plural Societies* (The Hague, Mouton, 1975).

—— 'Ethnicity and Resource Competition in Guyanese Society', in *Ethnicity* ..., (The Hague, Mouton, 1975).

—— 'Towards a Theory of Ethnic Phenomena', in *Ethnicity* ... (The Hague, Mouton, 1975).

—— 'Ethnicity and Ethnic Group Relations in Guyana', in *The New Ethnicity*, J.W. Bennett, (ed.), (St. Paul, West Pub. Co., 1975).

Devos, George, 'Social Stratification and Ethnic Pluralism: An Overview from the Perspective of Psychological Anthropology', *Race*, XIII, (4), 1972.

De Waal Malefijt, A., *The Javanese in Surinam: Segment of a Plural Society* (Assen, van Gorcum & Co., 1963).

Dodge, Peter, 'Comparative Racial Systems in the Greater Caribbean', *Social and Economic Studies*, 16 (3), 1967.

Drummond, Lee, 'The Cultural Continuum: A Theory of Intersystems', *Man*, vol. 15, N.S., 1980.

——, 'Ethnicity, "ethnicity", and culture theory', *Man*, vol. 16, N.S. 1981.

Duffy, James, *Portugal in Africa* (London, Penguin Books, 1962).

Dumont, L., 'Caste, Racism and Stratification', *Contributions to Indian Sociology*, 5, 1961.

Dunning, Eric, 'Dynamics of Racial Stratification: Some Preliminary Observations', *Race*, XIII (4), 1972.

Ehrlich, Allan S., 'History, Ecology and Demography in the British Caibbean: an Analysis of East Indian Ethnicity', *Southwestern Journal of Anthropology*, 27 (2), 1971.

Farley, Rawle, 'The Rise of Village Settlements of British

Guiana', *Caribbean Quarterly*, 3 (2), 1953.
—— 'The Rise of a Peasantry in British Guiana', *Social and Economic Studies*, 2 (4), 1954.
—— 'The Shadow and the Substance', *Caribbean Quarterly*, 4 (2), 1955.
—— 'The Unification of British Guiana', *Social and Economic Studies*, 4, 1955.
Floyd, Barry, 'Plurality in the Caribbean: Some Spatial Aspects', *Plural Societies*, 4 (3), 1973.
Franklin, John Hope (ed.), *Color and Race* (Boston, Beacon Press, 1969).
Frazier, E. Franklin, *Race and Culture Contacts in the Modern World* (Boston, Alfred A. Knopf, 1957).
Freedman, M., 'The Growth of a Plural Society in Malaya', *Pacific Affairs*, 33, 1960.
——, 'The Handling of Money: A Note on the Background to the Economic Sophistication of Overseas Chinese', *Man*, 59, 1959.
Fried, Morton H., 'Some Observations on the Chinese in British Guiana', *Social and Economic Studies*, 5 (1), 1956.
Frucht, Richard (ed.), *Black Society in the New World* (N.Y., Random House, 1971).
Furley, W.W., 'Protestant Missionaries in the West Indies: Pioneers of a Non-Racial Society', *Race*, VI (3), 1965.
Furnivall, J.S., *Netherlands India: A Study of Plural Economy* (London, Cambridge Univ. Press, 1939).
——, *Colonial Policy and Practice: A Comparative Study of Burma and Netherlands India* (London, Cambridge Univ. Press, 1948).
Glasgow, Roy A., *Guyana: Race and Politics among Africans and East Indians* (The Hague, Martinus Nijhoff, 1970).
Goveia, Elsa V., *A Study on the Historiography of the British West Indies to the End of the Nineteenth Century* (Mexico, Instituto Panamericano de Geografia e Historia, 1956).
——, *Slave Society in the British Leeward Islands at the end of the Eighteenth Century* (New Haven, Yale Univ. Press, 1965).
Green, William, 'The Apprenticeship in British Guiana, 1834–38', *Caribbean Studies*, 9 (2), 1969.
——, *British Slave Emancipation: The Sugar Colonies and the Great Experiment, 1830–1865.* (Oxford, Clarendon, 1976).
——, 'The Perils of Comparative History: Belize and the British Sugar Colonies after Slavery', *Comparative Studies in*

Society and History, 26, 1984.
Greene, J.E., *Race vs. Politics in Guyana* (Kingston, I.S.E.R., 1974).
Guerin, Daniel, 'Racial Prejudice and the Failure of the Middle Classes in the West Indies', *Black Society in the New World*, R. Frucht (ed.), (N.Y., Random House, 1971).
Hall, D.G., *Free Jamaica, 1838-1865* (Barbados, Caribbean Universities Press, 1969).
——, *Five of the Leewards, 1838-1865* (Barbados, Caribbean Universities Press, 1971).
Hall, Stuart, 'Pluralism, Race and Class in Caribbean Society', in *Race and Class in Post-Colonial Society*, (UNESCO, Paris, 1977).
——, 'Race, Articulation and Societies Structured in Dominance', in *Sociological Theories: Race and Colonialism*, (UNESCO, Paris, 1980).
Harper-Smith, J.W., 'The Colonial Stock Act and the British Guiana Constitution of 1891', *Social and Economic Studies*, 14 (3), 1965.
Harris, C.A., and J.A.J. de Villiers, *Gravesande: The Rise of British Guiana* (London, Hakluyt Society, 1911).
Harris, Marvin, *Patterns of Race in the Americas* (N.Y., Walker, 1964).
Hazareesingh, K., 'The Religion and Culture of Indian Immigrants in Mauritius and the Effect of Social Change', *Comparative Studies in Society and History*, 8 (2), 1966.
Higman, B., 'Theory, Method and Technique in Caribbean Social History', *Journal of Caribbean History*, 20 (1), 1985-6.
Hoetink, H., '"Colonial Psychology" and Race', *Journal of Economic History*, Dec. 1961.
—— 'The Concept of Pluralism as Envisaged by M.G. Smith — Review Article', *Caribbean Studies*, 7 (1), 1967.
—— *Caribbean Race Relations: A Study of Two Variants* (London, Oxford Univ. Press, 1971).
—— *Slavery and Race Relations in the Americas: An inquiry into their Nature and Nexus* (N.Y., Harper & Roco, 1973).
—— 'Resource Competition, Monopoly, and Socioracial Diversity', in *Ethnicity and Resource Competition in Plural Societies*, Leo Despres (ed.), (The Hague, Mouton, 1975).
—— '"Race" and Color in the Caribbean', in *Caribbean Contours*, S.W. Mintz and S. Price (eds.), (Baltimore, Johns Hopkins Univ. Press, 1985).

Horowitz, Michael (ed.), *Peoples and Cultures of the Caribbean* (N.Y., Nat. Hist. Press, 1971).
Hutton, J.H., *Caste in India: its Nature, Function, and origin* (London, Oxford Univ. Press, 1961).
Imperial Indian Citizen Association, *Indians Abroad* (Bombay, IICA., 1927).
I.N.C.I.D.I., *Ethnic and Cultural Pluralism in Intertropical Communities*, (Brussels, 1957).
Jayawardena, C., *Conflict and Solidarity in a Guianese Plantation* (London, Athlone Press, 1963).
—— 'Culture and Ethnicity in Guyana and Fiji', *Man*, vol. 15, N.S., 1980.
Johnson, Howard, 'The Anti-Chinese Riots of 1918 in Jamaica', *Immigrants and Minorities*, 2 (1), 1983.
Kiernan, V.G., *The Lords of Human Kind: European Attitudes to the Outside World in the Imperial Age* (London, Weidenfeld & Nicolson, 1969).
Klass, M., 'East and West Indian: Cultural Complexity in Trinidad', *Social and Cultural Pluralism in the Caribbean*, V. Rubin (ed.), (N.Y., Annals N.Y. Acad. Sci., 1960).
—— *East Indians in Trinidad: A Study of Cultural Persistence* (N.Y., Columbia Univ. Press, 1961).
Knox, Graham, 'Political Change in Jamaica (1866–1906) and the Local Reaction to the Policies of the Crown Colony Government', in *The Caribbean in Transition*, F. Andic and T. Mathews (eds.), (Puerto Rico, Univ. of P.R. Press, 1965).
Kuper, Hilda, 'Strangers' in Plural Societies: Asians in South Africa and Uganda', *Pluralism in Africa*, L. Kuper & M.G. Smith (eds.), (Berkeley, Univ. of Calif. Press, 1971).
Kuper, Leo, and M.G. Smith (eds.), *Pluralism in Africa* (Berkeley, Univ. of Calif. Press, 1971).
Kuper, Leo, 'Plural Societies: Perspectives and Problems', *Pluralism in Africa* (Berkeley, Univ. of Calif Press, 1971).
—— 'Ethnic and Racial Pluralism: Some Aspects of Polarization and Depluralization', *Pluralism in Africa* (Berkeley, Univ. of Calif Press, 1971).
—— *Race, Class, and Power: Ideology and Revolutionary Change in Plural Societies* (London, Duckworth, 1974).
La Guerre, J. (ed.), *Calcutta to Caroni* (London, Longmans, 1974).
Laurence, K.O. 'The Evolution of Long-term Contracts in

Trinidad and British Guiana', *Jamaica Historical Review*, 5 (1), 1965.
—— 'The Establishment of the Portuguese Community in British Guiana', *Jamaican Historical Review*, 5 (2), 1965.
—— *Immigration into the West Indies in the 19th Century* (Barbados, Carib. Univ. Press, 1972).
Levy, Jacqueline, 'The Economic Role of the Chinese in Jamaica: The Grocery Retail Trade', *Jamaican Historical Review*, xv, 1986.
Lewis, Gordon K., *Main Currents in Caribbean Thought* (Baltimore, Johns Hopkins Univ. Press, 1983).
Lind, Andrew, 'Adjustment Patterns among the Jamaican Chinese', *Social and Economic Studies*, 7 (2), 1958.
Lowenthal, D., 'Range and Variation of Caribbean Societies', *Social and Cultural Pluralism in the Caribbean*, V. Rubin (ed.), (N.Y., Annals N.Y. Acad. Sci., 1960).
—— 'Race and Colour in the West Indies', *Daedalus*, Spring 1967.
—— *West Indian Societies* (N.Y., O.U.P., 1972).
—— and L. Comitas (eds.), *Slaves, Free Men, Citizens* (N.Y., Anchor Press, 1973).
——, *Consequences of Class and Colour* (N.Y., Anchor Press, 1973).
Lutchman, H.A., 'Patronage in Colonial Society', *Caribbean Quarterly*, 16 (2), 1970.
Malinowski, Bronislaw *The Dynamics of Culture Change: An Inquiry into Race Relations in Africa* (New Haven, Yale Univ. Press, 1968).
Mandle, J.R., *The Plantation Economy: Population and Economic Change in Guyana, 1838–1960* (Philadelphia, Temple Univ. Press, 1973).
Marshall, W.K., 'Metayage in the Sugar Industry of the British Windward Islands, 1838–1865', *Jamaica Historical Review*, 5 (1), 1965.
—— 'Social and Economic Problems in the Windward Islands, 1838–1865', *The Caribbean in Transition*, F. Andic & T. Mathews (eds.), (Puerto Rico, Univ. of P.R. Press, 1965).
—— 'Peasant Development in the West Indies since 1838', *Social and Economic Studies*, 17 (3), 1968.
—— '"Vox Populi": The St. Vincent Riots and Disturbances of 1862', in *Trade, Government and Society in Caribbean History*,

1700-1920, B.W. Higman (ed.), (Kingston, Heinemann, 1983).

McKenzie, H.I., 'The Plural Society Debate: Some Comments on a Recent Contribution', *Social and Economic Studies*, 15 (1), 1966.

Menezes, M. Noel, *Scenes from the History of the Portuguese in Guyana* (London, The Author/Victoria Printing Works, 1986).

Mintz, Sidney W., 'The Plantation as a Socio-Cultural Type', *Plantation Systems of the New World*, Social Science Monographs VII, 1959, Pan American Union, Wash., D.C.

—— 'The Question of Caribbean Peasantries: A Comment', *Caribbean Studies*, 1 (3), 1961.

—— *Caribbean Transformation* (Chicago, Aldine Pub. Co., 1974).

Mintz, S. and Price, S., (eds.) *Caribbean Contours* (Baltimore, Johns Hopkins Univ. Press, 1985).

Montagu, Ashley, 'The Concept of Race', *American Anthropologist*, 64 (5), 1962.

Moohr, Michael, 'The Economic Impact of Slave Emancipation in British Guiana, 1832–1852', *The Economic History Review*, 2nd. ser., XXV (4), 1972.

Moore, Brian L., 'Review' (A.H. Adamson's *Sugar Without Slaves*), *The Hispanic American Historical Review*, 54 (2), 1974.

—— 'Colonial Politics and the Preservation of Planter Hegemony in British Guiana after Emancipation', *Some Papers on Social, Political and Economic Adjustments to the ending of Slavery in the Caribbean*, C. Campbell (ed.), (Jamaica, Assoc. Carib. Historians, 1975).

—— 'The Social Impact of Portuguese Immigration into British Guiana after Emancipation', *Boletin de Estudios Latinoamericanos y del Caribe*, No. 19, 1975.

—— 'The Retention of Caste Notions among the Indian Immigrants in British Guiana during the 19th Century', *Comparative Studies in Society and History*, 19 (1), 1977.

—— 'Walter Rodney: His Contribution to Guyanese Historiography', *Bulletin of Eastern Caribbean Affairs*, 8 (2), 1982.

—— 'Review' (W. Rodney's *A History of the Guyanese Working People*), *Journal of Caribbean History*, 18 (1), 1984.

—— 'Review' (M.G. Smith's *Culture, Race and Class in the Commonwealth Caribbean*), *Jamaican Historical Review*, xv, 1986.

Morner, Magnus, *Race Mixture in the History of Latin America* (Boston, Little, Brown, 1967).
Morris, H. Stephen, 'Indians in East Africa: A Study in a Plural Society', *British Journal of Sociology*. 7, 1956.
—— 'The Plural Society', *Man*, Art. 148, 1957.
—— 'Some Aspects of the Concept of the Plural Society', *Man*, 2 (2), 1967.
Murdock, George, *Social Structure* (N.Y., Macmillan, 1949).
—— *Culture and Society* (Pittsburgh, Univ. of Phil. Press, 1965).
Nath, Dwarka, *A History of the Indians in British Guiana* (London, Nelson, 1950).
Newitt, M., *Portugal in Africa* (London, Hurst, 1981).
Nicholls, D., 'The "Syrians" of Jamaica', *Jamaican Historical Review*, xv, 1986.
Niehoff, Arthur, *East Indians in the West Indies* (Milwaukee, Milwaukee Public Museum, 1960).
Noguiera, Oraey, 'Skin Colour and Social Class', *Plantation Systems of the New World*, Social Science Monographs VII, Pan American Union, (Washington, D.C., 1959).
Padilla, E., 'Contemporary Social-Rural Types in the Caribbean Region', in *Caribbean Studies: A Symposium*, V. Rubin (ed.), (Seattle, Univ. of Washington, 1960).
Post, Ken, *Arise Ye Starvelings: The Jamaican Labour Rebellion of 1938 and its Aftermath* (The Hague, Martinus Nijhoff, 1978).
Prado, C., *The Colonial Background of Modern Brazil* (California, Univ. of Calif. Press, 1971).
Purves, James, 'The Portuguese in Bermuda', *Bermuda Historical Quarterly*, vol. 3, pt. 3, 1946.
Ragatz, L.J., *The Fall of the Planter Class in the British Caribbean, 1763–1833* (N.Y., Octagon, 1971).
Rex, John, 'The Plural Society in Sociological Theory', *British Journal of Sociology*, 10, 1959.
—— *Race Relations in Sociological Theory* (London, Weidenfeld & Nicolson, 1970).
—— 'The Plural Society: The South African Case', *Race*, XII, (4), 1971.
—— 'A Working Paradigm of Race Relations Research', *Ethnic and Racial Studies*, 4 (1), 1981.
—— 'Racism and the Structure of Colonial Societies', in *Racism and Colonialism*, Robert Ross (ed.), (The Hague, Leiden Univ. Press/Martinus Nijhoff, 1982).

Riviere, W. Emanuel, 'Labour Shortage in the British West Indies after Emancipation', *Journal of Caribbean History*, IV, 1972.

Roberts, G.W., 'Emigration from the Island of Barbados', *Social and Economic Studies*, 4 (3), 1955.

Roberts, G.W. and Johnson, M.A. 'Factors involved in Immigration and Movements in the Working Force of British Guiana in the 19th Century', *Social and Economic Studies*, 23 (1), 1974.

Robotham, D., 'Pluralism as an Ideology', *Social and Economic Studies*, 29 (1), 1980.

Rodney, Walter (ed.), *Guyanese Sugar Plantations in the Late Nineteenth Century* (Georgetown, Bovell Printery, 1979).

──, *A History of the Guyanese Working People, 1881-1905* (Baltimore, Johns Hopkins Univ. Press, 1981).

Ross, Robert, (ed.) *Racism and Colonialism: Essays on Ideology and Social Structure* (The Hague, Leiden Univ. Press/Martinus Nijhoff, 1982).

Rubin, Vera (ed.), *Social and Cultural Pluralism in the Caribbean*, Annals of the N.Y. Academy of Science, Vol. 83, Art. 5, 1960.

── *Caribbean Studies: A Symposium* (Seattle, Univ. of Wash. Press, 1960).

── 'Culture, Politics and Race Relations', *Social and Economic Studies*, 11 (4), 1961.

Ruhomon, Peter, *Centenary History of the East Indians in British Guiana, 1838-1938* (Georgetown, Daily Chronicle, 1947).

Runciman, W.G., 'Race and Social Stratification', *Race*, XIII (4), 1972.

Saunders, Kay (ed.) *Indentured Labour in the British Empire 1834-1920* (London, Croom Helm, 1984).

Shahabuddeen, M., *Constitutional Development in Guyana, 1621-1978* (Georgetown, Guyana National Printers, 1978).

Skinner, E.P., 'Group Dynamics and Social Stratification in British Guiana', *Social and Cultural Pluralism in the Caribbean*, V. Rubin (ed.), (N.Y., Annals N.Y. Acad. Sci., 1960).

── 'Social Stratification and Ethnic Identification', in *Peoples and Cultures of the Caribbean*, M. Horowitz (ed.)., (N.Y., Nat. Hist. Press, 1971).

Smith, Douglas, 'Origins of Porknocking', *McGill Studies in Caribbean Anthropology*, Occasional Paper No. 5, McGill Univ., 1969.

Smith, M.G., *The Plural Society in the British West Indies* (Berkeley, Univ. of Calif. Press, 1965).
—— 'Institutional and Political Conditions of Pluralism', and 'Some Developments in the Analytic Framework of Pluralism', in *Pluralism in Africa*, L. Kuper and M.G. Smith (eds.), (Berkeley, Univ. of Calif. Press, 1971).
—— 'Some Future Directions for Social Research in the Commonwealth Caribbean', *Social and Economic Studies*, 33 (2), 1984.
—— *Culture, Race and Class in the Commonwealth Caribbean* (Kingston, U.W.I., 1984).
Smith, R.T., 'Land Tenure in Three Guianese Villages', *Social and Economic Studies*, 4 (1), 1955.
—— *The Negro Family in British Guiana* (London, Routledge & Kegan Paul, 1956).
—— 'Some Social Characteristics of Indian Immigrants to British Guiana', *Population Studies*, 13 (1), 1959.
—— 'Family Structure and Plantation Systems in the New World', *Plantation Systems of the New World*, Social Science Monographs VII, 1959, Pan American Union, Wash., D.C.
—— 'Review' (of *Social and Culture Pluralism in the Caribbean*), *American Anthropologist*, 63, 1961.
—— *British Guiana* (London, Oxford Univ. Press, 1962).
—— 'Culture and Social Structure in the Caribbean: Some Recent Work on Family and Kinship Studies', *Comparative Studies in Society and History*, 6 (1), 1963.
—— 'Ethnic Difference and Peasant Economy in British Guiana', *Capital Savings, and Credit in Peasant Societies*, R. Firth and B. Yamey (eds.) (London, Allen & Unwin, 1964).
—— 'People and Change' *New World*, Guyana Independence Issue, 1966.
—— 'Social Stratification, Cultural Pluralism, and Integration in West Indian Societies', *Caribbean Integration*, S. Lewis and T.G. Mathews (eds.), (Puerto Rico, Univ. of P.R. Press, 1967).
—— 'Race and Political Conflict in Guyana', *Race*, 12, 1971.
—— 'Race and Class in the Post-Emancipation Caribbean', in *Racism and Colonialism*, Robert Ross (ed.), (The Hague, Leiden Univ. Press/Martinus Nijhoff, 1982).
Speckman, J.D., 'The Indian Group in the Segmented

Society of Surinam', *Caribbean Studies*, 3 (1), 1963.
—— *Marriage and Kinship among the Indians in Surinam* (Assen, van Gorcum & Co., 1965).
Temperley, Howard, *British Anti-Slavery, 1833-1870* (London, Longmans, 1972).
Thompson, Edgar, 'The Plantation as a Social System', *Plantation Systems of the New World*, Pan American Union, (Washington, 1959).
Thompson, Leonard, 'Historical Perspectives of Pluralism in Africa', *Pluralism in Africa*, L. Kuper and M.G. Smith (eds.), (Berkeley, Univ. of Calif. Press, 1971).
Tinker, Hugh, *A New System of Slavery* (Oxford, O.U.P., 1974).
Tucker, Terry, *Bermuda: Today and Yesterday, 1503-1973* (London, Robert Hale, 1975).
U.N.E.S.C.O., *Race, Science and Society*, Leo Kuper (ed.), (Paris, UNESCO, 1975).
——, *Race and Class in Post-Colonial Society* (Paris, UNESCO, 1977).
—— *Sociological Theories: Race and Colonialism* (Paris, UNESCO, 1980).
Van Amersfoort, Hans. '"Minority" as a Sociological Concept', *Ethnic and Racial Studies*, 1 (2), 1978.
Van den Berghe, Pierre, *Race and Racism* (N.Y., John Wiley & Sons, 1967).
—— *Race and Ethnicity* (N.Y., Basic Books, 1970).
—— 'Pluralism and the Polity: A Theoretical Exploration', *Pluralism in Africa*, L. Kuper and M.G. Smith (eds.), (Berkerey, Univ. of Calif. Press, 1971).
—— 'Race and Ethnicity: a Sociological Perspective', *Ethnic and Racial Studies*, 1 (4), 1978.
Van Lier, R.A.J., *The Development and Nature of Society in the West Indies* (Amsterdam, Koninklijk Instit. voor de Tropen, 1950).
—— *Frontier Society: A Social Analysis of the History of Surinam* (The Hague, Martinus Nijhoff, 1971).
Wagley, Charles, 'Recent Studies of Caribbean Local Societies', *The Caribbean: Natural Resources*, C. Wilgus (ed.), (Gainsville, Univ. of Florida Press, 1959).
—— 'Plantation America: A Culture Sphere', *Caribbean Studies: A Symposium*, V. Rubin (ed.), (Seattle, Univ. of Wash. Press, 1960).

Webber, A.R.F., *Centenary History and Handbook of British Guiana* (Georgetown, Daily Chronide, 1931).
Weber, Max, *Essays in Sociology*, H.H. Gerth and C. Wright Mills (eds.)., (London, Kegan Paul, Trench, Trubner & Co, 1947).
Weller, Judith, *The East Indian Indenture in Trinidad* (Puerto Rico, Univ. of P.R. Press, 1968).
West, Katherine, 'Stratification and Ethnicity in "Plural" New States', *Race*, XIII (4), 1972.
White, Naomi Rosh, 'Ethnicity, Culture and Cultural Pluralism', *Ethnic and Racial Studies*, 1 (2), 1978.
Wilkinson, H.C., *Bermuda from Sail to Steam: The History of the Island from 1784 to 1901*, 2 vols. (London, O.U.P., 1973).
Will, H.A., *Constitutional Change in the British West Indies, 1880–1903* (Oxford., Clarendon, 1970).
Williams, Eric, *The Negro in the Caribbean* (Washington, Associates in Negro Folk Education, 1942).
—— *The Historical Background of Race Relations in the Caribbean* [pamphlet] (P.O.S., 1955).
—— *British Historians and the West Indies* (London, Andre Deutsch, 1966).
—— *From Columbus to Castro: The History of the Caribbean, 1492–1969.* (London, Andre Deutsch, 1970).
Wittermans, Elizabeth, *Inter-Ethnic Relations in a Plural Society* (Groningen, J.B. Wolters, 1964).
Wolf, E.R. and S.W. Mintz, 'Haciendas and Plantations in Middle America and the Antilles', *Social and Economic Studies*, Sept. 1957.
Wood, Donald, *Trinidad in Transition: The Years after Slavery* (London, Oxford Univ. Press, 1968).
Young, J. Allan, *Approaches to Local Self-Government in British Guiana* (London, Longmans, 1958).
Unpublished Theses and Papers.
Bisnauth, Dale, 'The East Indian Immigrant Society in British Guiana, 1891–1930', Ph.D. Thesis, U.W.I. 1977.
Campbell, Carl, 'Immigration into a Divided Society: A Note on Social Relationships in Trinidad, 1846–1870', 4th Conference of Caribbean Historians, Jamaica, 1972.
Ciski, Robert, 'The Vincentian Portuguese: A Study in Ethnic Group Adaptation', Ph.D. Dissertation, University of Massachusetts, 1975.
Fraser, P.D., 'Education and Social Values in British Guiana,

1870–1914', D.Phil. Thesis, Sussex University, 1977.
Goslinga, Cornelius, 'Immigration into Surinam, 1865–1939', 4th Conference of Caribbean Historians, Jamaica, 1972.
Key, Leslie, 'East Indians and the Afro-Guyanese: Village Settlement Patterns and Inter-Group Relationships, 1871–1921', 4th Conference of Caribbean Historians, 1972.
Key Potter, Leslie, 'Internal Migration and Resettlement of East Indians in Guyana, 1870–1920', Ph.D. dissertation, McGill University, 1975.
Laurence, K.O. 'Immigration into Trinidad and British Guiana, 1834–1871', Ph.D., Cambridge Univ., 1958.
Moore, Brian L., 'Social and Cultural Complexity in British Guiana, 1850–1891', Ph.D., Univ. of the West Indies, 1973.
—— 'The Problem of Stability in a Racially Segmented Society: Plantation Guiana after Slavery', Seminar Paper, Dept. of History, U.W.I., 1983.
—— 'Chinese Immigrants in 19th Century Guiana: Sociocultural Adaptation in an Alien Environment', UNESCO Conference on Migration and Culture Contact in the Caribbean, Barbados, April 1984.
—— 'Sex and Marriage among Indian Immigrants in British Guiana during the 19th Century', Third Conference on East Indians in the Caribbean, Trinidad, August-September 1984.
Moore, Robert J., 'East Indians and Negroes in British Guiana, 1838–1880', D.Phil., University of Sussex, 1970.
Ramnarine, T., 'The Growth of the East Indian Community in British Guiana, 1880–1920', D.Phil. Thesis, University of Sussex, 1977.
Skinner, Elliott, 'Ethnic Interaction in a British Guiana Rural Community: A Study of Secondary Acculturation and Group Dynamics', Ph.D., Columbia University, 1955.
Wagner, Michael, 'Structural Pluralism and the Portuguese in Nineteenth Century British Guiana: A Study in Historical Geography', Ph.D. dissertation, McGill University, 1975.
Waldron, P.N., 'The Salience of Race in the Politics of Guyana', M.A., University of Cincinnati, 1972.

INDEX

Absentee planters' (1851) meeting 86
Acculturation, Creole elites 21, 23, 132
Adamson, Alan H. 1, 100, 101, 106, 118, 120, 179–180, 187, 202, 218
Administrator General 193
Africa 9, 11, 143–144
Agricola 101
America, plantation 9, 11
Americans
  black immigrants 52
  white residents 44
Angel Gabriel, *See* Orr, John Sayers
Anglican church 126, 199
Annandale plantation 171
Anti-Slavery Society 45, 118
Antigua 31, 32–33, 39, 43
Arabian coast 35
Armed forces 203ff
  planter control of 61
Articles of Capitulation 53, 78
Asia 9, 11
Attorneys 52
Augier, Roy 82
Azorean immigration 43

Bagotstown 101
Bahamas 74, 78
Barbados 11, 31, 32–33, 44, 47, 78, 126
Barbarism, fear of 55, 61
Barkly, Henry 55, 56, 86, 112–113, 115
Beaumont, Joseph 61
Beckford, George 10, 11, 26, 29, 53, 111, 164

Bel Air plantation 199
Belgrave 123
Belize 36
Bellevue plantation 181
Benn, Denis 10
Berbice 35, 40, 41, 54, 58, 101, 121, 153, 178, 183, 199
Bermuda 74, 143
Beterverwagting 98, 119–120
Bisnauth, Dale 2, 222
Black majority rule, prevention 56, 61
Blacks and coloureds (*Also see* Creoles) 67–68
  racist Victorian attitudes towards 80
Blankenburg plantation 40
Boeke, Julius 13
Bolland, O. Nigel 36
Bourda 214
Braithwaite, Lloyd 17, 22, 23, 24, 25, 27, 191, 219
Brathwaite, Edward 23, 27, 191, 199, 202, 219
Brazil 9
  competition in sugar 31
Brereton, Bridget 1, 133, 145, 181, 183
Brighton 177
Britain 32, 42, 52
British Government 32, 43
British Guiana, unification 54
British Guiana African Association 123
British imperial troops, and race 207–209
British Isles, *See* Britain
British market 31, 32

Bronkhurst, H.V.P. 122, 124, 131, 132, 192
Broomhall plantation 57
Buxton 96, 98, 101, 102

Cane farming 119–120
Canje 180
Cape Colony 64
Cape de Verde 44
Capital, scarcity 33
Caribbean 1, 2, 9, 31ff, 116, 213
  historiography 1
  social history 1, 2–3
Carlyle, Thomas 81
Carmichael, Major-General 83
Carus 81
Caste (-status system) 24, 28
Central Board of Health, *See* Villages
Central Board of Villages, *See* Villages
Central government, and villages (*Also see* Villages) 95ff
Centralization, and race (*Also see* Villages) 97, 100, 103
  impact on villages 100, 104–105
Charlestown 214
Chase, Julia 154
Chefa lottery 181
China 45, 161, 213
Chinese chap. 8 *passim*
  and Christianity 202
  attitude to schooling 202
  creolization of 202
  female shortage 161
  land settlements 176, 178
  licences 174–175
  nocturnal gangs 128, 182–183
  number of immigrants 161
  occupations 175–176
  overseas 144
  population statistics 161
  retailers in Jamaica 148
  secondary colonists 139
  T'ai P'ing rebellion 162
Chinese government, *See* China
Chinese New Year festival 180
Churches, racial discrimination 126
Civil List, and power politics 71, 84

Civil service, and race 123–126
Class status 109
Class stratification, 22, 23–25, 27, 75
Clergy 53
Cob, *See* Creoles
Codrington College 126
Coercion, and creolization 25, 211
  emphasis on 203, 204, 205, 210
  in plural society 18, 19, 22
  in stratified society 25
Coffee 33
College of Financial Representatives 54, 57, 72
College of Kiezers 54, 56–57, 72
Colonial Bank 57, 62, 64
Colonial Office 77, 180
  and civil service 125
  and electoral college 56
  and local government 99
  and membership of legislature 60
  and political reform 70–71
  and white rule/planter dominance 79–80
  attitude to blacks and coloureds 79ff
  exploitation of race issue 85–86
  preservation of imperial authority 80
  racial bias 81, 82
Colonies, types 51
Colour bar 21
Combined Court, fiscal policies 114–117
Compensation Award 32
Compulsory education 159, 200, 201
Consensus, and religion 196
  of values 21, 25, 191, 215
  thesis 23
Constitution, and planter power 53ff, 78
Constitutional Reform Association 68, 69, 71, 72, 73
Continuum, creole 23, 219
  societal 29, 221–222
Corentyne 35, 121, 177, 180
Cotton 33
Cotton Tree 177
Council of India 45

INDEX

Court of Policy 45, 53, 54, 59–60, 72–73
Credit, See Capital
Creole, culture 23
  definition 110
  labour 120–121
Creoles, acculturation 132
  Afro-Creole culture 198–199
  and Barbadians 111
  and Civil Service 123–126
  and missionaries 197
  and taxation 114–118
  christianity and schooling 198–199
  colour gradations 110
  common law marriages 199
  crime 127–128
  cultural ambivalence 211
  divisions 111
  economic activity 120–123
  elites in politics 74–75
  emigration to Surinam 121
  incomplete creolization 199
  liberal professions 126–127
  population statistics 110–111, 274
  rural settlement 111–114, 121
  social mobility 131–132
  socio-economic status 127, 134–135
  urban settlement 121–122
Creolization, incomplete 23, 199, 202
  process of 23, 184, 185–186, 191, 218
Cross, Malcolm 4, 17
Crown, legislative power 83
Crown colony 78
  government 82
Crown lands 34, 35, 36, 37, 61, 111, 112–114
Cuban sugar producers, 31
Cultural institutions 14–15, 17
Cultural minority, dominance of 15, 19, 75
  integration of subordinate elite into 74–75
Cultural pluralism 15–16, 159, 219
Cultural sections 17
Culture, definition 14
Cumfo 198

Cummingsburg 214
Curtin, Philip 1, 131
Cuvier 81

D'Agrella, Antonio 155
D'Urban, Governor 83
Darwin, Charles 81
de Groot, J. van Ryck 69
de Gobineau 81
Dead Tree Farm 177
Demerara 35, 40, 53, 58, 62, 95, 96, 101, 153, 177, 178, 183, 199
Despres, Leo 3, 16–17, 18, 22, 25
Devonshire Castle plantation 173, 206
Dissertations, See Theses
Doctors 52, 131
Domination, forms of (Also see Planter dominance and Plantation system) 20
Dominica 39, 43, 44, 79
Drainage 46, 95
Drysdale, Robert 69
Dual society/dualism 13
Duff, R. 124
Dummett 66
Dutch residents, See Whites

East Africa 139
Education 2,200
Election rigging 55
Electoral college, See College of Kiezers
Emancipation 24, 32
Emery, John 62
England 52
Essequibo 35, 39, 40, 53, 58, 121, 128, 129, 153, 175, 177, 178, 183, 206
Estate system 26–27
Estates Armed Force 204
Ethnic cleavages 24
Ethnic diversity (Also see Multiracialism) 12
Europe 31, 33, 213
Ex-slaves, adjustment to emancipation 32ff
Executive Council 72
Exploitation colony 51

Farley, Rawle 34

Fileen, J.D. 69
Financial College, *See* College of Financial Representatives
Fiscal policy, as instrument of repression 114–118
Fortes, Meyer 15
France 42
Franchise 54–55, 73
Fraser, Peter D. 2
Free trade 32
Freedman, Maurice 144
French colonies 31
Friendship 98, 101
Froude, James 81
Furnivall, J.S. 6, 12–13, 157, 194
Fustee, *See* Creoles

Georgetown 57, 58, 62, 63, 70, 72, 149, 153, 154, 158, 175, 178, 205, 206, 214
Germany 42
Gilbert, J.T. 65, 66
Gladstone, John 44
Glenelg, Lord 112
Golden Grove 105
Gonsalves, Manoel 154
Gordon, John 58
Gormanston, Lord 71
Government officials 53
Governor, powers of 53, 72, 86–88
Green, William A. 32, 36
Grenada 33, 35, 37, 42, 43, 44, 45, 47
Grey, Earl 87, 112, 115
Guadeloupe 31
Guianas 9
Guyanese polity, uniqueness of 78
Guyanese society, change in 67–68, 218–219
  classification of 222–223
  plural and class features 211
  ethnic diversification of 213
  stability and coercion 202, 216

Haiti 61, 81
Hakka 186
Hall, Stuart 3, 17–18, 19, 20, 23, 24, 27, 191, 219
Havana 43
Haynes, Richard 57, 60, 62, 64
Henry plantation 39

Heterogeneous society 15–17
Hewick, Magistrate 129–130
Highbury plantation 181
Higman, Barry 1, 2–3
Hincks, Francis 98–102, 119
Hindi 186, 201
Hinds, W.H. 69
Hintzen, Percy 4
Hoetink, Harmannus 3, 20, 28–29, 191–192, 196
Homogeneous society 15
Homogenization, racial/cultural 28, 192
Hopetown 181
Huis t'Dieren and Middlesex 177, 180
Hunt 81
Hutson, D.M. 69

Immigration 41–46
Immigrants 23
  African 43–44
  Chinese 45–46
  Indian 2, 44–45
  role of 42, 163
  schools for 200–201
  West Indian 44
  white/Portuguese 42–43
Imperial power, and political integration 89
  role in colonial society 77–78, 215
Imperial trusteeship, objective of 80
Indenture system 24, 164–173
  and differential incorporation 187
  and racial separation 179
India 28, 161, 165, 213
Indian Mutiny 207
Indians (*Also see* Immigrants) chap. 8 *passim*
  caste composition 162
  Christianity and schooling 200–202
  creolization of 201–202
  economic activity 174–176
  female shortage 161–162
  indenture contracts 164–165
  indentured population 187
  land settlements 176–178

INDEX

Muslims 162
  number of immigrants 44–45, 161
  population statistics 161
  secondary colonists 139
  value of property 178
Inspector-General of Police 193, 206
Integration
  and culture 202
  and language 186
  biological 27–28, 196
  limited 210, 215
  role of common economy 194–196
  social and cultural 23, 24, 28, 217
Ireland 42, 52
Irving, Henry
  and political reform 70
  and villages 103–104
  and Crown lands 113–114
  land sales to Indians 177
  tax policy 116–117
Italian Jesuits 158, 159
Ithaca 101

Jamaica 1, 26, 31, 33, 34, 35, 37, 38, 39, 40, 42, 43, 44, 45, 46, 68, 74, 79, 81, 82, 139, 148, 175, 209
Jenkins, Edward 163, 206
Johnson, Howard 148
Judiciary 61
Jumbi 199
Justices of the Peace 52

Ketley, Joseph 64
King's Chest 84
Kingsley, Charles 81
Kingston 214
Kirke, Henry 74, 131
Knight, Franklin 51
Kroo Coast 43
Kuper, Adam 4
Kuper, Leo 12

La Belle Alliance plantation 129
La Bonne Intention plantation 119–120
Labour (free)
  availability of 31–33, 37
  enticements to 37
  1842 regulations 40
L'Amitie 180
Lacytown 214
Land
  and labour 32–37
  and power structure 36–37
  hunger of ex-slaves 34–37
  individualization 94
  parcellization 94
  planter control of 61
  restriction of joint purchases 96–97
Laurence, K.O. 43, 44, 144, 148, 156
Leeward Islands 11, 47
Legislature, *See* Court of Policy
Leonora plantation 173
Letter Kenny 177
Levantines 139
Levy, Jacqueline 148
Liberia 43
Light, Henry 55, 95–96, 112, 124
Local government (*Also see* Centralization, Central government, and Villages) 96, 99–100, 102–103, 105–106.
London Missionary Society 62, 64, 115, 118, 119, 126, 197
Long, Edward 81
Low-a-si 171
Lytton, Secretary of State 210

MacFarlane 123
Madeira 42–43, 141, 144, 149, 151
Magistrates 170
Malgre Tout plantation 171
Malta 42
Mandle, Jay 2
Manumission policy 31
Maria's Lodge 177
Marriage, inter-racial 214
  black/white 130–131, 132–133, 217
  Creole/Chinese 181–182
  Creole/Indian 181–182
  Portuguese/Creole 156–157
Marshall, W.K. 38
Martinique 31
Marx, Karl, theory of 25

INDEX

Massiah 177
Masters and Servants Act 40–41
Mayor(s) 62, 131
McDavid, E.N. 124
McKenzie, H.I. 22
Mediterranean 9, 213
Menezes, M.N. 1
Merchants 53
Metairie system/metayers 38–39
Militia 203–204
Milliroux, M.F. 129
Mingling, biological-cum-social 28, 192
Mintz, S.W. 10, 31, 161
Miscegenation 110
Mixed population 196
Mohurrum festival 180–181
Montserrat 39
Moore, R.J. 2
Mortality of immigrants 42–43, 45
Mulatto, *See* Creoles
Multiracialism 11–12, 29, 47, 213
Municipal Corporation Act 99
Murdoch, J.A. 69
Mustee, *See* Creoles

Napoleonic Wars 31
Negro, *See* Creoles
Nevis 38, 39, 43
New Amsterdam 58, 63, 72, 175
Newcastle, Secretary of State 165
Nigger, term of abuse 111
Nooten Zuill 176, 180
Nurnay 180

Obeah 181, 199
Octoroon, *See* Creoles
Onderneeming 128
Open voting 74
Orr, John Sayers 151, 152–153
Oudkerk/Oudkirk 123, 124
Overseers 52

Pacific 9, 11
Padilla, Elena 9
Pakington, John 60, 87
Parliamentary Select Committee, report of (1849) 85, 86
Parsons 52, 131

Particularistic-ascriptive values 21, 23, 217
Peasant/small-farming sector 119
Plaisance 96, 105
Plan of Redress 53, 59
Plantation colonies, of exploitation 51
Plantation economy, integrative function 194–195
Plantation managers 52–53
Plantation society 23
  and pluralism 11–12, 13
  critique of 10
  definition 9
  multiracialism in 11–12
  usefulness as general theory 11
Plantation system 9
  as total system 10, 11, 163–164
  characteristics of 9
  dominance of 9, 10, 11, 53
  fortunes of 31–34, 46–47
  importation of unfree labourers by 9, 41–46, 161
  operating conditions of 10, 31
Plantations 32–34, 37, 42, 46
Planter class *See* Planter dominance and Planters
Planter dominance 10, 31, 215
  and centralized government 93
  and local constituencies 58–59
  and race 56–57, 59, 60–61
  as distinct from white supremacy 58
  dissolution of 74
  pervasiveness 61
  preservation of 73–74
Planter hegemony, *See* planter dominance
Planters
  and immigration 41–46
  attitude to immigrant schooling and conversion 199
  attitude to Irving's village scheme 104
  attitude to labour 38ff
  fears of 32
  financial power of 83–84
  losses 33
  refusal to raise taxes 83, 85
  reluctance to sell land 34
  solvency of 37

INDEX

Planting interest, *See* Planters and Planter dominance
Plantocracy, *See* Planters and Planter dominance
Plural society
  and social change in 220-221
  centralized government in 93
  characteristics of 13
  coercion in 191
  conflict in 21-22
  Despres' classification of 17
  economic interdependence in 191
  institutional structure 14-15
  stability of 19, 21-22, 191
Pluralism
  and coercion 19, 211
  and political power 19
  application to Caribbean 13
  concept of 12
  conflict model 12
  dissolution of 28
  equilibrium model 12
  theoretical development 14
Pneumatic pans 46
Police Force 205-206, 209
Political power, and race 83
Politics
  crisis, 1887 70
  planters vs. Crown 82ff
Political institutions
  non-white membership 57-58, 60, 69, 131-132
Political reform
  agitation for 68-71
  and economic recession 68
  and ex-slaves 62, 66
  and Indian and Chinese 67
  and Portuguese 66-67, 69-70
  and race 65
  and the Press 66, 70
  Peter Rose's proposals 63-64
  petitions for 64-65, 66, 67, 71
  planter opposition to 62, 71
  public meetings for 62, 64, 66, 68, 71
  voter registration drive 69
  1849 law 54-57, 58-59
  1891 law 72-73
Political Reform Club 68-69, 70, 71

Pomeroon 121
Population, density of 32-33
Portuguese 1, 2, chap. 7 *passim*
  and indenture 140-141
  and politics 66-67, 69-70, 75, 157
  as social buffers 150
  Benevolent Society 149
  business failures 146-147
  conduct of business 145-146
  ethnicity/ethnic identity 139, 149-150, 157-159, 196, 219
  forestry and charcoal manufacture 148
  in Bermuda 143-144
  language 158-159, 196
  licences 117, 142-143
  male-female ratio 157
  moneylending and pawnbroking 146
  nationality 159, 196
  population statistics 139
  race and immigration 140
  reasons for success 142-143, 144
  religion 157-158, 196
  retail trade 141ff
  return to Madeira 141
  secondary colonists 139, 144
  small farmers 141
  social clubs 158
  Society of St. Vincent de Paul 149
  socio-political role 216
  spirits trade 147-148
  the indigent 149
  wealth and property 149
  withdrawal from estates 140-141
Post, Ken 26
Potter, Leslie Key 2
Power structure, and land 36-37
Praedial larceny 128
Press, planter influence 61
Prices, land 34, 35
  sugar 33, 46
Production of staples 33ff, 46-47
  costs of 32
Professionals 53
Proxy voting 55-56
Public Works Department, *See* Villages

308 INDEX

Punti 186

Quadroon, *See* Creoles
Queen's College 124

Race
  and divide and rule 193
  and economic competition 195
  and immigrant settlement
    179–180
  and imperial armed forces
    206–209
  and indenture system 164
  and occupational
    specialization 194–195, 214
  and pluralism 20–21
  and residential separation
    213–214
  and social change 217
  and social segmentation 192,
    214
  and societal destabilization 194
  and white power 89–215
  obstacle to integration 178
  recession of 74–75
  salience in society 184–185
Race relations
  and pluralism 20–21
  Barbadian-Indian 183
  black-Chinese 182–183
  black-Indian 2, 42, 182–187
  black-Portuguese 42, 148,
    150–155
  economic inputs 150–152
  in plantation society 11
  types of 21
  white-black 41
Race theories 81
Racial attitudes, 178–179
Racial stereotypes 80, 130, 152
Racism
  and white dominance 192
  in colonial society 20
  of whites 129–131
Ramnarine, T 2
Rates
  and Irving's village scheme
    103–104, 104–105
  and subordination of
    villages 101
  imposition on villages 98

"war" against 101, 102
Recession
  economic 33, 41
  of race 74–75
Reform Association 62–66
Representative government 62ff
Retail trade
  Indian and Chinese 174–175
  Portuguese dominance 142–143
Rex, John 20, 26–27, 29, 139, 144,
  150, 163, 194
Richards, Stephen 66
Rio (de Janeiro) 43
Riots
  anti-Portuguese 151, 152, 153,
    154–155
  by indentured immigrants 173
Riviere, W.E. 35, 39
Rodney, James 81, 129
Rodney, Walter 1, 26, 61, 120,
  126, 183–186, 194, 218
Rodway, James 66
Rose, Peter 57, 62, 63, 64, 65, 69,
  118
Rubin, Vera 24
Rural Constabulary 205, 209
Russell, William 119–120

Sacred Heart church 158
Schembri, Benedict 158
Schomburgk, Richard 130
Schoon Ord plantation 171
Scotland 52
Scott, Governor 113
Secondary colonists 139, 144–145
Secret ballot 73, 74
Segmental pluralism 15–16, 157,
  219, 188, 220
Segmentary/segmented society 13,
  75–76
Segmentation, social 213
Segregation 21
Settler colony 51
Shahabuddeen, M. 2
Sierra Leone 43
Singapore 182
Slave trade 31, 43
Slaves and slavery 20, 24, 32, 34
Smith, Lionel 83
Smith, M.G. 4, 14ff, 19, 20, 25, 27,
  29, 77, 109, 139, 157, 159, 163,

INDEX

164, 191, 211, 221
Smith, R.T.   3, 22–23, 25, 27, 162, 163, 191, 211, 219
Social Darwinism   81, 129
Social distance   21, 131
Social mobility   21
  and structural change   110, 133–134
  of Asian immigrants   187
  of Creole elite minority   131–132, 217
Social pluralism   14–15, 21
Social science theory   2–3, 220–221, 223
Social values, absence of   22
Societal types, criteria for classification   15–17, 221–222
Society of St. Vincent de Paul, *See* Portuguese
Somatic norm image   28, 191–192, 196
South Africa   213
Southeast Asia   12, 13, 139
Special Improvement Board, *See* Villages
St. Domingue   31
St. Helena   43
St. Kitts   31, 32–33, 43
St. Lucia   33, 35, 38, 39, 44, 45, 47, 78, 175, 209
St. Vincent   33, 39, 42, 43, 44, 45, 47
Stanley, Lord   45, 112
State churches, social aims   197
State power, and planters   31, 53
Statutory Boards, planter dominance   61
Steam clarifiers   46
Steam draining pumps/engines   46, 95, 97–98, 118
Stipendiary Magistrates   41
Stone, Carl   4
Straughn, David   69
Structural pluralism   94, 109, 216
Subjects, and citizens   109
Subordinate population
  lack of cohesion   93
  subjugation of   215–216
Sugar Duties Act   32, 33
Superintendants of Rivers and Creeks   37

Surinam   1, 47, 121, 147

Taggart, John   62, 64, 153
Tamil   186, 201
Task-gangs   38
Taxation
  indirect   114–117
  licences   117
  poll tax   117–118
Taylor, Henry   79, 81, 87–88
Tenancy-at-will system   39–40
Theoretical debate, pluralism *vs.* stratification   1, 3–4, 22
Theses   2
Thompson, Edgar   9, 10, 53, 111, 119, 161
Thompson, Leonard   51
Tobago   35, 38, 39, 47
Town councils   131
Trinidad   1, 25, 33, 34, 35, 37, 40, 41, 42, 44, 45, 47, 78, 82, 133, 139, 176, 181, 182, 183, 191, 218
Triumph plantation   119
Trollope, Anthony   81
Tuschen de Vrienden plantation   39

United States   9, 132, 213
Universalistic-achievement values   21, 24, 132, 217
Urdu   186

Vacuum pans   46
Vagrancy law   128
van den Berghe, Pierre   18, 20–21, 22, 25, 191, 194, 221
van Lier, R.A.J.   1, 13, 194
Vatican   158
Versailles plantation   171
Victoria   101–102
Villages (*Also see* Rates, Central government, Centralization, and Local government) chap. 5 *passim*
  and private sector   118–119
  and socio-political segmentation   93
  and structural pluralism   94
  as broker institutions   93, 107
  Central Board of Health

102–103, 105, 106
Central Board of Villages
  98–99, 102, 103, 104
commission of enquiry on 98
commissioners 98
councils 102, 105
expropriation of lands 104
flooding of 95, 105
fragmentation of 94, 118
government loans 98
incorporation of 97
institutional role of 106–107
intregrative function of 93, 107
legal classifications 99
loss of self-management 99, 104
management committees 95
partition of 96
poor drainage of 95–118
Public Works Department
  103–104, 105
revolt against plantations 34
socio-political significance 93
Special Improvement Board 98
Voluntary Subscription
  Immigration Society 44
Volunteer Force 205
Volunteer Militia Force 209
Vries 123

Wages 37, 41
Wagley, Charles 9, 11
Wagner, Michael 2
Wakenaam 183
Wales plantation 181
Wallbridge, E.A. 62, 64
Waterloo plantation 181

Wealthy urban interests and
  politics 58–59
Wesleyan Methodist Missionary
  Society 126, 197, 199–200
West Africa 31, 139, 213
West India regiments, and
  race 206–209
Westley, Rev. 101–102
White aristocracy 52–53
White domination role of imperial
  power 88–89
White immigrants, mortality 42–43
White, James 45
Whites (*Also see* Americans) 51, 52
  fear of black bush
    settlements 112
Widows and Orphans Fund 125
Williams, Dr. A.W. 70
Wills, S.E. 69
Windward Islans 33, 34, 35, 38, 46, 47
Witter, Michael 26
Wodehouse, Philip 118, 151, 207–208
Wolf, Eric 10, 31, 161
Women 37, 57, 131, 161–162, 207
Wong, Evan 175
Wood, Donald 1, 181
Work culture 186
Wu-Tai-Kam 181–182, 199, 202

Young, Alan 2, 101

Zeelandia plantation 183
Zemindar 177

For Product Safety Concerns and Information please contact our EU
representative GPSR@taylorandfrancis.com
Taylor & Francis Verlag GmbH, Kaufingerstraße 24, 80331 München, Germany

www.ingramcontent.com/pod-product-compliance
Lightning Source LLC
Chambersburg PA
CBHW052148300426
44115CB00011B/1573